THERE IS NO TRUCE

THOMAS MOTT OSBORNE

THERE IS NO TRUCE

A LIFE OF
THOMAS MOTT OSBORNE

BY

RUDOLPH W. CHAMBERLAIN

 BOOKS FOR LIBRARIES PRESS
FREEPORT, NEW YORK

First Published 1935
Reprinted 1970

STANDARD BOOK NUMBER:
8369-5418-1

LIBRARY OF CONGRESS CATALOG CARD NUMBER:
74-124229

PRINTED IN THE UNITED STATES OF AMERICA

TABLE OF CONTENTS

v

3. The Prison Reformer

BOOK III. SPLENDID DEFEAT

ILLUSTRATIONS

EPILOGUE

I

IT is one of the coldest days of winter, unseasonable in its severity. The mercury hovers near zero, and the wind whips out of the north with a ferocity that pinches the nostrils and chokes the breath. The ancient pile that is Auburn Prison rises gray and somber against the December sky. Atop the bastile Copper John, the Continental soldier who has kept solitary vigil for a century, looks down upon the scene with sculptured serenity.

To the casual observer there is nothing strange or out of place here. The few pedestrians, bracing themselves against the blast, scarcely note the familiar sights. Why should they? It is an old story, this grim façade with the grated windows and the silent figure, powdered with snow, that watches above. Even if they should pass through the iron-barred gate and enter the warden's office, there would be nothing to indicate that this day is different from any other. The same atmosphere of suspended doom, communicated from thousands of waiting men. The same hush in which voices and footfalls are quickly engulfed. The same coming and going of guards and clerks and trusties. Routine—the same yesterday, to-day, and to-morrow.

And yet, in the galleries where, tier on tier, the cells rise with terrible uniformity, there is an expectant hush. Waiting men. Waiting for what? Death? Freedom? Commutation? Or—

Trouble!

The word, vague yet menacing, flashes from guard to guard. There is nothing definite. A sixth sense warns them that there is something unnatural in this calm. It may, of course, be imagination. Ever since the abortive attempt at a delivery four months before, they have been keyed to the breaking point. In the yard the blackened ruins of shop buildings bear witness to the desperation of imprisoned men. Nearly two thousand inmates are crowded into quarters designed to accommodate about twelve hundred. Some convicts sleep in the corridors. It is impossible under such conditions to segregate habitual criminals from first offenders. Hard-boiled repeaters, some of them bearing that anomaly of legal obtuseness, a double life sentence, in easy communication with youngsters serving their first stretch. Mob leaders, whose only hope is violence, side by side with morons, fertile stuff for the promptings of any mad agitator. And through it all, resentment against the common enemy, society, growing to lunatic proportions.

Last night the hash was sour, and the complaint has reached Warden Jennings. Nothing surprising about that. Rotten stuff, anyway. But what can you do if the Legislature will not come through with an appropriation for decent grub? You can't maintain discipline in prison on a perpetual bellyache.

It is ten by the clock in the Warden's office. Before making his usual morning round, Jennings glances through the frosted windows toward the outer gate. The gatekeeper is sitting in his little cubicle trying to keep warm. On the wall, at the corners, sentinels stand watch. There is nothing amiss in the scene; yet what impulse prompts the Warden to strap his gun-pouch under his coat? He himself cannot say. It is not his regular custom. But to-day—well, it can do no harm. Besides, he must inspect the new construction work at the far end of the yard.

Through the outer corridor into the guardroom. A turn to the left and down a flight of stairs to the mess hall and kitchen; thence to the yard. Here, taking what exercise they can, are three hundred men, the "idle company," composed of the riff-raff of the prison, men who either cannot be trusted in the shops or are incompetent. Now that the prison is overcrowded and some of the shops are in ruins, there are not jobs enough for everybody. The best men are sent to work. The rest cannot be left to rot in their cells. Dangerous as they are, they must be given daily exercise in the yard. They would be more dangerous without it. Inmate members of the Mutual Welfare League act as marshals for the idle company.

At the carpenter shop Jennings pauses to inspect a new sample coffin. He has demanded something better than the rough boxes in which the poor devils who die in prison are laid to rest. This is better. Then on to the construction work. At last the State is making modern improvements and additions to the more than century-old institution. Oh, well, better late than never. That last riot helped to underscore the need, too.

On the return trip, near the foot of the stairs, the Warden observes three inmates approaching him, one carrying what seems to be a piece of paper. A petition, probably. As Jennings wipes his glasses, steamed by the heat of the building when he entered from the yard, he feels something pressed into his stomach and has to look twice before he recognizes what it is. A gun! Smuggled into the prison despite all precautions. Behind him another convict presses into his neck the point of a wicked-looking knife fashioned from a file. A third displays a razor.

For a moment the Warden is speechless. No inkling of serious trouble has reached him. Only when he is disarmed and used as a shield to overpower the guards in the vicinity does the significance of the revolt break in upon him.

"We're going through with this, Warden," one of the convicts tells him. "We're going to release the men in the punishment gallery and make a break for it. We've got plenty of guns and ammunition."

Things begin to happen. As the Warden and captive guards are marched along the corridor and up the stairs, Jennings hears a fusillade of shots behind him. That is something. The attempt at a break has been discovered, and soon the news will be broadcast over the state.

In the punishment gallery more guards are captured, and the rioters are reinforced by a dozen of the forty-odd inmates being disciplined for infraction of prison rules. The remainder elect to keep clear of trouble. One of the released men, a misshapen, apelike creature, smashes his fist in the Warden's face. With an oath, the convict guarding Jennings, one Sullivan by

name, thrusts the man back, announcing roughly that he is
"taking care of the Warden." To the convicts it means "This
man is my meat. I'll deal with him." But Jennings wonders. He
has been pretty decent to Sullivan several times in the past.
Something in the man's voice now makes him hope that perhaps . . . But it is a chance in a million.

Even this ray of light soon flickers out. Two convicts enter
bearing a third between them. There is a gaping hole in his
chest, and he breathes with difficulty.

"Put him out of his misery," whispers someone, sticking a
gat to the wounded man's head. Others pull him away.

"Warden," Sullivan says solemnly, "your men got one of
us, but we got one of them. The P. K."

Jennings' heart sinks. So that was the shooting he heard.
And the Principal Keeper got his. With horror he realizes
that only a miracle can save them now. Blood has been shed.
For these desperate criminals there can be no turning back.
It is freedom or death—death by a bullet from an officer's gun
or death in the electric chair. Every one of them had rather
be shot than "burn." Their faces are stern with the sternness
of a desperate purpose. Human life means nothing to them now
except as a commodity for barter. Life for life. Death for
death.

Tied together in fours, with an armed convict behind each
man, the hostages are marched up the stairs. Just short of the
wicket door that opens to the guardroom, advance is checked
by a screen partition, pierced by an aperture for parcels. A
civilian employee, captured during the mopping-up process,
is forced through the opening to summon the prison authorities
for a parley. He yells loudly through the little wicket in the
steel door, but gets no reply. Minutes pass. The convicts
chafe at the delay. Their nerves are on edge. Now that the
die is cast, they want action.

Someone suggests that the Warden write a note incorporating the demands of the rioters. He refuses, and the men get
ugly. There are threats of violence. Finally, they compose a
note and ask Jennings to sign it. He reads the scrawl and
declares it won't do. Again the demand that the Warden write

the note himself. In a low voice Sullivan advises Jennings to yield.

It is a difficult situation. The Warden has a double responsibility. Control of the prison population. The lives of the guards who are in the power of maddened criminals, some of them hopped up with dope. He must try to do justice to both. His only hope is to stall, to prolong the negotiations until the forces outside the prison are organized. There is an understanding among prison officials that orders given by a warden under such circumstances are to be ignored. The acting warden assumes full authority. A note will bring delay, and at the same time inform the administration forces of the nature of the emergency.

Jennings takes the pencil handed him and begins to write. He bears down hard so that the point breaks. More delay until a knife can be found and the pencil sharpened. Leisurely now the Warden takes down the demands of his captors. The gates shall be opened, and the rioters given safe-conduct to automobiles waiting for them at the curb. If there is any sign of violence, the Warden and the guards will be killed immediately. If allowed to pass through to the waiting cars, the convicts will take their captives with them until safe from pursuit. Then the officers will be released.

Jennings smiles grimly to himself as he writes that last item. Small chance that any one of them would leave those cars alive, even if the prison authorities should accept the terms. Already some of the convicts are waiting for an excuse to kill their hated enemies, the "screws." There would be slaughter before the fugitives dumped their prisoners into a ditch on some remote byway.

As a sop to the convicts, Jennings adds the words: "Don't shoot." Sullivan grabs the paper, glances it over, and prefixes the word *Please* to the last sentence. A masterpiece, that amendment. "Please don't shoot" gives an impression of despair and shattered morale.

The civilian beyond the screen partition throws the note through the wicket. As time drags on without a reply, the convicts grow restive. Some of them have broken into the Principal Keeper's room overlooking the front wall. From this point of vantage they can see the mob surrounding the gate. A motley group it is. Police officers aiming high-powered rifles over automobile hoods. National Guardsmen patrolling the streets trying to hold back the crowd. State troopers, cool and efficient, stationed at strategic points along the wall. Automobiles dashing up at reckless speed bringing reinforcements from near-by barracks.

The situation is not without a certain ghastly humor. Embattled citizenry, excited and disorganized, are brandishing a strange assortment of weapons. They come with six-shooters, double-barreled shotguns, and ancient blunderbusses. Some wear hunting coats and have their license buttons pinned to their caps as if eager to take advantage of the open season on convicts. In the excitement, one civilian presses the trigger of his gun and narrowly misses shooting off the leg of the man in front of him. Periodic alarms that the convicts are coming send streams of heroic minutemen scampering to cover.

But there is nothing humorous in it for the little group in gray watching from the P. K.'s window. The delay has destroyed all element of surprise in a sortie. The only hope for freedom rests in a bargain with the besiegers, the lives of Jennings and the guards being the medium of exchange. To these latter it is only too plain what fate is in store for them. In the mind of each there is a vivid memory of that bloody day in Canon City, Colorado, when revolting prisoners slew their captured guards one after another and hung their bodies on the walls in the hope the authorities would relent. The authorities did not relent. They will not relent now. Jennings has realized this from the beginning. Blood and blood alone will be the price of this day's violence.

In the P. K.'s room the convicts have broken into the lockers. They find handcuffs and lock Jennings and the guards in fours. Sullivan discovers a keeper's uniform and puts it on. He makes a splendid-looking officer in his stolen clothes, tall, well set-up, almost handsome. It is hard to realize that instead of being on the side of law and order he is a ringleader of a criminal gang who will fight their way to freedom or die in the attempt. In all probability, when night comes out of the cold sky, all or most of these living beings, officers and convicts together, will be stretched in the stark attitudes of death.

As time passes, the tenseness becomes almost unbearable. Someone manages to snap the lock of the screen partition, and there is a surge toward the steel door that bars the way to the guardroom. An officer on duty without explains about the delay. It is taking time to make all the arrangements. Automobiles have to be procured. Measures must be taken to hold back the crowd at the gate, already difficult to control. For a time this satisfies the mutineers. But not for long. They suspect treachery. When the Catholic Chaplain appears at the wicket to urge that they give up their mad enterprise and to promise his personal influence in obtaining leniency, he is greeted with oaths.

"Are you another Canon City priest?" sneers one. It is a reference to the report that it was a priest, under protection of his holy order, who carried the dynamite with which to blow open the doors of the Colorado penitentiary. But the Chaplain stands his ground. His sincerity wins recognition.

"I am a Catholic," volunteers one of the leaders. "We respect you and don't mean what we said. But it is too late. We must go through with it. Even if you could save us, we had rather die than be sloughed into cells and eat swill the rest of our lives."

After this there is constant demand for drastic action. One of the guards is particularly detested by the convicts.

"Kill the son-of-a-bitch!" shouts one of them. "And paste him up on the door. Let 'em see what we'll do to the others if they don't open up." A moment later Jennings is startled by the sudden crack of an automatic. He turns just in time to see a guard sink to the floor, his face ghastly pale. So, it has come at last. There is a moment of tense silence. Even the rioters are sobered. "We didn't fire that shot," a convict puts in defensively.

"Pick him up and take him to the hospital," orders the Warden. "You wouldn't treat a dog like that."

To his amazement the men assent. Yet even as they stoop

to lift him, the guard struggles to his feet, unhurt. When the shot was fired, aimed apparently at the ceiling in a moment of exasperation, he fell in a dead faint. The strain had been too great. The incident brings, however, a foreboding of what soon may happen.

The long wait is almost too much, for convicts and guards alike; and there is a shout of jubilation when word comes from the P. K.'s room that the front gate is open and empty cars are waiting at the curb.

"Warden," exults one of the convicts, "I'll either have beef-steak and onions for supper to-night, or you and I will be in hell."

At last the bar of the steel door is lifted, and a key ring is tossed in. As it tinkles on the corridor floor, there is a general rush for it. With eager hands the convicts unlock the mechanism, then pause. It is the supreme moment. Ahead of them freedom or death. Behind them only death. The choice is simple; yet now that the time has arrived it is not so easy. Each one realizes what a desperate chance it is. Are they being tricked? If there is crooked work, by God, the Warden and the guards go too!

The leaders begin to organize their forces. At Jennings' suggestion, the captured guards are split into pairs. The Warden tells them it will be easier to get into the cars. The line of march is formed with Jennings, handcuffed to the civilian, at the head. Behind each officer stands a convict, his gun pressed into the back of the man in front. Sullivan is still "taking care of the Warden." Before the procession starts, the order is given that if anything happens each convict is first of all to shoot his man. Then the steel door swings open, and the column advances slowly into the guardroom. Almost opposite the door leading to the main corridor and exit Jennings pauses, and the whole line halts.

"Don't forget," the Warden reminds them, "you promised to lock that wicket door after you."

Whether some sense of honor remains to these desperate criminals or whether they still recognize the voice of old authority, it is difficult to say, but they comply. Now comes the most difficult test. One of the keys on that ring unlocks the last barrier to freedom. There is a moment's hesitation as though all are fearful to try the issue. In that instant the guardroom is filled with blinding, strangling fumes. From the main door a small round object like a baseball is rolling toward Jennings. It is a smoke bomb. Others are thrown through a smaller door near the rear of the procession. The break has failed.

Everything is pandemonium. The last the Warden remembers is a terrific blow on the head that knocks him unconscious, full on the smoke bomb at his feet. Simultaneously there is a burst of pistol shots. The convicts have obeyed orders, sending bullets crashing into the heads of their captives—all except one guard who is too quick for his man. In spite of his fetters he succeeds in wrenching the gun from the convict before falling in a stupor in the fumes. The rioters rush back to the comparative safety of the corridor, leaving one of their number gasping in death agony beside the prostrate Warden. It is Sullivan.

Willing hands lift up the Warden and the wounded guards. Strange, that none of the bullets fired from such close quarters is fatal! As for Jennings, he is unhurt, except for the blow on the head, shock, and gas fumes. But who dealt that blow? Sullivan, dead with a convict bullet in his heart? Did he save the Warden and take the lead himself? It seems fantastic, but Jennings still wonders.

It is shortly after noon. Until darkness comes mercifully down, Auburn Prison is an abattoir. The man hunt is on. A contagious frenzy for killing, partly thirst for revenge, partly an elemental urge, grips the invaders. Some of the convicts have barricaded themselves in a cell block and are shooting it out with the state troopers. "Come and get us, you so-and-so's!" they shout in maniacal derision.

Men fall sprawling on floors slippery with blood and rise again to pump more lead into human bodies. One of the rioters is captured, manhandled, threatened with death, and forced through the crack of the door behind which his comrades are making their last stand. He has been ordered to clear away the obstructions which have been piled on the other side, but his own pals shoot him down without mercy. As he breathes his last, a sturdy priest gives him the last rites of the Church, and the battle goes on.

The convicts entrenched in the topmost gallery know it is the end. Their numbers are up, but they will not surrender. Better to die fighting than to sit on "the hot seat" in the death room at Sing Sing. One by one they are picked off by the trooper sharpshooters. A lone survivor makes a mad rush and receives a .45 bullet in the breast from a distance of a few feet. He falls in a pool of blood, and the riot of December 11, 1929, is over.

II

The riot was over, but not the shouting. During the weeks that followed, the hubbub outside was almost a match for that twelve-hour hubbub inside. Everyone had a reason for the riot. Everyone had a remedy. Only there was no unanimity on reasons or remedies. The press took it up and filled its editorial columns with inveighings and exhortations. During the riot the most preposterous rumors had been circulated. One newspaper reported that the citizens of Auburn had packed all their belongings and were prepared for flight to distant parts. After the riot, rumors persisted. Dr. Kieb, state commissioner of correction, was forced to deny reports that authorities were contemplating indicting *all* the inmates of Auburn Prison for complicity in the murders of the nine dead. Fictitious tales of what had happened during the siege were spread, nor did the trial of seven of the conspirators—three of whom went to the electric chair—clear up the mystery of what actually occurred.

Everything was vague and conflicting. Acting Warden George H. Sullivan, who temporarily replaced Warden Jennings, blamed the uprising on lax discipline. "This is going to be a tough prison," he was quoted as saying, "so long as I am in charge." Dr. Hastings H. Hart of the Russell Sage Foundation thought "too strict prison discipline" responsible, along with elimination of one-third time off for good behavior. Dr. Kieb believed the riot was due to long-termers and advocated complete isolation. Senator Caleb H. Baumes defended his law which automatically imposed life sentences on fourth offenders, blaming overcrowding and idleness. The New York *World*, after conducting an investigation into causes of the riot, asked Governor Roosevelt and Dr. Kieb why "no adequate steps were taken to prepare for an outbreak of which there had been ample warning." Six weeks before its occurrence the revolt had been predicted by the New York State Commission of Correction. Warden Jennings was quoted as saying, "I am sitting on a volcano." There was work enough for only two or three hundred men; the rest spent most of the time in cells three and one-half by six feet, sunk deep in the masonry of the century-old bastile. One hundred men were sleeping in corridors. The food was bad; sanitation, worse. Between forty and fifty men had rotted for over four months in improvised segregation cells and had sworn there would be trouble. Yet the authorities seemed indifferent. When disaster came Governor Roosevelt announced that there was no basic fault in the New York State prison system. "We shall go right ahead with our program," he said, "and relieve the crowded conditions in our prisons."

These many voices gradually resolved into two voices. One heard the remark: "If Tom Osborne had been alive, there would have been no riot." One also heard the remark: "If it had not been for Tom Osborne and his mollycoddling of prisoners, there would have been no riot." There was the issue, clearly drawn, even though presented in an exaggerated and inaccurate form. Tom Osborne did not preach mollycoddling; he simply substituted for the punitive principle that of security for society and rehabilitation for the convicted man. It is doubtful, however, that he could have prevented the riot or checked it once it had begun. Conditions over which he could have had small control had developed, bringing with them changes in legislation and a different attitude in malefactors.

Still, the two voices persisted. Of the prisoners' association which Osborne had founded, Acting Warden Sullivan said: "The Mutual Welfare League is through. The men in this institution have been coddled too much." Mayor Charles D.

Osborne of Auburn, son of the penologist and president of the National Society of Penal Information, called attention to the fact that, while the League could not prevent a few desperadoes from attempting a delivery, it did take charge of the rest of the inmate population and maintain absolute order in the yard.

The contention grew until the New York *Times* was constrained to weep editorial tears that "the Auburn riot should have stirred the embers of a bitter controversy that raged in this state fifteen years ago when Thomas Mott Osborne was conducting his experiments in prison reform." But that could not stop it. Osborne was the very pith of the dispute. In death, as in life, he lifted men out of indifference to heights of enthusiastic indorsement or bitter denunciation. "What manner of man is this?" asked an inmate of Auburn Prison one Sunday in 1913 when the Gray Brotherhood first realized that Tom Osborne was of his own will to become one of their number. What manner of man is this who from the grave still answers the call of the trumpet and the thunder?

III

It was inevitable that Thomas Mott Osborne should be remembered by the world at large for his contributions to the theory and practice of penology. The last third of his life, after he had reached the height of his powers, was devoted to the redemption of criminals. His own downright seriousness and intensity made it impossible for men to accept his crusades otherwise than seriously and intensely. Because of his unswerving purpose, he was regarded by conservatives with fear not unmixed with awe. He became the center of innumerable controversies that left him more determined than ever, a pugnacious and occasionally quixotic knight errant who disturbed respectable people by jarring them out of their comfortable habits of thinking.

There was, however, another Osborne—a sensitive, gracious, youthful figure, enjoying the amenities of congenial comradeship; a conversationalist of infinite charm who could draw on a vast store of classic and modern culture for his themes; a gregarious person among his peers, whose delight in the arts was spontaneous and contagious; in short, a man as different from the reformer the world knew as day is from night. In his later years, many of Osborne's most intimate friends, especially those who had known him in his youth, found it difficult to reconcile the preoccupied, stern, and often sad man with the boy they had loved. Occasionally, in a carefree moment, there would be a flash of the old gayety; but such interludes were brief and grew more infrequent as the years passed. His devotion to humanitarian projects demanded its sacrifice in normal human relations. It set up a barrier that was never fully realized by Osborne himself. Old friends, meeting him by chance after years of separation, experienced a sudden sense of loss, as if someone very dear had been taken away from them.

This feeling of bereavement transcended any mere consideration of agreement or disagreement with Osborne's ideas. It was largely that the messianic urge in him brooked no partnership. The warm, humble, inconsequential things that make life pleasant for most of us were crowded out by the importunities of a great cause. It was difficult for him to cast off his preoccupation. He had seen a vision, and his eyes were set upon the distant horizon.

To Osborne's friends it was but scant consolation that his degree of success in prison reform was due largely to this very concentration. Best friends are always selfish friends. They are won and held by human qualities of personality, not by abstract ideals. And though some approved of the crusade to which Osborne had consecrated himself, they could not forget the Tom they had known of old, so gifted with social graces, so light-hearted, so appreciative of all good things that stimulate the mind or warm the heart.

It is a temptation to explain these vastly different Osbornes —the poet and the reformer—on the basis of dual personality. There were in him, it is true, striking contrasts; yet the differences were largely superficial. There was much of the reformer in the poet, and even more of the poet in the reformer. The creative force in him merely changed its direction. Its operations were transferred from one sphere to another. The Tom Osborne who delighted in nocturnal excursions in disguise, much to the distress of a scandalized family, and the Tom Brown who donned a gray uniform and suffered voluntary confinement in Auburn Prison as Convict No. 33,333x, were essentially the same.

The youth, almost abnormally sensitive to the emotional appeal of heroes and heroines of literature and strangely exalted by the mysticism of music, was in a Wordsworthian sense the father of the man whose whole being vibrated to the injustices he saw in the world about him. It is but a step from "Oliver Twist" to a school where wayward boys are taught the responsibilities of citizenship; and another pace from the satires of Gilbert and Sullivan to a program of political and social reform.

Osborne took those steps. He was one of those individuals whose emotions, once aroused, demand a practical outlet for expression. There was no buffer between his brain and his heart; nothing to absorb the shock either from vicarious adventures in the realm of illusion, as of books and the theater, or from the actual experience of living. A book played a part in deciding Osborne to make prison reform his chief object in life. Confinement in Auburn Prison, working at the same bench with convicts, eating the same food, doing the same menial tasks, and finally suffering the tortures of "solitary" gave impetus and direction to his efforts.

These contrasts, which at bottom are different manifestations of the same impulse, may be attributed in part to factors of heredity, training, and environment; but when all of these are noted and analyzed, one feels there is a residue of individual force still unexplained—something which eludes all scientific formulas, and whose origin may only be guessed at.

At first thought, the personality of such a man seems amazingly complex; yet the truth may be that it is amazingly simple. Simplicity is most difficult to understand. Variety of interests and activities does not necessarily denote intricacy of mental processes. Often, as with Osborne, it furnishes different aspects of the same creative energy.

Emotionally and imaginatively Osborne was a Romantic. Intellectually he was a Realist. Sometimes these two parts of his nature were in open conflict. Sometimes they were allies. Yet because the Romantic element is so much more theatric in its manifestations, Osborne's reliance on reason and sound judgment has been too often ignored. Without the combination of the two in a high degree of development there could have been no Tom Brown.

To begin with, he stood squarely on the fundamental principle of Romanticism: the inherent goodness of human nature. The early Christian dogma that man is born in sin and can achieve the miracle of grace only through humility was swept aside with an impetuous gesture. Man is born good. He becomes evil through environment and associations. The inevitable corollary is that regeneration is possible only through an appeal to latent decency. In this struggle of the individual to regain self-respect and a sense of social responsibility, society is obligated to help by providing wholesome and inspiring conditions.

The tempestuous quality of Osborne's nature was another phase of the Romantic temperament. The same uprush of emotion which inspired his crusades was equally manifest in his antipathies. If he loved with ardor, he hated with bitterness. There was no middle ground. He was all for a man, or all against him. By the same token, he was practically incapable of compromise. It was all or none. At critical moments in his career, refusal to concede a minor point lost him the chance of preferment—once perhaps, the nomination for governor of New York State. Sudden estrangements with men of great force of character, like Theodore Roosevelt, men who in the main professed the same principles he espoused, hindered him in his work, and, nourished like Achilles' grievance, filled his life with bitterness and contention.

The intensity of Osborne's likes and dislikes was heightened by an absolute confidence in his own perceptions. It is inaccurate to say that Osborne possessed ideas. Ideas possessed him. The assumption of infallibility which his assertions often carried was not, however, the dogmatism of an opinionated man. He rarely took credit for inventing an idea. He presumed only to uncover or restate a truth which had always existed. It was something outside himself, having an independent existence of its own, like one of the eternal verities. Once it was freed from the dust of centuries, anyone could see it and understand it.

The man who accepted its validity and acted upon it was welcomed by Osborne not only because he had demonstrated his personal loyalty but because he had aligned himself with truth and righteousness. The man who rejected it was stigmatized as an enemy of social progress, unwilling for selfish or vicious reasons to concede what he knew in his heart to be true. Thus Osborne was prone to judge men who disagreed with him as either unbelievably stupid or morally corrupt. In either case, a rupture was invariably the result.

It would be forcing an hypothesis too far to insist that Osborne's trusts and distrusts were founded only on this adherence to an abstract ideal. The human element entered in. Like most of us, he was susceptible to flattery. More than one parasite found that a play on his natural vanity was the key to his sympathy and generosity. Others discovered that to wound this amour-propre was to arouse a hostility of unexpected virulence.

There was, however, a curiously disarming quality in Osborne's vanity. It was so lacking in self-consciousness. He made no attempt to conceal it or disguise it with false modesty. Instead, he took a whole-hearted joy in his accomplishments. All taint of a cheap exhibitionism was removed by the childlike simplicity of his enthusiasm. He was always ready, with or without invitation, to run through a Gilbert and Sullivan score with that facility which delighted him quite as much as his listeners. He loved conversation of a literary turn, for his knowledge of the classics was encyclopedic. When he took part in costume plays or operettas, he was enchanted by his magnificent appearance. He never failed to derive and exhibit a naïve pleasure in donning the uniform of lieutenant commander in the Naval Reserve, a rank he attained during the World War through appointment as head of the naval prison

at Portsmouth, New Hampshire. Such unfeigned zest in life
is contagious. Osborne's buoyant spirits were communicated
to those about him, so that others found themselves enjoying to an equal degree the amusements which he found so
entrancing.

Democratic though he was by instinct and training, his
pride of caste, nourished by association with the Brahmin
circle of Harvard and Cambridge, was manifest in his social
contacts. Yet it was not to this group of the socially elect, or
to an intellectual aristocracy, that he looked for progress. He
believed that in the long run the great mass of common
people is wiser than the privileged few. Between his inclina-
tions for congenial companionship and his convictions as to
the promise of human betterment Osborne drew a distinct
line. He even suspected that the propensity of the American
people to hero-worship is dangerous. In the spring of 1908
he wrote in a political article:

"While craving leadership, the American people should be-
ware they do not idolize their leaders, as they are too prone
to do. Is it wise to fool ourselves into believing that any man
is a god? . . . We must restrain ourselves from undue devotion to our heroes lest we find ourselves deceived."

The integrity of this declaration as a general truth may be
slightly undermined by the suspicion that in part at least it
was *argumentum ad hominem*. The allusion to Theodore
Roosevelt is inescapable. Osborne had no use for the hero of
San Juan Hill. The man was getting out of hand. There had
been talk of a third term. The Bull Moose was a-borning.
Roosevelt—the man who would be king! And the people loved
it. Osborne could trust democracy in everything but its infatu-
ations.

Notwithstanding this personal bias, the doctrine is wholly
in keeping with Osborne's philosophy. The judgment of the
many remains unselfish; that of the few is perverted by ambition and greed. To the lines quoted above he added:
"There is something better than a splendid theory—and
that is the Truth. . . . In a multitude of counselors there is
safety."

Many of Osborne's well-wishers have deplored his bent for making enemies. In a sense, that is shortsighted. While it is true that he alienated men whose coöperation might have meant a great deal both in personal advancement and in the furtherance of his humanitarian projects, the same passion that precipitated his feuds was the secret of his power as a leader. Without his conviction of absolute rightness, without his impatience at contradiction, his impress on society would have been far less deep. The imagination of the public was captured by the tremendous sincerity of the man. As he was never lukewarm toward others, so others were never lukewarm toward him. He inspired either unswerving loyalty or aggressive opposition. The weakness and the strength of genius spring from the same source. As Sainte-Beuve sagely remarked, "Nothing so much resembles a hollow as a swelling."

The hallmark of the Romantic is his dream of a world shaped nearer to the heart's desire. Osborne had his dream, his "tower of ivory," and cherished it to the last. Neither disappointment nor mockery could shatter it. The saddest of all spectacles is the disillusioned idealist who seeks refuge from his despair by deriding the thing he still worships. Osborne was made of different stuff. Disappointment never turned into cynicism. Through all the turmoil, misunderstanding, and vilification, he clung to his vision—a world in which the common people, realizing their power and responsibility, shall find their own way to wisdom. He fortified himself with a battle cry, a shibboleth, that recurs so often in his speech and writing that we can accept it as an epitome of his creed. The words are those of Gladstone, spoken in relation to Ireland: "It is liberty alone that fits men for liberty."

This ringing pronouncement that man's salvation lies within himself became the guiding maxim of Osborne's career. In government he was against the tyrant. In politics he was against the boss. In the education of youth he was against a too rigorous imposition of discipline from without. In penology he was against a system that placed criminals under the jurisdiction of petty officials, the guards, whose judgment in meting out penalties for infractions of prison rules was not to be trusted. "No man," he quoted Lincoln, "is good enough to govern another man without that other man's consent."

It is to the everlasting credit of Osborne that he was not content with these negations. For him, to be *against* one thing obligated a man to be *for* something else, militantly, perseveringly. He applied himself to the task of righting wrongs with all the enthusiasm of the visionary; but, with the logic of the rationalist, he checked his theories with practice, often after personal experimentation. That his enthusiasm sometimes carried him further than the inertia of public opinion would stand for is no reflection upon his program. Leadership entails the conception of ideas and the advocacy of courses of action not immediately manifest to the crowd. Otherwise there would be no necessity for leaders.

In view of the revolutionary character of his reforms, it is astounding that Osborne should have obtained public sanction for his policies to the extent that he did. No man without his faculty for making himself and his principles spectacular could have accomplished it. His friend, John Jay Chapman, in a monograph on Osborne a few months after the latter's death, remarked that "the general public must be saturated with an idea before any practical improvement which embodies the idea can be introduced." It is conceivable that all the lecturing and importuning that Osborne undertook in behalf of his prison crusade would have come to nothing had it not been for the excitement produced by his self-imposed incarceration in Auburn Prison. That experiment had the double value of providing him with first-hand information about the psychology of the prisoner and of startling the public into recognition of his purposes. Even the newspapers that held him up to ridicule assisted in preparing the ground for cultivation.

Of even greater significance than public reaction, so far as the infallibility of a principle is concerned, is the test of application. More than once Osborne found that the process of translating ideas into methods of practical operation was complex and baffling. He met these crises with a decisiveness which revealed no trace of the disappointed visionary—only the man of action, the Realist. Had he been able to bring the same eagerness and practical insight to the treatment of routine detail as he brought to the great problems, his task would have been easier and his success greater. He had neither liking nor capacity for the exacting duties of administration, whether in the factory or in the warden's office. His mind was concentrated on fundamentals, and details had for the most part to take care of themselves or to be taken care of by subordinates. He was too impatient to be bothered by trifles and was inclined to confuse the essential minutiæ of organization with red tape. Nature rarely produces that hybrid, the grubber and the creator.

The fate of such a man is to be misunderstood. People responded, favorably or adversely, to his dream of a better world, but only infrequently took the trouble to study his plan for realizing that dream. They were willing to feel with him, but not to think with him. And it was his thinking that gave value to his emotions. Read earnestly and without prejudice, his carefully deliberated utterances carry the authority of sound reasoning. Imagination is disciplined by an orderly mind. Hypotheses are tested. An insatiable student, Osborne buttressed his arguments with the testimony of earlier writers and with the evidence gathered from his own observation and experience. Yet the public in general has grasped only a fragment of the whole. It has been Osborne's misfortune to be applauded by the sentimental and pilloried by the hard-boiled, with the result that misguided well-wishers have often done his cause more harm than have his forthright enemies.

More and more in recent months, however, the validity of the fundamental principles he enunciated has been acknowledged. The controversy he started now tends to center upon the manner in which these principles shall be applied. Though never prompt to concede even a subsidiary point, Osborne was practical enough to apprehend that in the process of realizing the ideal certain adjustments in the machinery might be necessary.

If it was inevitable that Osborne should be misunderstood, it was equally inevitable that he should be betrayed. Even if it be granted in all its implications that man is inherently good, it is too much to hope that in every case an appeal to his better nature will miraculously change the direction of reflexes built up by the habits of a lifetime. The marvel is that Osborne was not more frequently disappointed in his trusts. The world remembers the defaults, forgets the payments. How many men have found a new promise in life because of his inspiration, we shall never know; from his point of view, if but one or two of those to whom he reached a helping hand had dragged themselves from the mire and placed their feet on solid ground, it would have been worth while.

Osborne could rise above betrayal with undimmed faith, but he could not escape the sorrow that such treachery evokes. Sorrow and indignation—the two were blended. Remembering the circumstances of environment and association which had played their part in driving a man back into vice or crime, he could pity the culprit. Realizing, too, the moral responsibility which opportunity for rehabilitation placed upon such an individual, he could not withhold his wrath. To surrender with victory in sight was the act of a coward. Though his capacity for forgiveness was infinite, his patience had its limits. Again and again he would rescue a protégé from the consequences of his misdeeds. He would pay his debts, fight his legal battles, and start him once more along the straight road. The time would come, however, when patience was exhausted. "I wash my hands of you," he told one who had too often betrayed him. "Don't come to me again until you have proved yourself worthy of my confidence." Even this banishment was implicit with hope.

BOOK I

REVEILLE

. . . He calls me by the thunder,
The trumpet sounds within my soul.

CHAPTER I

THE HIGH-VAULTED PAST

AUBURN is quartered by two main roads. One, Genesee Street, runs east and west. The other intersects Genesee Street at the center of town, its two segments being known respectively as North and South streets.

Business has made little headway along South Street. After one block of office buildings and retail stores, you strike immediately into the best residential section. Here stands the Seward mansion, where Lincoln's secretary of state lived. Beyond, extending almost to the city limits, are the residences of Auburn's oldest families—fine structures notwithstanding the "bastard architecture" whose ugliest lines time has softened or partially concealed in the shade of conifers and elms. Most of them are still in possession of descendants of the original owners, for Auburn is like a tree that holds its moss. In the geographical and social group that occupies South Street and its immediate environs there have been comparatively few breaks in continuity. Families cling to the ancestral domain generation after generation. Even when pressure of economic conditions or revolt against the disturbing turmoil of day and night traffic has recommended a change, they have rarely strayed farther than the outskirts of the city, or at the most, the rural region bordering Owasco Lake. A few unkind critics have implied that lethargy rather than loyalty or nostalgia has kept this group intact, but there is *something* which works for uninterrupted succession.

The group consciousness of the "South Street aristocracy" is not simply a matter of social distinction or wealth. Based on tradition and common interests, it has been bulwarked by intermarriage. Nearly all of its members are related in one degree or another. Unless a newcomer has the patience for

27

intensive study of kinship in all its ramifications, he is likely to find himself in a state of perpetual embarrassment. Prick South Street at one end, and it bleeds at the other. Nor should the newcomer be deceived by the masochistic joy the group derives from mortifying itself periodically through petty jealousies, cruelly perceptive criticisms of one another's foibles, and occasional feuds that run their course and disappear into the limbo of forgotten passions. This is a prerogative reserved for itself alone—a sort of communal hair shirt, good for the soul but to be donned *only* at the pleasure of the joint owners.

Into this circle, by virtue of his successful pioneering in industry, came Osborne's father, David Munson Osborne. Here, too, Osborne was born, and his sons, and his sons' sons. Through nearly a century the family has occupied a place of distinction both in the circle and in the community. And yet, in one respect they have been singularly aloof. While the sons and daughters of other South Street families were intermarrying, the Osbornes invariably went afield for their mates, with the Boston area as the favorite trysting ground. Not once since the first generation have they mingled their blood with that of the group with which they are otherwise so intimately connected. They are like some old castle, a conspicuous part of the scenery yet insulated from their surroundings by a moat.

Perhaps this freedom from blood ties has helped to build up a detached attitude; certainly it is partly responsible for the clan feeling which through all vicissitudes and family discords sustains a cohesive loyalty among them. If an ideal were needed as a focal point for this tribal allegiance, already strong because not diffused through lesser relationships, it has been furnished by the career of Thomas Mott Osborne.

To the student of heredity he presents a rather curious problem. He was born September 23, 1859, in Auburn, New York, the third of four children in the family of David Munson and Eliza (Wright) Osborne. So far as personality and conduct show, he owed little to his ancestors on his father's side. Himself an only son, he could trace his line back through the eldest son in each generation to that Richard Osborne of Sheffield, Bedfordshire, who in 1634 sailed from England and settled temporarily in Hingham, Massachusetts Bay Colony. This Richard, founder of the American branch of the family, was apparently the only Osborne down to the generation of Thomas Mott who felt the urge of the wanderlust and exhibited characteristics at variance with the accepted code of society. That he may have proved something of a trial to Bay Colony authorities is indicated in the records, in which the following entry appears:

"June 6, 1637, Richard Osborne was enjoyned to give an account to the constable weekely how he doth impve his time; and if he neglect, further order to be taken by puting him in the Castle."

This admonition had apparently a salutary effect, for Richard, after brief residences at Windsor and New Haven, settled in Fairfield, about midway between New Haven and New York City, where he became one of the largest landowners of the commons of the town, a citizen of means and importance. Though he later moved to Westchester, New York, his direct descendants clung to the Fairfield estates for generations.

Few of the Osbornes achieved either great distinction or great notoriety. Some of the younger sons were active in colonial affairs, rendering able if not exceptional service in the councils of government. Richard's son, Captain John Osborne, was fairly prominent in military affairs, and a great-grandson, Deacon Daniel Osborne, a graduate of Yale College, served briefly and without special merit in the Revolutionary War.

Most of them, however, were content to remain on their own lands, accepting the petty town offices that fell to their lot as men of substance and integrity. This was especially true of the eldest sons, who inherited the bulk of the estates and spent their time raising large crops and larger families. They intermarried with many of the distinguished families of the period, the Burrs, Wards, Wakemans, Couches, Sturgeses, and others, the various lines joining, separating, and joining again in bewildering fashion.

The Revolutionary War started the decline of the family fortunes. At the beginning of the conflict, Deacon Daniel was one of the wealthiest men in the community; but one night in

July, 1779, Tryon and his men fell upon Fairfield and left the thriving town a mass of smoking embers. Deacon Daniel lost nearly everything he owned. Not long after the latter's death in 1801, his grandson, John Hall Osborne, who had inherited half the property, sold all his holdings in Fairfield and moved to Westchester County, New York. There he married Caroline, daughter of Gershom and Hannah (Raymond) Bulkley, and raised a family of eleven children, of whom David Munson Osborne, Thomas Mott Osborne's father, was the eldest son. It was this David Munson Osborne who was to become one of the romantic figures of our early industrial epoch and lay by the fortune that gave his only son, Thomas Mott, not only special advantages in the way of education and travel, but money and leisure for philanthropic experiments.

Thomas Mott Osborne had little in common with these paternal ancestors. There was in him a restless urge, an original as well as versatile genius, and an almost fanatical devotion to ideals. The Osbornes, too, had their ideals—honesty, industry, a sense of obligation to the community that prescribed public service and public benefactions; yet they were content to possess these qualities without seeking to impose their convictions on others. They had little of the missionary spirit that characterized the other side of the family.

Of these intangibles Thomas Mott Osborne inherited uprightness, generosity, and a capacity for indefatigable labors. Though he probably did not realize it until later years, he received also a family motto, part of the heraldic emblem of the English Osbornes: *"Quantum in rebus inane."* How much frivolity in human affairs! That phrase was peculiarly applicable to Tom Osborne's attitude toward his generation, though the implied cynicism was tempered in an almost paradoxical way with faith in that same generation to work out its own salvation—given proper leadership. He was under deep conviction that the time was out of joint and that he, among others, was born to set it right. He had, however, none of Hamlet's indecision and reluctance to act. He accepted the call with eagerness, even gusto.

In a more material way, he owed much to his father, through

whose vision and initiative the manufacturing firm of D. M. Osborne & Co. prospered mightily. As a boy Tom had everything money could buy, though he was taught to spend wisely and share generously. As a man, he used the fortune he inherited to play the rôle of patron of the arts, benefactor of budding genius, and apostle of social uplift. He seemed to come naturally by the notion that opportunity creates obligation.

If the Osbornes provided the substance wherewith these expensive if praiseworthy tastes could be indulged, it was the distaff side that was responsible for the spirit and inclination. Tom's mother was Eliza Wright, daughter of David and Martha (Coffin) Wright. Both the Wrights and the Coffins had been prominent in the Society of Friends since the early days of the colonization of America. David Wright's ancestors had come from England with the William Penn colony and had settled in what is now Bucks County, Pennsylvania. They were a hardy, stubborn race, and David was a hardy, stubborn man. While still in his teens he had left Bucks County for Aurora, New York, a little town on the east bank of Cayuga Lake. There he married Martha Coffin, widow of Captain Peter Pelham, and settled permanently at Auburn, the county seat. Nearly three-quarters of a century later he still took his place at the head of the Osborne table, a defiant, crotchety nonagenarian, four times a great-grandfather, with an indomitable will and an assertive individuality. Much of this tenacity of purpose was transmitted to his daughter, Eliza, and through her to Thomas Mott Osborne.

David's wife, Martha, came from that branch of the Coffin family famous in the history of Massachusetts, and in particular of that little island, Nantucket, so long a center of the whaling industry. She was descended on both sides of the family from several of the original purchasers of Nantucket, among them Tristram Coffin, Sr., the organizer of the purchasing company. Until his retirement to Boston, Martha's father was a sea captain in the China trade, exchanging sealskins for the silks and nankeens of old Cathay, a typical Nantucket skipper who spent most of his life on the ocean. On one of his long cruises his ship was seized by the Spaniards off the Pacific

Coast of South America, and his family heard nothing of him for three years. Anna Coffin, his wife, was one of the "Tory daughters" of William Folger, an obstinate conservative who stood by his king though it cost him most of his property when the Revolutionary War broke.

Stanch Quakers, these Coffins, living in simplicity and godliness, yet in them the germ of revolt: dissenters in religion, nonconformists in speech and dress, abolitionists in the slavery controversy. Nor was it wholly a doctrine of passive resistance. Quakers have been greatly misunderstood. Their quaint ways and conscientious objection to bearing arms disguised a militant, though not a military, spirit, and they were identified with most of the important reforms of the nineteenth century, including penal reform.

The Coffin family contributed its share of the great leaders of the period. Martha herself was one of the early champions of woman's suffrage, but her fame is overshadowed by that of her sister, Lucretia Coffin Mott. Lucretia, who married James Mott, was a preacher in the Society of Friends. She was known both in the United States and in Great Britain as one of the most powerful exhorters for the freedom of the slaves. Early in her married life she had induced her husband to give up a lucrative cotton business because cotton was a product of slave labor. Between loss of income and extra expense incurred by trading only at "free labor stores" the Motts were nearly ruined, but Lucretia's determination carried them through half a century until Lincoln's Emancipation Proclamation took the taint from cotton and sugar.

She must have been a vital personality, courageous, domineering in a quiet, unanswerable way. An extreme individualist, she broke from the orthodox Society of Friends and united with a liberal Quaker wing. She lectured fearlessly on abolition in slave states where it was dangerous even to admit such views. William Lloyd Garrison and Lucy Stone were her intimate friends. Evoking both scorn and adoration, she was not daunted by the one or cozened by the other.

It was her experiences in London in 1840 as a delegate to the World's Antislavery Convention that led Lucretia Mott to undertake another great crusade. When she and her Quaker sisters found themselves barred on account of their sex from active participation in the convention, Lucretia for the first time realized the inferior and humiliating position women had been compelled to occupy for centuries. Then and there she compacted with Elizabeth Cady Stanton to call a Woman's Rights Convention as soon as practicable after their return to the States. Eight years later this vow was fulfilled, and the first convention for the emancipation of women held in America met at Seneca Falls, New York, July 19 and 20, 1848. Lucretia's sister Martha, Thomas Mott Osborne's grandmother, was chairman of that historic convocation. In the next generation, Osborne's mother, Eliza Wright, took up the battle for the political and economic independence of women.

Osborne's earliest recollections were associated with distinguished men and women of liberal tendencies who gathered at his parents' home in Auburn—Elizabeth Cady Stanton, Susan B. Anthony, the Motts, Garrisons, and others. Sometimes Tom was allowed to accompany his mother and father on visits to these people. Later, when he went to a preparatory school near Boston and thence to Harvard, he was thrown into the very citadel of liberalism. There were giants in the land even in those days, for many of the great spirits of the early and mid century had not yet passed away. About Boston there lingered the afterglow of its Golden Age, waning, it is true, but radiant enough still to fire the idealism of youth.

Liberalism and militant revolt were thus a family tradition with Osborne's maternal ancestors. They gravitated naturally to the left, so that each generation had its apostle of reform either by birth or by adoption. New links with liberals were continually being forged. Eliza Wright's sister Ellen married William Lloyd Garrison, Second, son of the great abolitionist, and drew the two families still closer. James Russell Lowell, who with Whittier invoked the poetic muse in behalf of the antislavery cause, was an uncle of Osborne's wife,. Agnes Devens.

Tom, therefore, felt an influence both biological and intellectual. Not only did the blood of reformers leap in his veins, but from early youth he was exposed to the inspiration of famous progressives associated with his family. What was at first mere hero worship became strong conviction. He studied their careers and their philosophy, and could quote verbatim numerous passages from their written works. Particularly was he attracted by Lowell, whose broad culture and classic poise formed a contrasting background for trenchant democratic sentiments. Above all he was fond of quoting those lines from *The Present Crisis:*

Once to every man and nation comes the moment to decide,
In the strife of Truth with Falsehood, for the good or evil side.

Before many years he was to realize that only too often in this opposition of forces it is: "Truth forever on the scaffold, Wrong forever on the throne."

The moral struggle was always very real to Osborne. For him, life was an old morality play with vice and virtue battling for the soul of man. Through his conscience spoke generations of Quakers, abolitionists, and reformers. He had their strength and their weakness. Once his mind was made up, Osborne was immutable. He was inclined to be categorical in his judgments and arbitrary in his actions. Few men could reason with him, for he was impatient of disagreement. The other side was always the wrong side. He spoke, as did his maternal ancestors, in the vocative mode, asking little, demanding much.

Coupled with these harsher traits there was a great tenderness and sympathy, as well as an unfeigned delight in social and intellectual diversions. He was a reformer, but no ascetic.

Born of liberals, raised in liberalism, with tradition and inclination urging him on, he might be deemed preordained for the course he was to follow. And yet, had not a tragedy severed the ties that bound him to a happy domestic life, the militant spirit in him would have been under control. A progressive he would have been in politics and social theory. He would have responded to the cry of the oppressed. But the Savonarola touch would have been wanting. That was as much a product of circumstances as of disposition.

CHAPTER II

APRON STRINGS

It had come at last. In the autumn of 1859 when Thomas Mott Osborne was born, few could doubt that civil war was inevitable. Abolitionists were clamoring for the establishment of a separate northern republic free from slavery. A southern republic founded on the institution of slavery was the dream of extremists below the Mason and Dixon line. Slowly but surely the centrifugal forces in the United States had increased until they equaled the centripetal. Only a touch was needed to destroy the balance and fling the two segments apart.

Attempts to plug the hole left in the Constitution by its framers had been in vain. It was too late now to solve the problem of slavery by rational means. Hate and bitterness engulfed the nation. Emotion ruled. Oratory and statesmanship had failed. Compromise and legislation had failed. Both Clay and Webster were dead, and in the White House was a man with no gift for either compromise or strong action. He simply observed that Congress had no power to prevent any state from withdrawing if it wished, and washed his hands of the matter.

There were two residents of Auburn, New York, who were to play a large rôle in the impending struggle; one conspicuously as a statesman, the other unobtrusively as a manufacturer. William H. Seward had served two terms as governor of New York State and had twice been elected to the United States Senate. In 1860 he was to be Lincoln's strongest competitor for the Republican nomination for President, and thereafter during the progress of the war was to head Lincoln's cabinet as secretary of state. David Munson Osborne, on the other hand, lived quietly at home, perfecting and merchandising his mower and reaper. Until years later, many

35

failed to realize how important a factor the latter had been in the success of the Union forces. The prime requisite in war time is man power. Second only to man power is food supply. The farm machines that D. M. Osborne & Co. manufactured and distributed throughout the northern states released men for military service who otherwise would have been compelled to plant and harvest the crops. For once at least the transition from manual labor to machine labor was accomplished with no disturbing economic unrest. Instead of throwing men from the wheat fields to the bread line, the invention of harvesting machines threw them from the wheat fields to the battlefields. It had come at the psychological moment for the northern cause, and the South was severely handicapped.

When Tom was born, his father was just beginning to establish himself in the new industry. For the first time in his life, D. M. Osborne knew what it meant to be reasonably free from financial worries. As a boy of fifteen he had been compelled to leave his father's farm in Rye, New York, to fend for himself. For a time he clerked in a grocery store in New York City; then he entered the hardware business. From the first he had no childhood such as most boys enjoy. It was work and responsibility always. The only opportunity he had for education came during his New York residence. He would leave the grocery, get a bite to eat, and pore over his books in night school. That left little time for recreation. Besides, he soon had other worries. His father died, and at the age of eighteen David Munson found himself the guardian of his brothers and sisters, responsible for their upbringing and part of their maintenance. The one-seventh portion of the estate which fell to each child was hardly enough to keep them.

The first turn in fortunes came while he was working in the hardware store. His firm did business with Watrous & Hyde, hardware merchants of Auburn. Watrous met young Osborne and was impressed by his ability and seriousness of purpose. When Hyde died in 1848, Watrous offered Osborne a junior partnership in the Auburn firm, an opportunity that was promptly accepted.

Within a few years, however, Watrous retired, and a new partnership was formed, Osborne, Barker & Baldwin. When this firm failed a year or two later, Osborne decided to start in manufacturing on his own. Purchasing a plot of land on the main business street of Auburn, he began to make straw cutters and corn shellers.

Those were lean, lean years. Struggle as he might, business did not improve. One picture of him in those days is preserved for us. He is sitting in his little office, dividing a month's profits of five dollars with Henry Kosters, faithful aid in the construction of his plant and in the running of the business. Soon there were no profits at all, and his first experiment as an independent manufacturer failed dismally.

With a debt of several thousand dollars, and a wife and two daughters to support, he left Auburn for Buffalo to start over again. There he met William Kirby, an employee in the factory where the Forbush machine was being made. Kirby had invented a combined reaper and mower, and Osborne immediately saw its possibilities. Borrowing $4,000, he obtained an interest in the patent rights and began production. In 1856 seven machines were built, the trials being held on the Sherwood farm in Cayuga County. Success was immediate. Osborne returned to Auburn, took possession of the old building in Genesee Street that had been the scene of his former failure, and established a new company, with Charles P. Wood and Cyrus C. Dennis as partners. By the end of the second year of operation profits permitted him to pay off all debts, and when the Civil War began, D. M. Osborne & Co. was equipped to furnish harvesting machines to most of the northern states.

In these days of massed capital and organized labor it is difficult to appreciate the relationship which existed between D. M. Osborne and his employees. Osborne watched over his men in the shops with the solicitude of a father, and they repaid him with a loyalty that would be incomprehensible to most of our employers. There were no strikes because there was nothing to strike for. Men spent a lifetime in the Osborne works and, when retired at last, cherished memories of little kindnesses they had received from "the old man." In 1930 the dedication of a new city hall in Auburn, the gift of Mrs. Frederick Harris and Mrs. James J. Storrow in memory of their father, D. M. Osborne, brought a flood of letters to the newspapers from old shopmen recalling their experiences of fifty and more years before when they had worked at the plant. The keynote of these reminiscences was their personal touch. The head of the firm had had direct contact with the lowliest puddler apprentice.

For all his benevolence, D. M. Osborne was a dominating personality, a paternal autocrat. Whatever the personnel of the firm, his word was final. In the contract for the partnership of Osborne, Barker, & Baldwin he had incorporated the following article: "In case of disagreement among the partners, the said D. M. Osborne shall decide." It was the same with the new company. All decisions were referred to him. Nothing was done without his sanction. In all his long career as a manufacturer he relied upon his own judgment for the conduct of the business, and only once did he fall into grave error. Then, as if Fate were jealous of such undiluted success, the business was nearly ruined.

One may assert with confidence that the establishment and development of D. M. Osborne & Co. was a one-man job. It had meant years of hardship and disappointment at first; later, a concentration that excluded almost every other interest. The rest of his family gave him little support. When Wood retired in 1862, David Munson took his younger brother John into the firm. John was always dependent on his brother for support. He was an eccentric character, a fussy, pompous person who added little or nothing to the business. But though he was a joke at the office, no one dared suggest that he be ousted.

Even Mrs. Osborne could not comprehend fully her husband's engrossment in business. Sometimes he would come home dog-tired and drop down for a nap, leaving word to be called at a certain hour for an important appointment. But Mrs. Osborne had no conscience about appointments. Often he would awake to find he had overslept an hour or more.

DAVID MUNSON OSBORNE

Portrait by Orlando Rouland

ELIZA WRIGHT OSBORNE

"You needed the sleep," his wife would remark laconically. Giving her a glance, half-amused, half-sorrowful, he would leave the house without a word.

During the Civil War Osborne went to London to exhibit his machines at the World's Fair. The business was prospering, and branch offices were being opened in the principal cities of the United States. In 1866, shortly after C. H. Burdick had succeeded to the firm upon the death of Dennis, the second national trial of farm machines was held in Auburn under the auspices of the New York State Agricultural Society. Out of forty-four mower entries, Osborne & Co. won first prize, and out of thirty reapers, second. Both fame and fortune had arrived.

By this time, the Osborne family was complete. Tom, an only son, had three sisters, two older than he, Emily and Florence; and one younger, Helen. He was named after Thomas Mott, the husband of his mother's half-sister Marianna, Martha Coffin's daughter by her first marriage to Captain Peter Pelham. An extraordinarily beautiful child, a bit girlish with a passion for pretty things, Tom was something of an enigma to his parents. He looked out on the world with large brown eyes, wistful and appealing. Marking the soulful gaze, a friend of the family exclaimed, "Eliza, how do you expect to raise a child with an expression like that?"

Even as a little boy Tom took delight in his clothes. He was sensitive to color and loved to blossom out in a brand-new jacket. One of his earliest attachments was a straw hat trimmed with a purple velvet ribbon. It became the very apple of his eye. One day at a picnic Tom was taken for a boat ride on Owasco Lake. A gust of wind snatched the lovely headgear and sent it sailing overboard, never to be retrieved. "Oh, my purple velvet!" he wailed. "Oh, my purple velvet!" And he would not be comforted.

He never did get over his fondness for fine feathers. As a man beyond the prime of life, he reveled in the gorgeous costumes of period masquerades and the pageantry of the theater. One sees him returning to a friend's home in Syracuse where he is to spend the night after appearing in one of the principal rôles of an opera. He is dressed in hunting clothes, red coat, white breeches, high boots. A disturbingly handsome figure out of an old print. The good nights are said, and the party prepares to retire. At the head of the stairs Osborne is confronted by a great pier glass in which he sees a full-length reflection of himself. He is enchanted; he nearly swoons with delight. For another half-hour he attitudinizes before the mirror, wholly absorbed in that marvelous creation he has become, entertaining the tired hosts with rapid-fire comment on music and the stage, interpolated with naïve exclamations of self-admiration.

Again he is conducting an orchestra in a theater concert, unconscionably aware of the spick-and-spanness of his naval officer's uniform worn with such address that he is easily the most conspicuous person in the auditorium. Military garb set off his erect figure to the best possible advantage, and he loved it as he had loved his "purple velvet." Even after the Armistice he often used this uniform for formal occasions, and in it sat for his portrait to the painter Orlando Rouland.

Women were fascinated by this passion for beautiful clothes, but men were rather taken aback and embarrassed. They could not understand it, and were a little ashamed that one of their sex should go into ecstasies over a bit of finery. The masculine code enjoins a high scorn for such things or, at the very least, reticence. Osborne, untrammeled by inhibition or prohibition, never hesitated to rhapsodize whenever the spirit moved him. The very transparency of his nature deluded many into believing that this was mere front, and that behind the simplicity there were unfathomable depths of mystery.

Tom was born in a large wooden house in South Street, still one of the most beautiful thoroughfares in central New York. Lofty elms on either side interlaced their topmost branches, forming a natural nave. Fine old residences with well-kept lawns bordered the unpaved street, with carriage blocks and iron hitching-posts hospitably inviting calls from the neighbors. Farther down the road was the Seward mansion in the building of which, a half-century before, the young apprentice, Brigham Young, had labored, blissfully unaware of his prophetic mission. Occasionally Secretary Seward himself, resting from his heavy duties in Washington, would ride forth in his coach for a drive in the cool of a summer evening, greeting his old friends with a bow and a smile as he passed.

The Osborne yard was a gathering place for the children of the neighborhood. On the piazza was a rope swing that could gradually be "worked up" to an arc of such magnitude that one could touch his toes to the ceiling, as a large spot innocent of paint attested. Behind the house the garden and stable beckoned to young explorers, and a bough apple tree with sprawly branches demanded climbing.

Unfortunately, these attractions did not wholly suffice. Mrs. Osborne watched over her brood like the proverbial hen, and if Tom played anywhere he played at home. As he could not roam the streets or visit other playmates, most boys soon tired of his companionship. Not even a rope swing and a bough apple tree can hold the male cub for long. He is too restless and questing. Mrs. Osborne may have been too strict in ordering her son's life, but she was by no means the usual type of oversolicitous mother. Though her capacity for dominating a situation made her at times rather formidable, she had a truly noble spirit and a kindliness that no autocratic manner could disguise. Her strong features were tempered by eyes which responded sympathetically to distress. Hundreds blessed her for her generosity, and many others held a deep respect for her executive ability. It was but natural that a woman of her force of character should seek, above all, to provide for her only son that protection she was so amply qualified to give. Even when Tom had grown to manhood, she still thought of him as her little boy, her Timmie, in need of her guidance in the fashioning of his life.

As a consequence of the restrictions placed upon him, young Tom came more and more to indulge his own tastes, which were feminine to begin with. He learned to sew, knit, and crochet better than most girls, and was so undisguisedly fond of his craft that his sisters were embarrassed. Then, too, he played with dolls much longer than most children, boys or girls. His sister Emily was often out of patience with him for insisting on joining her own little group in playing house. "I should have been the boy," she would complain bitterly, "and you the girl."

Tom was not at all abashed by these rebuffs. In the make-believe land of dolls he found an irresistible appeal. When he was twelve years old he headed his Christmas list with two things upon which he had set his heart; a set of Shakespeare and a wax doll. It may have been childish; again, it may have had a deeper significance. So long as he lived, the representation of other characters, whether by puppets or by living persons, was intensely alluring; and by a natural transition he came to look upon himself as an actor in one of the world's great social dramas.

More in the boy tradition were the days spent at Willow Point, the Osborne summer home on Owasco Lake. In after years Tom remembered these excursions as the happiest times of his childhood. Early Sunday morning the coachman would draw up at the carriage porch, a big luncheon basket would be stowed in the phaëton, and the whole family started on the long drive to Willow Point. Here the boy found real enjoyment in rambles through the woods, hunts for crawfish in the shallows of the lake, and all the outdoor diversions a healthy youngster can invent.

While still in his thirteenth year Tom took the first of his many trips abroad. It was an extended tour, lasting well over six months, including England, Wales, and most of the countries on the Continent. Christmas was spent in Dresden. In his reading and games Tom had already shown juvenile symptoms of the historian and the artist. Now he had his first opportunity to correlate names and things. His grandest achievement was the collection of photographs of all the kings of France, with their queens and mistresses. In his lexicon of youth the scarlet words of French court life had no sinister meaning. A queen was like your mother, and a mistress was a sort of favorite aunt. With perfect innocence he would explain these distinctions to whoever would consent to look through his album with him.

Again the following year the family went abroad, but the

great panic of 1873 brought Mr. Osborne home before the others. When he landed, he found conditions much more distressing than he had imagined. Many banks regarded as impregnable had failed. Some of the wealthiest men in the country had gone into bankruptcy. To his great relief, Mr. Osborne learned that his own business, though suffering some losses, was in no great danger.

As he saw the poverty about him, men and women used to all that luxury could bring living in single rooms, their carriages and horses and mansions swallowed up in a moment by the collapse of the nation's financial structure, he realized what he had escaped. With gratitude in his heart he drove to the new house he was building, farther out South Street at the outskirts of the town where soon, thanks to the soundness of D. M. Osborne & Co., he and his family would be established. Looking out of a western window on the second story, he could see the sun shining on the snow-clad hills beyond Seneca Lake, thirty miles away, and felt strangely comforted. Only one thing bothered him—the cost. That was growing beyond all his calculations. When the bills reached $100,000, he paid them and destroyed the records. No one, he vowed, would ever know just how much he had spent.

The new house was an imposing structure of brick covered with gray mastic, the largest and most substantial residence in town. Built in the hybrid style of the mid-Victorian era, with heavy, severe lines topped by a mansard roof, it had the somber, aloof air of a magistrate. Within, high ceilings and thick walls deadened sounds, a phenomenon that was reflected in the diminuendo of people's voices unconsciously hushed to comport with the palpable sobriety of the surroundings. An atmosphere of respectability judiciously combined with elegance permeated the rooms. The mantels were of marble. The woodwork was black walnut, with Circassian walnut and curly ash inlays. In the drawing-room a great glass chandelier imported from London looked down with scintillating hauteur, its magnificence being reflected in two pier glasses that filled the wall spaces at the side and end of the room. On the newel post in the hall a bronze damsel, discreetly scarfed, upheld a lamp to light the feet of visitors entering the great double door.

To this temple of Victorian splendor Tom Osborne returned after a few months in Europe that had included a visit to the World's Fair at Vienna. It was great fun for the children to explore their new home and its grounds; but it was the attic that captured their youthful fancy. There during long winter afternoons or on rainy summer days they slew the chimera with the aid of a sawhorse Pegasus, or played charades, or acted little operas and fairy stories that Tom adapted from the originals. He was always the leader in the theatricals, being a born stage manager. Even his little sister Helen, conscripted to play tragic rôles, was overwhelmed with pride when Tom reported that "Baby died splendid."

The dramatic entertainments received a great impetus at this time, for in Paris the young producer had purchased a toy Punch and Judy theater. For years afterward he delighted to give shows for the sisters and cousins at the holidays; and his sons, with children of their own, have perpetuated the custom. Every Christmas Eve the small boys and girls in the neighborhood are invited to the same house in South Street to see Punch and Judy pop out of the same little box and renew their three-century-old quarrel.

Most boys and girls enjoy "dressing up." It is a passing phase in normal development, an expression of the dramatic impulse always most active in primitive races and in children. But Osborne never outgrew it. Unless we realize at the outset how strong in him was this impersonation complex, we can never grasp the full significance of his later career.

Life at 99 South Street ran on in the usual fashion of the mid-Victorian era. It was sedate, yet not stifling, and Tom enjoyed himself in his own way. Sometimes he would go for a solemn drive with the Osborne coachman. At other times he would ride his own cream-colored pony, though he never really cared much for horses or any pets for that matter. His sister Florence, on the other hand, had a passion for mothering all the stray animals that crossed her path. Her special weakness was cats, but almost any waif could find refuge with her. She once found a tiny chick with a broken leg and placed it tenderly in a canary cage. It chanced that Mrs. Osborne was called away from home for several weeks. Upon her return she was taken to see how much the chick had grown. When she saw the creature she nearly collapsed, for as such birds will, it had grown into a rooster and its head, attached to an incredibly long neck, was pressed uncomfortably into the wires of the cage top. Had Tom been interested in such things at the time, he might have learned a lesson in ingratitude: for this same rooster turned into a most shrewish fowl that chased the youngest of the family with fell intent.

Though Tom Osborne was five years older than his sister Helen, he turned naturally to her for companionship. Emily, the present Mrs. Frederick Harris, and Florence, who died in her young womanhood, were sent to boarding school at an early age, leaving the two youngest of the family together. There was nothing patronizing in Tom's attitude toward his sister. He could find enjoyment in building a dark house out of blankets flung over the dining-room table; or cutting out paper dolls; or doing tapestry work. About this time, he suffered several illnesses. During one convalescence he learned to make wax flowers, the masterpiece being a group of artificial water lilies arranged on a round mirror, the whole covered with a half-sphere of iridescent glass. The finishing touch was a halo of red chenille. For years this *objet d'art* occupied a conspicuous place on a table in his mother's room, and in the minds of its creator and his sister represented the fulfillment of the æsthetic ideal.

Young Osborne's artistic impulse found its first real satisfaction in music. After a few lessons with such teachers as a small town afforded, it was evident that he had a phenomenal gift for the technique of the piano. He read music with speed and assurance, could play by ear, and remembered a composition accurately once he had mastered it. One winter he spent with his mother in New York City, studying with a renowned instructor; and he continued his musical studies in college.

Yet even his sister Helen, now Mrs. James J. Storrow, cannot remember seeing Tom practice. Mere formal exercises were always distasteful to him. As soon as he learned facility, he began playing everything he could lay his hands on, regardless of its suitability to his stage of development. Before long he had a repertory of which, for mere variety, a concert artist might be proud.

In spite of a talent that amounted almost to virtuosity, his touch was rarely pleasing to the sensitive ear. When he sat down to a piano, he attacked it with the same impetuosity he exhibited in all his avocations. He played with brilliance and dash and an air of excitement, but was inclined to overaccentuation. Under his strong fingers the notes sounded hard and metallic like those of a player-piano. There was a machinelike perfection without the shading that distinguishes the performance of a great artist.

The most stimulating feature of his playing was his own undisguised enjoyment in it. He would sit at the piano for hours, forgetful of time and circumstance. Yet he liked to have an audience. Whatever Osborne did was usually the better done for public observation. The showman in him responded to imaginary footlights. Recognition, whether favorable or unfavorable, acted upon him like a stimulant, and he was at his best when holding the center of the stage. Once in a great while, however, when he was alone or in the presence of an intimate friend, a different spirit controlled him. The brittleness of tone vanished. There was a delicacy of touch, a tenderness of expression in harmony with some inward mood, that transformed his playing. The true artist, not the showman, spoke through his fingers. As he played, he often would recite poetry as a sympathetic accompaniment, especially Browning's "Rabbi Ben Ezra," which he loved. The few who were privileged to see him under such a spell felt they had witnessed a revelation, that for a few moments an Osborne they only vaguely suspected had opened a secret place in his heart, usually so cautiously guarded.

Occasionally he approached this mood of inspiration when playing for great musicians, for he was welcome in their company. Their acceptance of him as a kindred spirit evoked his genius. Before the literary and musical group that surrounded Mrs. Spencer Trask at Yaddo, her estate in Saratoga Springs, or in the home of Walter Damrosch, or at a privileged concert in Carnegie Hall, he seldom showed that self-consciousness which makes for pretense. He was at home among his peers; he forgot the crowd; he played from within, with the quiet joy of self-expression through the most fluid of arts.

It was far different in Auburn. There he seemed to feel an unspoken antagonism. Once he wrote: "Running counter, as I always have, in politics and in many other respects, to the prejudices of this community, I am regarded as a very erratic and wrong-headed person in most intellectual matters." In his desire to make an impression, he unconsciously adopted a flamboyant style, with the result that his prodigious skill rather than his true talent, was most appreciated. For many, of course, this was quite sufficient; but it seems strange that with a few exceptions those who knew him best realized least his potential genius in music.

Although his sisters attended boarding schools, Tom Osborne was sent to No. 2 Public School in Auburn, where Miss Julia Ferris, a teacher of much spirit and common sense, taught him her doctrine of "gumption" as she was to teach it to three generations. She was an assertive little body, radiating energy and will power, with a mind like a steel trap and a wit caustic and provocative. The passing years failed to impair either her memory or her alertness, and in her eighties she would greet her old pupils with droll reminiscences of their school days.

From her inspiring tutorage, Tom passed into high school, where he spent a year or two. He was a handsome boy, rather overgrown and plump, keeping much to himself and entering little into the strenuous sports of his comrades. It could not be said that he was generally popular. His tastes were finical, and he had such a highly developed sense of propriety in speech and conduct that he could never quite forget himself in the homely pastimes of his playmates. One day he was invited to a party at the home of one of Auburn's prominent families. With his usual solicitude for personal appearance, he dressed in his best and summoned the Osborne coach. To his dismay, on arrival he was ushered to the rear of the house, where he found a kitchen party in progress in the absence of the master and mistress. This bit of unconventionality so disgusted him that he stalked out of the house and walked home. Still, he was not a recluse. Some intimate contacts with his fellows he must have had, for he founded a secret society, known to the world as the D. S., which flourished for years. Only when the members had grown to maturity was the full name revealed: "Da Scherzo," which they had imagined meant, "For Fun."

How much of Tom's fastidiousness was innate and how much the product of his mother's overwhelming surveillance one cannot be certain. That he had half-unrealized longings for a life of unrestraint may be assumed, for his reading was largely in the realm of action, history, period romances, novels of chivalry and brave deeds. He must have had dreams of which no one guessed, in which he rode into adventure with flying plumes and blaring trumpets. The day was to come when he would break the spell that had been woven about him and lead a charge against walls as impregnable and accursed as Merlin's castle.

CHAPTER III

ADAMS ACADEMY

JUST before his sixteenth birthday Tom accompanied his father on a visit to a number of the eastern preparatory schools. The decision of Mr. and Mrs. Osborne to send their son away from home to continue his education was a turning point in his career. His mother was a cultured woman who had inspired him with her love for good books and fine music. She had given him an example of high-minded service in liberal causes and of generosity in philanthropic and community enterprises. Yet there was danger that her dominating spirit would encompass his own, mold it into an imitation instead of letting it develop as a free and independent thing.

What he needed was a chance to rub shoulders with his youthful peers and make his own way among them. This opportunity came when Adams Academy at Quincy, Massachusetts, was preferred among the preparatory schools visited. It was a fortunate choice. Founded in 1872, fifty years after John Adams, second President of the United States, had bequeathed land for the purpose, Adams Academy maintained the classical tradition in education. The terms of the grant provided that "as soon as the funds shall be sufficient, a schoolmaster should be procured, learned in the Greek and Roman languages." The trustees were faithful to this ideal, employing Dr. William Dimmock, teacher at the Boston Latin School, as the first headmaster.

Osborne found Adams Academy much to his liking. There he received a thorough grounding not alone in the dead languages, but in Greek and Roman history, oratory, and kindred subjects. Relations between the students, then fewer than one hundred, and Dr. Dimmock were unusually close, for all except the older boys were kept under the headmaster's wing. There were supervised study periods even in the evening. On Sunday morning, church attendance was required, and in the afternoon "short homilies" by Dr. Dimmock continued the process of edification.

Tom, however, escaped much of the Sabbath ritual, for he was permitted to spend his Sundays with the William Lloyd Garrisons in Roxbury, with occasional visits to the Hallowells in Medford.

The town of Quincy, one of the oldest settlements in New England, appealed to Osborne's historic sense. The school itself was built on the site of John Hancock's birthplace. The Josiah Quincys and James Otis had occupied the old house in turn, and the memory of John Adams and John Quincy Adams was closely associated with the institution. Once a year in October, Founder's Day was celebrated with appropriate ceremonies.

It was an uphill fight for Osborne to win the complete confidence of his fellow students. Notwithstanding his pleasant manner and interesting conversation, there was something about him the boys could not fathom. They felt and resented a certain assumption of superiority. Tom was a natural leader, yet in many respects strangely aloof. He carried his own atmosphere with him. To the young bloods of Adams Academy a boy who had no slang or small talk, regarded smoking as a crime, boasted of no bad habits, and took pride in accomplishments that belonged, in their opinion, to a young ladies' finishing school was a phenomenon outside their experience. When, under the stress of emotion, Osborne folded his hands across his breast and ejaculated "Oh, my!" the expletive struck them as inexcusably inadequate.

Yet, whatever the criticism spoken or implied, Osborne went his own way. He loved the adulation of his fellows, but would not cater to it. A strong sense of propriety as well as a congenital dislike for anything vulgar governed his actions. One evening as he was writing a letter to his sister Emily amid frequent interruptions from a group of schoolmates, a Harvard freshman, Adams Academy graduate, burst into the room with the suggestion that they attend a dance given in the town. The idea was received with enthusiasm by all except Tom. He wrote to his sister:

I like a good boy refused, partly because I have some lessons I must get but mostly because the dances here are not so select as they might be, and when I dance I like to dance with the best. I must confess I have a very strong dislike of lowering myself, so to speak. I am ready to enter into higher society, but I will not go into lower.

With most boys, such a letter might be construed as written expressly for home consumption, but in this case it was an expression of honest conviction.

Tom's second year at Adams Academy was marred by the first real tragedy to strike the Osborne family. In February, he received word that he should come home immediately as his sister Florence was seriously ill. Throwing a few things into his traveling bag, he rushed for the station, only to miss the train by seconds. The next day, accompanied by his aunt, Mrs. Garrison, he set out for Auburn. As he entered the great doorway of his home, the hush struck a chill to his heart. It was like a tomb. Slowly he mounted the stairs to the sick-room and turned the knob. For a long moment he stood there looking at the still face so white against the white pillow. Then softly he closed the door. His sister was dead.

To Mrs. Osborne, Florence's death was a shock from which she never fully recovered. The memory of her daughter became one of the most precious things in life, and the room where she had slept was preserved for years exactly as it had been in the past. When Osborne brought back a bride to live in the old home, the spot was still hallowed ground filled with whispers of the dead.

Though apparently robust, Tom was subject to repeated attacks of sickness aggravated by chronic catarrh. Back in Quincy following the burial of his sister, he was twice taken seriously ill. At the second attack, his parents took him out of school for a rest. A summer at Bar Harbor and a jaunt into the Adirondacks failing to restore his health, it was decided that he should spend a year in travel. With an older cousin, William Morris Davis, then instructor at Harvard and later an eminent geologist, he journeyed round the world, starting west to the Pacific Coast, thence to Japan, China, India, Ceylon, Egypt, Malta, and the countries of Europe.

Now, at the age of eighteen, he was a seasoned traveler making his fifth voyage overseas. With infinite care and no small amount of pride he recorded the impressions of the trip in letters home. These were voluminous missives, written in a light informal vein yet with some pretense to literary style. The amazing thing, however, is the extraordinary background they reveal. He not only described vividly the scenes he visited but commented with considerable acumen upon the history, art, architecture, social customs, religion, and general character of the peoples of the Orient and of Europe. Original pen sketches illustrated his points.

Mrs. Osborne was so pleased that she had Frank R. Rathbun, a draftsman, transcribe them in longhand on fine paper, with illuminated lettering and designs, the whole sheaf being bound in four large leather and board volumes entitled, "A Year from Home, or the Circuit of the Globe." Twenty-five years later Osborne published selections from these letters in the local newspaper, the *Auburn Bulletin*, and was delighted with their reception by the public.

It had been planned that after his return from abroad Tom should spend a year in Cambridge studying with tutors for the Harvard examinations, but this program was given up as impracticable. It took two years more of study at Adams Academy to prepare him for entrance to college. At Quincy, Tom found that Dr. Dimmock had been superseded by Dr. William Everett, son of the famous statesman, orator, and author, Edward Everett. The new headmaster was a nervous, irascible, little man, just under forty, whose eccentricities had the spark of genius. It was afterwards discovered that his humors were the result of a curious affection of the ears, which were disparately tuned so that a single sound, like a piano note, was transmitted to the brain as two sounds, one-eighth to one-quarter tone apart.

For this choleric pedagogue young Osborne formed a genuine attachment, comparable only to that greater friendship with Dr. Charles W. Eliot, president of Harvard College. Dr. Everett in his explosive way was most ingenious in contriving aphorisms, which Tom in boyish admiration hoarded in his memory. One in particular made a deep impression, to which in his highly controversial career he often resorted: "When I'm in a minority, I'm pretty sure I'm right. When I'm in a very small minority, then I *know* I'm right." Osborne was so often in a very small minority that on the basis of this major premise he could argue that he was nearly always right.

Of necessity, recreations were limited in Adams Academy. There was no baseball, no boating. Tennis, "that funny game from England," was popular with only a few. Basketball had not yet been invented. The students concentrated on one major sport, football, and in that they excelled. For two years they won every game, trouncing all the big preparatory school teams and even challenging the Harvard Varsity. Harvard would not play, and surviving members of the Adams Academy eleven still aver they would have "licked the stuffing out of 'em."

It was football that changed the boys' attitude toward Tom Osborne. Tom was a large fellow, but a little soft and disinclined either to receive or to give buffets. An incentive to participation in the manly sport of the gridiron was provided by the example of his new roommate, Harry R. Woodward, familiarly known as "Fuddy." Woodward was a handsome young giant, a football star, and the idol of the whole academy. In spite of the contrasts in their natures, the two boys took a great liking to each other from the start. Each recognized something wholesome and genuine in the other. Realizing Osborne's potentiality as a football player, Woodward induced his roommate to try out for the team, with the result that each afternoon found Tom in the thick of the scrimmage on the playing field. Whole-heartedly he set out to win a place as a "rusher" in the line, a position that exposed him to a lot of mauling from both friend and foe.

In those days football was not the open game it is now, hedged in with rules and penalties. It was more like a free-for-all fight, with bruises, black eyes, and not infrequently broken bones the guerdon of victory. When he took all this punishment without a whimper, the young men of Adams Academy revised their opinion of him. He wasn't so effeminate after all. There was good stuff in him.

For his part, Tom gloried in his scars. When he made the team he wrote home:

I am on the football eleven. To be sure, I haven't done anything to justify the fact yet, but nevertheless it is true as various kicks and bumps on my poor frame can testify; for instance: item one—dig in the eye (small); item one—lump behind the left ear (size of a small chestnut); item one—claw at the muscles of my arm, two finger marks plainly to be seen; item one—strained wrist (slight). I forebear to proceed.

Though these were small matters compared to what was to follow in the big games, he would have done better to keep them to himself. The family was horrified. Mrs. Osborne could not bear to think of her Timmie making such a vulgar spectacle of himself, to say nothing of risking life and limb. Even Mr. Osborne disapproved. Weren't there other pastimes more gentlemanly and less strenuous?

For the first time, perhaps, Tom refused to obey his parents' injunctions. Possibly he realized the transformation that the rough and tumble of athletics was working in him. At any rate, he was obdurate. Play he would, no matter what the cost. Time and again the subject came up at the family councils during vacations until at last Tom adopted the diplomacy of silence. Even as late as his sophomore year in college the controversy was still raging. He confided to his diary:

Papa said he should expect me not to play tennis or football when I went back—or words to that effect. As I fully intend to do both, I did not say anything. Dear me, life is a burden sometimes, and I am ready to get back to Cambridge where life is not so heavy a burden as elsewhere.

Osborne had begun to direct his own destiny.

Yet the longing to get away from home was only a passing mood. More often, as the only son, he felt a growing responsibility for sharing his father's burden both in business and in the family circle. In a family in which each member stands out as highly individual, self-willed to the point of stubbornness, and fond of dominating the situation, frictions are inevitable. Osborne himself has given us a glimpse behind the scenes in one of these heated discussions.

Present: Mother, Father, Helen, and I. Dangerous ground occasionally, but no collision. Did my best to help things through. Helen not much good as waterworks were turned on, not in full force however. Talked with Papa alone and curious to see how much freer and kindlier he was. He thinks just as much of Mother, but keeps squelching not her exactly, but her ideas—and these Mother treasures up and makes worse. I feel more and more as if my place were home here.

Whatever dissensions might temporarily mar the serenity of domestic life, as a group the Osbornes were compact, loyal to one another, and proud of their composite accomplishments. Though worshiping his mother, Tom as he grew older conceived a great admiration for his father's quiet strength and calm judgment. His own mercurial temperament often needed a prop, and he could always rely on Mr. Osborne for sound advice.

To return to Adams Academy. Once Tom had broken into athletics by way of football, he turned eagerly to other forms of sport. To begin with, he bought a bicycle and nearly broke his neck in the gymnasium trying to master "the bone-breaker," that new-fangled toy which had but recently been imported from England. In the end he conquered his unruly steed and wrote proudly: "You should see the calmness and coolness with which I now mount my bicycle and speed away before the admiring eyes of the Q. M's (Quincy Micks)." Tennis appealed to him too, though he was momentarily appalled at having to pay six dollars for an imported racket. It became his favorite sport. "I am not going to belong to any old archery club," he declared. "Tennis is the game for me."

In the winter there were dancing parties in the neighborhood and occasionally amateur theatricals in the big school boarding house. Osborne loved to dance. He had a natural grace and sense of rhythm. But some of the new steps offended him.

Of the polka redowa he wrote: "It is very jolly but so horribly ungraceful that it is painful to watch—*although very nice to dance.*" It was the conscience of 1879 speaking. Critics of the next generation were to pass the same judgment on a rhythmic progression that began with the turkey trot and bunny hug and continued through such artfully named contortions as the black bottom and snake's hips.

In the meantime something was happening to Tom Osborne. It had been delayed longer than is the case with most boys, even when they have been subjected to close parental supervision. The masculine side was coming to the fore. Even now he was marked with distinctive mannerisms and prejudices, but the boy in him was gradually being emancipated. Harry Woodward had considerable to do with this transformation, as even Mrs. Osborne was quick to recognize. Shocked as she was to hear her son ejaculate "Hell!" when he jammed his finger in the door, she realized that the forces at work in him were wholesome. "You have your faults, Fuddy," she said to Woodward one day, "but at least you are no hypocrite. I guess in the main you're not a bad influence for Tom."

Both boys were musical, and Woodward had a fine baritone voice. Tom could neither sing nor whistle, but his skill at the piano made him popular with the students if not with the faculty. It seemed to the latter that he was always playing.

One day as Osborne was running through his usual repertory, the cry of "Fire!" resounded through the corridors of the old lodging house. One of the boys had tipped over his oil lamp and set fire to the wooden structure. For a time it looked as if the buildings were doomed, but quick action by the firemen extinguished the flames in half an hour. Tom had interrupted his playing long enough to make sure that the fire could be put under control; then he returned to the piano. As Dr. Everett arrived on the scene, breathless and anxious, he heard one of the melodies from Gilbert and Sullivan's "Sorcerer" floating from an upper window. The learned Doctor did not need to be told who it was. "That boy Osborne," he muttered, shaking his head, "would keep on playing if the house burned down about his ears." After prayers he summoned the young

Casabianca and stood glaring at him, a wrathful Napoleonic figure with a rage too great for his body. Finally he exploded: "Now I know what it was like when Nero fiddled while Rome burned."

Osborne's first attempt to pass the Harvard examinations was a failure. Though he did collateral reading far beyond the requirements, he found it difficult to buckle down to the dull routine of the curriculum. When success finally crowned his efforts at the end of his fourth year in Adams Academy, he was eager for the experiences which life at Cambridge would bring, especially since "Fuddy" Woodward was to room with him again. Yet he always had a tender spot in his heart for the Academy. He never forgot that at Quincy he had felt the first thrill of independence: that in the democracy of student life he had by his own efforts earned a right to the friendship and good will of his fellows. Whatever the future might hold, he was the better prepared to meet it.

CHAPTER IV

FAIR HARVARD

WHEN Tom Osborne went up to Harvard in the autumn of 1880, Boston and its environs was still the hub about which, from the New England point of view at least, the intellectual life of America rotated. Most of that famous group which had brought the first touch of native genius to American literature were still alive. Emerson, the Sage of Concord, lingered on. Longfellow was at Cambridge, revered both as university savant and as household poet. Now and again Oliver Wendell Holmes issued from his Beacon Street house and took "the long path" over Boston Common. Whittier was at Amesbury. Lowell, the bantling of the brood, had just been appointed minister to England.

When a great man dies, he becomes a name, and History throws over him its inescapable shroud of legend. Except for those who knew him intimately, he becomes curiously unreal, until we are not quite sure whether he actually existed or we only invented him. To Osborne, these men were living beings still, not literary symbols.

Yet even an undergraduate must have felt the portents of disintegration. They were in the air, in the wind that swept in from the sea. Emerson, an intellectual ruin, standing at Longfellow's grave unable to remember the name of him who was being buried. Whittier, an Ichabod whose glory had departed, piping thin pastoral notes on a reed that was once a trumpet. A decade more and on the brink of his own grave he would write of Oliver Wendell Holmes:

> *The hour draws near, howe'er delayed and late,*
> > *When at the Eternal Gate*
> *We leave the words and works we call our own,*
> > *And lift void hands alone. . . .*

Void hands. Already they were uplifted when the Eighties began, yet many could not tell whether in benediction or despair. In a year or two they would be folded in that eternal posture with which we feign resignation to the divine will.

Neither William Dean Howells nor Henry James could save for New England the laurel wreath she had worn for half a century. Other voices, importunate and lusty, were catching the ear of the republic. Walt Whitman was sending his barbaric yawp over the roofs of the world. Mark Twain, hiding a consuming cynicism beneath jest and jape, was blowing smoke rings at idols he could not quite believe in. Bret Harte had blazed a trail through the wild and still woolly West. In the South, Sidney Lanier, F. Hopkinson Smith, and Joel Chandler Harris were beginning to speak, each in his own tongue. Only Chicago and the Middle West were inarticulate.

Meanwhile, over Boston there hung the nimbus of mild decay. There was a certain splendor in it, and in the stiff-necked Yankee resistance to the noise and brawl of the new epoch. The word "propriety" had not yet assumed derogatory overtones. Refinement was a native commodity, and wit needed no apéritif. Life moved slowly, sedately, and with a grand aplomb, its tempo reflected in the horse car that after the better part of an hour's jolting deposited a customer at the gates of New England's temple of culture, Harvard College.

To Osborne, as to many another young man, Harvard represented the meridian of intellectual superiority and Brahmin caste. Yale existed, but as an athletic not an educational rival. It was the same with Princeton. Other colleges were upstarts and a trifle boorish. Among the undergraduates in Cambridge there existed a homogeneity now impossible, the doctrine of higher learning for average intellects having as yet made little headway. The young men who gained admittance into that historic institution were made to feel that they were a select and privileged class, as indeed they were.

As a group, however, they were not vastly different from the student body of any reputable college of to-day. No amount of beard, burnsides, and mustaches could hide the fact that beneath the hirsute embroidery there was a boy, full of ideals, deviltry, and hero-worship; student by compulsion, and not deeply impressed by the momentous changes taking place around him.

Osborne entered Harvard with entrée into the homes of many of Boston's and Cambridge's socially elect. As in his Adams Academy days, his week-ends were usually spent with the Garrisons in Roxbury or with his Quaker cousins, the Hallowells, in Medford. Occasionally he visited the Hoars, friends of the family residing in Concord. Most Sundays, however, found him at the home of Mrs. William Lloyd Garrison, Second, the great liberator having died the year preceding Tom's matriculation. Aunt Ellie, as he called her, was greatly attracted by this handsome, whimsical youth, whose knowledge of literature, music, and art made him welcome in company far beyond his years.

Nevertheless, it was the young people who demanded most of his time. Children were always fascinated by Osborne. He knew how to meet them on their own level without seeming to stoop. His sense of humor was akin to that of childhood, reveling in extreme absurdities. His chief delight was to gather the five young cousins about him and read aloud during the whole of some rainy Sunday afternoon. Dickens was his favorite, but the children liked Scott best. Tom had traveled all through the Scott country and, as he read, would describe the background of the poems and novels—Kenilworth, Marmion's Gate, Edinburgh, Loch Katrine, and Ellen's Isle.

If he was a favorite with the young cousins, he was a godsend to their parents. They could leave home for the afternoon, knowing the children were well taken care of.

Tom was equally welcome in Medford. The Hallowells made a rite of Sunday afternoon "coffee," a sort of open house for young people, especially the college students. There were three families—one that of Mrs. Richard P. Hallowell, granddaughter of Lucretia Mott—and the Sunday "coffee" rotated from one house to another. At these informal gatherings Tom was in his element. His gift for guiding conversation into fascinating channels made him the center of interest, and when supper was served there was likely to be some rivalry for a seat at his table.

Even then Osborne had a faculty for attracting people of various types, both young and old. Later he was to be father and brother to undisciplined boys and hardened criminals. It is a commentary on his individuality that in Harvard the contacts most difficult for him to make were those with the average student group who had little reverence for sober deportment or Norman castles.

From the first, Osborne was conspicuous at college; partly because he had an almost unconscious talent for making himself conspicuous; partly because he gained a reflected glory from his roommate, "Fuddy" Woodward; but most of all because all who met him recognized something essentially different in his make-up. Tom was older than most of the boys in Harvard, being twenty-one when he matriculated. He was tall, well built, with a certain nobility of countenance that attracted attention. The expanse of brow and the dreaminess of the eyes, which would light suddenly with enthusiasm or scorn, suggested the poet.

Mentally as well as physically he was cast in a different mold. Except for the years spent at Adams Academy, his training had little in common with that of the other undergraduates. Natural boyish interests had been largely submerged in music and art studies, travel, and other pursuits more edifying than humanizing. He knew the churches of Paris better than he knew the young men of Harvard. He could describe accurately the background of Scott's novels, but was only dimly and censoriously aware of certain byways of Cambridge frequented by the sporty element among the students.

The same traits that made him conspicuous tended at first to restrict his popularity. His room was a natural resort for the sober-minded and the musically gifted, but there were some who looked upon him as narrow and captious. The reformer in him was already in evidence. He never smoked and was inclined to read lectures to those who did. This antipathy to tobacco remained with him until he was nearly sixty, and then it took a world war and the United States Navy to corrupt him. He drank rarely and always temperately, a second glass having not the slightest allure for him. He would not countenance coarse language or ribald stories. He never "went out with the boys."

The libertines thought Tom Osborne something of a prig, with a holier-than-thou complex; yet, whether they liked him or not, the majority accepted him for what he was. No one expected Tom to enter into any of the less admirable of extra-curricular activities. Aside from principle, he found vice in any form unattractive. His own roommate often felt that Tom deserved little credit for being good. Nothing seemed to tempt him. Because of his sincerity, however, he won the respect and often the liking even of those who were rather repelled by his austerity.

And yet, if Tom was not widely popular in college, he was a favorite in his own coterie. Among the classmates who derived a keen enjoyment from his companionship were such men as John Jay Chapman, Samuel A. Eliot, son of the president of Harvard, Louis McCagg, and Leigh Bonsal—lifelong friends all of them, and in later years deeply interested in Osborne's prison reform work. Still another group of intimates met at table at Mrs. Mooney's boarding house, ten in all, among them George Agassiz, Gordon Abbott, Allen Curtis, Thomas Jefferson Coolidge, and Harry Woodward. Here there was no restraint, practical jokes and college gossip furnishing the best of sauce for the Mooney fleshpots.

Through Sam Eliot, Tom met Dr. Charles W. Eliot and became a frequent visitor at the president's home. A genuine affection sprang up between the boy and the man, evidenced in many ways through the coming years. When Tom came to graduate, Dr. Eliot wrote the father, D. M. Osborne, thanking him for sending his boy to Harvard: such a fine influence, so manly, unusually gifted.

On his side, Osborne was profoundly influenced by the liberalism of Harvard's famous educator. Possibly no single personality whose orbit intersected his own made such a lasting impression on his mind. In Dr. Eliot, Tom at last found the

OSBORNE AS A HARVARD
UNDERGRADUATE

TOM OSBORNE AT THE AGE
OF TWELVE

incarnation of those virtues he had been taught to revere—independent thinking, progressivism, moral stamina, optimism bolstered by energetic action. The ideals and traditions of his forbears met in a man at such a time and in such a sphere that the youth could not fail to be deeply stirred.

The association with the Eliots, father and son, continued after graduation. Nearly every season Osborne spent a week or two at Asticou on Mt. Desert Island, the Eliot summer home in Maine, often bringing his children with him. In 1924 when Dr. Eliot, stricken with quiet grief at the death of his wife, wanted someone very near and dear to the family to speak at the memorial services, he thought naturally of Thomas Mott Osborne. With the Rev. Samuel McChord Crothers, beloved pastor of the Cambridge First Church, Unitarian, Osborne spoke those last words of farewell to the dead.

Those who knew Dr. Eliot will realize what an extraordinary thing this intimacy was. To most people, especially those like Osborne many years his junior, he seemed cold, aloof, impersonal. Few ever penetrated the shell of reserve in which Dr. Eliot took refuge. He was one of those men who, feeling deeply, are inwardly restrained from giving expression to their emotions. With Osborne it was different. Their two natures made harmonious contact that neither inhibitions nor disparity in age could disrupt.

There was, too, a natural attraction between Tom and Sam Eliot. They were together a great deal in college, having many interests in common, and kept in close touch afterward. In 1907, after Osborne had broken with Tammany and, with his "honor Democrats," had elected a Republican, Charles Evans Hughes, governor of New York State, the younger Eliot published in the *Outlook* an unsigned tribute to the courage and integrity of his friend. When other classmates pooh-poohed Osborne's penal reform ideas as impracticable and visionary, he saw in them the promise of a new era. And at the last, when the time came for Osborne to become "a part of earth and the dumb things that the tides push," it was Dr. Eliot, now famous in his own right as eloquent preacher and president of the American Unitarian Association, who came to say a requiescat over the bier of his comrade, as Osborne had done when Mrs. Eliot passed away.

Although social and family ties in and about Cambridge tended to draw him away from some of the undergraduate activities, Tom had all the enthusiasms of a typical college boy. His scrapbook is filled with programs of athletic events, all carefully preserved as if history were to change its course because the Harvard nine defeated Princeton on a June day in 1881.

By dint of hard practice and encouragement from "Fuddy," he made the freshman football team, but his prowess on the gridiron failed to impress. Woodward, however, was snatched from the "frosh" to play a stellar rôle on the varsity with the result that the Yale freshmen that season administered one of the soundest thrashings ever visited on Crimson yearlings. From then on Osborne's athletic interests were largely vicarious, though he kept up his tennis with moderate success.

The relentless energy which never ceased to dominate him found other outlets. Soon after his matriculation it was noised about the Yard that a freshman up in Thayer Hall was a jim-dandy at the piano. Tom was all of that. He could glance over a piece of difficult music he had never seen before, throw it aside, and play it off fluently from note memory, a feat few have been able to master. He knew by heart the words and music of hundreds of operas, old ballads, nursery rimes, sonatas—an olla podrida of light melody and classical composition. Above all, his readiness to play—any time, anywhere, anything—brought him into great demand among his classmates.

This facility on the piano gave Osborne the warm comradeship he longed for; it opened doors that would otherwise have been closed to him, or that he would not have cared to enter. He began to blossom out, became more boylike, less stand-offish. During his first two years in Harvard his room was a meeting place for two different crowds: the jolly, happy-go-lucky group who idolized Woodward, and those who came for music or to lay plans for the next club or class theatricals.

It was good for Tom, this mingling with various types of

young men; yet he never lost his keen sense of right and wrong. Once a boy had made a slip, Tom had no further use for him. The idea of a second chance had not yet penetrated his prejudice against any sort of impurity or dishonor. His antipathy to such characters was undisguised. Occasionally some one of whom he disapproved would drop into the room for a chat. The chances were that Osborne would throw down his book, grab his hat, and stomp out of the room, leaving embarrassment and amazement in his wake.

By the beginning of his sophomore year, he had won a distinct place for himself in the Yard. Recognition came through election to practically all the important college societies. Early in the term he was chosen among the second "ten" for the Institute of 1770, a social club that offered the first step toward college fame. It was no small honor to be chosen so early in the elections, though his roommate Woodward, ever the white-headed boy in such matters, had preceded him in the first "ten."

Shortly afterward Tom was taken into the subsidiary of the Institute, the Δ K E, or the Dickey as it was commonly called, one of those prodigiously secret organizations of which one spoke with hushed breath. Indeed, so secret was it that some of the old members resented the few paragraphs of revelation Owen Wister permitted himself in his volume, "Roosevelt: The Story of a Friendship." They felt it was not quite cricket to draw aside the veil from so venerable a mystery.

To this inner circle one was initiated by devilish rites that only an undergraduate brain could conceive. They were especially designed to inspire anguish and humiliation in the human breast, though some torments of the flesh were included. The official schedule called for the "drowning, hanging, and burning" of the victim, but a consoling clause was added that "care will be taken that you be rescued before life is extinct." As might be expected, the tortures were greater in anticipation than in experience, the worst of the inflictions being the branding of the left arm in four places.

Whispers of this hazing evidently penetrated to the editorial sanctums of the Boston press, for one indignant scribe composed for his paper a solemn article entitled "Savage Rites at Harvard."

The custom [he wrote of the branding] has been in vogue for some time, and it is said that many students whose arms have been thus disfigured, instead of being ashamed of the folly, actually take pride in showing the scars on all possible occasions. The branding is no slight affair, the students sometimes fainting under the infliction. We presume that this matter must be in some way outside of the province of the authorities of the college, else it would have stopped long ago. We understand that the son of one of the highest officials of the college [Sam Eliot?] has already entered upon his initiatory exercises. Certainly the college officers can instruct the students that such methods of self torture by way of showing fortitude and devotion are the disgrace of savage tribes, and that giving up the crucifying of the flesh has been one of the steps in the march of civilization.

I am afraid that the march of civilization, however handy as an editorial utility, did not bulk very large in the minds of the Dickey acolytes.

Most of the hazing, however, consisted of the usual horseplay indigenous to the American campus. Neophytes were obliged to learn a ritual far from flattering to their self-esteem and had to patter it off on request.

"What's your name?" some full-fledged Dickey member would gruffly inquire.

"Fool Osborne, sir," would be the reply, "a man of licentious passions and all hell on the piano."

There were other ordeals required of the candidates, such as idiotic fagging for upper-class men, appearing in public in outlandish costume, or proposing matrimony to every young lady who passed a certain corner during a specified hour. Naturally, the unwilling suitor was not allowed to take into account race, color, or previous condition of servitude. Moreover, the ogre of disqualification was always before him. Refusal to obey commands or failure to remember the prescribed ritual meant a black mark, and seven black marks supposedly eliminated the candidate from further consideration. In reality, the demerit system was just another trick to scare the initiates into submission.

Osborne, always meticulous in social conventions and abhorrent of imposed authority, resented the "running" to which he was subjected. Yet, eager to qualify, for the Dickey roll call was the equivalent of a "Who's Who" in the Yard, he performed with smoldering wrath the foolish, embarrassing, though in the main harmless capers required of him. Once he was a bona fide member, however, the psychology that so often governs in such cases turned Tom into one of the most conscientious persecutors of Dickey novices, and he "ran" the poor devils with a zeal worthy of the Inquisition.

In the same year he was taken into the membership of the Alpha Delta Phi Society, then a chapter in the national fraternity. Later, when Greek letter societies were abolished at Harvard, the same group carried on as the Fly Club. There had been an earlier chapter of Alpha Delta Phi which, after relinquishing its charter, had been continued as the A. D. Club. By Osborne's time the A. D. Club was one of the two most select societies in the college, and election to it was a coveted honor conferred only on a few students in each class who had notably distinguished themselves in undergraduate activities. Osborne's admission in his senior year testifies at once to the position he had attained, and to the fellowship he enjoyed. Achievement alone would not have assured him a bid.

One distinction in particular contributed greatly to his prestige. This was his election in his sophomore year as conductor of the Pierian Sodality, the college musical society. The choice of an under-class man for that position was unprecedented, but Osborne justified his selection. The concerts given under his leadership received more than local attention and raised the Pierian Sodality to a prominence it had not hitherto enjoyed. In addition, he was accompanist for a class quartet that won considerable fame during its existence, consisting of Samuel A. Eliot, Louis B. McCagg, Paul Thorndike, and Richard F. Howe.

Though Osborne was a great success in Harvard as an instrumentalist, he was a notoriously poor singer. In a group he would join lustily in the harmony, but his voice was never pleasing, often distinctly disagreeable. Once, while directing a rehearsal of a college show, he undertook to instruct one of the principals in his part. He went through the lines and business for him, even to the point of singing his special number. An orchestra from Boston had been hired for the occasion, and the leader imagined all this was part of the performance. Buttonholing Osborne after the rehearsal, he inquired gravely if Tom didn't think that his solo should be accompanied by the cornet.

It was only natural, therefore, that for the time being the Glee Club was content to get along without Tom's services. After his success with Pierian Sodality, however, it jumped at the chance of drafting him for its non-singing leader. His skill in conducting and his experience in arranging programs were large factors in the increased popularity enjoyed by the Glee Club during his régime.

With Osborne's musical talent, this deficiency in singing is rather odd, for his speaking voice was exceptionally good, the tones being clear, well modulated, and, though rarely raised to philippic vehemence, audible in large assemblies.

There was one college activity, enjoying a tremendous vogue at the time, peculiarly adapted to Osborne's talents. Ever since as a child of twelve or thirteen he had put through their paces those bloodthirsty puppets, Punch and Judy, he had been fascinated by the art of impersonation. In the garret he had produced and directed his own adaptations of stories and operas. As he grew older he found a keen enjoyment in charades and masquerade balls, spending weeks prior to his school vacations planning brave entertainments for the recess.

Adams Academy had offered few opportunities for dramatic diversions, but the Cambridge of 1880 was alive with amateur acting societies. While still a freshman, Tom made his début as *Mr. Barker* in "My Uncle's Will," a performance given by the Game Club, a Cambridge society group not associated with the university, and the following year he became an active member. Later he took part in plays produced by the Cambridge Dramatic Club in an old building in Arsenal Square.

It was in the college amateur theatricals, however, that Osborne made his greatest triumphs. Musical burlesques were the favorite vehicles of the period, being, in the parlance of reviewers, mélanges of melody and fun. The wit was often pretty terrible, tending to sophomoric puns whose assumption of erudition aggravated their atrociousness. Occasionally a production of real merit sprang full-formed from the brain of some undergraduate Zeus—for example, Owen Wister's "Dido and Æneas"; while sometimes even the puns had a skylarking note of genius, as in the title "Helen, or Taken from the Greek." But usually the average came closer to the following program notes in the dramatis personæ:

Scarabæus (surnamed Scabby, king of beetles—a demon tyrant, who not content with governing cockroaches also (h)encroaches upon others' rights. Seldom at rehearsals, though always re-Hearst). ....W. R. Hearst

Juno, (Queen of the gods, and Jove's spouse; otherwise known as little Samuel, who aspires to be a *Junior* next *June, Oh!* Fond of *Peacocks* that sing *Pea-hens* of joy while drawing her car). ....S. A. Eliot

Typical college humor, yet saved from the doldrums by its vivid contemporaneousness, the exuberance of the acting, and the incidental music.

To this particular genre Tom Osborne contributed much. He had a flair for absurdities and often added a whimsical touch to the broad claptrap of the libretto. While he was a moderately good actor and was ever eager to assume major rôles, it was his musical talent that brought him into chief prominence. Soon after his election to Δ K E he was chosen musical manager and accompanist for the Dickey Christmas theatricals, *"Ixion, or, the Man at the Wheel,* Extravaganza . . . altered and adapted by the funny men of Δ K E." His success on that occasion insured his selection for nearly every class, club, and college production during his Harvard career.

Drawing on a vast knowledge of all kinds of music, Osborne would select and arrange rousing choruses or lilting ballads to which "the funny men" wrote the lyrics and gags. In rehearsals he would train the cast both in song numbers and in dance routines. More than once in these amateur productions his resourcefulness was tested to the utmost. While acting as accompanist at a public performance in Boston, he was astounded to hear the chorus start one of the songs half a tone below the key. He promptly transposed the accompaniment to suit the voices, and no one in the audience realized how close had been disaster.

By his junior year Osborne had built up a reputation as actor and musical director that made inevitable his election to the Hasty Pudding Club, the college dramatic society that was the goal of all undergraduate Thespians. Again his chief duty was selecting and arranging the music for the score and directing the rehearsals, but sometimes he collaborated with John Jay Chapman and William Amory Gardner, later beloved teacher at Groton School, in writing the text. On one occasion, when the gag writers were at a loss for a few lines with which to round off a chorus for the burlesque of "Helen of Troy," Tom added the lines:

> *The sail is in the offing,*
> *The offing of the bay—*
> *We don't know what the offing is,*
> *But that's the thing to say.*
>
> *The bow is hard a-starboard,*
> *The wind is on the lee—*
> *We have to be quite nau-ti-cal*
> *In language, as you see . . .*

Typical Osborne quatrains with more than a faint flavor of Gilbert. The stanzas will be doubly appreciated by those who remember the author's high scorn for all things nau-ti-cal, especially the salty argot on which the amateur yachtsman usually prides himself.

Osborne not only acted as musical manager of all the Hasty Pudding Club productions of the year, but was a member of the casts as well. It is curious to note that in each instance he played a female rôle. He was not effeminate, but there was so much of the feminine in his nature that he was the logical choice for Trojan *Helen* or *Donna Elvira Sol*. Probably, too, his inability to sing had something to do with his repeated selection as leading lady for the Hasty Pudding theatricals.

In the meantime, Osborne attended practically all the professional productions that found their way to Boston. For him the glitter and illusion of the stage never lost their attraction. Although he echoed the sentiment of *Tony Lumpkin's* pot-companion, "O damn anything that's *low*, I cannot bear it," his tastes were catholic. He enjoyed Edwin Booth in "Othello" and the Vokes Family in "The Belles of the Kitchen"; Dion Boucicault, then at the height of his popularity, in "The Shaughraun," and Harrigan and Hart in "Squatter Sovereignty." He rarely missed an opportunity to hear grand opera and never, if he could help it, skipped a performance of Gilbert and Sullivan.

This delight in impersonation, whether as actor or as spectator, was perhaps the most significant characteristic of the man; a fundamental urge that, inexplicable in itself, explains much of what later occurred. Osborne dramatized so many things, even his own life and the causes he espoused. He was the protagonist in a cosmic drama; his adversary, an Antichrist. But more than anything else it was a gesture toward getting outside himself into somebody else's skin. He put on a convict's livery to see with the convict's eye. He clothed himself with tatterdemalion garb to feel as the hobo feels.

No one realized better than he how inadequate such artifices are; yet they served as well as anything a mortal can avail himself of to unshackle the bolts of identity and give the illusion of another self. I firmly believe that he came closer to actual dissociation in these moments than most people realize; not as the trained actor, submerging his emotions, sure of his technique, to project through voice and gesture the character he has assumed; but as the amateur, giving himself unreservedly, awkward, yet so earnest to wrap himself completely in another personality that he feels surging up within him impulses, alien and potent, that half frighten him with their implications.

Unless we grant Osborne a unique capacity for putting himself in another's place, mystically rather than intellectually, there is no explanation for his deep sympathy with his fellow men. To suggest that he was a poseur would be to ignore the facts. No man sacrifices the best part of his lifetime, his leisure, his peace of mind, and a large share of his fortune merely to put on a show. Though always conscious of the dramatic aspect of his behavior, like a playwright attending one of his own first-nights, Osborne was moved by a force that transcended petty motives.

In his junior year Tom lost his roommate, Harry Woodward. He and "Fuddy," though constitutionally different in make-up, had made an excellent team, each contributing to the other a wholesome influence. During four years of rooming together a true affection had grown up between them, grounded in respect and admiration for each other's qualities. Woodward, football idol, crew man, glee club singer, and all-round campus hero, carried with him, wherever he went, a sane boyish atmosphere that won friends and disarmed enemies.

Through this companionship Tom mellowed, learned a little how to play as boys play, came closer to the normal average strain of human nature than before or after; for in him there was a curious gravitation toward the extremes of society: the upper reaches of intellectuality and refinement; the lower fringes of abnormality and crime. For the one he had a natural inclination; for the other, what amounted to a passion, partly reaction from the sheltered world in which he had lived, but mostly a sympathetic urge to give succor to those on whom society had turned its back.

After Woodward left college, Osborne roomed alone for a time; then joined with Leigh Bonsal, for whom he had a high regard. Bonsal was a practical, level-headed youth, sharing Osborne's ideas of rectitude, but lacking the boisterousness and bonhommie that had made Woodward popular in so many diverse groups. As a consequence, Tom adhered more and more to his own crowd, losing some of the contacts with the free-and-easy life of the college. Yet in many ways the association was a happy one. The two had much in common, including in later years an interest in penal reform.

Osborne's judgments of men were always uncompromising.

As an upper-class man he felt the responsibility of using his influence for the improvement of club and college morals, and his outspokenness frequently brought upon him the maledictions of those who found the primrose path pleasant in spite of the thorns. More than once in A. D. Club elections he sat up all night to blackball candidates of whom he did not approve. One man in particular he detested with a passion that was almost medieval in its violence.

William Randolph Hearst entered Harvard in Tom's junior year, a gangling, large-headed, big-nosed boy who made free with college traditions and refused to be squelched by upperclassman dignity. So long as Osborne held the power of veto, Hearst was not admitted to the charmed circle of A. D. Club membership. From the beginning Tom was repelled by the Hearst manner, the prodigality with which he flung his money about, his manner of living, and the complacency with which he accepted the world as his oyster. In after years, when he had acquired a newspaper of his own, Osborne regarded Hearst as the high priest of yellow journalism, a jingo in politics, a force for evil in the republic.

There were others in Harvard, however, who found in Billy Hearst qualities to admire. His affability and generosity were as much responsible for his popularity as the family millions. Moreover, he had a ready sense of humor. When Harry Woodward was trying to put the Harvard Athletic Association on its feet financially, Hearst volunteered to solicit subscriptions and promised to contribute personally an amount equal to the total obtained. John Jacob Astor, another young plutocrat, was enrolled in the Scientific School, in those days considered a refuge for the dull-witted. He had been approached in vain, and Hearst tackled the wealthy hold-out for a donation. Astor hemmed and hawed, finally capitulated, and proffered ten dollars.

Hearst looked aghast. "My God, Jack!" he exclaimed. "You can't afford that!" and refused to accept it.

Hearst was too much the hail-fellow, well-met type to be kept out of the social clubs for long. His talent for theatricals, coupled with ability in clog dancing, won him election to the

Hasty Pudding Club. The A.D. Club took him in after Osborne was graduated. Many, deprecating the conduct and policies of the flamboyant Hearst of to-day, have pleasant recollections of a slender, sometimes shy young man who blushed easily, spent liberally if unwisely, and took what life offered without compunction.

Another Harvard man who, unfortunately for both, was later to become an adversary of Osborne's was Theodore Roosevelt. As Roosevelt took his degree in the spring of 1880, Tom, entering in the autumn, knew him only by reputation. More than fifteen years were to slip by before their paths crossed, and then a political quarrel, largely the work of that shrewd boss of New York State Republicanism, Tom Platt, engendered a bitterness that rankled in Osborne's soul till the last.

James J. Storrow was a class behind Osborne: a retiring, silent youth who left the impression of vast reserve power. Even in those days in spite of a sense of humor sometimes disturbing in its penetration, he was inclined to be serious-minded. When directed to compose an original essay as part of the initiation rites of a certain college society, he complied with a dissertation on "Worms." Some of the members still recall the utter gravity with which he pronounced the central theme: "It is a terrible thought that the earth for some distance beneath our feet has passed through the bodies of worms." He was wholly in earnest about it. No tongue-in-the-cheek drollery marred the perfect lugubriousness of the composition.

Notwithstanding his reserve, there was something magnetic about Storrow that gave him both friendship and mastery. He was a born leader and a keen judge of men; unassuming, yet in his quiet way exerting a strong influence over his fellows. Whether winning glory as captain of a victorious Crimson eight or organizing the General Motors Corporation; smashing the tradition of Hasty Pudding Club hazing or fighting a political ring that had Boston hog-tied, Storrow was a dominating personality.

Class lines were rather sharply drawn at Harvard, and Tom Osborne, '84, saw little of Jim Storrow, '85, during his college days. Besides, temperamentally they had little in common.

The one was expansive, volatile, subject to sudden enthusiasms and prejudices; the other, reticent, self-controlled, practical, with a good sprinkling of Yankee conservatism thrown in. It was a vacation trip in Switzerland that indirectly brought the two closer together, for on the ascent to Zermatt, Storrow met Tom's sister Helen and fell in love with her. Although their engagement was announced shortly after his graduation, it was not until 1891 that they were wed; for Storrow clung to the old-fashioned notion that a man should be able to provide a comfortable living for a bride before the banns were posted.

Though bound by family and business ties, Osborne and Storrow rarely saw eye to eye with each other. The idealist scorned the pragmatic philosophy of Big Business. The practical man of affairs was irritated beyond words at the dreamer's obliviousness to certain well-established principles. Yet each had a wholesome respect for the other's attainments, and the association, for all its controversies, was a pleasant one.

In some of his studies Osborne was far from brilliant, but he was held in high regard by members of the faculty and administration. He had a talent for making himself agreeable in cultured society, liked teas, conversed easily on a variety of topics, became quite the social lion, dining often with the Lowells, Thayers, Greenoughs, Gilmans, Lees, Bowleses, and other families in and about Boston.

There was, however, a curious quality in his attitude toward women. He liked the society of the opposite sex, indeed cut quite a figure with the ladies; yet for a long time he was immune to the witchery of any one particular charmer. One friendly critic suggested that he treated women with too much respect, an illuminating commentary on the real sentiments of the Victorian era. But Osborne had been raised by women, had grown up with three sisters, two of them older than himself, and had come to accept females as a perfectly natural part of the divine scheme. He appears to have skipped that period of adolescence when sex seems miraculous and woman the supreme miracle.

Perhaps, too, the streak of femininity in his own nature was partly responsible for the faintness of that romantic aura with which a young man usually surrounds his favorites of the lovelier sex. Women, intelligent women, made fine comrades. Their tastes were likely to coincide with his, and their homage was sweet to a youth not a little proud of his accomplishments. Beyond that, he was only mildly interested.

Of the demimonde he had no experience, nor cared to have any; and he found it hard to forgive those who pursued the light ladies occasionally seen flitting near the outskirts of the Yard. It was more than principle with him. Something within him revolted at the mere thought of carnality. Youth is little inclined to count the cost or rue the day. It sheds few tears over withered camellias or the soon-to-wither ladies who wear them. But Osborne, attending a ballet in Paris, wrote sadly in his private journal: "The sight was to see some of the 'women' of Paris in the gallery between the acts. But it makes me feel blue." Characteristically he added: "I enjoyed the ballet, however." Even the portrayal of seduction in literature nauseated him. As a young man of twenty-five he wrote in his diary: "Read all day. *Within an Inch of his Life.* Horrid, immoral French novel of Gaboriau's. Never shall read another." Outright facetious or erotic literature held no attraction. He was disgusted by it.

All his life Osborne preserved his ideal of purity. When in later years his political enemies sought to frame him on charges of unspeakable depravity, his old college mates, many of whom had been antagonized by his prison crusade, were so shocked and incredulous that they planned to come to court in a body as character witnesses. Such was the impress Tom Osborne left on his Harvard contemporaries.

Of the possibility of gentle dallying with girls of his own class Tom never dreamed; yet long before the Petting Age was ushered in by the rumble seat and the hip flask there were maidens whose pulses beat to an Anacreontic rhythm when moonlight and music conspired together—sometimes when they didn't. On the way home from a party one evening a younger but more sophisticated boy ragged Tom about a certain girl to whom he had been attentive.

"Arm around her waist and all that sort of thing, eh, Tommy?" he inquired.

And Tom, with that characteristic gesture of crossed hands on the breast when slightly shocked: "Oh, my, no! She's not like that."

Subsequently, several young gentlemen of Auburn discovered that the lady was not so immune to masculine blandishments as Tom Osborne had imagined.

This blend of intimacy and aloofness must have baffled more than one damsel eager to penetrate beyond the Platonic corridors. At least one, nameless now forever more, kept her head though she lost her heart. On St. Valentine's Day she wrote Tom:

> *Were you as good as you are proud,*
> *'Twould be a good deal better.*
> *(Today, you know, a girl's allowed*
> *To write a saucy letter.)*
> *I'd tell you you were handsome, but*
> *I fear 'twould make you vainer—*
> *To vanity the gates are shut*
> *And Satan is the gainer.*
>
> *Your playing's said to be "immense"*
> *With plaudits always greeted.*
> *(I tell you this in confidence,*
> *It must not be repeated.)*
> *To seem too bashful you're inclined*
> *Yet cheek you have in plenty,*
> *While lots of girls say you're unkind—*
> *And, Tom, you're only twenty.*
>
> *They say a neighbor took to drink*
> *Distracted by your riot.*
> *How do you make the proctors think*
> *You are so very quiet?*
> *You ne'er shall be my valentine*
> *While thus you act the Hindoo;*
> *Your sentence take and don't repine,*
> *But act as other men do.*

Though "lots of girls" thought Tom unkind, his capitulation, when it came, was complete. One Easter vacation—his sophomore year—he and Harry Woodward boarded the train for Auburn to spend the holidays. Across the aisle Tom noticed a passenger who merited more than a passing glance. She was a tall, willowy girl of about sixteen, not pretty, yet with singularly attractive features. A cascade of red hair fell with unruly grace upon her shoulders. And they were beautiful shoulders, in a few more months to become the admiration of many a ballroom of Cambridge. Woodward, already acquainted, presented his friend, and the little god of romance was content. Within two years the engagement of Miss Agnes Devens, daughter of Arthur Lithgow and Agnes (White) Devens, to Thomas Mott Osborne was announced, and in another two years they were married.

Most of us mortals fare variously in the reports of our contemporaries. We have our advocates and our detractors. Agnes Devens had advocates only. There was a warmth in her nature, a sincerity and openness in all her dealings, that dispelled jealousy while winning friends. She was blessed with a rich sense of humor, loved a good time, sports, dances, repartee, and all that is part of youth. She had too an independence that was refreshing. With her friend, Susan Smith, she learned to play tennis at a time when it was considered improper for young ladies to indulge in such hoydenish capers; but she did everything with such grace and good spirits that everyone was charmed.

Tom Osborne could not have found a better mate. She brought him one thing he had always lacked: poise, sense of proportion, balance—whatever you wish to call that faculty for putting things in their proper light and evaluating them with calm judgment.

It was his only love affair. Agnes Devens was the one woman who ever aroused in him the fire of a grand passion. Before his engagement he sometimes contemplated the subject of matrimony, but never with any ardor. He was more apt to feel bewildered or repelled by the attentions of feminine admirers. In his junior year diary he wrote of a party: "Had a nice talk with Alice Gray, and one with Kitty Noble. She is very nice, and I wonder if—. I must be careful anyhow. I do not want to make any girl care for me that I don't care for. It seems to me I might for Alice Gray."

Though Agnes Devens Osborne died when Tom was a comparatively young man, he remained true to his first love. For him she always represented ideal womanhood, and he was incapable of accepting another in her place.

In the meantime, there were happy parties at home during the college vacations. At Christmas and Easter the big and, from without, rather forbidding house in South Street resounded to the laughter of young people. At night the chandeliers, ablaze with the refracted light of pendent prisms, shone down on formal dinner parties, gay dances, boisterous masquerades. In summer there were house parties at Willow Point, with boating and swimming. Tennis, too. Tom had cajoled his mother into having constructed on the Willow Point lawn the first tennis court in those parts, an object of much curiosity mixed with scorn.

"What's Tom Osborne got that fish net out in the front yard for?" people would ask, determined to be witty at any cost when that namby-pamby game was mentioned.

To tell the truth, some of the pictures of the period at least partially exonerate those who sat in the scorner's seat and hurled the cynic's ban. They reveal heavily draped ladies in polka-dot veils, one hand daintily lifting a voluminous skirt with buckram ruffles; the other clamped to the haft of a racket, stiffly poised as if in the act of swatting a fly. It took a quarter of a century to raise the game of tennis from the croquet class to the status of a masculine sport; and another twenty-five years to raise the hem of a woman's skirt to a point that made locomotion feasible. The grudging admission that females are possessed of such practical accessories as knees was a turning-point in our national life.

Over these festivities Tom's mother ruled with a high hand. Her word was law, and the way of the transgressor was hard. Everyone loved her, feared her, bore away memories of a *maîtresse femme* to whose tyranny all submitted without protest. Mrs. D. M. Osborne inspired obedience by force of character. She exerted a sort of moral coercion on the mind, so that thoughts of mutiny withered and died. It would be lese majesty, no less, to defy her commands. And she had a tongue that enjoined respect. One night at dinner she turned suddenly on a college friend Tom had brought home for a visit.

"Paul Thorndike," she announced, fixing him with a stern eye, "there are three things I don't like about you. You part your hair in the middle. Your side-whiskers are too long. And you wear button shoes."

In the background was Tom's father, taking little part in the gayety, yet in his quiet way enjoying it all, chuckling to see his wife "manage," contemplating the merry-making with recollections of his own boyhood, so hard, so empty of care-free moments. He never watched the fun without feeling that at last he had found his own youth in the frolics of his children. The young people who spent their vacations with Tom and his sister saw little of Mr. Osborne. He seemed a remote figure, already a little dim and legendary, a patriarch indulgent yet preoccupied with greater affairs than whist and sleigh rides.

Sometimes Tom spent his vacations in travel. One summer he accompanied his father on a tour of D. M. Osborne & Co.'s branch offices in the West. Not that Tom cared about the business side of it. He had no leaning toward commerce. "Strikes me in this business," he wrote, "one is in a perpetual state of having to see some man and then when you do see him at last, having nothing of any importance to say."

Mr. Osborne was disappointed that his only son did not share his enthusiasm for manufacturing. Soon—sooner than anyone realized—Tom would have to assume responsibility for the great industry his father had built up. The thought of it oppressed him. Only a strong sense of filial duty and family pride constrained him to prepare for a career "at the works."

A kind Providence, however, turned this particular trip from a bore into a lark. On the train from Fargo to Bismarck, Tom met a General Armstrong who, with a Boston minister and

two Civil War veterans, was on some mission to the Crow
Agency in southeastern Montana. Afterward, they planned
to push on to Yellowstone Park through country that was
little more than wilderness. Tom obtained permission from
his father to join the party, and the next day started on one
of the great adventures of his life.

By train through scorched prairies that burst into flame as
if for Tom's special benefit; through the Bad Lands, where
the air lay so heavy he could scarcely breathe; and by stage
and wagon to the valley where the Big Horn empties into the
Yellowstone. Beyond lay the mesa, and beyond that the
Rockies, serene, remote, like white-haired old men who dream
and wish not to be disturbed.

Here was the real West, the young and turbulent West of
which Bret Harte was writing such glamorous tales: frontier
towns, streets lined with saloons where local John Oakhursts
played stud-poker and bespangled ladies of dubious age and
more dubious virtue sang smutty songs; mining camps, railroad settlements, scattered ranches, and government forts.
In the reservation Tom saw Indian braves riding naked along
forest paths, painted warriors dancing about the fire in his
honor, squaw men, half-breeds, sphinx-eyed papooses. One
young buck, a chief's son, presented him with a handsome belt
and was with difficulty restrained by the agent from handing
over his sole article of raiment, a buffalo robe on which Tom
had laid envious eyes.

From the reservation they continued on horseback to Yellowstone Park, Tom astride a charger he had rechristened
Richard Cœur de Lion; riding through cañons railways were
one day to pierce; camping by streams and lakes; irreverently
naming mountain peaks and rivers after themselves. Nature
often appealed to Osborne in terms of music. Of Yellowstone
Cañon and its falls he wrote: "If Niagara is the Third Symphony, the Yosemite the Fifth, Fujiyama the C Major, this is
the Seventh."

At last the purple peaks and the sagebrush and the geysers
and the greasy breakfasts began to pall. For a tenderfoot
Osborne had stood the hardships of the trail fairly well, but

his tastes were fastidious and he longed for the comforts of civilization. During the trip he had clung to a bottle of *eau de cologne* with which he sprinkled his handkerchief on dusty roads until a native filched the precious aromatic for some mysterious purpose of his own. Some years later, after a number of visits to the West, he observed: "My general impression has always been the same. The West is undoubtedly large, but was not made to live in."

More to his liking were the jaunts about Europe, where already he was quite at home. Even there "horrid" people and "nasty" food took some of the joy out of life. During the vacation prior to his senior year in Harvard, Tom in company with his mother, his sister Helen, and a party of friends whom they met in Paris, made his sixth tour abroad. He had a loathing for guides of all nationalities and preferred to act as cicerone himself. This arrangement was always agreeable to his fellow travelers, for he knew all the interesting things about pictures, cathedrals, and historic places, and in addition had an uncanny knack for hitting upon treasures out of the beaten track of tourists.

In the party were Beth Hoar, soon to marry Sam Bowles, whose engagement to Tom's sister Florence had been so sadly terminated by the latter's death; and Allen Curtis, a college classmate. Osborne piloted them through the Louvre, explaining the glories of the old masters; introduced them to the majesty of Notre Dame de Paris; explored the country about Chartres, Amiens, Rouen, and conjured up a vision of Marie Antoinette playing milkmaid in the Petit Trianon, and of gorgeously arrayed ladies and gentlemen walking in the gardens of Versailles.

In Germany there were rambles about the medieval towns of Heidelberg, Munich, and Nuremberg, with a stopover at Bayreuth for the Wagner memorial celebration. With Curtis he scaled the Schilthorn in Switzerland, drank a bottle of wine on the summit, and discovered that even sacrificial libations are better observed at low altitudes. This may partly account for the tremendous thrill he got from the glissade on the descent.

Everywhere they went, Tom met old friends and made new ones. This was long before the day of "tourist third," but it was a convention that all young men and women of means make the "grand tour" once or twice before taking up business or matrimony. Harvard College had unofficial ambassadors all over the Continent. Evert Wendell, Frank Bacon, Owen Wister, "Rod" Plummer, and others kept bobbing up at unexpected moments like *Captain O'Hay's* ubiquitous *Ernie*.

For Tom these were happy days, speeding all too quickly. He seemed to have a presentiment that when this "sweet fifth lustrum" of his life ran out, it would put a period to hours of careless freedom. He even grudged the weeks spent abroad, merry and exciting though they were, and the shorter excursions to Charleston and the Maine coast, because they stole so much time from his stay at home. It was there his real affections lay.

Thoughts of Willow Point never failed to arouse in him a romantic nostalgia. Returning to the old house by the lake shore late one summer after all had left, he wandered through the empty halls, feeling strangely lonesome, peopling the several rooms with the shades of comrades who had lately stayed there—"George Ledlie . . . good old Billy Goodwin . . . Billy Williams, Bob Minturn, Amory Gardner . . . dear old crazy Jack Chapman." He wrote in his journal:

I wonder if the Point will ever again see such jolly days! I fear me not. . . . Can I ever again have my friends here and be without care and happy? Oh, these next two years I must hang on to every day and not let it go until it has given to me all it can. I may be happier again but I don't believe I can be.

College friendships meant more to Tom Osborne than they do to most men. Until he went away to school, he had few intimates among boys of his own age. His first experience of genuine companionship was at Adams Academy. At Harvard intimacies did not spring up easily, but when they did they gripped him completely. They satisfied an unrealized hunger in his soul. It was nothing short of tragedy that the humanitarian task to which he later dedicated himself entailed a sacrifice of many of these early associations. Some of his college chums were alienated by his reform program; the rest, with few exceptions, found him so immersed in his theories that the old familiarity was impossible.

Osborne graduated with the class of 1884, making a brilliant record in everything except, possibly, studies. He had had little time to devote to curricular matters. Theatricals and music took up most of his leisure. Club life and society accounted for many of the remaining hours. Besides, he was a regular attendant at Papanti's famous dancing classes, a member of a whist club, an editor of the Harvard *Daily Echo,* a founder, director, and finally treasurer of the Harvard Co-operative Society. He belonged to the O. K. Society, the college literary guild; to the Harvard Art Club and the Harvard Historical Society. With the restless energy that always characterized him he flew from one activity to another and still found time to do a prodigious amount of reading of his own choosing.

Small wonder that Tom was always in a sweat before examinations. In his freshman year only the grace of God and low scholastic requirements saved him from being thrust into the cold world without the blessing of John Harvard. From time to time his professors sent him little reminders that his work had "not been such as to assure a passing mark." By his junior year, however, Osborne had found himself; that is to say, had accommodated himself to the American system of education as applied at Harvard. So far as education in a broad sense is concerned, he was the superior of most high honor men. Probably no one in the undergraduate body had read so widely or traveled so extensively and with such keen perceptions. His retentive memory treasured up scenes in all their detail, and he could describe temples, landscapes, towns, and people with a minuteness that made them vividly real.

His remarkable acquisitiveness was strikingly illustrated in his reading. Osborne could gallop through a book in a few hours, apparently only skimming the surface. Months afterward he would suddenly quote with accuracy a long passage that had been engraved on his brain. It was the same with music. The only things he could never remember were those that concerned his own business and well-being. He had something of that quality of Coleridge, of whom Hazlitt once said: "He is capable of doing anything that does not present itself as a duty."

Osborne would have been a highly educated man without any formal schooling. He had the gift of self-instruction, absorbing knowledge from its sources without the aid of an intercessor. Had he chosen to apply himself to the assignments of his instructors, he might have been one of the scholastic leaders of his class. He chose to draft his own curriculum. As it was, he gained honors in his two favorite studies, history and music, and was graduated with a *cum laude* degree, an amazing achievement considering his outside interests.

Class Day brought a pang of sadness. Tom's school days were over. The Dickey burlesques, the Hasty Pudding Club shows, the hours of song around the piano in his room, the camaraderie of the Yard, the strolls along the Charles River, the football games and the cheering—all a part of a glorious interlude, so long in prospect, so brief when it is done. We know that he felt unaccountably downcast when he thought of breaking college ties, as if already he heard voices bidding him prepare for an arduous and solitary pilgrimage.

Fortunately, he had little time for brooding. There descended upon him all the sisters and the cousins and the aunts, come to see their darling receive the benediction of Alma Mater. Tom bore up well under this avalanche of consanguineous affection. He squired his relations individually and in groups through a series of Commencement functions with a conscientiousness that must have exasperated less dutiful candidates for a sheepskin. To tell the truth, he rather enjoyed it. He was dramatizing life again. This three-day celebration was like a Greek trilogy, and he was stage manager and protagonist in one. Adulatory kinswomen provided a chorus that would have satisfied Euripides himself.

One of the Class Day events was a forerunner of the modern college "rush." A large elm in the Yard was decorated with a band of flowers so placed that one had to jump to reach it.

At a given signal, all the graduating class charged the defenseless tree with a determination to wrest from the garland as many blossoms as possible. Lucky indeed was the young lady who received one of these tokens from a husky admirer. Tom, being tall and hefty, managed to snatch a large handful of the posies, which he proceeded to divide meticulously among his relations. Agnes Devens, his fiancée of a few months, received no more than her just share. To say that the sisters and the cousins and the aunts were delighted with this thoughtfulness is to understate the case. Tom always had been and always would be their idea of a proper young man.

And so it all came to an end at last. Hostesses put away their best silver and china with a sigh of relief. Overworked professors yawned and thought of the sea. Workmen started cleaning up the Yard litter. Express carts rumbled to and from the station. And some two hundred young men, half-stupefied with good advice, tucked their diplomas under their arms and sauntered through the Yard gates looking for dragons, windmills, and good jobs. Among them was Thomas Mott Osborne, A.B.

CHAPTER V

APOLLO AT A DESK

It was July, 1886. The new president of D. M. Osborne & Co. sat in his office regarding with disfavor the pile of unopened mail on his desk. It was hot, and besides his new duties lay heavily upon him. Less than two years since, he had entered the business as a clerk in the collection department with the uninspiring task of addressing envelopes. Within a few months he had been transferred to the rolling mill department in charge of office work. Another year had found him assistant superintendent and vice president of the company. To-day at the age of twenty-six he sat at the president's desk, the titular head of a great industry.

But Thomas Mott Osborne was not happy. His rapid promotion, he realized, had been due solely to force of circumstances culminating in the death of his father only the week before. That tragedy had not only saddened him but thrust on him responsibilities for which he had no liking. A business career was the last thing he desired. In college, the unfolding of his special talents had brought hazy ambitions, linking up with thoughts of music and creative writing. Even during his Adams Academy days doubts had assailed him. What was he to do? There were the mills, brick and mortar monuments to his father's inventive genius, representing years of unremitting labor, anxiety, and self-sacrifice. It would break the old man's heart if his only son failed to carry on. There was no one else in the family. For Tom Osborne it was the old struggle between duty and inclination. And duty won. Two years before he entered Harvard, he had written home from his round-the-world trip:

And now, Father, *please* don't worry about what I am to do. You speak in your letter as if I had a settled idea that I am going to be idle all my life. I don't want to be idle and I never shall be idle, but I want to find out what it is I can hope to succeed in best, and then go to work and succeed. I know you have always felt bad about my not displaying any mechanical genius, but "a leopard cannot change his spots," and I know you don't want to force my inclination at all. . . . I know very well that happiness and contentment generally come to those whose minds are busy and have no time for discontent, so don't think that I will ever be idle. I will be a poor professor of history or anything rather than that.

No one could ever say that Osborne was idle. A man of more diverse activities it is difficult to conceive; not by the farthest reach of imagination, however, could he be called a typical business man. For details of business procedure he had a profound distaste. His success, not inconsiderable in view of the record of the company, came largely through his intuitive grasp of the problems that presented themselves. Others had to take care of the general routine.

During those last years at college the decision he would soon have to make had disturbed him greatly. In spite of his own expanding genius in cultural and intellectual fields and a hesitancy on the part of his father to "force" his inclination, he was only too painfully aware of the logic of circumstance. Everything pointed to the advisability of maintaining the family name in the business. He could not hope to turn his musical and literary accomplishments into immediate cash, and no other opportunity for lucrative and congenial employment presented itself. Moreover he was engaged to be married. Finally he reconciled himself to destiny with the reservation that it was only a temporary arrangement. The chance to follow his own bent would come sometime, somehow. In two years he found himself chained to an office chair with apparently no prospect of evading responsibility. Proud though he was of the industry his father had built up and of his own hereditary position in it, he felt that life had cheated him, and that the great world of facts and figures was about to engulf him. He wondered if after all the life of a "poor professor of history" were not more desirable.

When Tom Osborne came home after graduation to take his place in the factory, he had been struck with his father's failing strength. The firm step and erect carriage were gone. Signs that the strain of years had taken their toll were unmistakable. To this decline two incidents had contributed.

In 1876 John Gordon had come to Auburn to build his self-binding harvester for D. M. Osborne & Co. Gordon was one of the inventors who had answered the demand for a machine that would eliminate the laborers who followed the reaper and bound the bundles of grain by hand. With almost human dexterity his machine took the cut grain from the reaper platform, wrapped a wire about it, snapped off the wire at the proper length, twisted the ends into a sort of knot, and threw the sheaf to the ground. To the farmers of the Seventies, the Gordon binder was a godsend. It solved, apparently, all the harvesting problems. For several years it held the market, competing with the Withington self-binder manufactured by McCormick. With business increasing by leaps and bounds, prospects for continued prosperity were bright indeed.

Then one day in 1880 John F. Appleby appeared with a device for binding grain with twine instead of wire. Full rights on this invention were offered D. M. Osborne & Co. for a song, and all the members of the firm, except David Munson himself, were eager to take it up. Tenacious of opinion, he beat down opposition and stuck to the old Gordon. Wire, he thought, was more practical. Twine was only a fad.

His fatal mistake was soon evident. Somewhere in the Middle West a cow died, and the report was circulated that a piece of wire found in her stomach was the cause of death. Millers began to protest that bits of metal were injuring their machinery. Although these stories were probably gross exaggerations, it was evident that the wire binder was outmoded. Twine was cheaper and easier to manipulate. In a last effort to retrieve his error, Osborne attached a twine device to his old Gordon. In 1882 some 6,000 of these machines were sold to farmers. They failed to give satisfaction, and Osborne at a great loss took back and replaced every one at the firm's expense.

Possibly no competitor at the time would have made so generous a gesture, but Osborne would consider no other course. It was part of his character to give value for value. Once the mistake was evident, he accepted responsibility. The fault was his. He would make good. But it nearly ruined the firm.

He never fully recovered from the strain of that year. It was not merely that when he turned down the Appleby twine binder he lost the chance to become a multimillionaire, or that his firm was set back thousands and thousands of dollars by the failure of his own device. It was a blow at his pride, at his judgment which for so many years had been unerring. Even so, his rugged frame might have withstood the stress had it not been for an acute nervous shock suffered about the same time.

In the early eighties D. M. Osborne & Co. sued the Mc-Cormick Harvesting Machine Co. of Chicago for infringement of patents. After long litigation, the Auburn concern was awarded approximately $225,000 in damages, a large sum for those days. Mr. Osborne was called to Chicago for settlement. On arrival at his hotel, he got in touch with representatives of the McCormick Company and was given an appointment for that night in the factory offices.

At the appointed time he was met and conducted to the factory, situated in a tough section near the railroad. As they passed through the dingy streets, Osborne saw strange figures lurking in the shadows. All the sordidness and crime of a great city seemed pent up in these few blocks, already astir as creatures of the night went their mysterious ways. Turning a corner, his guides led him up a dark alley at the end of which an unlighted building hid the stars. It was the factory, forbidding in its unwonted silence, looking down upon him with vacant eyes. He stumbled up stygian stairways to the top floor, where in a little office a light was made. From the safe his companions took a sheaf of bills and laid it on the table. "Take it," they said. "It's yours."

Osborne counted the money. Two hundred twenty-five thousand dollars, all in cash! He waited the next move, but there was none. They were watching him in silence. Suddenly it dawned upon him that he was dismissed, that he should find his way back alone. Concealing his apprehension, he packed the money in a satchel and started down the stairs. He had to feel every inch of the way.

Outside, the fresh air revived his spirits. He was glad to get away from the unholy atmosphere of the factory. Then his situation flashed upon him. Here he was in Chicago's notorious tenderloin with nearly a quarter of a million dollars in greenbacks! For the first time it occurred to him that it might be premeditated. That seemed the only explanation. Else why drag him down to the red-light district and pay him in cash? They were going to murder him and get their money back.

Behind him he heard the soft thud of feet. He fought down an impulse to run for it, and breathed a sigh of relief as the footsteps died away. He was just imagining things. It was fantastic to think they would kill him.

A stealthy movement at the next corner caught his eye. Someone was there! Waiting for him! Someone who would pounce out and stab him as he passed. All around him now he heard things and saw things. It was like a nightmare. A cold sweat drenched his clothes. He tried to hurry, staggered, and almost fell. He must get to his hotel. Hotel! It kept ringing in his ears as he pushed along, block after block, a prey to nameless fears. Sullen faces peered at him curiously, contemptuously. Did they know? He thought they did. They all knew. They were just waiting for the right moment. Any time now . . .

Late that night an old man stumbled into the hotel. His face was ashen and he was trembling so that he could barely stand. In his hand he clutched a little black bag and would let no one touch it. From that moment D. M. Osborne was never a well man. His health was broken. A trip to the West Indies failed to bring improvement. Doctors were of no avail. The terrors of that night, groundless though they proved to be, were too much for a constitution already undermined by worry and exhaustion. He died July 6, 1886, mourned by the whole city but by none more sincerely than the men in his shops. They perhaps knew him best: an exacting employer, demanding the full measure of a man's capacity, yet generous, faithful to his word, unassuming, gentle. Though the son was to win loyalty and respect in his own way, he never held quite the same place as his father in the affections of the working-man.

However generously one interprets the act of the McCormick officials, the tragic consequences make it difficult to condone. In his recent book, "The Century of the Reaper," Cyrus McCormick, grandson of the inventor, explains that the McCormick Company paid the old man in small bills, fearing that a check for $225,000 in settlement of the claim might be photographed for hostile advertising purposes. He adds with apparent satisfaction that "Mr. Osborne stayed late to count the money, carried the satchel containing it to his hotel for the night, lugged it back to Auburn, and there enjoyed what triumph he could by exhibiting it to his men."

Even if Thomas Mott Osborne had been business-minded, the task that confronted him as executive officer would have been appalling. In 1886, D. M. Osborne & Co. was not only the greatest industrial enterprise in Auburn but the largest manufactory of harvesting machines in the world. In twenty-five years it had grown from a single shop employing twelve men to a self-contained city of a score of buildings giving employment to nearly fifteen hundred men. In the first year of operation one hundred fifty machines had been fabricated. In 1886 the output was approximately one hundred fifty machines per day. Mowers, reapers, and self-binding harvesters were sold all over the United States and exported to nearly every country of the world.

In spite of these evidences of prosperity, all was not well with the firm. Each year a large sum was expended in royalties for the Appleby binder device. Competition was growing keener, with Cyrus Hall McCormick, William Deering, and others fighting for supremacy in the agricultural implement field. Price wars cut down profits, orders were slowing up, and credit was hard to obtain.

With the removal of the senior Osborne's steadying influence, frictions arose within the firm itself. David Munson's

brother, John H. Osborne, was secretary. Though he had
been sidetracked to the collection department, he was an indefatigable busybody and kept the whole office force in turmoil
by his persistent interference. His assumption of importance
was a stock joke, and nobody paid any serious attention to
him. A curious figure, this Uncle John, with a mania for writing to the newspapers. Often he vented his spleen in articles
printed under the caption: "What My Little Brass Monkey
Told Me." Still more unconventional were his journalistic
vagaries in connection with a little sheet, *The Index,* which
from time to time he printed on a small hand-press in his
cellar for private distribution. *The Index* advertised itself as
"published whenever necessary"—which prompted one victim
to complain that "whenever necessary seems pretty damned
often!" Tremors of apprehension ran up and down South
Street whenever a number appeared, for Uncle John did not
hesitate to retail gossip of the most personal nature.

Another source of trouble was the general manager, Gorton
W. Allen, Osborne's uncle by marriage. Allen had won to a
post of great responsibility in the firm partly by natural ability
and partly by sheer bravado. He had a blustering manner that
was often impressive, and exercised his authority with a swagger that intimidated little men and antagonized men of spirit.
Though he was a hustler, he lacked some of the quieter virtues
of a business executive. Bad accounts were allowed to run on
the books for years until it was impossible to know just where
the company stood.

So long as D. M. Osborne was alive, Allen used some discretion; but when the death of the father brought the son to
the presidency, he became a veritable tyrant. For Tom
Osborne he had not the slightest use. What did that piano-
playing son of D. M.'s know about business, anyway? The
more he kept out of the way, the better. Allen took delight in
humiliating the youthful executive on every possible occasion.
For the most part he ignored him, making a pretense of con-
sulting him only when a presidential signature was required.
It was his custom to be on hand when the mail arrived, snatch
the letters addressed to the president, and rush into his private

office to read them, as if Osborne were a mere figurehead incapable of understanding the problems of a big business.

Whatever Osborne's failings as an executive, he had spirit and an eagerness to qualify. The treatment to which he was subjected by Allen exasperated him beyond measure, but for a time he bore it in silence. Then one day he called Allen to his office and told the manager he was through and could leave as soon as convenient.

Allen could scarcely believe his ears. Under the old régime he had gradually assumed more and more responsibility for the direction of the company until he thought himself indispensable. D. M. Osborne was not primarily a business manager but an inventor and skilled mechanic. He took care of the factory end and left the rest to his deputy. Allen felt he was the backbone of the business, and now a mere boy had the effrontery to discharge him like a common clerk!

Osborne well knew what a risk he was taking in ousting his general manager. Business was at a low ebb, and the shops were running part-time, eight to ten months in the year. The firm's credit was tottering. Only a small setback might send D. M. Osborne & Co. into bankruptcy. It was even feared that Allen, whose rage knew no bounds, might undermine the confidence of banks with which the company did business. But Osborne was determined to be free of Allen's dictation. Besides, he had by this time some ideas of his own about running a business.

At this critical juncture the Osbornes held a family conference, attended by Frederick Harris of Springfield, who had married Tom's sister Emily, and James J. Storrow, recently wed to his sister Helen. It was Harris who recommended that Colonel Edwin D. Metcalf, whom he knew in Springfield, be brought to Auburn to straighten out affairs. The suggestion was adopted, and a new era began.

According to the original plan, Metcalf was to remain a year with the firm to put through a big deal, negotiations for which had been begun under Allen. In order to protect themselves from losses incurred by cutthroat competition, a number of the farm machine companies planned a gigantic amalgamation to be called the American Harvester Company. In this trust D. M. Osborne & Co. was to participate, and it was Metcalf's job to arrange the matter. Unfortunate as it seemed at the time, the deal failed to go through. Wall Street, over-cautious as the events of the next decade were to prove, turned down the $50,000,000 bond issue required to launch the project. It seemed too ambitious an undertaking.

In the meantime Metcalf had become interested in the Osborne situation. He saw prospects of rebuilding the business and promptly accepted an offer to remain as general manager. Acquiring a large block of stock, he proceeded to reorganize the company along his own lines. Ruthlessly he wrote off the books accounts which were dubious or impossible. He got down to rock bottom and began to build up again. From eastern banks with which he was connected he obtained credit. A more aggressive sales and advertising policy was adopted. The shops began to run full time, and profits increased.

Metcalf turned out to be a genius, with a fine grasp of the technique of business administration. Having put D. M. Osborne & Co. into shape, he began to branch out on his own. With some associates he formed the Columbian Cordage Company, which manufactured twine and sold it to the Osborne Company for their binders. He invested heavily and wisely in Auburn real estate, and in a few years became one of the most powerful factors in the life of the city.

When Colonel Metcalf became general manager of D. M. Osborne & Co. in 1891, Tom Osborne breathed a sigh of relief. He felt as if a millstone had been lifted from his shoulders. Better than any one else he realized that business was not his element. In the early days of his presidency visitors found him apparently busily engaged in solving some knotty problem of administration. He sat frowning at a sheaf of papers on the desk before him, now and then jotting down a note for reference.

Closer inspection would have disclosed that his labors had no concern with reapers or binders. He was drawing up a tentative cast for an amateur play soon to be presented at the Academy of Music. The first year after Osborne's return

from college he had founded the Auburn Amateur Dramatic
Club. This was long before the day of the Little Theater
movement, and organized amateur drama was largely confined to the university centers. Osborne, however, could not
bear to relinquish his rôle of actor-manager, played so bril-
liantly in Cambridge. Having formed his Dramatic Club, he
chose the plays, cast them, coached the actors, directed
the music, and usually appeared in one of the important
parts.

While this interest made life tolerable for a young man
who had no heart for the practical affairs of business, it was
often disconcerting to his associates. Osborne was forever
engrossed in some problem connected with theatricals. His
desk was covered with scripts and scores and layouts of programs. When a member of the firm entered his office with a
question of immediate moment, he was likely to be sidetracked
with a query concerning Mr. So-and-So's aptitude for the part
of the judge in "Trial by Jury." In the middle of a serious
conference, Osborne, who had been preoccupied during the
discussions, would suddenly grab his hat and excuse himself
to attend a rehearsal. Ultimate decision of the matter in hand
had to be postponed until the errant executive could be seques-
tered in a quiet moment.

To Mr. Harris and Mr. Storrow this perpetual state of
abstraction was incomprehensible. Both were busy men, practical, intensely serious about business matters. During the
critical years preceding the merger of D. M. Osborne & Co.
with International Harvester Company, they formed an unofficial advisory board that proved the mainstay of the firm.
With considerable self-sacrifice and even more personal incon-
venience, they would catch a sleeper for Auburn for a day's
deliberation and return by sleeper the next night. Having gone
to all this trouble for their brother-in-law, they were at first
astounded and then exasperated to find that at the height of
the negotiations, Tom Osborne had fallen quietly and uncon-
cernedly asleep.

With such provocation it was only natural that two men
whose time was worth a lot of money to themselves and others

should find Osborne's conduct inexcusable. Relations were sometimes strained. Dissensions arose. Yet both Storrow and Harris had an undisguised admiration for Osborne's attainments outside the business field. On his side, Osborne had a profound respect for their earnestness, ability, and uprightness.

It was simply that he could never look at life from the angle of Big Business. He was inclined to consider the bustle over inventories, margin of profit, surveys, and statistics as a tempest in a teapot. His theory of industry was simple: make something worth while and sell it for a decent profit. That is an unavoidable accessory of existence. But the business of living is tremendously more important.

And yet, in a larger sense, Osborne was a successful business man. Notwithstanding his other preoccupations, he contributed a great deal to the success of D. M. Osborne & Co. When he actually buckled down to work, he accomplished what two men could do in the same time, rarely showing signs of fatigue. During his presidency the business trebled in size. Much, but by no means all, of this progress was due to able colleagues. His own personality was a great asset. He lectured on business management at Cornell University, represented the Auburn Business Men's Association at a number of national conferences, was a vice president of the New York State Agricultural Society, acted for a time as executive officer of the machinery department of the State Fair, and was a member of the reorganization committee of the New York Life Insurance Company following the enforced resignation of President Beers.

With the exception of his correspondence, the vehemence of which often required retraction and apology, he was an ideal negotiator for a thriving business. "There is no line I know of," he said, "which separates my business from the rest of my life. . . . What is right and wrong elsewhere is right and wrong in business." That principle was strictly adhered to. When one of his own departments was contemplating a strike but could get no hall for a meeting place, Osborne promptly offered the directors' room as the proper place for the discussions. Such a thing was unheard of, and many employers felt it was carrying democracy too far. *But there was no strike.*

From the outset, the younger Osborne recognized the right of workingmen to organize for their own protection, and he was always willing to deal openly with union representatives. Not that his own men needed much protection. His sense of justice was a sure guarantee against the appalling conditions that prevailed in many other places in the 1890's. On one occasion, a group of his employees demanded an increase in wages. Though the Company declared itself willing to investigate the case, the men were impatient and the strike was called. It was a complete failure. In a short time the malcontents voluntarily returned to work at the old scale. In the meantime, Osborne had been making a survey of the wage matter. Calling the men together, he reported that his study had convinced him of the justice of their grievance. Though they had failed in the strike, the wage increase they had demanded would be granted.

Stark, staring mad he was thought by many; but the allegiance D. M. Osborne had maintained in the old days was preserved by his son in the new social order.

One more task was to confront him. In 1902 the International Harvester Company was formed, with the McCormick plant as the central unit. Systematically it proceeded to gobble up competitors, throwing a vast amount of capital into the campaign. Though D. M. Osborne & Co. could not hope to stand the strain of a price-cutting war very long, it refused to submit without a struggle. Metcalf met I.H.C. price cuts with still greater slashes until the trust realized it had a battle on its hands.

It was only a gesture, and Osborne and Metcalf knew it; but they had the satisfaction of seeing their company get from International Harvester an approximation of their terms. In 1903 D. M. Osborne & Co. sold out for a good price. The deal, however, was kept under cover until 1905, when a public announcement was made. Seven years later there was a sequel to this transaction. In its anti-trust suit against International Harvester, the federal government produced documents to show "that for two years the defendant concealed and denied its association with the Osborne Company," widely advertising it as "the largest independent company in the country and independent of any trust."

As an interested party in the merger, the Columbian Cordage Company agreed to manufacture no twine for binder purposes until ten years had elapsed. Metcalf reorganized the business as the Columbian Rope Company and began to manufacture on a large scale various grades of rope. To-day it is one of the largest rope and twine factories in the world.

Though several of the one-time Osborne shops are still running, much of the glamour of the old, independent days has evaporated. A large share of the business has been transferred to International Harvester headquarters in Chicago, leaving the Auburn plant a far less important factor in the industrial life of the city than before. But it was not simply this remote control that Osborne deplored; it was the pervading influence of the McCormicks. He always felt they did not deserve their reputation in the reaper industry.

Early in 1897 he protested to the United States Treasury Department against a proposed issue of notes bearing the portraits of Cyrus McCormick, Robert Fulton, and Samuel Morse as the three great American inventors. Osborne argued that McCormick was a farsighted promoter but not an inventor. He had simply appropriated Obed Hussey's patent and developed "a machine of his own which was quickly superseded and which marked no epoch in the history of the trade whatever." For proof he referred to an investigation conducted by the *Farm Implement News* of Chicago, and to the affidavit of Mr. McCormick's own brother that the main invention bearing the McCormick name was not original. It had always angered him to read in history textbooks about McCormick's priority; now it enraged him to find the Treasury Department intent on perpetuating "this fiction."

"It would be a falsification of history," he wrote, "an outrage upon the public, if the United States government set its seal of approval upon the claims of Mr. McCormick to these honors."

It should be added that the portrait of McCormick has never appeared on a United States Treasury note.

With the merger of D. M. Osborne & Co. with the trust, Osborne's first major enterprise terminated. Financially it had been a success, but from another angle it was disappointing. He had sacrificed his hopes for a career in the arts that he might keep the family name in the business his father had founded. It had meant turning from things he craved and applying himself to things he detested. Relieved as he might be to have the load off his shoulders, he could not help feeling that the effort of nearly twenty years had at last come to nothing. The Osborne name was now lost in the anonymity of a trust. He had made his sacrifice in vain.

CHAPTER VI

THE GOLDEN AGE

THE decade between 1886 and 1896 was nevertheless the golden period of Thomas Mott Osborne's career, a time of normal domestic experience, of social and cultural flowering. In October of 1886 he was married to Agnes Devens at the First Church, Unitarian, Cambridge. It was a quiet wedding, for his father's death less than four months before had cast a shadow over the nuptials.

His wife brought him the greatest happiness he had ever known. He responded to her natural vivacity and found a balm for taut nerves in her cool, understanding judgments. More and more he took his place in the social life of the community. His work at the office was not exacting; at least, he rarely permitted it to interfere with agreeable avocations. His town house and his summer residence at Willow Point became noted for their hospitality. From this period until his death, his home was a rendezvous for distinguished persons—musicians, artists, educators, judges, political leaders, authors, reformers.

Music was still his greatest relaxation. By this time he had collected an immense library of four-handed music, and each evening he and his sister Helen would play for an hour, taking each composer systematically in turn. At the end of three years they had proceeded only three-quarters of the way through the list. When Miss Osborne was married to James J. Storrow in 1891, the partnership was broken, and they never did finish the program they had outlined.

Osborne was one of the first competent interpreters of Richard Wagner in America. Even in his undergraduate days at Harvard he had delivered an address on the German composer before the Boston Art Student Association, now the Copley

Society. In the autumn following Wagner's death in 1883 he had witnessed the production of "Parsifal" at the commemoration exercises at Bayreuth and had been stirred by the surge and transcendent beauty of this masterpiece. From then on he was a devoted student of the great iconoclast. Something of Wagner's romantic extravagance struck an answering chord in his soul. He was enraptured not alone by the grandeur of the stage effects but by the Wagnerian theory of operatic composition: the leitmotif, or guiding theme, woven into a plan as lofty and intricate as a Gothic cathedral; and the association of certain instruments with one or more of the characters.

In the Eighties and Nineties the controversy over Wagner still raged hotly. To profess a liking for, and an understanding of, his works was considered dangerously modern. Osborne championed him with enthusiasm, giving a series of lectures at Cornell University where a short time before he had spoken on a curiously alien subject, business management, and talking at music and art club gatherings. Often there were delightfully informal musicales at home. Assembling a select circle of friends in the music room, he would explain the *Nibelungen* tetralogy, illustrating his talk by playing snatches of the operas on the piano. Sometimes his young son David, a mere babe, would be brought downstairs in his bassinet to imbibe with his bottle of milk some of the glories of "Die Walküre." The frolicsome Gilbert and Sullivan were not forgotten, but for years Wagner was Osborne's absorbing passion.

He had other hobbies, too. On the side, he was a philatelist, spending much time in picking up rare stamps at home and abroad. Unfortunately he was unable to pass on intact to his sons the valuable collection he acquired. Years later when an ex-convict, established in the Osborne home as a sort of factotum, took French leave, the best stamps in the album mysteriously disappeared. The natural inference has never been completely confirmed.

These interests alone, however, could not satisfy him. The old urge to be doing things, to have a finger in every pie, led him into one enterprise after another. In 1885 he was elected to the Auburn Board of Education, "an office accompanied by considerable work, much abuse, and no salary." Most of his later activities could be characterized by the same words. As Commissioner of Education he served three terms of three years each, being twice elected president of the Board. Defeated for a fourth term, he remarked: "That's one of the best things that ever happened to me." Possibly so, yet privately he was deeply mortified. He had temporarily withdrawn his children from public school because of ill health, and it hurt him to think that this action could be so misrepresented as to cause his defeat. His bitterness, however, did not prevent him from refurnishing one of the schools as a memorial to his wife.

The post on the Board of Education was his first public office. It gave him an insight into the vagaries of public opinion and a glimpse as well of state politics, for he headed the committee that lobbied the high-school construction bill through the Legislature at Albany.

One assignment led to another. The chronic civic uplifters found Osborne a gift from the gods and laid endless responsibilities on his willing shoulders. Yet his flair for contention was already strong. To J. A. Schweinfurth, Boston architect, he wrote:

"With the exception of that classic ass, Dogberry, as Shakespeare drew him, I know of no one who takes himself quite so seriously as Mr. ———. It must be thoroughly delightful to believe in oneself so absolutely. I wish I could."

He was referring to a co-member of a committee in charge of building a memorial chapel at Fort Hill Cemetery, Auburn; but the last sentence somewhat underrates his own self-assurance. On most questions of art he was inclined to be dogmatic, even though in a minority of one. When the Chapel Committee insisted on a slight change in plan, Osborne promptly resigned and refused to reconsider until he convinced himself it was for the good of the city (and of the architect, whom he had sponsored) that he should not withhold his advice.

To do him justice, his taste in matters of art was apt to be instinctively right; except that he had little faith in modern developments. Of so-called "artistic posters" he reported:

"This extraordinary Aubrey Beardsley-Yellow Book style of thing with its pseudo-Japanese style of flat coloring is, I think, on the whole the most distressing artistic (?) development that our generation has yet seen." He was to shudder even more violently when jazz turned music into a delirium of cacophonous spasms.

Sensitiveness to beauty was one of the criterions by which he judged a man. Even if one did not have, as he did, a natural instinct, it could be developed by study and training. When one of his sons, growing a little bored by "doing" the cathedrals of Europe, complained that he did not like stained-glass windows, he was taken to task by his father:

It is a reflection on one's own capacity of appreciation not to enjoy beautiful things. It often arises from a lack of knowledge as to what to look for. . . . If you don't like the old stained glass that the rest of us find so beautiful, don't give yourself away. Keep quiet in public until you have thoroughly tested your powers of appreciation.

Osborne never did learn to spare himself. He took on new burdens with cheerful disregard of consequences. While still in his twenties he was elected trustee of the Auburn Savings Bank, the Board of Trade, the City Club. Wells College drafted him for a trustee. He just could not resist any appeal to "join," even when accompanied by a "please remit" card; and it is not surprising to find him a bona fide member of the Dolphin Boat Club and the Toboggan Club though he scarcely knew a sloop from a sled and scorned both as pleasure vehicles.

"I am ready," he confessed ruefully, "to join anything that comes along except the Salvation Army."

The flippancy of this reference to the Salvation Army is evidence that as yet he had no inkling of the part he was to play in the regeneration of down-and-outers. No doubts of society and his relation to it had come to torture him. The world was a pleasant place, and the people in it were pleasant people. It was sufficient to live honorably, to enjoy the society of your intellectual peers, to discharge your duty to others by engaging in worthy civic projects and helping impecunious young men and women to develop their talents.

This Osborne, blissfully content in surroundings of domesticity and peaceful intercourse with his fellow men, was in striking contrast to the Osborne of the later period who carried with him an atmosphere of the arena and strode among men, wary, belligerent, as if suspecting a foul blow. It was a magnificent interlude between the uncertainties of college days when the necessity of choosing a career hung over him and the dark violence of his crusade. He had not heard the still sad music of humanity. He had not been disillusioned by corruption or embittered by betrayal. His contacts with people had been gentle and gratifying, and he had found outlet for his energies in the serene pursuits of a man of culture and wealth.

By far the greatest factor in this adjustment to normal living was his wife. She brought him sanity and moderation. Under her wholesome influence his extremist tendencies lay dormant; and they might have remained so had she lived. Domestic responsibilities soon engrossed him. During the decade of their married life, Mrs. Osborne bore him four sons: David Munson, Charles Devens, Arthur Lithgow, Robert Klipfel. Only one thing disturbed the serenity of this ideally happy household.

After his marriage, Osborne acceded to his mother's wishes by bringing his bride to live in the old home at 99 South Street. It was a great mistake. Agnes Devens Osborne, for all her even temper and good humor, was a woman of spirit. She would not brook interference in marital affairs even from such a benevolent autocrat as her mother-in-law. For her part, Mrs. D. M. Osborne could not bring herself to acknowledge that her only son, her Timmie, had grown to man's estate and that another had taken her place as intimate adviser. She attempted to exert over the man the same influence as over the boy, and to direct the rearing of his children. She felt, we may be sure, that no woman was quite good enough for him. When she saw him one day helping his wife with her overshoes, she exclaimed: "You can't put on any woman's rubbers. I won't have it."

Osborne was torn in his soul between reverence for his mother and love for his wife. His loyalties were sadly confused. Yet there was never an open break. Both women were too sensible for that. At last after seven years of intermittent discord Osborne took a step he had long contemplated. A few doors away he began the construction of a new house in which he and his family might live their lives in their own way.

Sorrow has its big moments and its own vocabulary but joy is elusive and hard to portray. It hangs upon trivialities that are of significance for the individual alone. In the building of his house Osborne reveled in happy anticipations. A stone added to the foundation, a joist fitted or a beam laid, seemed of tremendous import. If he fretted at every delay, he exulted in every sign of progress. When at last it was finished and the day of the housewarming came, he led his wife proudly across the threshold and into the parlor. There he lighted the first fire on the hearth and with pleasurable apprehension watched the smoke curl up the chimney.

"It draws like Adelina Patti in one of her first farewells!" he exclaimed jubilantly.

The idyl that began about this fireside was all too brief. In 1895 his wife became pregnant. With happy prospects they planned a vacation trip abroad, but on the day before the start was to be made, Mrs. Osborne complained of a pain in her breast. The local physician advised bringing a specialist from New York immediately. The following day a consultation was held.

Though Osborne awaited the verdict with anxiety, he was totally unprepared for the severity of the blow: "Your wife," the great doctor said, "is beyond human help. The child will be born, but she will die soon after. It will be better not to tell her."

It would have been a shock to any man. To Osborne it was catastrophic, incredible. His whole world seemed suddenly to have crumbled around him. He could not conceive what existence would be like without Agnes Osborne.

"I have lived my life," he told a friend. "From now on there is nothing ahead of me."

It was torture to see her sitting there, so happy in her secret thoughts, unaware of impending doom. And he could do noth-

AGNES DEVENS OSBORNE WITH HER SONS, CHARLES, DAVID, AND LITHGOW

ing. At first he could not bear to face her, with his dreadful knowledge. It cried for utterance. But there was iron in him. All day long he kept by himself at the office, striving to screw up his courage for the ordeal. In the afternoon he would come home whistling and smiling. He dressed for dinner with the same meticulous attention to detail as usual. During the meal he told droll stories, and laughed heartily as if he had not a care in the world. Not by the slightest word or action did he betray the horror that was upon him.

Together they laid plans for the postponed trip abroad. It would be a second honeymoon. In the quiet evenings the scrapbooks were brought out, and they looked over pictures of an earlier tour they had made. "We must go there again," she would say when some snapshot revived memories of a pleasant sojourn; and he would assent. With a pretense of excitement, he permitted her to make a complete new wardrobe for a trip which he knew she would never take. To the last, Osborne carried on this drama. The grim irony of it tortured him, but he played the part. Mrs. Osborne never knew the truth until death was close at hand.

It happened as the doctor had foretold. An operation failed to bring relief. Early in February, 1896, the child Robert was born; and in March Mrs. Osborne died.

The tragedy of those days was to remain with Osborne forever. Long afterwards he wrote to Representative Sereno Payne, whose wife had just died:

I do not know whether such a loss is greater when it falls upon us in younger or in older manhood. Had my own wife lived until today, would it have been harder to bear the separation? That is a question without an answer. I only know that the grief I bore fifteen years ago and have borne ever since gives me a keener sympathy with those who are called upon to suffer today.

When his sister, Mrs. Storrow, urged him to consider marrying again for the sake of the children, the suggestion hurt him deeply. "It would be bigamy," he said.

CHAPTER VII

CALLED BY THE THUNDER

OSBORNE was thirty-six when his wife died.

He is in his prime physically and mentally, tall, well proportioned, darkly handsome. The face has a classic beauty that in some moods is almost feminine. The features, nobly formed, are dominated by the eyes, moderately deep-set beneath a lofty brow. He wears a trim black mustache, discarded in later years. At the corners of the mouth barely perceptible lines suggest sympathy and humor, transforming a countenance that otherwise would give an impression of austerity.

Until now his lot has been that of the average man born in good circumstances: travel, college, business, marriage, children. Tragedy breaks this natural progression. The latter half of his life hardly seems to fit the former. The two parts might belong to different men. The change that comes over him bewilders and then alienates many of his old friends, for the conventional man is much more agreeable to live with than the unconventional. Osborne's unconventionality consists in his stepping beyond the stage of deploring social conditions into the realm of action calculated to change those conditions. That means loneliness, especially if one has a zeal which conservatives can construe as fanaticism.

Still, it is not a new Osborne miraculously created, but the old Osborne with a new vision. For thirty-six years he has been absorbing all that life has to offer. Now he turns to repay the debt. He has intensity as well as versatility, an unusual combination.

"I am gifted," he confides in a friend, "with an unhappily restless disposition which will not let me rest—partly a natural disposition and partly the result of the sorrow which settled on my life and which has driven me into restless activity."

The various pursuits to which he devotes himself during the next three decades are not mere hobbies; each in itself is a single purpose prosecuted with a diligence, a violence even, that would demand the entire resources of a less dynamic being. Loneliness whips his natural zeal into greater ardors. Though he has many friends, intimates are few. He has always kept a certain part of himself to himself. Only his wife held the key to that innermost chamber, and she is dead.

In this spiritual solitude he finds relief by giving free play to the restless surge within him. He throws himself into politics, social reforms, philanthropies. The pressure of business is still on him. He has four sons to whom he must be both father and mother. As he comes more and more into national prominence, his services are in demand for important public assignments. The tax on his strength is terrific, yet he does not seem to mind. He revels in it. Even when warned that he must slow down if he would live long, he drives himself on as if racing against time. To the last he is vigorous and aggressive, fighting battles that are lost before they are begun, facing defeat with unflinching fortitude. He is called by the thunder, and the trumpet sounds within his soul.

BOOK II

CHAMPION OF LIBERTY

. . . True freedom is to share
All the chains our brothers wear,
And, with heart and hand, to be
Earnest to make others free!
—James Russell Lowell.

1. THE POLITICIAN

CHAPTER I

BAPTISM OF FIRE

THE Auburn *Daily Advertiser* for March 10, 1879, triumphantly announced the election and seating of a new Republican mayor, David Munson Osborne. During the campaign it had hailed its candidate as friend of the workingman, a stanch Republican, and a high-minded citizen. Twenty-five years later this same daily was paying its respects, grudgingly, sometimes bitterly, to another Mayor Osborne, Thomas Mott, Democrat. "Mr. Osborne is a splendid young fellow," it had said after characterizing the Democratic slate as a mongrel ticket, "and outside of politics the ADVERTISER has always liked him immensely." Exactly a quarter of a century after the report of this Democratic victory, the *Advertiser-Journal*, Osborne-owned but keeping its Republican traditions unimpaired, congratulated Charles Devens Osborne upon his election to the office which his father and grandfather had held before him.

Three generations of mayors. Fifty years in the political limelight and fifty years of political controversy. Whether in or out of office the Osbornes moved in an atmosphere of conflict. There were factional fights within the party and partisan battles in the campaigns. High words exchanged in the heat of conflict sometimes threatened to break, sometimes actually did break, long-standing friendships. Yet whatever the turns of political fortune, the family retained a position of recognized importance, first in the community, later in the state and nation.

This prominence was both a family and an individual victory. The Osborne name meant much, but this alone would not have sufficed in a city and a county which can be taken as perfect specimens of what is called rock-ribbed Republicanism. Even in the case of David Munson, who was a bona fide member of the Grand Old Party, there was another and perhaps a greater factor in his success at the polls. Feeling the strong partisan sentiments engendered by the Civil War and representing also the conservative industrial element, he had gravitated naturally toward the party of Lincoln. Yet he was not a "line Republican." Occasionally he jumped the traces, as in 1883 when he voted for Grover Cleveland for governor of New York State. That this defection did not materially injure his party standing is demonstrated by his designation the following year as delegate to the National Republican Convention in Chicago at which James G. Blaine, ex-senator from Maine, was selected as the Republican standard-bearer.

Though it is not surprising that a man of Osborne's prominence and political leanings should have been the choice of the people for mayor back in 1879, it was his appeal to the workingmen that in a large measure accounted for his victory. The employees of D. M. Osborne & Co. delivered an almost full quota of votes for their boss, not from fear of losing their jobs but from deep-rooted loyalty. The individual was for them more important than name or party, and as a unit they rallied to his support.

The first Mayor Osborne's term, however, was not so serene as one might imagine. He was a firm believer in public improvements at a time when thrift in government was far more popular than it is to-day. A quarter of a century before the automobile turned the attention of legislatures to highway conditions and the necessity of "getting the farmers out of the mud," D. M. Osborne was advocating a program of good roads. One morning in 1878 the peace of the community was shattered by the appearance of a juggernaut that clattered its way over the unpaved streets with protestations of escaping steam and grinding gears. It was a steam roller, the first to be seen in those parts. The whole town came out to jeer the operator. "Osborne's Folly," they nicknamed it, parodying the phrase that had been applied to the purchase of Alaska by another

Auburnian, William H. Seward. In spite of ridicule, in spite of acts of malicious violence resulting in the mayor's report that the steam roller "has been relieved, by some unknown person or persons, of all its loose pieces of brass," Osborne's Folly proved its practicality. In his inaugural address Mayor Osborne remarked that the "much-abused steam roller is vindicating the judgment of those who advocated the purchase," and at the same time recommended the use of asphalt for paving. This project was also too far ahead of the times to gain widespread support, for asphalt pavements were then little known except in the great cities of the world, such as London, Paris, and Washington.

The strife of active politics did not appeal to the elder Osborne, and at the end of his term he was content to give his whole attention once more to business affairs. When Thomas Mott came along, times had changed. The labor problem had become more serious. The unions were growing more active. One could no longer count on the same spirit of harmony and understanding between employee and employer. Besides, the second Osborne had not quite the same appeal to the working-man that his father had had. There was a larger gulf between them. D. M., the quiet, practical, paternal autocrat, spoke directly to his men in a language they understood. T. M., high-minded, emotional, with a Harvard vocabulary and a Cambridge manner, was sometimes baffling to men who spent most of their waking hours in the shops.

Another factor against the second Osborne as a political candidate was his party allegiance. To his father's disappointment, he had rejected Republicanism and allied himself with what he considered the progressive party. This, to begin with, might be considered a tactical blunder in a city where Democrats were so far outnumbered, but it was only a small part of the burden which Thomas Mott Osborne assumed. At that time the local Democratic organization was split with a factionalism more bitter than interparty enmity. The side defeated in the caucus took its revenge by spiking the regular candidates at the polls. It was not a pleasant prospect for beginning a political career, yet Osborne was twice elected mayor and was defeated for a third term by a narrow margin.

Late in the summer of 1892 the press of New York State carried news items and editorials reporting and commenting upon the political conversion of Thomas Mott Osborne. The position of the family and the Republicanism of David Munson Osborne contributed to the stir which the announcement made. Osborne himself was a little surprised and more than a little amused at the circulation given this news item, for the conversion, if it could be called such, had been in process for eight years. In fact, he had left Harvard a Democrat in principle if not in name. His academic studies had made him a free trader. His nonconformist spirit rebelled against the established solidarity of Cayuga County Republicanism, even though his own father was a prominent representative of the party in control. Ever since the days of William H. Seward, Auburn and the surrounding country had been "regular." Regularity was always anathema to Osborne. Besides, he found in the Democratic Party, at least nationally, what he believed was the best promise of progressive and liberal government.

The first application of these sentiments came but a few months after graduation. It was 1884, and there was preparing a presidential campaign that for nastiness and vulgarity has had no equal in the United States. The Republicans at Chicago had nominated James G. Blaine of Maine. The Democrats, looking for a man who could draw votes, picked Grover Cleveland, whose chief distinction at the time was that unexpectedly he had been elected governor of New York State by a majority of 192,000. Though the issue was supposed to be the tariff, this was almost lost sight of in a welter of personalities. To young Osborne, fresh out of college, his ideals still unsoiled by contact with the seamier side of political life, Blaine's crooked dealings with the railroads counted for more than the dirty story of Cleveland and the widow. Shorn of its trimmings, the latter narrative reduced to an unfortunate alliance with a dipsomaniac. Blaine's manipulations were irreducible on any count. Particularly Blaine's famous letter to Warren Fisher, enclosing an exonerating statement composed by himself and intended for publication under Fisher's signature, made a deep impression. "Burn this letter," Blaine had added as a postscript. Time and again in later years Osborne recurred to these three incriminating words.

If further stimulus were needed to make Osborne bolt his father's party, it was furnished by the Rev. Dr. Samuel D. Burchard, New York City clergyman who has won the dubious honor of coining the most maladroit phrase of any campaign. At the head of a delegation of ministers, Burchard visited Blaine at the Fifth Avenue Hotel. "We are Republicans," he intoned, as the weary candidate made a pretense of listening, "and don't propose to leave our party and identify ourselves with the party whose antecedents have been Rum, Romanism, and Rebellion." That was the death blow for Blaine. It offended not only Catholic voters but many others of liberal thought. Among these was Osborne. He turned Mugwump and cast his first vote for Cleveland. "Rum, Romanism, and Rebellion" lost New York for Blaine, and New York's votes in the electoral college won the presidency for Cleveland.

Osborne was not ready, however, to ally himself formally with the Democratic Party. He still thought he was more a Republican than a Democrat. For every office except that of president he voted the straight Republican ticket. The following year he voted in the Republican caucus. At this time he obviously did not suspect how fundamental his Democratic principles were and fully intended to unite with the Grand Old Party as soon as certain conditions, which he believed transient, had changed. They did not change. It might be more accurate to say that Osborne did not change.

He soon had his first glimpse of practical politics. As a member of the Auburn Board of Education he had become deeply interested in the erection of a new high school, long needed. In 1886, as head of a committee to obtain favorable legislation for this project, he paid a number of visits to Albany, lobbying successfully in behalf of his bill. This introduction to the devious paths of politics, he admitted afterward,

depressed him, but at the same time it whetted his appetite for
active participation in the affairs of government. It may be
added that in June, 1888, he had the satisfaction of presiding
at the dedication of the new high school, an occasion made
memorable for him by the delivery of his first public address.

It was Cleveland's tariff policy that finally won Osborne to
open support of the Democratic Party. In 1888 he presided
at a tariff reform meeting, and later cast his vote for Cleveland
at the polls. Four years later, with Cleveland again a candidate for the nomination, he excited the editorial comment
previously mentioned by enrolling as a Democrat. In reply to
a query from the New York *World*, he wrote:

> Believing that our present tariff is a serious hindrance to the
> country's natural and prosperous development, I find that I can
> honestly join the Democratic Party. I do this the more heartily as
> I find myself in the company of so many former Republicans, whose
> motives I revere and in whose judgment I trust.

Not content with halfway measures, he stumped Cayuga
County for Cleveland, making his first campaign speech before
a gathering of farmers whose Republicanism seemed about as
permeable as the Rock of Gibraltar. Consequently, when the
election returns showed that the Republican majority in the
county had been reduced from its average of 3,500 to 2,500, he
indulged in a little gloating on his own account.

Republicans were at a loss to understand such enthusiasm
for a low tariff. Osborne was a manufacturer and stood to gain
by keeping tariffs at a protective level. In supporting Cleveland and Democratic tariff policies he was working against his
own interests and those of his family and associates. Some
thought it was high idealism. Others said it was just plain
foolishness.

Osborne's brand of Democracy was not, however, popular
with the other Democratic leaders in Auburn. He introduced
a discordant note. He would not play ball with the regular
organization. He made contacts with the rebellious element
of the party in the state. To one he wrote: "The Democratic
Party here is entirely unworthy of trust or confidence." As an
afterthought he inserted with a pen the word *almost* before

entirely. Some light is thrown on the meaning of this emenda-
tion by another letter which states: "I am going to make an
endeavor to start a new Democratic organization in this place,
which I hope may lead to some good."

This impudence from a man who had just turned thirty and
who, moreover, had been an enrolled Democrat for but a few
months, was too much for the pride of the petty bosses. They
fought him, used him, double-crossed him—whichever served
their purpose best. Yet if they had foreseen the extent to
which the independent movement in the state would spread
and what part Osborne would play in it, they would have read
him out of the party at the outset. Instead, they delayed for
eighteen years.

Cleveland's victory in 1892 encouraged Osborne to greater
efforts. He had formed a Tariff Reform Club modeled after a
similar club in New York City. Though it was ostensibly a
nonpartisan association, Osborne used it with good effect to
buck the intrenched Democratic organization in Auburn.
Through his connections in New York and Washington,
notably Charles A. Hamlin, newly appointed assistant secretary of the treasury, he began to exert an influence on local
appointments. At his own expense he made frequent trips to
Washington to interview cabinet members regarding postmas-
terships. Though the jobs were petty enough, involving appointments in villages of but a few hundred residents, this
extraordinary energy coupled with his ability to make contact
with important personages in the national capital soon won him
considerable reputation. Candidates for jobs began to seek
Osborne's patronage, and the Old Guard was worried. Every
man Osborne succeeded in placing was discovered to favor low
tariff, civil service reform, and other crazy notions detrimental
to the health and prosperity of the bosses.

The latter did not know just how to meet this opposition. In
the first place, they were not sure what this interloper was
after. Idealism was all right to talk about in public, but they
knew better than to suppose that was all there was to it. There
must be some ulterior purpose. To a friend who had asked for
help in getting a certain appointment, Osborne wrote a stern

refusal. He would not countenance the removal of the incumbent. "It would seem to most people, under ordinary circumstances," he wrote, "that if a man has done his work well for two years, that would be the best reason in the world for continuing him in the position." What kind of man was this, anyhow, who turned down friends on such a flimsy excuse as the merit of the office holder?

When Osborne succeeded in maneuvering the appointment to the Auburn postmastership, the second biggest plum in the local orchard, it was realized that steps must be taken. Even the warden of the State Prison began to feel anxious about his own sinecure. As the chief of the regular Democratic organization, he knew that Osborne was aiming at his political head. While it might be dangerous to fight openly, there were other methods that rarely failed to work. Consequently, one day in January, 1895, Osborne received a letter from the warden with the suggestion, paramount to an offer, that he accept the mayoral nomination "unanimously at the hands of the united Democratic Party."

To the amazement of the warden, this bait did not even get a rise. Osborne probably realized that the purpose back of the offer was his own reclamation to party loyalty, but he was actuated by a still more powerful motive. Even though as mayor he might be able to put through some of the reforms he believed in, he could not and would not compromise. Differences were not to be settled but to be fought out. Halving a principle destroyed its integrity. Already he had reached the conclusion that city government should be conducted on a nonpartisan basis, with no party labels attached to candidates for office, and he told the Democratic moguls that unless he could be nominated on a citizens' ticket which had no connection with state and national politics, he would not run. Secretly, he hoped that this nomination on a nonpartisan slate was not far off.

It was largely as a result of these activities that Osborne found himself in July, 1896, a delegate from New York State to the Democratic national convention at Chicago. From this point on the tempo of his life increased rapidly. The death of his wife in March, instead of inducing lethargy, threw him into a belligerent frenzy. He changed from an advocate of reform into a militant apostle. Figures in national life became personifications of good or evil.

Looking back, one realizes that, whatever might have been the issue—tariff, imperialism, social justice—it would have claimed Osborne's whole being. It happened to be currency, a matter of financial policy, yet he made of it a great moral issue. As early as 1893 he had written to Hamlin: "I should think that the silver fanatics would begin to realize where they are driving us." When he learned he was to be a delegate to Chicago, he felt a great responsibility to do something "to save the party from dishonor and ruin."

Osborne went to the convention as a Crusader to the Saracenic wars. Because of his contacts with farmers in every section of the United States, he realized more than most easterners just how serious a struggle the country was facing. The free coinage idea had been spreading rapidly. To the South and the West, the East was typified by Wall Street, and Wall Street was unholy. To the East, the Free Silverites were a mob of unthinking or unreliable bankrupts eager to manipulate a repudiation of debts. The explosion which followed the impact of these two forces at the Chicago convention startled the country.

Osborne, however, was more angered than surprised—angered not so much that the Bryan faction stampeded the convention as that it completely upset convention procedure to accomplish it. He saw the National Committee overruled in its traditional function of establishing the temporary organization and Senator Daniels of Virginia installed as temporary chairman in place of the Committee's nomination, David B. Hill of New York. He heard a drunken southerner shout: "To hell with the East." In a convention only slightly free-silver in sentiment, he watched the maneuvers that gave Bryan and his crowd the required two-thirds majority of the delegates. The Nebraska delegation of sixteen, committed to the gold standard, was unseated in favor of Bryan and his free-silver delegates, though in the Nebraska election the latter had received about half as many votes as the sound-money Democrats. Michigan's delegation of twenty-eight was also on the side of sound money until the unseating of four free-silver members gave the whole delegation to the opposition. The unit rule required that all the votes of the state be cast in accordance with the will of the majority of the delegation.

As if this were not enough, the free-silver majority on the floor hammered through a resolution to increase from two to six the votes allowed each territory in the convention. As the territories were solidly free-silver, this tripling made doubly sure the two-thirds majority required by the West. How much simpler, thought Osborne, to have voted to triple the votes of all the free-silver states! That would have been no more irregular than the tactics adopted.

Now that the convention was in the hands of the free-silver men, the stage was set for the play of personal ambition. As if he had been in the wings waiting for his cue, there appeared upon the rostrum a man, a few months younger than Osborne, whose voice suddenly quieted the milling throng on the floor. With uncanny distinctness, as if the day of amplifiers had been anticipated, his words penetrated every corner of the vast auditorium. One moment twenty thousand people sat in stunned silence. Another, and they were on their feet shouting acclaim. They ceased to be individuals; they were a single entity, a mob, swayed from one emotion to another by the magic of one man's oratory. When the speaker reached the peroration, which he had practiced upon many a smaller audience in his barnstorming campaign until he knew every inflection that would strike deepest response from his listeners, Osborne's heart sank, for he realized that William Jennings Bryan would be the next Democratic candidate for President.

"You shall not press down upon the brow of labor this crown of thorns. . . ."

The voice boomed over the multitude with apostolic fervor. Twenty thousand people felt their temples prickle under an imaginary crown of thorns.

"You shall not crucify mankind upon a cross of gold!"

Twenty thousand people groaned beneath the weight of a

golden cross and then shouted defiance to the powers of evil.
They cheered and cried and pummeled one another. It was
the frenzy of hypnotism. From that moment there was no
doubt of the outcome. Even those who kept their wits felt that
somehow they had all been bewitched. Osborne himself felt the
spell. Speaking of it later, he described the address thus:

> Without a single thought above the commonplace, without
> scholarship or lofty ideals, without humor and with only a cheap
> attempt at pathos, beginning with claptrap and ending with blas-
> phemy, it was nevertheless a great, a wonderful speech.

The very qualities which Osborne criticized were responsible
for its effect. It was commonplace. It did lack humor. It may
even have been blasphemous. But it was timed to the psychological moment. It expressed all the protests that the toiler
had been unable to put into words, and suddenly "the cause
of humanity" seemed very real to thousands of people who a
moment before and an hour after were but hard-boiled politicians.

When a draft of the proposed platform was released, there
was only one thing for Osborne to do. That it would be
adopted, he knew. Free silver, the revival of the greenback
agitation, the abolition of life terms for judges and civil service
men, the debasement of the Supreme Court from an independent body to the creature of the executive, and finally the
studied insult to President Cleveland—against all this Osborne
revolted. It seemed a most vicious betrayal of Democratic
ideals, a negation of everything the party stood for. Surrendering his credentials to ex-Governor Flower, chairman of the
New York delegation, he left the convention commenting cyni-
cally that "if the outcome of the convention had been as satis-
factory as the badges, there would have been little complaint."

He did not, however, accept defeat supinely, but began
immediately to organize a third-party movement. Neglecting
his work at the Osborne plant, furnishing his own expenses, he
launched into a campaign for a "real Democratic convention."
"I intend to throw myself into this work for all there is in
me," he publicly avowed. Liberal leaders in New York and

Massachusetts began to hear from him. He sent his appeals as far west as Colorado, and followed them up vigorously. There is little doubt that his importunate demands had much to do in crystallizing sentiment in New York State for a Gold Democrat ticket, and that indirectly his influence was felt much farther afield. The specific job he chose for himself was the organization of the interior counties of the state. To accomplish this more effectively he formed the National Democratic Club of Cayuga County, imported speakers of note, stumped the region himself, reported conditions regularly to state headquarters, and generally made such a to-do that he was presently recognized as a vital force in the liberal wing of the party.

Early in September, following a state convention in Syracuse, he went as New York State delegate to the sound-money convention at Indianapolis. Ex-Governor Flower was also a delegate. From this assembly Osborne returned with renewed enthusiasm. "Nothing so hopeful has taken place in American politics within my recollection," he wrote a friend jubilantly. Appointed a member of the finance committee of the state, he began a series of addresses that immediately brought him public attention. Toward the end of the campaign he spoke practically every night for three solid weeks. They were good speeches, far above the average political harangue. A man who can hold a packed house for an hour and a half on a subject dealing with currency is worth watching.

Osborne himself began to have an inkling of his potentiality. He was enjoying himself thoroughly. With naïve modesty he apologized repeatedly for his poor oratorical powers, but he protested too much. He was exhilarated by his success and felt the stirring of political ambitions. He dropped hints of his own availability. "I see the National Democrats have done themselves the honor of nominating you," he wrote a fellow Democrat. "I might have been in the same boat had I not sternly repressed the enthusiasm of my supporters." Of the state convention he had remarked: "We shall nominate a good Democrat—if I have to run myself."

He was fully aware that even a scattering vote for Palmer

and Buckner would mean not only defeat for Bryan but the election of McKinley. McKinley he despised. But he feared Bryan. As between the two the choice was simple. Bimetallism represented the greater danger. "If I lived in a doubtful state," he declared, "I should not hesitate to cast my vote for McKinley."

Such outspoken invitation to irregularity alienated many Democrats even among the supporters of the third ticket. To them, this disaffection was an emergency measure. After it was over, they would return to the fold. Osborne thought that he was witnessing the rebirth of the party and that a permanent organization of the National Democrats would displace the old machine. He was wrong. He underestimated the inertia of the rank and file. Years later, when he was the popular choice in the state for Democratic candidate for governor, these things returned to plague him. Tammany licked him on the charge of treason. Yet he might have answered in the words he used to explain his position in the Bryan campaign. Conceive a party, he argued, that has been duped and betrayed by rascals bent on destroying the old ideals and substituting a program that will eventually mean the ruin of the nation.

Then would we be expected to bow the head meekly and say: "It is for the majority to decide! . . . What I have always called honest I will disavow; what I have believed to be honorable I will throw aside; what I think to be dangerous to my country I will accept. I will do all this that I may be called regular."

A born fighter never lacks an opponent or a *casus belli.* When McKinley was elected, Osborne turned to battle against the man he had helped put into the White House. Tariff, imperialism, civil service, the income tax—these were the issues that now struck fire from flint. But first he turned his attention to solidifying the reform movement in New York State, seeking to establish an independent organization that would enlist the support of enlightened voters of both parties. Though he failed he could never be dissuaded from his conviction that but for the betrayal of one man the political history of both state and nation would have been written differently.

CHAPTER II

A TILT WITH A ROUGH RIDER

IF ever two men were equipped for joint action in political and social reform, it was Theodore Roosevelt and Thomas Mott Osborne. Both exhibited an exceptional courage, a disregard for opposition in high quarters, and an intense individualism. Both came of good family and had high social standing. Both felt that the privileges conferred by birth, fortune, and education enjoined a definite obligation to society, a responsibility that could not be evaded. And finally, both were intensely interested in the physical and moral welfare of their generation.

Only two years after Roosevelt had left the academic cloisters of Cambridge he threw a bomb into both Republicans and Democrats of the New York State Assembly by demanding the impeachment of Judge Westbrook of Newbury "on the ground of corrupt collusion with Jay Gould and the prostitution of his high judicial office to serve the purpose of wealthy and unscrupulous stock gamblers." If he failed in his purpose it was not for lack of courage or fighting spirit. The old guard rose en masse to circumvent the young upstart from Harvard who in his first term in the Assembly dared to defy the authority of the bosses.

Roosevelt, backed to a large extent by Governor Grover Cleveland, next launched an attack upon the very citadel of Tammany, forcing through the Legislature a series of bills revamping municipal government and seriously restricting Tammany's corrupt control of New York City. A decade later, when he was appointed president of the police board by Mayor Strong of New York, Roosevelt not only enraged the liquor interests but alienated many influential leaders by rigid enforcement of the Sunday liquor laws. Indeed, he made himself so obnoxious by his perseverance in reforms that nearly all the politicians and editors were against him, including those of his own party. With only lukewarm support, he fought organized corruption with grim courage, though his own interests were jeopardized.

At this time too Roosevelt made those night pilgrimages with Jacob A. Riis through New York's tenement and tenderloin districts, learning at first hand the needs of the poor and discovering vice conditions that were winked at by the authorities. Osborne himself would have delighted in these exploits. He was to carry personal investigation to a more startling and unorthodox extreme.

Though not an apostle of the "strenuous life" as conceived by the robust, outdoor enthusiast Roosevelt, Osborne could not withhold a grudging admiration for the man. He hated to admit it—was in fact exasperated by it—but there was a sort of temperamental kinship between the two. As late as 1911 he wrote: "Roosevelt is going around like a roaring lion, and the papers print pages of his performances. He bores me so I don't know what to do; and the worst of it is he's so often *right* in what he says! He's simply maddening."

Osborne too was endowed with a spirit of restless activity that manifested itself in crusades against the dragons of intrenched authority and oppression. When he dealt a blow, all the force of his arm was behind it. He never pulled his punches. Roosevelt's "unforgivable sin" was soft hitting. "Do not hit at all if it can be avoided; but never hit softly." Osborne never hit softly, yet the adjective he was most fond of applying to the hero of San Juan Hill was "barbaric."

For a brief moment it looked as if these two dynamic personalities were to unite in a struggle against the tyranny of the political machines. Osborne hated Tammany as unreservedly as did Roosevelt. Roosevelt despised the autocratic Tom Platt and his control of Republican destinies in New York State. Both were sound-money advocates. Yet something in each of them made collaboration impossible. When it came to a practical method of putting their ideas into execution, they were as far apart as the two poles. To gain political power Roosevelt did not hesitate to compromise with party leaders whom he detested. He would even compromise with his own conscience. Osborne would do neither. He spurned compromise even though it might serve a good end. There was always but one *right* thing to do, and he did it with the stiff-necked stubbornness of a Puritan.

In 1898 the independent movement in New York State grew to such proportions that the time was conceived ripe for the presentation of a state ticket. In both parties there was resentment against the arrogance of the bosses. Platt had built up a one-man power that was as absolute as a dictator's. He could name his own candidates in the state and sometimes swing a national convention through his instructed delegates. Richard Croker was using strong-arm methods in elections without compunction. When Tammany elected a city official or a judge, Croker expected him to do his duty—to Tammany and Croker. Only infrequently was there insubordination, and then retribution was swift. When Justice Daly of the Supreme Court refused to appoint one of the Tammany incompetents as clerk, Croker denied him renomination. He brazenly explained that, when he put a man on the bench, he had "a right to expect proper consideration at his hands." There was nothing subtle or mysterious in the Croker domination. Since there were a lot of people who would stand for it, and since those who wouldn't couldn't do anything about it, what the hell? That was his philosophy. He had no more need of finesse than a mud turtle has of wings.

Open and prolonged flouting of public decency, however, is eventually challenged. In New York City the Citizens Union, a nonpartisan group working for municipal reform and home rule, saw an opportunity to extend its influence. The previous year it had thrown a scare into both Platt and Croker by sponsoring Seth Low as independent candidate for mayor of Greater New York. Low was defeated by the Tammany candidate, Robert Van Wyck, but ran nearly 50,000 votes ahead of Benjamin F. Tracy, Platt's hand-picked man. For a time Platt's leadership was threatened. He had refused to endorse Low though he knew that the independent candidate had nearly one-quarter of the voters of Greater New York behind him. First and always a boss, Platt preferred handing Tammany the mayorship to accepting a man he might not be able to control.

Dissatisfaction with Platt was reflected upstate as well as in New York City, with most of the large cities electing Democratic mayors. In the Assembly, the Democrats nearly doubled their representation. Republicans grumbled, blaming Platt for betraying the party for the sake of his own skin. But the independents were encouraged in spite of their defeat. They had shown unexpected power. What they needed was a permanent state organization, with a name and an emblem, to acquire legal standing as a continuously existing party.

With a gubernatorial election impending, the Citizens Union maneuvered a coalition with the independent forces upstate. The name and emblem of the Citizens Union were adopted by the greater organization and plans were laid for a state-wide canvass. To this standard were attracted most of the anti-Tammany Democrats and the anti-Platt Republicans, a group large enough to merit the notice of leaders of the major parties. They already had decided on a candidate for lieutenant governor—Thomas Mott Osborne of Auburn. Though he had been active in politics for a scant six years and had held no political office, his conspicuous rôle in political reform and his influence upstate made him a logical choice for second place. If an outstanding candidate could be induced to head the ticket, the impetus of the reaction against machine politics might well carry the whole slate into office. The chief problem was to find the right man.

As the summer waned the eyes of more than one harassed politician strayed toward Montauk Point. There at Wikoff Camp were Roosevelt and his Rough Riders waiting to be mustered out. But it was not the same Roosevelt who four months since had resigned his post as assistant secretary of the Navy to organize a national volunteer cavalry regiment. Then he had been a strenuous but by no means impressive figure on the American horizon. The picturesqueness of the Rough Riders first captured the public imagination. Then came San

Juan, or hills to that effect, and the miracle of democracy was performed. In an explosion of patriotism the crowd seized upon Teddy as the national hero. Overnight he became the most significant person in public life.

Tom Platt watched this development with uneasy eye. He did not like Roosevelt, yet he would have to use him. There was no way out. T. R. was the only possible candidate for governor on the Republican ticket. Before Platt could act, however, a delegation from the Independents journeyed to Montauk Point and approached the hero of San Juan. Their proposition was simple and unmistakable. Roosevelt was bound to receive the Republican nomination. Let him first accept the gubernatorial designation on the Independent ticket, with Thomas Mott Osborne as his running mate. His election thus assured, he would not be obligated to Platt and his henchmen; Platt and Croker could be pried loose from their foothold; honest government by the people would replace the corrupt despotism of the bosses.

Reputable witnesses have testified from personal knowledge that Roosevelt accepted this offer with alacrity. Oswald Garrison Villard of the *Nation;* John Jay Chapman, editor of the *Political Nursery,* a periodical that was born with this Independent movement and that died shortly after Roosevelt struck his fatal blow. Though the histories are curiously silent on the subject, there seems to be little doubt that Roosevelt considered the time opportune for such a step. He did not change his views until after the memorable meeting with Platt in the Fifth Avenue Hotel. What occurred at that interview one can only surmise, but four days later Roosevelt declined to allow his name to be used on the Independent ticket. With the Republican nomination in his pocket, he denied having given his consent to the reform delegation or having visited Platt at the Fifth Avenue Hotel.

Osborne and his friends were stricken almost to tears. Until their champion deserted, it had seemed a golden opportunity. Never again did Osborne place confidence in the integrity of Roosevelt. He could admire but not trust. "Just for a handful of silver he left us," was his lament, "just for a riband to stick in his coat." Roosevelt could "resist everything except temptation." The *Political Nursery* observed that Roosevelt had been dragooned, and that the power which could so school him once could do it again.

If the Independents underrated Roosevelt, they in turn were misprized by him. It was for them he invented his famous phrase, "the lunatic fringe." Reformers were mostly "silk stockings" with æsthetic rather than moral reasons for opposing the bosses. The candidate they put forward was usually "some rather inefficient, well-meaning person, who bathed every day, and didn't steal, but whose only good point was 'respectability,' and who knew nothing of the great fundamental questions looming before us." This sounds like a paraphrase of Horace Porter's *bon mot* in the Cleveland-Blaine campaign of 1884. "A mugwump," defined Porter, "is a person educated beyond his intellect." And yet both these definitions are kinder than the modern version describing a mugwump as a sort of bird that sits on a fence with his mug on one side and his wump on the other.

The question of Roosevelt's veracity in regard to his rejection of the Independent nomination is a curious one. In his *Autobiography* Lincoln Steffens asserts that "Roosevelt's lies were unconscious. He was an honest man; he could not tell a lie until he made himself believe it." As an illustration, he testifies that he, Steffens, suggested that if Roosevelt read his statement denying the interview with Platt at the Fifth Avenue Hotel twice before breakfast, once after, once before luncheon and twice after, and just before going to bed, he would wake up some morning and find he believed it. The efficacy of this treatment was slightly disturbed when Steffens asked two days later: "Well, Colonel, have you got that lie so you believe it yourself?" Whereupon, according to the narrator, T. R. flew into a rage and swore Steffens had put him back a day or two.

With crushing defeat a certainty, Osborne and the substitute candidate for governor, Theodore Bacon of Rochester, still carried on the fight. It was hopeless from the start, and they knew it. Between the hurrah vote that Roosevelt carried to the entire Republican slate and the stand-pat Tammany vote that supported Van Wyck, the Independents received only a few scattering ballots. Even in Cayuga County, Osborne polled but 222 votes out of a total of nearly 15,000. Still he felt less the personal humiliation than the blow given to reform. Good government and clean politics had been set back years. Viewing the situation in the Democratic and Republican parties, he could not help crying: "A plague o' both your houses!"

CHAPTER III

A GENTLEMAN OF THE MINORITY

"WE will not renounce our part in the mission of the race, trustee, under God, of the civilization of the world. . . . Of all our race, He has marked the American people as His chosen nation to finally lead in the regeneration of the world."

So spoke Senator Albert J. Beveridge of Indiana a few days after the turn of the century, voicing the thought of the majority of his fellow countrymen. For the first time since the establishment of the republic, the eyes of the nation looked outward upon the world with visions of empire. A little war and two little islands had wrought the change. Men were fired with dreams, and a catchword could intoxicate them: our little brown brothers; disinterested protection; benevolent assimilation; our imperial destiny. What Germany believed herself to be before 1914, the United States was convinced she was in 1900: the servant of God with a sword in hand. Listen to Beveridge: "Pray God the time may never come when mammon and the love of ease will so debase our blood that we will fear to shed it for the flag and its imperial destiny."

What caught the imagination was not only territorial aggrandizement; it was the mission of saving backward peoples from their ignorance and squalor. For the Republicans, with the exception of a group led by Senator Hoar of Massachusetts, "imperialism" became the magic watchword. It stirred men's souls. It also stirred voters' souls. At the head of the anti-expansionists was Bryan, still silver-tongued, still preaching free silver. Eloquent as he might be in denouncing the evils of dominion, there was another who spoke more clearly in the common idiom. That was Mr. Dooley.

"Whin we plant what Hogan calls th' starry banner iv freedom in th' Ph'lippeenes," remarked this political philosopher to Mr. Hennessy, "an' give th' sacrid blessin' iv liberty to the poor, down-throdden people iv thim unfortunate isles—dam thim—we'll larn them a lesson!"

When Mr. Hennessy inquired what should be done with Aguinaldo, Mr. Dooley replied, "Well, I know what they'd do with him in this ward. They'd give that pathrite what he asks, an' thin they'd throw him down an' take it away fr'm him."

To Osborne this state of affairs presented a dilemma. His brain told him that Bryan and the free-silver plank which once more had been inserted in the Democratic platform were not to be tolerated by intelligent persons. His heart told him that the imperialism of McKinley was tantamount to the authorization by the United States of a new form of slavery. He believed the Philippine War would forever be a blot on the record of a republic whose first article of faith is liberty.

At first he had hopes that a new independent party might rise from the ruins of the old. But the National Democratic Party was dead. Its members were either fascinated by the dream of empire or reconciled to Bryan as the lesser of two evils. Osborne's attempt to organize a third party that would not be dominated by New York City came to nothing, and he was faced with a choice between two theories that were revolting to him. For once, he refused to make a positive decision. He could not conscientiously support either Bryan or McKinley, and there was no other asylum except the Prohibitionist ticket. He liked the state gubernatorial candidates no better and determined not only to keep out of the campaign but to abstain from voting. His letter to the local Democratic boss, Dr. M. P. Conway, then state committeeman, defining his position had two effects. It emphasized his independence. It caused a rift with the party machine that was not to be healed until he himself became the head of it. Though he considered himself a Democrat still, his critics might have quoted what a waggish editorial writer said of a similar declaration by David B. Hill in the campaign of 1896—"Yes, very still!"

Hurt and disgusted as he had been by Roosevelt's desertion of the Independents in 1898, he was honest enough to recognize that Roosevelt had a sincere purpose. He even accepted appointment as delegate from New York to the Conference on

Trusts in Chicago. "I know nothing of trusts," he admitted, "but I am willing to please our erratic and barbaric governor." To Oswald Villard he wrote: "While I think Roosevelt is a pitiable object and will fail in his endeavors to use the Machine for worthy political ends, among them his elevation to the presidency, I think that nothing is to be gained by underrating what good he is achieving." Again, having breakfasted with the governor, he reported: "I do not agree with him by any means, but he is genuine, and I will forgive a good deal to a man who is that."

Here, aside from different political leanings, is the one thing that kept Osborne and Roosevelt from working in harmony. Osborne would make no concessions to the machine for the sake of promoting reform. For him the end never justified the means; but he was mistaken in his faith that an enlightened democracy would accept the stone which the builders refused and make it head stone of the corner. The very stars in their courses fought for Roosevelt; for when the crafty Platt side-tracked him in the vice presidency, destiny intervened and raised him to the supreme office. Osborne in the meantime, stubborn and uncompromising, saw the power he craved elude his grasp and fall into the hands of those who would make at least a slight genuflection toward the priests of the inner temple. Nor was any miracle performed to demonstrate that his was a righteous cause. He might override machine opposition in his own bailiwick, but the influence of the bosses in state and nation was great enough to keep him out of posts in which he might undermine their authority.

Few men have ever been so unerring in their choice of the losing side. Osborne seemed to take without the proverbial grain of salt Dr. Everett's doctrine that the minority is always right, especially if it is a very small minority. When the lines of battle were drawn he was always to be found waving the banner of some doomed legion. Yet, almost uncannily, he foresaw that these defeats were not fruitless, but part of a campaign whose ultimate success was secure. In later years he might rejoice in victories so long delayed that his own part in them was almost forgotten.

CHAPTER IV

ENTER HARUN-AL-RASHID

BEFORE the advent of prohibition you could walk down State Street, Auburn, and enter any one of many swinging doors through which was exhaled an odor of stale beer and sawdust. It is different now. The swinging doors are gone, and the passing crowd is free to gaze upon the relicts of the Noble Experiment quaffing their favorite brews perpendicularly, or otherwise, as the law may decree. In 1904 a man could be sure of privacy—from the knees up.

More than once in that Presidential year, which happened also to be a mayoral year in Auburn, convivial groups which gathered about the bars of these establishments would cast a curious look at the man who had unobtrusively joined them. He was a queer-looking duck, tall, rather well built, yet patently down at the heel. His clothes hung loosely upon him; he stooped; even his jaw sagged as if the heavy beard were a burden. He certainly looked like a bum, yet he did not act like one. For instance, he lacked the thirst that belongs to one of his ilk. He seemed content to lean on the bar gazing vacantly into space or sit hunched over at one of the small tables. Harmless, at any rate. He never caused any trouble. After a little, he would get up and go quietly out.

The others soon forgot him. There were more important things to talk about, especially after another glass had kindled the polemic fire. Roosevelt had been renominated and was going to sweep the country. No doubt about that. And Tom Osborne was fool enough to run for mayor again. Did he think he could check the Republican landslide that was preparing to sweep Teddy and candidates of his political creed into office? Not in good old Cayuga County!

Probably Tom was thinking he could repeat his triumph of two years ago. That had been a surprise. In a city which gave the Republicans an average majority of 1,500 Osborne had been elected mayor with a lead of 1,179 votes over his opponent! Not even the complaint of irregularity lodged by his own party machine had been able to hold him down. Calling for nonpartisanship in municipal government, he coaxed enough Republicans into his column to carry every ward in the city and every election district but one.

For a year he fought a lone battle against a Republican board of aldermen and hostile city officials. Then came another surprise. The following November saw the election of a Democratic city judge and a Democratic recorder, together with seven Osborne aldermen out of a total of ten. For the first time since the days before the Civil War, Auburn was under full Democratic control.

But those had been off years. This was a Presidential year with a Republican candidate whose popularity had grown to tremendous proportions. It was folly for Tom Osborne to think he could buck against that in a town like Auburn.

So thought the groups gathered about the saloon bars. So thought many another citizen who was rather favorably inclined toward the mayor's militant crusade. What ran through the mind of the unobtrusive stranger no one knew or cared. If, however, a mildly curious group could have followed him up South Street to the mayor's residence and, unseen, accompanied him to the little room above where beard and clothes and padding were packed carefully away, they would have been stunned. For Harun-al-Rashid had come home.

It was not the first time that Osborne had resorted to disguise. There had been whispers early in his administration that he was investigating the music halls incognito in order to launch a clean-up campaign against them. These rumors had been quashed as preposterous, and one can only surmise the truth. Ever since his college days the urge for impersonation had been on him. Amateur theatricals failed to satisfy his craving sufficiently. They were too obviously make-believe. He wanted to *be* some one else for a time, and in that character to play the part to the hilt unhampered by the four walls of a stage.

In view of the slanders that were to be spread later, it is worth recording that Osborne exhibited not the slightest trace of transvestism, that strange urge which drives some persons to dress in the costume of the opposite sex. Not once did he put on a female disguise. To him that would have been an unnatural act.

Only a few intimates knew of his eccentricity. His family guarded the secret in mortal terror of disgrace. To them it seemed incredible that so fastidious a person as he could stoop to such antics. Even when he disguised himself as a peddler and showed his wares at his own door at Willow Point, they could not forgive him, though his boys shrieked with delight at the eventual unmasking. In London, Osborne once donned some outlandish costume and called at his hotel room. When his wife answered the summons, she was startled by the uncouth individual who stood bowing before her. Recognition came swiftly. In deep mortification she slammed the door in his face, bolted it, and delivered an ultimatum to the effect that he would never enter that room until he changed into decent Christian garb. Since Osborne's clothes were behind that very door, the situation was deadlocked until a rapprochement could be effected.

After his entrance into politics he was delighted to find justification for his masquerades. It was worth while to learn about conditions at first hand and to sound out public sentiment where he was sure it was undiluted.

When Osborne discovered from his nocturnal ramblings that odds were being asked in wagers on his reëlection, he redoubled his efforts. Night after night he addressed crowded houses on his new charter, based on greater home rule for the city and a separation of legislative and administrative functions. Though now he rarely spoke for less than an hour and sometimes spoke three hours at a stretch, he held his audience through long discussions of budgetary problems. If the truth must be told, the people who flocked to hear him did not care much more about finances and charter provisions than the average group of citizens. They came to see the fireworks. Osborne could be counted on to lash out at his adversaries with a fury that was almost vindictive, and he had a way of barbing his shafts with such irony that his victims squirmed.

In the heat of a campaign he sometimes made statements that, true or not, were highly indiscreet. Early in his first term he accused one of the Republican candidates for office of having filched a small sum from a poor widow. He charged that his opponent, a lawyer, had induced a local physician to remit half a fee in favor of his (the lawyer's) client; that he had then collected the full amount from the widow and pocketed the other half. Though Osborne would assert the amount of this alleged peculation had nothing to do with the matter, it was an unlucky moment when he was prompted to make public accusation. In the first place, the sum involved was only five dollars. In the second place, the rights of the matter were so obscure that the $70,000 libel suit brought against him dragged along for over two years, with two hung juries, heavy public and personal expense, and a bitterness between the two litigants that spread to their respective adherents. Finally, only two days before the case was abandoned because of jury disagreements, one of Osborne's witnesses, a brilliant young doctor with a family of four children, committed suicide. In no way involved, except as the veracity of any witness may be questioned by opposing counsel, he became momentarily unbalanced by the strain. Three days later his father died from the shock.

Five dollars!

The mayor's uncle, John H. Osborne, helped to complicate matters by continuing to issue his privately printed sheet of gossip, *The Index*. This eccentric man had now turned his attention to politics, and his frankness in retailing both fact and rumor kept him in continual hot water. At one time there were libel suits totaling approximately $150,000 pending against him, the plaintiffs being the city recorder, a county supervisor, a state senator, and the chairman of the State Prison Commission.

The mayor's mother, Mrs. Eliza Osborne, contributed her

share to the general atmosphere of belligerency. To begin with, she did not approve of Tom's political confederates by any means. Still loyal to the Grand Old Party, as her husband had been, she cast a suspicious eye on the local Jeffersonians with whom her son was consorting. One evening Osborne planned to hold a Democratic rally at 99 South Street, the old home whose spacious rooms would accommodate a crowd. The faithful, being duly assembled, marched in a body to the rendezvous, but were brought up short at the front porch. There stood Mrs. Osborne, fire in her eye.

"This is a Republican house," she admonished them, "and no Democrats are going to hold any meeting here!"

Considerably abashed, the marchers retreated in disorder to more secure positions.

The spirit of this woman was a joy to every disinterested observer, but it sometimes caused embarrassment to the ambitious son. When the telephone company erected poles in the street adjacent to her residence, she complained that they were ruining her trees. Nothing being done about it, Mrs. Osborne took matters into her own hands and had the poles cut down. The result was another lawsuit.

And to cap everything, the Mayor was charged with stealing water from the city for D. M. Osborne & Co.!

All this added fuel to the flames of an already hot campaign. The Republican machine was exerting every effort to regain lost patronage. The Democratic faction under Dr. M. P. Conway, who had lived to regret he ever supported Osborne for mayor, worked tooth and nail to discredit its own candidate. On his side, Osborne had Charles F. Rattigan, editor of the Democratic newspaper, the *Bulletin,* and successor to Dr. Conway as state committeeman. This internal feud was far more bitter than the Democratic-Republican rivalry. In response to the mayor's denunciation of Dr. Conway, the latter replied with an attack on Rattigan as "a shabby, vulgar, unprincipled hack," the implication being that Osborne was the brains of a vicious cabal.

Election Day came, and with it a Republican landslide. In Auburn, Roosevelt received a majority of nearly 2,000. With one exception, every elective post in the city was filled by a Republican. That exception was the office of mayor. The votes of 107 citizens sufficed to keep Osborne in the City Hall. Though his ambitions were to carry him into larger fields, this scant victory over tremendous odds was really his greatest political triumph.

By a previous amendment to the city charter, Mayor Osborne's second term had been limited upon his own recommendation to one year in order to bring city elections in off years. When in 1905 Osborne was nominated a third time on a Democratic ticket whose nonpartisan claims were attested by the presence of three Democrats, three Republicans, and one Independent, he fell victim to a fault that sometimes took on the proportions of a vice. He was too disputatious, too denunciatory. Though he was justified in many cases, more than once his fervor led him to extremes and even to unfairness.

The trumpet is an instrument that demands some discretion of the player. Economy becomes a cardinal virtue. Blow it once, twice, or even thrice, and an army may rise overnight or the walls of Jericho crumble in ruins. It is not, however, adapted to chamber music or to prolonged solo parts. Osborne's trumpet had first aroused an indifferent public; now by its persistence it began to irritate. The Republican candidate, a staid and highly respected citizen, felt the change and sat tight. During the entire campaign he scarcely opened his mouth, while Osborne charged from one rostrum to another, literally talking himself out of office. When it was over and the ballots were counted, Osborne had lost by 152 votes.

"It has been an excellent lesson for me," he had the grace to confess, "and a good thing for the city."

Unfortunately both these assertions are open to doubt. Though he never did learn the full value of restraint, it is certain he gave Auburn an administration that pointed the way for his successors.

CHAPTER V

THE NONPARTISAN MAYOR

A SURVEY of his achievements as mayor shows one significant thing: the possibility that an ideal may be translated into practical operation. He was first elected to office on a pledge of nonpartisanship in local government. Nonpartisanship had never stood a chance in Auburn before he sponsored it. It has been an egregious failure since his time. In politics as in other fields, reform seems to be contingent upon the force of a single individual acting upon the sentiment of the mass— which may or may not explain the impermanence of so many reform movements.

Osborne's first step was to take with him to the City Hall his own private secretary, a young man known to be a stanch Republican. The idea of a Republican in such a confidential position, privy to all the secret maneuvers of administration, was too much for the line Democrats. That was going too far, even in the interests of nonpartisanship, which most of them had looked upon simply as campaign window dressing. Undaunted by such criticism, Osborne continued to horrify by putting into practice what he had preached on the hustings. As chief of police he appointed from the ranks another young Republican, a man with a great reputation as a gambler. This double violation of accepted policy brought a storm of protest. A gambler as chief of police! But the mayor knew what he was doing. He could not have picked anyone with better knowledge of conditions. Besides, he was a student of character and lived to see his appointment justified in nearly a quarter of a century of efficient service. By conferring a sense of responsibility Osborne turned a potential hell-raiser to the side of law and order.

At this time, the reform groups and in particular the church organizations were not wholly in sympathy with the mayor. He was not rabid enough to suit them. In his campaigns against vice resorts and liquor dives, he refused to go further than the law sanctioned. Not revolution, but creation of public sentiment, was his doctrine. He even doubted the efficacy of much legislation. "There is not and cannot be any such thing as reform by wholesale," he told the State Charities convention at Buffalo. "The individual must catch the spark of sacred fire." This was to be his guiding principle during all the years of prison work. His strong faith in democracy was never laid upon the masses, but on the individual persons who make up the masses.

With the adoption of his new city charter, conferring greater authority in home rule and transferring local elections to off years, Osborne made other Republican appointments, among them that of police commissioner and city engineer. By this time Dr. Conway and his cohorts had moved from bitterness to panic. Disappointed in their expectation of dictating appointments, they were aghast to see one Republican after another given important assignments. When it came to the primaries, however, the mayor and Rattigan showed complete control of the situation.

Osborne's flair for the spectacular was invaluable in holding his advantage. The Bartels' case is an example. One night while making his rounds a patrolman became suspicious of what was going on in a local brewery. Entering, he found distributed through the building innumerable cans of benzine, open. On the top floor he discovered a forty-four-gallon cask, with benzine dripping through a partly opened spigot. Holes had been bored in the floors to permit the fluid to spread below. Walls and beams were saturated. The touch of a match would have turned the ancient structure into an inferno, endangering the whole city.

Attempted arson was the only inference, for the brewery concern was in financial straits, and there was nearly $50,000 insurance on the plant. Nevertheless, Osborne found his efforts to obtain indictments thwarted at every point. Men of wealth were financially interested. The district attorney refused to take any action on the ground that he had no authority to spend public money until *after* a culprit had been apprehended. There the case would have remained had not Osborne at his own expense hired detectives from Chicago to investigate. The upshot was a confession on the part of several conspirators and a prison sentence for Herman Bartels, chief owner of the brewery. It cost the mayor nearly $1,000 to bring the culprits to book. When he applied for reimbursement from the county, the supervisors refused to allow one cent.

There were other startling things of which the public knew little or nothing. Saloonkeepers who broke the closing laws found themselves suddenly and inexplicably in the toils of the law. Too late they would realize that the smuttied, overalled workman who parked his dinner pail in a corner and sipped a glass of beer was not what he seemed to be. Thinking of the incident afterwards, they had their suspicions.

One Sunday a certain barkeep was doing a thriving though illicit business. His place was crowded, for thirst grew apace under the Sabbath taboos. In such an establishment there is always room for one more. When a shabby stranger knocked at the door, his very appearance was a sufficient credential, and he was admitted. His addition to the assembly, however, meant no great profit for the house. One small beer satisfied him. It was a few minutes after this that the officers at the police station, just turning out for inspection, were amazed to see a disheveled-looking individual running toward them waving his arms. They were still more amazed when he began shouting orders about raiding some saloon. After the first shock of surprise the chief recognized His Honor the Mayor. The raid was executed and the proprietor apprehended. It may be added, though with no intent to imply a consequence, that in a few years this same proprietor became a detective in the police force of a near-by city.

Until the autumn of 1900 the City of Auburn had no fire engine. Protection against fire loss was low, and insurance rates were correspondingly high. At that time D. M. Osborne & Co. presented the city with its new Silsby steamer, a sturdy engine that was to give years of service. Nevertheless, during Osborne's term as mayor there were two serious fires. The second, which nearly destroyed the high-school building, turned the city's attention to its water supply, pumped from Owasco Lake. Because low pressure during the night had severely handicapped the firemen in fighting the flames, it was first thought the pumping system was breaking down.

Though in favor of mechanical improvements, Osborne suspected something else. Finding the Water Department hostile to his proposed investigation, he called once more upon Harun-al-Rashid. Dressed as a bum, he came loafing up the pier to the pumping station one night and begged the engineer for a place to sleep. But he did not sleep; the engineer slept, and Osborne watched the gauges dropping lower and lower. Next day the city was rocked by the mayor's sensational charge that the engineer at the pumping station was accustomed to sleeping most of the night, a dereliction that had cost the city thousands of dollars in property damage. The general public did not know where the mayor got his information, least of all the culprit.

Osborne's make-up on these night rambles usually defied detection. He once called in disguise upon his own private secretary, engaged him in conversation on the plea of needing financial help, and was finally obliged to declare himself. "Bill," he said, "you never knew me. I just wanted to see how safe I am." With that he departed. It was the only time his secretary ever saw him in disguise, at least to know him. Few others guessed that their own mayor was walking the streets of Bagdad, impersonating the caliph incognito with much the thrill small boys derive from playing cops and robbers.

If the citizens missed these little dramas, they beheld enough public spectacles to keep them interested. Osborne fought a gas merger to the very doors of the state capitol. He was in continual controversy with the trolley company and the light and power company over their franchises. He introduced a new financial system and inaugurated a program of capital improvements without materially increasing the taxes. Both the country and the metropolitan press took him up, printing his messages and inditing editorials on "the Auburn system." He found time to establish a newspaper of his own, the *Citizen,* dedicated to a policy of absolute nonpartisanship in treatment of local affairs and to independence in state and national politics. If this ideal was not wholly attainable, human nature being what it is, at least it established a principle that has served as a guide for nearly thirty years.

Osborne's evident sincerity in promoting nonpartisanship in local government, together with his success in surviving the practical operation of his system, brought him into great demand as a speaker throughout the East. Municipal reform was in the air. Osborne took place with Mayor Weaver of Philadelphia as a champion of good business in government and an enemy of graft and incompetence in public officials. Several large cities adopted the Auburn plan as a model. When Boston was engaged in drafting a new charter, Osborne was persuaded to coöperate with the special charter commission in laying the foundation of the new government.

In spite of the fact that he refused to replace a Republican machine with a Democratic machine, at his departure Osborne left the Democratic Party in Auburn stronger than it had ever been. After one Republican administration, the city reverted to Democratic rule with one of his lieutenants as mayor. Never after, however, did the nonpartisan idea thrive. With his passing, the system passed; for it had been based on the personality of a single individual.

There was, it is true, a partial revival. In January, 1928, his son Charles took office as mayor. Elected on a platform which included a plank providing for a nonpartisan ballot in municipal elections, the younger Osborne set an example by retaining several appointees of the preceding Republican administration. During the course of his term, a referendum on the issue brought public sanction, and the nonpartisan system was formally established. So completely, however, are both parties dominated by the partisan idea, that abolition of party labels has made little difference. "Regular" candidates endorsed by the Republican and Democratic organizations respectively are invariably successful in the primaries, and the theory of party responsibility is apparently as strong as ever.

CHAPTER VI

DOGS AND CURS

THE summer of 1906 found Thomas Mott Osborne once more on the warpath. His arch-enemy, William Randolph Hearst, had blossomed from a callow youth, strafed by the academic disciplinarians of Harvard, into a great social force. That this force was inherently evil, Osborne never doubted. He watched with growing alarm the extension of that type of journalism which had transformed the San Francisco *Examiner* from a moribund newspaper into a lusty, loud-mouthed shouter of cheap slogans. The terrifying thing was the success which was the reward of these methods. Prodigal as ever, conscienceless as ever to Osborne's way of thinking, Hearst went triumphantly from one field to another. New Yorkers were reading the diatribes and exhortations of the *Evening Journal*. In the Loop, Chicagoans lapped up the scandals, business, political, and domestic, served under mammoth headlines in the *American*. In an increasing number of population centers the masses were finding a champion for their discontent and a purveyor of salacious gossip.

That one man could so impress his opinions upon millions of people throughout the country seemed monstrous to Osborne. And now Hearst had ambitions to be governor of New York State—yes, and ambitions to be President of the United States. Success in the gubernatorial election would make him the logical nominee for Democracy, from a strategical standpoint at least. More than once the governorship of New York had proved to be a stepping-stone to the portals of the White House. With his presses pouring out more campaign material than any national committee ever dreamed of, the publisher might confidently make a strong bid for election.

From the first, Osborne took the threat of a Hearst victory at the polls in all seriousness. In the Democratic national convention of 1904 the publisher had received 263 votes for the Presidential nomination. The following year the united opposition of Tammany had only barely defeated him in the New York City mayoralty contest, the vote being so close as to warrant a recount. Confronted with the possibility of an even more aggressive campaign, and fearing pre-convention tactics not endorsed by the Marquis of Queensberry rules, Osborne decided to appeal to the more liberal leaders of up-state Democracy. His call for a meeting at Albany for early September was answered by many of the most distinguished Democratic leaders in the state.

Though this Albany Conference disavowed endorsement of any particular candidate and mingled the popular phrases "muckraker" and "octopodicide," or "trust buster," with the usual political palaver, the intent of the conference was never in doubt. It was betrayed in the call Osborne had sent out, explaining that the purpose of the conference was to prevent the completion of a deal to sell the Democratic name and organization. It was still more obvious in the wording of an appeal issued a fortnight later by a committee of the conference urging Democratic voters to repudiate the bosses' every effort "to obtain control of the party organization by purchase, by intimidation, or by hired agents." In the conference, mention of Hearst by name was carefully avoided. Yet everyone knew that, however earnest was the desire to build an intelligent Democratic leadership, the immediate purpose was to prevent Hearst from grabbing the nomination.

It fell upon Osborne to organize the anti-Hearst forces for the big battle in Buffalo. About two weeks before the convention, the Independence League Party, a Hearst-controlled organization, nominated its leader for governor. This I.L.P. nomination was construed by its opponents as in fact an Inside Left Pocket nomination, and W. R. Hearst was subjected to the criticism that he was trying to cow the Democrats into naming him for the head of the ticket. There were much more serious accusations. It was asserted by Osborne and his Albany

colleagues that Hearst used violence and bribery in the cau-
cuses; that when he could not buy he would intimidate. The
long arm of the Yellow Press was seen at work everywhere.

Whatever the justice of these charges, there was a terrific
explosion when the delegates assembled in Buffalo the last
week in September. Contested delegations—and there was no
lack of them—had to submit to the decision of a committee
headed by Senator Thomas F. Grady, Tammany leader. With
a regularity that is curious, to say the least, the Hearst and
Tammany delegates were certified by the Committee on Contested Seats; the majority of the dissenters were kicked out.
"It is the dirtiest day's work I ever did in my life," Grady
is reported to have confessed when it was over. Whether the
remark attributed to him is indicative of remorse or pride one
can only surmise; but on the floor of the convention he had
bellowed at the indignant minority: "I am proud of the political tag and collar I wear!"

It was clear now what was happening. Tammany, which
held the balance of power, had completed "an iniquitous and
treasonable bargain" with Hearst. In all his turbulent career
it is doubtful that Osborne ever attained such heights of righteous wrath as at this moment of realization. In placing in
nomination the name of John A. Dix, a man who "does not
straddle two platforms in order to grab a nomination for governor," he flayed the Tammany legion with a ferocity that
turned the convention into bedlam.

"You dogs!" he shouted. "You who lick the hand and fawn
at the feet of the man who has lashed you, you think you are
to have a victory. You will be struck down by the very hand
you now lick!"

Neither Hearst nor Tammany ever forgave him for that.
The point was too shrewdly taken. Only a short time before,
Hearst had declared he had "nothing in common with the
Tammany leader, Mr. Murphy." In a speech on October 29,
1905, Hearst himself had called the Tammany leader "as evil
a specimen of a criminal boss as we have had since the days of
Tweed. Murphy grows rich and insolent on corrupt con-
tracts." On November 10 of that year Hearst's *Evening*

Journal had printed a cartoon depicting a wolfish, cowering Murphy in prison garb, with the caption: "Look out, Murphy! It's a short lockstep from Delmonico's to Sing Sing." The accompanying copy read in part:

> Every honest voter in New York WANTS TO SEE YOU IN THIS COSTUME. You have committed crimes against the people that will send you for many years to State prison, if the crimes can be proved against you. . . . YOU KNOW THAT YOU ARE GUILTY. The PEOPLE know it. . . . Look out! If you ever sit in the prisoner's dock, you will not come out, except in striped clothing.

In the months that followed, a striped Murphy glowered regularly from the pages of the Hearst papers.

Now that Murphy and Hearst had swallowed each other's insults and joined hands, it seemed to Osborne that two evil genii had suddenly coalesced into one gigantic afreet. Nor, observing them, could he make that choice with which Bourke Cockran illuminated the cynicism of the period: "As between rottenness and riot, give me riot!"

With the departure of the delegates from Buffalo, exultant over their complete Hearst slate, the influence of the Albany Conference became militant: not merely against Hearst, but for the Republican candidate, Charles E. Hughes. It was aided by a number of Democratic bolters who could not stomach the Hearst-Murphy alliance, among them Senator Patrick H. McCarren, leader of the Kings County Democracy, who got himself investigated for his pains. On the other side there were, chiefly, the fist of Tammany and the Yellow Press. And Bryan. A lukewarm Bryan who found no enjoyment in contemplation of the shadow cast across his path by the bulky publisher. At first opposed to Hearst for fear his own Presidential chances would be impaired, he finally gave notice that, though he could not come to New York on a speaking tour, he would be glad to have his friends support Mr. Hearst.

It needed more than a Bryan to put Hearst over. Osborne and his liberal friends refused to accept Hearst as a Democrat at all. Up and down the state they preached that it was loyalty to Democracy, not treason, to vote this interloper down. When the ballots were counted, the results of this campaigning were apparent. Hearst brought a mere 77,000 majority from New York City to meet upstate opposition. It did not suffice. While every elective position in the state except that of governor was filled by a Democrat, Hughes turned back the head of the ticket with a plurality of 57,000. In a Democratic year, the Democrats had lost the greatest prize of all.

Perhaps old Richard Croker, sojourning in Ireland, had the right of it. Asked to what he attributed Hearst's defeat and the repudiation of Murphy, his successor as chief of the Wigwam, he ejaculated:

"God Almighty!"

Even the Almighty, however, makes use of human instruments to achieve his purposes. Osborne, filled with divine wrath, had for once whipped the Tiger to its lair. Hearst's Presidential ambitions went glimmering. It looked, for a moment, as if there were justice in the world, even in politics; and Osborne, invited by friends eager for his personal advancement to unite with the Republican Party, refused with no regrets. He had work to do. There was promise that in the party of his choice a new spirit was at work that would evoke great leaders dedicated to the true principles of Democracy. And who was better fitted to answer this call than Thomas Mott Osborne?

CHAPTER VII

PUBLIC SERVICE COMMISSIONER

WHILE Charles Evans Hughes could not have been insensible to Osborne's share in his victory at the polls, he was not a man to let political debts determine his appointments. Nor was Osborne one to accept appointment on the basis of service rendered. When the new governor selected Osborne for upstate member on the new Public Service Commission, he was moved by a desire to obtain an independent Democrat of high character and outstanding ability for this bipartisan body. When Osborne refused the post three distinct times, he was sincere in his belief that he was not wholly fitted for the assignment. Even before he had been mentioned as a possible candidate, he had written Governor Hughes recommending for his consideration the name of a high-grade engineer. The state of his health, impaired by the strain of the last months, dictated a complete rest. Though the office carried an annual salary of $15,000, quite a munificent stipend when it is remembered the governor himself received but $10,000, Osborne was not tempted. He never sought office for financial gain. Even when his personal fortune was fast dwindling, he remained sublimely oblivious of opportunities for adding to his income through public service.

In late June he started for Europe on a well-earned vacation, with a final injunction to the Governor to dismiss his name from consideration. The appointment was to take effect on July 1. Osborne would not return until the middle of September. Nevertheless, on arrival in London he received word that Governor Hughes had insisted on naming him Public Service Commissioner. Characteristically, he was not ill pleased and returned from his trip eager to undertake his new duties.

The bill creating a Public Service Commission had been forced through the Legislature by Governor Hughes against stiff opposition. There were two districts, each with five commissioners. The first district comprised Greater New York; the second, all the rest of the state. Even after the Commission had proved its value in controlling the financial set-ups of public utilities and supervising their operations in respect to service rendered, antagonism was loud-spoken. The Democrats were particularly voluble. In 1908 the Democratic state platform declared: "In the two Public Service Commissions which have been brought into existence at his [Governor Hughes'] suggestion and dictation, he has created office-holders who have woefully failed to better the condition of affairs confided to their charge." The Democratic candidate for governor voiced his opposition with equal force: "I favor to the fullest extent practicable doing away with what is familiarly known as 'government by commission.'"

Osborne did not follow his party. He believed in the Public Service Commission and said so openly. More than that, he believed in Governor Hughes. Between these two men there arose a feeling of mutual confidence and respect that was lacking in most of Osborne's political contacts. To Osborne must go a large share of the credit for shaping favorable public opinion. In his public addresses and magazine articles, notably his able analysis for the *Atlantic Monthly,* he presented convincing evidence of the actual and potential value of the Public Service Commission Law of New York State.

In spite of his ardor in championing the system, Osborne was not blinded to the danger of paternalism toward which it tended to gravitate. When the Public Service Commission of the Second District denied the application of the Buffalo, Rochester & Eastern Railroad Company for a certificate of convenience and necessity to build a railroad from Buffalo to Troy, he wrote a dissenting opinion. The New York Central, having preëmpted the one perfect railway route from the Hudson valley to Buffalo, convinced the majority of the Commission that competition through the establishment of a road on the one practicable alternative route was undesirable.

Osborne disagreed. In a minority report that was of extreme importance in establishing the general principles underlying the operation of public service commissions, he attacked the doctrine of extending protection to public utility monopolies beyond guarding them from blackmail and unfair competition, and laid down the rule that the Commission was not called upon to decide upon the wisdom of the investment to be made. On the one hand, service to the public should be the prime consideration; and on the other, prevention of fraud, dishonesty, and overcapitalization. It was, however, no function of the Commission to prevent people from making bad investments, as that was bound to lead to all forms of extravagant paternalism.

Favorable reaction to this report was immediate. The people of the fourteen counties through which the proposed railroad was to run were naturally behind him, and others, less biased, recognized the soundness of his premises. At last Osborne had found a field of public service for which he was eminently fitted. His business training, his capacity for going directly to the fundamentals of a problem, and his almost fanatical sense of justice presented a combination not too common among political appointees. Moreover, he liked the work, for he did not confine himself strictly to the clerical and administrative duties of the post. When a complaint was filed against the reduction of crews on certain freight trains of the Pennsylvania Division of the New York Central Railroad, Commissioner Osborne was selected to make the investigation.

It was too good an opportunity to miss. Dressed as a workman he rode the freights to gather his information at first hand. He was in his element. Riding in the cab with the engineer, clambering over the cars, sweating under the grease that smutted his face and overalls, he momentarily forgot the commissioner in this new and engaging identity he had assumed. One can imagine his satisfaction when his exhaustive report, describing the regulations and practices on this division as "inadequate and unsafe," was adopted by the majority of the Commission.

There were other adventures during this period. Osborne

was interested in the problems presented by thugs and bums who hung about the railroad yards and hopped freights for anonymous destinations. Dressed as a tramp, he mingled with this floating population, learning its vernacular, sleeping in freight cars, playing the rôle of caliph in disguise with the same old zest. With him on these excursions he took a young man whom he had found in a reform school and established as a sort of handy man in his ménage. Louis Schaedeline claimed Indian descent through his mother, and his physique bore out his contention. Solidly yet gracefully built, with dark skin and strong aquiline features, he was a perfect physical specimen. He had, too, a diversity of talents that approached genius. He dabbled in painting and rigged up a studio in the attic of his patron's home. He posed for the figures of the Indian murals in the Osborne Hotel grill room—though they libel his anatomy. He sank a lot of his own money and more of Osborne's in an airplane which he invented and built in the back yard of 115 South Street. This Darius Green fashioned his machine along the lines of a bird, but unfortunately the inanimate thing failed to find the air its natural medium and folded up its wings against a tree the first time he tried to coax it aloft.

A vagabond by nature, Schaedeline appealed to the roving instinct in Osborne. His special delight was to tear around on a motorcycle hell-bent for election, a sport for which the Public Service Commissioner soon developed an equal passion. Together they disturbed the peace of many a quiet village, for though Osborne demanded a cautious pace when another was driving, once he was in command he drove like a wild Indian. There were canoe trips and automobile tours, but the supreme sport was riding freights. Here Schaedeline was in his element. Always equal to any emergency, he was an ideal vizier for Harun-al-Rashid—though worth more as a protector in time of trouble than as a counselor against getting into trouble.

Ostensibly the purpose of the jaunts in hobo-land was to gather data for the Public Service Commission. It is likely, however, that in spite of the very real value of his investigations, Osborne would have found some other justification for them had this one been lacking. Long ago Ben Franklin wrote: "So convenient a thing is it to be a *reasonable creature,* since it enables one to find or make a reason for every thing one has a mind to do." Osborne could no more resist the excitements of masquerading than a toper can resist his stimulant. It was his way, and his only way, of snatching a few hours of illusion from the compulsions of reality.

I am convinced, too, by a notation he made, that at this time he contemplated writing a book on tramp life. He was always fascinated by the antipodes of society, and in the knights of the road he found a subject of absorbing interest. Pursuit of material, however, led occasionally to embarrassing situations.

The circus was in Auburn. With it had come the hangers-on, the pickpockets, thieves, and prostitutes who in those days found rich pickings along the carnival routes. Patrolmen had received orders to inspect carefully all doors and windows along their beat. When headquarters received word that a store near the railroad yards had been entered, the night captain assigned a sergeant and a young patrolman to investigate. Only a few bananas, they found, had been taken. The trail led down to the tracks. Someone had seen two suspicious-looking persons heading for the line of open coal cars that stood on the siding. Car after car was examined with the aid of a flashlight.

It was Patrolman Mike Kelley who finally found them. They were hiding in a dark corner of one of the empties, having scooped a refuge out of a pile of loose coal. Mike put his gun on them and ordered them out. Handcuffs clicked, and the quartet headed back toward headquarters. Under a light the officers had a good look at their captives. Tramps, obviously. One was a big fellow, coat tucked into his overalls, a slouch hat pulled low over his eyes. Incongruously, he wore kid gloves.

"Say, officer," he said, "we don't want to spend Sunday in that lock-up of yours. Let us go. We haven't done anything."

No reply. A moment later he tried again.

"I've got a letter in my pocket from Chief Bell saying I'm all right. You can't take us to headquarters."

"Oh, can't we!" said Mike, knowing his regulations. "We've picked you up, and we got to report. Anyhow, there ain't time to read any letters." And he hustled the pair along.

After a short distance, the big fellow stopped and grinned. He turned to the sergeant.

"Hello, Parker!" The voice was changed somehow. "You didn't know me, did you? Nor you either, Mike." With that he pulled off his hat and wig.

"Tom Osborne!" ejaculated Mike. Then his jaw set. "And who might you be?" he asked, snatching off the other tramp's cap. "Hm! Louis Schaedeline! A fine pair to be hanging round the railroad yards! It's you for headquarters, the two of ye. I'd book you if 'twas the Pope himself."

Only the intervention of Sergeant Parker saved them from this fate; but the story leaked out in various garbled versions. Whether they actually intended to ride the cars that night, or whether, under Louis Schaedeline's impish urging, they had staged a make-believe burglary to see what would happen, has never been established. It might easily have been either. Whatever the nature of the escapade, it was one of the more bizarre adventures of Osborne's railroad investigations. Years later Chief of Police Bell revealed that he had known all about the hobo jaunts and had issued letters to the Public Service Commissioner addressed to police chiefs and railroad detectives of New York State explaining the situation and asking for their coöperation in the work. In this instance, the need for such protective measures was only too well established.

"It was the first time I ever had a gun pulled on me," Osborne told Mike later. "It wasn't pleasant."

Still he held no grudge. When the hot-blooded Irishman lost an eye in a fracas with a real culprit and was retired from the police force, the ex-mayor paid him tribute as an officer whose sense of duty had made him one of the valuable men in the department.

About this same time occurred what came to be referred to as "the Syracuse incident." An Auburn man was standing one day near the railroad station at Syracuse. By chance his attention was drawn to a curious figure in a duster. In spite of the uncouth rig, there was something familiar about the stranger's carriage and facial features. Suddenly the resemblance became clear.

"Why!" ejaculated the Auburnian impulsively. "There goes Tom Osborne! I'll bet anything that's Tom Osborne!"

By some roundabout means word came to police headquarters that a stranger in disguise was hanging about the station. Officers assigned to investigate overtook the man, ascertained his identity, and let him go. Thomas Mott Osborne caught the train to Auburn.

That is the whole story of "the Syracuse incident" as vouched for by the officers who investigated; but it gave plausibility to the innuendoes of Hearst and others.

Even those who were aware of Osborne's vagary did not guess how often he resorted to masquerade as an escape from dull routine. Only recently a condensed diary of the years 1907 to 1909 has come to light. In it are brief jottings of his activities during his public service commissionership. Glancing through it, one notices time and again the Greek symbol ψ. Just what the classical reference may be is debatable, unless the Psi stands for pseudomorphos (disguising one's person); but the immediate meaning is clear enough, as the following entries for 1908 indicate:

Fri. Jan. 17. Ψ. To New York. 7-10. Bowery.
Sat. Jan. 18. Still Ψ.
Wed. Feb. 5. New York. To Albany. Hearings. Dinner. Ψ.
   Music halls, etc.
Tues. Feb. 25. B. R. & E. hearing. Ψ with Louis. Pete. The Kid.
Wed. July 22. Albany. Ψ hobo. N.G. at begging.

There are many other notations revealing that Osborne had more than a dozen characters in his repertory. C. P. Marsh, Jr., the Reverend Dr. Hurd, and MacDonald were definite identities. Probably no less definite in his own mind were the rôles he called Dude, Doctor, Old Gent, Mexican, Italian, and Colored Gent. To hear a Männerchor Concert in New York he went as a German. He attended an address by his chief, Governor Hughes, in the costume of a tramp. Often the jaunts climaxed a hard day of Commission hearings, work on magazine articles, dinner and the opera. During 1909 he was still at it, apparently never tiring of the process of making-up or of the long hikes:

Tues. May 11. Albany. Louis back from New York. Ψ Nig to Jungles.

Fri. July 30. Albany. Ψ. Buy brakeman's cap. Alone. Working on opinion. Ψ to Schenectady. Hobo to Utica. Fresh conductor. To Syracuse. Rest of night anyway.

The keynote of this diary, for all its telegraphic style, is ingenuous delight in his escapades. There seemed to be no particular effort to keep them a dark secret; sometimes he even forgot himself and wrote "Dress up" in long hand. Yet however innocuous these episodes might be, they were too unconventional to pass the local censors of conduct. Few seemed to apprehend the romantic impulse that prompted these expeditions into forbidden worlds. Even the most charitable found in them something abnormal. They *were* abnormal in the sense that everything that does not square with average behavior is abnormal. Osborne was not average, chiefly because he did not allow an accepted code to come between impulse and action. Where others would repress a maverick urge for fear of criticism, he would go exuberantly ahead, supported by his own sense of rightness.

It was inevitable that sometimes his disguises should be penetrated. He fully realized that, yet appeared to fear unmasking only because it might make future incognitos less effective and circumscribe the sphere of his operations. He loved the mystery of it as much as anything. Could he have foreseen how the story of the freight-yard episode was to be whispered among his friends, picked up by his foes, and with sinister construction made part of a malicious campaign against him at a critical moment in his career, he would have been shocked and saddened. I doubt that he would have been deterred.

When Osborne accepted the post of public service commis-

sioner under Governor Hughes, there had been a good deal of
sly winking and smiling among his foes in the Democratic
Party. "What did we tell you!" they exulted. "The only
difference between us and this man is that he's a high-brow.
But he's after the same things: money and power. Only we
never stooped to electing a Republican for the sake of getting
a job. Huh! Fifteen thousand a year for a betrayal." And
they chalked this up for future reference against him.

This fine theory suffered something of a blow, therefore,
when in January, 1910, more than a year before the expiration of his term, Osborne voluntarily resigned to accept a post
whose only compensation was hard work and criticism. As
Public Service Commissioner he never lost sight of his chief
goal—the rejuvenation of the Democratic Party as the party of
progress and liberalism. He had learned wisdom from defeat.
To be effective an appeal must be directed to the people at
large, not to a small group of intellectuals or political malcontents. It was this thought that had dictated his refusal to attend
an anti-Bryan conference in New York City early in 1908. He
said in his reply to the invitation:

> I should like to see some effective steps taken to have a broad
> and representative conference of New York State Democrats, not to
> gather in secret with the resultant liability to public misunderstand-
> ing of its motives, but to confer frankly and openly upon Demo-
> cratic principles; its action to help infuse new life and enthusiasm
> into a party which sadly needs it, after suffering uninterrupted
> defeat in this state for the past sixteen years.

The idea of holding a state conference persisted, and in the
spring of 1909 he took active steps to bring it about. At the
same time, unknown to him, a similar movement had been
started in New York City with such sponsors as Alton B.
Parker, Judge Morgan J. O'Brien, and S. Stanwood Menken.
The upshot was that Osborne maneuvered a consolidation
which resulted in a call being issued for a September meeting
in Saratoga. The prominence of the delegates as well as the
wide field they represented immediately stamped this conference as the most important Democratic gathering in years. As
chairman of the Executive Committee, Osborne opened the

meeting with an appeal to all varieties of Democrats to unite in a common cause: victory for the party through a purging of undesirable leaders. "In other relations of life one does not look to gather grapes from thorns or figs from thistles. Why," he asked, "should we ever believe we can do so in politics?"

Before adjournment, the delegates founded the Democratic League of New York State. For the first time a powerful instrument for combating boss control and amalgamating all the liberal elements in the state had been forged. To its influence may be traced the increase in Democratic victories in the 1909 elections and the reorganization of the Democratic State Committee with one of the League's directors, John A. Dix, as chairman. Greater prestige was added when Thomas Mott Osborne cheerfully relinquished a $15,000 job, easily the juiciest plum at the disposal of the Governor, to take over the unsalaried office of permanent chairman of the Democratic League. Between the two duties Osborne never hesitated. In fact, it was revealed that two years prior to this he had asked Governor Hughes to release him but had reconsidered for fear of damaging the Public Service Commission in the eyes of the public at a crisis in its early development.

Osborne's enemies were rather glum at this unexpected refutation of their attacks upon him, but their astonishment was no less than that of his friends. In the pæans of praise which editors of both political faiths lifted to the heavens the pervading note was surprise. It was outside their experience that any man in politics who had got his fingers on a choice morsel should relinquish his grasp of his own accord. Though they could not fully understand, and half doubted that much good could ever come of it, they hailed his action as at least a hope for better things. Typical of the comment is this excerpt from the New York *Sun,* a newspaper that more than once in the preceding months had cast ridicule and censure upon the Public Service Commissioner:

The Hon. Thomas Mott Osborne may not succeed in saving the Democratic Party, but in resigning a $15,000 state job we think he has placed his glory beyond the ravages of time.

CHAPTER VIII

BOOMED FOR GOVERNOR

THERE is never more than a vague demarcation between altruism and self-interest; the important thing is the quality of the self-interest. Osborne's political ideal was the preservation of American liberties through a regenerated Democratic Party, but it takes more than an abstraction to evoke such an ardor as his. As in all his reform crusades, he felt a personal responsibility, as if he had received his commission from God himself. His heart was set on being leader in the battle against intrenched privilege. He saw himself as the people's champion, the Moses who would show the way to the promised land.

Though there can be no doubt of his sincerity, it would be attributing to him a low order of intelligence to assume he did not realize how conspicuous his labors and sacrifices made him. He had not chosen the common path to prominence. Instead of serving an apprenticeship under petty political leaders, followed by gradual rise to influence through coöperation with the "regular" organization, he had immediately defied the bosses and fixed attention upon himself by a startling pugnacity. In March, 1907, reviewing Osborne's record as mayor and his fight against Hearst and Tammany, which resulted in the election of Hughes in a Democratic year, the *Outlook* had recommended him as "an honor Democrat," deserving promotion in the service of state and nation. His increasing facility as a speaker and writer on political subjects enhanced his reputation, until it needed only a sacrificial gesture, like his resignation of a $15,000 job, to make him "available" in a political as well as in an idealistic sense.

The first authoritative word spoken in his behalf as a gubernatorial possibility came from the New York *World*. In an editorial on July 1, 1910, entitled, "Thomas Mott Osborne for Governor," the *World* unofficially placed him in nomination:

Where will the Democrats of New York find a better candidate for governor than Thomas Mott Osborne of Auburn?

Where will they find a candidate who is a more faithful representative of independent Democratic thought and independent Democratic courage? Where will they find a candidate who would devote himself more completely to the work of giving New York a clean, vigorous, intelligent administration of public affairs? . . .

What the voters of New York will be looking for next fall is . . . a man who will bring to his task a trained mind like that of Charles E. Hughes and a rugged independence that is subservient to no boss, to no machine and to no corrupt corporation. That is the kind of candidate the Democrats must nominate, and that is the kind of man Mr. Osborne has proved himself to be. . . . He is the type of man that is worthy to succeed Mr. Hughes. . . .

THE WORLD presents his name and suggests his nomination without prejudice.

Almost with one accord the Democratic press of the state followed the *World's* lead, endorsing Osborne for governor. Newspapers in near-by states, and as far west as Kentucky, became interested; while in the national field both *Harper's Weekly* and *Life* went on record in his favor. Taking advantage of this enthusiasm, the Democratic General Committee of Cayuga County passed the usual resolutions, pledging themselves to his candidacy and urging the support of Democrats in all other districts.

Elated as Osborne was by the agitation for his candidacy, he was by no means blinded to the difficulties that lay in his path. He well knew that Murphy would have Tammany in solid array against him. He knew that in Auburn there were those who would stab him in the back if they had the chance. His chairmanship of the Democratic League was somewhat embarrassing, as it would allow his enemies to allege that he was using the organization to advance his own political fortunes. On the other hand, it would be a distinct victory for the Democratic League and the principles it stood for if one of its own officers could win the nomination. Besides, was not this the very opportunity for which he had been waiting: the chance to show that it is possible to "arrive" in politics by sheer force of character without kotowing to despots of the inner ring? Win or lose, it was worth while; and in an open letter Osborne accepted the call.

He was not far wrong in supposing he would find stiff opposition. In Auburn his old opponent, Dr. M. P. Conway, got busy in ways best known to politicians. In a letter sent to a number of the upstate committeemen, he shrewdly stressed Osborne's record as a bolter and threw in several guarded attacks upon his character. Indeed, the letter is so plausibly written that at least a portion deserves to be quoted here. Urging the importance of nominating a man for governor who could unite the whole party, Dr. Conway undertook a recital of Osborne's political career. In 1900 Osborne had practically read himself out of party, opposing both the Presidential and the gubernatorial candidate on the Democratic ticket. A few years before that he had run as a "rump" candidate for lieutenant governor against the regular Democratic nominee. Argues the good Doctor:

That a man should change his political views should not be urged against him, but when such change is coincident with a favorable opportunity to obtain a nomination on a ticket which seems to be reasonably sure of winning, one may be justified in asking whether the change is not the result of the opportunity.

When Mr. Osborne began, prominently, to reform the Democratic Party, the comment by Democrats in his own city was as follows: "Tom is out for the nomination." Whether events have justified this criticism it is for others to say, but I believe it is not unfair to suggest that the claim for entire disinterestedness in this movement would have a better justification if the principal mover in it did not appear as claimant for the principal reward. There are some Democrats who opposed Bryan; some who supported Hughes; some who thought Hearst was "very bad" and said so; and some who called Tammany "dogs" and "curs" in public speeches; but I can call to mind no man except Mr. Osborne who has done all of these things openly, and afterward presents himself as a candidate for governor upon the Democratic ticket. It is a good thing for a man to be better than his party, but if he is so much better than his party that he has never been able to support any of them for office, it may be fairly doubted whether he will command an efficient support when he, himself, becomes a candidate.

Although the general public was unaware of Osborne's chief eccentricity, reports of his masquerades were in circulation among his best friends and his worst enemies. The opportunity to make political capital out of them was too good for Dr. Conway to miss, and he took good care, under a guise of righteousness, that the state committeemen would not overlook this phase. To the letter quoted above he added:

Mr. Hearst, in a characteristic interview lately, animadverted upon Mr. Osborne's false whiskers. I do not believe in that kind of politics and Mr. Osborne will undoubtedly, if he sees fit, offer some explanation of the alleged Syracuse incident.

To Hearst the reports of Osborne's nocturnal ramblings were a godsend. Now at last he had a chance to strike back at the man who had robbed him of the governorship of New York State, and he did not hesitate to employ the weapon placed in his hands. Yet later he was to miss the most sensational story of all. Through the loyalty of Auburn reporters the great opportunity Hearst was looking for passed him by.

Dr. Conway was not content with circularizing the committeemen. He wrote Charles F. Murphy, Tammany boss, enclosing the letter and embroidering his case against Osborne. "I am sure," he told his chief, "that Mr. Osborne will never fool you because you already know him full well." Perhaps he was remembering how Murphy's thick red neck had grown thicker and redder as Osborne had lashed the Tammany boss in that hectic convention in Buffalo. Certainly Conway could have chosen no surer way of arousing Murphy's desire for revenge for that attack and the resultant loss of the campaign. The Doctor dared go further with Murphy than with the committeemen, whose credulity might have certain limits. To his indictment he added the charge that Osborne had stolen an Assembly convention in direct disobedience to a court order:

Surely no man who would dare do such a thing is a safe public man. Most of the citizens of Auburn, at least those outside "our walls," obey the law; there are some, however, who have not done so, and among this number is "Tom" Osborne.

In view of Tammany methods of packing a convention, it is perfectly understandable why Dr. Conway omitted this accusation in his letter to the committeemen. His attitude is best illuminated by the closing words of his letter to Murphy:

And then you know, I am the up-state fellow who always believed in the idea that Tammany should sit in the saddle.

I pray you, remember the porter!

Osborne has left one cryptic comment on the Rochester convention of 1910. In the brief outline for his contemplated autobiography he entered the following: "My great mistake in politics. Failure."

Perhaps it is possible to interpret this in connection with the collapse of his boom for governor. If he had been willing to make peace with Tammany, to show even a guarded willingness to play ball according to the rules of the political game, there would have been a good chance for his nomination. He had a big following upstate; sufficient in fact, as events proved, to prevent the selection of a hand-picked Tammany candidate. The press of the metropolis was behind him. It was the day of reform, in semblance at least, and the Republicans too were cleaning house after the régime of Platt and Odell.

But Osborne would not compromise or retract. Tammany men were still "dogs and curs." An alliance would be treason to the cause of good government. It would be a subversion of the principles of the Democratic League. The whole of his later career gives the lie to any interpretation based on regret that he did not make concessions to the Tammany delegates. Even if he could have been sure of being elected governor, with power to put into effect at least some of the reforms he advocated, he would have made no commitments to the opposition. Twice Murphy approached Osborne to see if he would run as lieutenant governor with a Tammany man heading the ticket, and twice Osborne declined. It was all or none with him, and "my great mistake" is the last thing he would call his defeat.

The logical explanation is that when it was all over Osborne realized he should never have permitted his name to be used in that campaign. Others besides Conway were quick to point out that the principal mover in the reform movement was appearing as "claimant for the principal reward." He found out too late that it was the vulnerable spot in his armor. As a result, some of the enthusiasm at his sacrifice of the commissionership began to wane. Doubt entered. Had he given up one post in the hope of snatching a better one?

Osborne had another reason for feeling he had made a mistake. Murphy had outsmarted him. When it was seen that the convention would be deadlocked between the Democratic League and Tammany, the only resort was a candidate not too offensive to either faction. After some haggling Murphy declared himself willing to accept John A. Dix, who in 1908 had been the Democratic candidate for lieutenant governor.

Osborne was only mildly elated. "In many respects," he conceded, "the choice is absurd, for Dix can't speak, he can't write, and he can't read. . . . On the other hand, he is a clean gentleman of fine presence and would make a good though not great governor."

In some ways, it looked like a victory. Though Tammany names filled the remainder of the slate, Dix was a member of the Democratic League and disposed to resist the tyrannical sway of the bosses. Also there were no strings tied to his candidacy. There had been no yielding of principle. What Osborne did not realize was that Murphy had already discounted this. The Tammany boss knew his man. Dix was a well-meaning person, but weak, easily influenced by the exigencies of the moment. Job Hedges, Republican humorist and tactician, had him card-indexed from the first. Hedges would appear on the platform at Republican rallies, just as the audience was beginning to show signs of tedium.

"Dix?" he would say, cocking a shrewd eye. "He's not a Republican Dix. Why, he's not even a Democratic Dix. He's just Mr. Murphy's appenDix!"

Though Osborne undertook an extensive campaign tour that autumn, he would speak for no one but the head of the ticket. In distress he wrote to his son Charles, "How am I ever going to make a speech for a ticket that I hope and pray may be defeated?" And a little later: "I'm getting reconciled to a Democratic victory." Conscientiously he voted for Dix and one other Democrat. For the rest he either supported Republicans or cast no ballot.

In justice to Dix it should be said that he wanted to be a good governor. Upon election, he asked Osborne to accept an appointment in his administration, to serve with Charles Edward Treman and William Church Osborn in a sort of advisory cabinet. This Osborne was loath to do, for he was tired and hoped to join two of his sons in Italy. The governor being insistent, a meeting was finally arranged at the home of Colonel William Gorham Rice in Albany. Present were Governor and Mrs. Dix, Senator and Mrs. Franklin D. Roosevelt, and Mrs. James Roosevelt. Dix pleaded his need of support in staving off Tammany influence, and at last, after an all-night session, Osborne gave his consent.

The result of these deliberations was the latter's appointment as Forest, Fish, and Game Commissioner, than which a more ridiculous assignment is difficult to imagine. Osborne detested both hunting and fishing and would admit with a laugh that he could hardly tell the difference between a bull-frog and a speckled trout. Besides having no relish for the conservation job, he had his eye on the Prison Department; yet when Dix offered him that a little later, he felt he could not with good conscience deprive another of his post after public commitments.

Back of his decision to take on the Forest, Fish, and Game commissionership was a feeling of responsibility for the governor. To all intents Dix was a substitute for Osborne, who had seconded his nomination in the convention with glowing eulogies and Shakespearean quotations. As a fellow leader in the Democratic League he deserved support that his record might be a credit to the organization. It soon became apparent, however, that the Governor was playing directly into the hands of the old gang. Murphy, counting on just such a situation, had seen to it that it was more comfortable for Dix to listen to advice from Tammany headquarters than to go elsewhere. Most of the appointments smacked of Fourteenth Street.

To Osborne this anticlimax seemed catastrophic. The showdown came during the fight over a successor to United States Senator Chauncey M. Depew. Popular election of senators had not yet arrived, and Tammany was able to exert a pressure, amounting to practical dictation, upon the Democratic members of the Legislature. Murphy, taking advantage of the Democratic majority, picked Attorney William F. Sheehan of New York as the logical man to perpetuate Tammany influence in the national field. This was "Blue-Eyed Billy" Sheehan, formerly of Buffalo, ex-speaker of the Assembly, ex-lieutenant governor, and at this time corporation lawyer close to Thomas Fortune Ryan and Charles F. Murphy. The brazen effort to hook up both Wall Street and Tammany with the United States Senate brought Osborne out of his brief refuge in the Forest, Fish, and Game Department. War was declared.

Fortunately he found an ally in a young man who was serving his first term in the State Senate. He had first met Franklin D. Roosevelt on a West Indian cruise some five or six years before. In the intimate contacts of life aboard ship before thirsty tourists made a Mecca of Havana, he had conceived a great liking for this buoyant, clear-eyed youth enjoying a vacation after graduation from Harvard. In the years ahead their paths were to cross, if not frequently, always dramatically. Now he was glad to build a political alliance on a warm friendship.

Though Roosevelt had been elected from a strongly Republican district only a few weeks prior to these events and was without political experience, he did not hesitate to jeopardize his future career by teaming with Osborne to thwart Murphy's plans. Together they organized a bloc of twenty-six insurgent Democrats in the Legislature, sufficient to hold balance of power. This group defied the old-school politicians by the simple expedient of refusing to attend the party caucus, where they would have been bound to support the candidate receiving the majority vote. On their side, the insurgents presented as candidate Edward M. Shepard, a man of scholarly attainments and liberal leanings. Although Shepard had once been a Tammany candidate for mayor, the Wigwam had rejected him as a gubernatorial possibility the autumn before and would not accept him now.

The deadlock that ensued lasted eleven weeks. During that time legislative business in Albany was almost at a standstill, attention being concentrated on the revolution being staged by the small band under Osborne and Roosevelt. The amazing thing was their success in holding the men in line. The defection of even one or two would have meant collapse. Though Tammany brought out all its bag of tricks to break down their morale, and though Murphy fumed, threatened, and cajoled, the phalanx remained unbroken.

Besides the insurgent senators, other political leaders swung to Osborne during this fight. Among them was William J. (Fingy) Conners, Democratic boss of Buffalo. Conners had risen from a dock walloper to a millionaire freight contractor and newspaper publisher. Until the battle over Blue-Eyed Billy Sheehan, he had been considered Murphy's right-hand man in western New York. Suddenly he changed his point of view. Slapping Osborne on the back, he said: "You're all right, Tom. From now on we're pals." In contrast to a majority of political friendships, this pact survived many a storm.

The discouraging feature was Governor Dix himself. From a Pontius Pilate attitude, in itself a revelation to the independents, he advanced to what was practical acceptance of Tammany dictation. Confined to his bed for a few days, Osborne diagnosed his malady thus: "My trouble is combined Grippe and Governor." Only too soon he came to the conclusion that "Murphy owns Dix—body, boots, and breeches." Bland promises came to nothing. Smooth explanations did not explain. In a spasm of vexation, he wrote:

How he can keep on as he does—lying with a perfectly straight face—when he must know that I know he's lying! I don't like to lie myself, and when I have to, it is always upon the assumption that the other man doesn't know it. But then, I don't think I'm a liar. I only lie occasionally in the interest of truth.

In spite of the governor's obstruction, the insurgents stood firm. Even when Tammany dragged Sheehan out of it and presented Cohalan, "Murphy's man Friday," they would not yield. Sheehan was wild with disappointment. He had been so sure his designation was cinched that it is reported he actually rented a house in Washington.

At the height of the deadlock, the Republicans began to cast about them for an acceptable Democrat they could support with the insurgents. Osborne wrote to his son: "There are two or three whom the Republicans would be justified in electing. One of them is your Pa." For a time he flirted with the idea, and it would not have taken much to convince him of the wisdom of announcing his candidacy. Although the insurgent group were a little staggered at the turn of events, they could be counted on for support if his name were proposed. The Republicans were urging him to accept, and designation was therefore assured. This would break the deadlock, prevent a hook-up between Tammany and Congress, and furnish a spectacular victory over his personal enemy, Murphy. And after the Senate, what? A man born to be conspicuous could not fail to make his mark in the upper house. That opened vistas.

In the end he declined. He remembered how enemies had turned his decision to be a candidate for governor the preceding autumn into the grasping of a selfish man for the chief reward of insurgency. His great mistake—not because it injured his chances for preferment, but because it hurt his self-respect and reflected on the organization he captained. He should not have given his critics an opening then: he would give them none now. Besides, he wanted to see the leaven of reform work *within* the Democratic Party. Appointment as United States Senator was contingent chiefly upon the unanimous support of Republicans, permitting the inference that he would take what he could get, whatever the means.

After rejecting this attractive proposition, he tried his best to maneuver the selection of his friend, John N. Carlisle, who at Osborne's urging had been chosen to succeed him as Public Service Commissioner. His efforts were of no avail. Though at the last moment after much backing and filling Dix had ostensibly switched to the insurgents' side, he did not exert himself. Suddenly the rebels marched into the caucus and compromised on James A. O'Gorman, a Supreme Court justice.

Osborne was disgusted. It seemed like yielding in the moment of victory, for O'Gorman basked in the paternal benevolence of Tammany. Only after careful investigation disclosed that the appointee had a reputation for fairness and independence did Osborne send him a belated letter of congratulation. Though O'Gorman was scarcely of senatorial caliber, he earned Osborne's gratitude a few months later by assisting in tying a knot in the Tiger's tail at the Democratic National Convention.

The real disappointment was not O'Gorman, but Dix. Deserted by his comrade-in-arms, Osborne found his position as Forest, Fish, and Game Commissioner no longer tolerable. He wanted to resign, but still felt a sense of responsibility toward the Democratic League. Finally a serious illness prostrated him, and upon his doctor's advice he put an end to the dubious relationship his post in the "cabinet" represented. Immediately he was recognized as leader in a new war against Murphy and Dix, the latter being by this time openly accepted as a Tammany confederate.

Though wounded by the betrayal of one man, he found consolation in the strength and incorruptibility of another. Together they had bested Murphy and by their stubborn resistance paved the way for election of senators by popular vote. From that time on Osborne watched over the political career of Franklin D. Roosevelt with an almost paternal solicitude. It is too much to ask, however, that he should discern in his boyish ally those qualities which twenty years later were to make Roosevelt President of the United States.

CHAPTER IX

MAKING A PRESIDENT

THOUGH soon another cause was to enlist Osborne's sympathy and lift him to more spectacular heights than politics had ever done, his active career as a crusader against bossism was not to end without a flourish. The year 1912 was a Presidential year and, in New York State, a gubernatorial year. For Osborne the impending conflicts were practically identical. It was not merely the liberals against the reactionaries, but the liberals against Tammany. In Washington as well as in Albany, Boss Murphy was digging in.

Osborne went to both the national and state conventions: to the former as a belligerent with no official capacity; to the latter as an accredited delegate. Though his name is rarely mentioned by historians of the Baltimore convention that nominated Woodrow Wilson, behind the scenes he played an active and influential rôle.

It is a warm night early in July, not many hours after the nomination of Woodrow Wilson at Baltimore. A procession of enthusiastic citizens marches up South Street, Auburn, and pauses before the residence of Thomas Mott Osborne. In response to the demands of the crowd, the former mayor appears on the porch. He is tired to the point of exhaustion, but he relishes this demonstration. It is like old times: the plaudits of his fellow townsmen; parades; cheering; a victory to be celebrated—and a moral victory at that. No chance for anyone to impute selfish ambitions now.

"I have never felt so happy, politically, since 1892," he tells his hearers. Since that date marked his formal conversion to the Democratic faith, the statement is both comprehensive and significant. Even more remarkable is the tribute he proceeds to pay to one who, until a few days before, he counted among the great enemies of sound liberalism in the United States:

There was one man in Baltimore to whom the Democratic Party owes a tremendous debt. That man is William Jennings Bryan. I differed with him in the past, but I want to say that he is the greatest Democrat in America today. His fight at Baltimore, for courage and shrewd political action, is the finest thing we have ever seen in the history of American politics.

The *past* to which Osborne refers in connection with his differences with Bryan can scarcely be called remote. Only four days prior to this utterance his own newspaper, the *Citizen*, characterized Bryan's resolution pledging the Democratic convention not to nominate a Wall Street candidate as "sound and fury . . . bull-ragging and demagogism . . . a circus stunt." A few hours have wrought a great change. Bryan is "the greatest Democrat in America!"

Osborne went to Baltimore with the purpose of making a last stand against the spread of Tammanyism. He was not a delegate, and he had no great following; yet his sincerity and persistence counted in the final outcome. In preparation for the struggle he had composed a history of the rise and fall of clean Democratic leadership in New York State. This he had printed in pamphlet form and sent to every national delegate and political leader in the country. It depicted Murphy as the archvillain of politics. Somehow Murphy had to be stopped. He was trying desperately to stick a thumb into the political pie in Washington. Only after months of stubborn fighting had his attempt to shove Sheehan into the Senate been foiled. Now, if he could dictate the Presidential nomination, Tammany's nest would be feathered only too cozily.

Osborne was convinced that the man best equipped to bring the Democratic Party back to its former prestige under Cleveland was Woodrow Wilson. Here at last was a man who combined scholarly attainments and independence with a practical knowledge of public affairs. If he could be nominated in the face of Tammany opposition, the split between Taft and Roosevelt augured well for his election.

Looking about him for allies in the pending battle, Osborne was delighted to find his young friend, Franklin D. Roosevelt, once more on the side of the liberals. Remembering the success with which they had blocked Murphy a few months before, he promptly selected Roosevelt as his first lieutenant. To his great satisfaction, possibly to his surprise, there was also Senator O'Gorman, the compromise candidate to succeed Depew, demonstrating his reputation for independence by supporting Osborne and the Wilson men against his former chief.

The situation, however, was not encouraging. Champ Clark, the leading candidate, had not only national prestige as Speaker of the House but a forceful personality. His type was far more familiar to delegates and voters than that of Wilson, the academician. Murphy, though nominally committed to Governor Judson Harmon of Ohio, was expected to shift to Clark at the proper time. Oscar Underwood of Alabama was also in the running. And then there was Bryan. That, to Osborne's mind, was the real tragedy. However mistaken Bryan might be on currency, it was incredible that he should play Murphy's game. Yet he was cornered. Clark, posing as a progressive, had headlined Bryan's support in the preliminary campaign, and the Nebraska delegation had been instructed for the Speaker. Because of the unit rule, Bryan could not bolt even if he wished.

Clark's strategy was to win a progressive following without losing the support of the old guard. It showed even in his choice of a campaign song. Day and night, in street, hotel, and convention hall, his backers bellowed:

> *I don't care if he is a houn'—*
> *You gotta quit kicking my dawg aroun'.*

With the spirit of liberalism in the air, it was far wiser to show solicitude for a houn' dawg than for a golden calf.

It looked to Osborne like an impossible situation, but he underrated Bryan's sagacity. Indeed, during the early days of the convention, few penetrated the strategy of the Great Commoner. Shrewdly aware of the futility of advancing his own candidacy, Bryan resisted all inducements to throw his hat into the ring. He knew where his power lay. No one could be nominated without his support. The old halo hung over him still, and thousands followed where he led.

His first move had antedated the convention. In a letter to the outstanding candidates, he asked each to support him in naming a progressive as temporary chairman in place of the reactionary, Alton B. Parker, selection of the committee. Of them all Wilson was the only one who did not evade the issue. Disregarding the protests of a close adviser, he threw down the gauntlet to the bosses and endorsed Bryan's proposition. It was Clark's refusal to take sides that first alienated Bryan. The latter's circular letter had not been entirely disinterested. He wanted the post of temporary chairman himself. When finally it went to Parker, he saw the sinister influence of Ryan, Sheehan, and Murphy. It roused his fighting blood. Yet he realized he must meet guile with guile. Craftily he bided his time.

His one aggressive move was to introduce the famous resolution committing the convention to oppose any candidate for President who was a representative of, or under any obligation to, "J. Pierpont Morgan, Thomas F. Ryan, August Belmont, or any others of the privilege-hunting or favor-asking class." A second paragraph provided, illegally under convention rules, for the expulsion of all delegates representing such interests. Bedlam broke loose. Bryan was subjected to all kinds of jeers and taunts. Even his own colleagues did not understand. Osborne himself could not help feeling it was an empty, grandstand gesture, a demagogic appeal for notoriety.

Nevertheless, after Bryan had withdrawn the last clause, as no doubt had been his original intention, the resolution was passed four to one. Few dared to vote against it—not even Murphy. How keen a thrust it was at Clark did not appear until later.

When the voting began, Clark had a comfortable lead. The first climax developed on the tenth ballot. New York shifted from Harmon to Champ Clark. "Mr. Murphy's ninety wax figures," as Bryan called them, swung into line behind the real Tammany candidate. For a time it looked as if Murphy were to dominate the convention. There was a gigantic demonstration; almost a stampede. Even Woodrow Wilson, resting at Sea Girt, thought it was all over. Then came the fourteenth ballot, and Bryan showed his hand. Denouncing Clark for docilely accepting Murphy's support, he invoked the authority of his resolution against a Wall Street candidate, and threw the Nebraska delegation to Wilson. It was a master stroke. Immediately the entire situation changed color. Wilson began to gain strength. By the thirtieth ballot he was in the lead. On the forty-sixth he was nominated.

Such, in brief, was the sequence of events as related by the historians and autobiographers. What is seldom mentioned is the frenzied activity of Osborne and his independent Democrats. Behind the convention maneuvering reported by William G. McAdoo, Joseph P. Tumulty, and others, there was another campaign. Though neither Osborne nor Roosevelt was a delegate, they worked among the delegations, exhorting, cajoling, threatening. Their main objective was winning Bryan's support for Wilson. When Bryan made his spectacular switch, Osborne turned his attention to Tom Taggart of Indiana and Roger Sullivan of Illinois, bosses only slightly beneath the stature of Charles F. Murphy. No less a competent observer than the late George Haven Putnam has given Osborne the credit for accomplishing in fact the nomination of Woodrow Wilson. In his "Memories of a Publisher" Brevet Major Putnam describes the Baltimore convention from the point of view of an active independent Democrat working for Wilson:

I helped in the organization of what was called the Wilson Conference Committee, the leader in which was Thomas M. Osborne, late Mayor of Auburn. His active lieutenant was young Franklin D. Roosevelt, a cousin of the great Theodore. Franklin's father was, I heard, a supporter of Theodore, but the son had been ready to mark out for himself his political course. The work of our Conference Committee was to make clear to the delegates at Baltimore

that the Murphy vote did not express the opinion of the State. . . .
It is probable, in fact, that Murphy as the leader of the only unbroken block of votes of ninety would have had in his hands the
actual selection of the candidate. The risk was serious that the Convention might have the mortification of accepting as a nominee a
man selected and controlled by Murphy and his financial backers, of
whom the most important, Thomas F. Ryan, was a member of the
New York delegation.

This result, which would have been a grievous disaster for the
country, was prevented only through the persistency, the courage,
and the intelligently exerted influence of our leader Osborne. He had
been laboring night and day with the delegates to make clear that
the representation of New York in the Convention did not voice
the opinion of the Empire State but was a travesty and a fraud. He
finally succeeded on the forty-fourth ballot in inducing the delegates
from Indiana, who had been giving their support to Marshall, to
agree to make a break if they could do this in company with one
or more other States. Osborne brought to the same way of thinking
the delegates of Illinois and of Kentucky, and the progress made on
the forty-fifth ballot secured on the forty-sixth the nomination of
Wilson. The surprise and disgust of the Murphy-Ryan group was
so great that they did not have the sense to swing the ninety votes
of New York into line in time to have these votes constitute a part
of the two-thirds required for the nomination. The national democracy had decided against Tammany Hall and from that point the
anti-Tammany Democrats of the State could, during the campaign
that was to follow, claim to be the "regulars" as against the Tammany "faction." . . .

Thomas Mott Osborne should in the political history of the
country receive due credit for heading off the disgrace of a White
House controlled by Tammany Hall.

Though in later years Osborne sometimes wondered why
these services were forgotten by the man who benefited most
from them, he never regretted the part he had played in Wilson's election. There were times, it is true, when Wilson seemed
to him altogether too willing to let Boss Murphy regain his hold
on patronage in New York State. The President's first appointments included only one man who could possibly be construed
as representing the upstate independents whose efforts had
counted for so much in the convention. That was Franklin D.
Roosevelt, picked for assistant secretary of the Navy. Finally
Osborne grew so exasperated that he wrote Wilson a confidential letter, intrusting it to Roosevelt for personal delivery.

The tartness of that letter may partially explain why he was passed over in the ministerial appointments of two administrations. Wilson liked contradiction no better than Osborne, and must have resented both the tone and the contents of the communication.

It was the appointment of Judge James W. Gerard as ambassador to Germany and that of Francis Burton Harrison as Governor General of the Philippines that most aroused Osborne's ire.

. . . Your attitude toward New York has been a matter of great surprise and deep disappointment to many of your friends in this state. The impression is gaining ground that you have chosen to ignore almost completely the "Up-state" Democracy. . . .

"Jimmy" Gerard was a lawyer of small account. . . . He had no claims whatever upon the Democratic party when he was made Judge—a position secured, it is asserted, in the approved Tammany fashion. No other explanation was ever given for his being raised to the bench. This is certainly not a creditable political record; and many have wondered what there was in it that entitled him to an appointment for an important diplomatic post. The fact that he was one of the largest, if not the largest, contributor to your campaign fund recalls the case of Mr. Van Allen of Rhode Island, whose appointment as Minister to Italy was withdrawn by Cleveland for just such a cause.

Either the President kept these outspoken remarks strictly confidential, or else the victim of the attack was liberal enough to overlook personal prejudice, for two years later Ambassador Gerard chose one of Osborne's sons for his private secretary. But if Osborne was incensed at the choice of Gerard, he was almost beside himself at the thought of Harrison's becoming Governor General of the Philippines. The anti-imperialist in him made him rate that post as the most difficult and dangerous the President had to fill, and Harrison seemed the least qualified of all available candidates. He lectured Wilson like a schoolboy, berating both appointer and appointee. In conclusion, he observed:

[This letter] is written because I simply cannot keep silent; I feel that it is my duty to call your attention to the wide difference between your words, which I believe truly represent your intentions, and your actions in New York State as they are being judged. Having drawn out of active politics, and having no political favors to ask of you or any one else, I can afford the luxury of speaking to you plainly without danger of being misunderstood; and if I did not feel that you were so broad and big a man that I may so speak, I should not write you at all.

As many another was to discover, efforts to influence Wilson were fruitless—though one must grant that in this instance the approach might have been more ingratiating. In 1916 Osborne was so disgusted that he decided not to vote for Wilson for a second term; but he changed his mind at the last moment. Not until the outbreak of the World War did he become an outright enthusiastic supporter of the man he had helped to make President. From then on he was once and for all a "Wilson Democrat."

CHAPTER X

JEREMIAD

FAR more spectacular, so far as Osborne's participation is concerned, was the Democratic state convention in Syracuse the following October. It was the valedictory of Osborne the Politician. It was too, in one sense, a climax; for the trumpet and the thunder had never swelled to such volume before. Only too late was he to realize that the victory he thought he had won was but the shadow, while the substance belonged to his ancient enemy, Charles F. Murphy.

In the days preceding the convention Governor Dix was hopeful of renomination. He knew the independents were against him, but Tammany would not throw him over. He had served the tribe too well for that. What he did not take into consideration was the ability of Murphy to diagnose public sentiment; to stop just short of the fatal step that would precipitate a revolution. Murphy was not particularly worried over the hostility of the independents, nor did he mind the scholarly frown with which Woodrow Wilson contemplated Dix. What he did pay heed to was the reports of upstate Tammany leaders, a majority of whom doubted that the governor could attract many voters in their districts. Though he did not realize it, or at least would not admit it, Dix was slated for the discard long before the clans assembled at Syracuse.

The Republicans had nominated Job Hedges and James W. Wadsworth, Jr., while the Progressives were presenting a strong combination in Oscar S. Straus, the philanthropist, and Professor Frederick M. Davenport of Clinton, former state senator. It was essential that the Democrats find someone who could prevent any formidable drift toward the Progressive ticket. Osborne, heading the Cayuga County delegation, anticipated a battle royal. In his own bailiwick the Tammany outfit, rejoicing in the name of the Cayuga County Democratic Association, chartered a special car to transport its members to the convention for the avowed purpose of "howling Osborne down." With Murphy still smarting from the lashing he had received at Baltimore, it was obvious that the conflict was to be between the Wilson Democrats and the Tammany faction.

Combing the state for indications of the trend, Osborne was disturbed by the lack of party harmony. By letter and telegram he pleaded with Wilson to stand by the Independents— or at least "to say or do nothing that will express approval of a wretched *compromise*." He declared Sheehan was conducting an under-cover fight to prevent the naming of any insurgent who had helped in the election of Senator O'Gorman, and he predicted a disastrous bolt to Straus, if Murphy succeeded in choosing the candidate. It was unnecessary for him to add that in such a contingency T. M. Osborne would be the first to bolt.

The first action taken by the convention Osborne counted a victory for the liberal wing. For temporary chairman the delegates chose Martin H. Glynn, whose pretension to independence had been loudly broadcast in his newspaper, the Albany *Times-Union*. As a matter of fact, this selection had been ratified weeks before by the political ring. Whatever the temptation to celebrate, it was soon quashed by the election of Alton B. Parker, generally conceded to be the mouthpiece of the reactionaries, as permanent chairman. The latter justified his reputation by lauding Governor Dix to the skies and pointing with pride to numerous, imaginary achievements of the administration.

Sickened by this hypocrisy, Osborne took the offensive. His first tilt was with Senator Robert F. Wagner, whom he finally forced to accept an amendment providing that all sessions be open to the public. That started the bad feeling. The rupture, however, became a chasm when the Resolutions Committee reported. Osborne was on his feet in an instant, clamoring for recognition to present a minority report. Shouts of "Put him out!" "Hurry up, Tom!" greeted him. Tammany representatives sought to have him expelled from the convention on the ground that he was not a Democrat. Patrick E. McCabe of Albany County seized the opportunity to bring up the matter of Osborne's appointment as Public Service Commissioner by Governor Hughes, and asked if the gentleman from Auburn did not recognize his obligation to the Republicans. "The obligation is the other way round," was Osborne's rejoinder.

Finally he won his point, was granted a hearing by Chairman Parker, anxious to restore order, and launched into an attack on the platform. Charging that on every crucial issue the document was a fraud and an evasion, he introduced a resolution calling for selection of state officers by direct primary, from the governor down. The plank endorsing Dix and his administration he characterized as contemptible hypocrisy. "If Dix is so good," he shouted, "why throw him out?"

The convention was in an uproar, but there was more to come. In words which were to be reprinted in newspapers and quoted in speeches for months to come, Osborne made a last savage attack on the man he held most responsible for the evils in public life.

You think we are fighting Dix. We are not, nor have we been. To do so would be to waste powder. His hour has struck. . . . You think we are fighting Murphy. We are in one sense, for he is the apparent obstacle to genuine forward progress. Yet really we are not. His hour is about to strike. The long delayed storm . . . has already burst; the lightning is already flaming; and already one great reputation has come crashing to the ground. Yet this man sits here now, surrounded by his satellites, dispensing favors, dictating policies, and distributing the nominations of a great party. Look at him well, for this is the last time you will see such a spectacle. For him, too, the hour is about to strike, and upon the ruins of his fall will arise the New York Democracy of the future. . . . Choose ye this day whom ye will serve. On the one side stand Woodrow Wilson and the principles of progressive Democracy; on the other, Charles F. Murphy and the cohesive power of public plunder!

He stopped, and for a moment there was absolute silence in the hall. Delegates were astounded that anyone could have the temerity to hurl such defiance in the very teeth of Murphy.

Then a storm of hisses and jeers broke. One leather-lunged Tammany delegate sitting just behind his leader yelled, "Three cheers for Charles F. Murphy!" The whole tribe jumped to their feet and made the rafters ring to their answering challenge. Senator Wagner almost ran to the rostrum, so anxious was he to counteract the effect of this startling prophecy.

"Oh, if the name of Osborne were displayed around for one of the gubernatorial candidates," he screamed above the tumult, "what patriots we should be!"

"Liar! Liar!" shouted Osborne, shaking his fist.

In all this din only one person seemed unmoved. Squat, pudgy, imperturbable, Charles F. Murphy sat quietly in his seat as if the dramatic pronouncement of his passing concerned someone in whose fate he had not the slightest interest. Possibly he was pondering the prediction, debating whether or not there was any truth in it. It is also possible that he discounted some of the effects which the oratorical outbursts of his adversaries might have on the final result. For this "uncrowned king," known in Syracuse as "the man in Room 216," pulled the strings that made the puppets jump; and he had one string of which few were aware.

John A. Dix did not enter much into his plans. While ostensibly backing the governor in conferences, Murphy had fixed the convention to give that gentleman a consolation vote. It was another he had in mind, and he was content to bide his time.

Although Osborne had first favored William G. McAdoo as candidate for governor, he turned with other independents to support Glynn. Glynn, who had served two years as state comptroller under Hughes and had been mentioned for governor in 1910, had built up for himself a reputation as an aggressive independent, a man of the people, and an enemy of the machine. Sentiment in the convention, however, was swinging toward William Sulzer, who for eighteen years had been congressman from a New York City district that in other respects was soundly Republican. Though connected with the Tammany organization since his entrance into politics, Sulzer was too much an individualist to "wear the collar." Even the independents were not averse to his nomination. Consequently, when Murphy pretended to yield on Dix, in favor of Sulzer, it was considered a good bargain, particularly since the arrangement included Glynn as lieutenant governor. Osborne reported to Woodrow Wilson: "While I think Sulzer is a demagogue—he is an honest one. . . . He really thinks the voice of the galleries is the voice of God."

When Sulzer and Glynn were nominated on the fourth ballot, it was the signal for rejoicing. Osborne was pleased, apparently. He went home and spread the news that at last New York State Democracy had found the right type of leadership. All the anti-Tammany men were pleased. Had not Murphy been routed and forced into a humiliating peace pact? Woodrow Wilson was pleased and said so in an open telegram to the victorious candidates. What few suspected, however, was that Murphy was also pleased. Furthermore, events show that he was justified.

Only nine months after taking office, Sulzer, whom Murphy could not handle, was impeached and removed from office. In his place went Glynn, the man whom Murphy had wanted from the beginning. As for Osborne's prediction that Murphy's hour had struck, the wily chief was to see his empire solidified from one end of the state to the other and his own power more firmly intrenched in spite of direct primary legislation. And could death leave still a consciousness of human affairs, he might, twelve years later, have flapped his wings in seraphic delight at the elegies his fellow men recited over his bier. When one day in April, 1924, he suddenly succumbed to an attack of acute indigestion, the encomiums, considering what Murphy had stood for, were almost nauseous.

The *Outlook,* once a mighty organ of liberalism, stammered weakly:

Judged by *any* standards, Charles Francis Murphy was the best chieftain that the tribe of Tammany ever had. He held its power longer than any other. He increased its influence. *He elevated its standards."* [The italics are mine.]

Governor Alfred E. Smith contributed this ethical gem: "Murphy made of his life a lesson and an example to the youth

of this country." This man, who had never held any office of
high rank, who had no visible occupation except that of horse-
car driver and saloonkeeper in his early days, who had done
no single act of public service and had distinguished himself
in none of the arts or professions, yet had held the destinies
of great men in his fist and had left a fortune of legendary
proportions—this man suddenly became a symbol of go-getting
America, and his career the epitome of our philosophy of success. In the face of an avalanche of eulogy the *Nation* stood
almost alone in denouncing this "mealy-mouthed" hypocrisy.
Quoting Osborne's phrase, "the cohesive power of public plunder," it lamented the only too palpable fact that no voice was
lifted to rally the independents and lead them against the
legions of Tammany.

What was it that turned the liberal victory of 1912 into a
rout and permitted Murphy to consolidate his positions?

Osborne, as already observed, went to Syracuse to fight for
the nomination of Glynn. He would have been astounded had
he realized that Murphy came with exactly the same purpose.
Murphy's advocacy of Dix was a blind, for no one knew better
than he that the Governor was through. With Glynn the Tammany chief is believed to have had a secret understanding, the
more effective because of the independent label Glynn wore.
As the time for balloting approached, Murphy realized that
even if Glynn were nominated, it would be difficult to elect
him. Should Sulzer turn to the Progressive camp, the situation
would be serious. The question was: Could Sulzer, if nominated and elected, be controlled? Murphy thought so. Sulzer
was in debt. If Glynn were given second place on the ticket,
there were possibilities. It was so arranged, though the independents thought they had done the arranging.

The events that led to Sulzer's impeachment and removal
are too complicated to permit more than an outline here. Yet
even an outline will speak for itself. In view of what occurred
the following conversation between Glynn and Jay W. Forrest,
candidate for Congress from the Albany-Troy district, is significant. The time is August, about six weeks before the Syracuse convention. Forrest himself is the authority.

GLYNN: Jay, I think I will be nominated for governor this year. If I am not nominated for governor I can surely be nominated for lieutenant governor. Would you advise me to take it?

FORREST: Yes, I would advise you to accept the nomination for lieutenant governor. There is always possibility of death and then you would be governor.

GLYNN (*instantly*): Yes, or removal.

This is by no means conclusive evidence that the plot against Sulzer was already being hatched. It is, at the very least, curious.

After Sulzer's election and inauguration, it seemed for a time that the new governor was to play Murphy's game in the same old style. His appointments led to that inference. Perhaps Murphy himself considered Sulzer's campaign declaration that, if elected, he would be *the* governor as mere election humbug. If so, Murphy was determined to make assurance doubly sure. With a knowledge of the governor's private affairs that was rather breath-taking, he offered to put up a sum rumored to be about $100,000 for payment of Sulzer's debts. He was insistent about it, but the Governor, though tempted, stubbornly resisted the offer. He knew that acceptance would forever after tie his hands at Albany. This intractability, however, sealed his doom. From then on he lived, politically, on borrowed time.

One is tempted to believe that Osborne's campaign enthusiasm for Sulzer was not as whole-hearted as it might have been. Not long after the inauguration of the new governor he realized a struggle was impending that would make or break Sulzer.

"I always thought him a good deal of a fool," he wrote, "and I have not changed my mind. But he certainly is up against it."

He did change his mind, however. He had obtained the governor's promise of the appointment of Charles F. Rattigan as warden of Auburn Prison. Because of the pressure put on Sulzer from other quarters, he doubted it would ever be fulfilled. When Rattigan was one day offered another post carrying a larger salary, this doubt seemed confirmed. Whatever Rattigan's sentiments may have been, Osborne desired for his friend only the warden assignment. Already vague plans were forming in his mind.

It is ridiculous, he wrote Sulzer, to think we can accept any other appointment. That would place us in the position of cheap office seekers. To his surprise, the governor responded promptly that such logic was unanswerable, and that he would keep his word, whatever happened. He did keep his word, and Rattigan was appointed in the face of stiff opposition. When Sulzer followed this by making Osborne chairman of a Commission on Prison Reform, the latter's notions about the governor underwent a radical change.

In the meantime, the split between Sulzer and Murphy was growing wider. The governor began to defy the bosses, make his own appointments, and crusade for legislation that threw Tammany into a panic. In the latter class three things stand out: his investigation of graft scandals, his fight for an effective direct primary law, and his signing of the full-crew bill. Osborne could scarcely believe his eyes as he watched this governor, reputedly a Murphy man, carrying out his (Osborne's) own program. It was Osborne who had scored Tammany graft with the greatest vehemence. It was Osborne who as spokesman for the minority on the Resolutions Committee of the convention had introduced a genuine direct primary plank. And finally it was Osborne who as Public Service Commissioner had urged the necessity of train crews sufficiently manned to insure safety.

William Sulzer paid the price of his independence. In August he was impeached by the Assembly on charges of filing a false statement of campaign contributions and using a portion of the money for private purposes.

When Osborne awoke to the situation and realized how the Independents had been sold, he took immediate action. He thought he had withdrawn definitely from all active politics, but he could not desert a man who had sacrificed himself in such a cause. Wearied and harassed, he canceled a trip to Europe and threw himself into this new conflict. Writing to J. P. Tumulty, Wilson's private secretary, urging the President's personal interest in the New York State situation, he said:

I have come to the place where I am so worn out, mentally and spiritually, that I can hardly respond to the most obvious call of public duty. (This state of mind is probably inconceivable to a successful young man like yourself. But wait until you have fought some *losing* fights against the forces of evil—and have come to be over fifty!) In spite of myself, however, Governor Sulzer's splendid struggle has roused all my flagging energies; and I shall do all that I can to aid him—even at the sacrifice of my own wishes and plans.

Two days after the impeachment Osborne was the chief speaker at a great protest meeting held in historic Cooper Union, New York City. Similar mass meetings were held in the principal cities of the state. But it was too late. The Tammany machinery was working smoothly. Martin H. Glynn had immediately taken over the acting governorship, refusing to submit to the courts the question of whether or not an impeached governor should continue in office until after the trial. "Government by investigation should now cease," he announced—an enlightening statement in view of Tammany's fright at what Sulzer's investigations might disclose. When in October the governor was brought to trial before the High Court of Impeachment, the alignment of liberal against reactionary was reflected in the personnel of the respective counsel. One of the foremost of Sulzer's staff was Louis Marshall of New York, eminent constitutional lawyer. Chief counsel for the prosecution was Alton B. Parker, law partner of Blue-Eyed Billy Sheehan.

The result was never in doubt. It was essential to Tammany that Sulzer be got rid of; otherwise, as one of Murphy's lieutenants is reported to have remarked, "he will send us all to jail." In October the governor was found guilty on three of the eight counts against him and was removed from office. That he was a victim of a Tammany conspiracy is scarcely to be doubted. Had he not refused to take orders from Murphy, there is reason to believe he would have enjoyed a comfortable administration, disturbed by nothing except his own conscience.

The truth of the charges brought against him is of less importance than the manner of their bringing. Perhaps he was guilty of filing a false statement of his campaign expenses. The court said so. Perhaps he was guilty of perjury in swearing this statement was true. The court said so. But there are several points to be noted. Sulzer was tried and convicted for acts which, if done, were done *before* he took office. No taint attaches to any of his acts as governor. He was tried and convicted *after* prosecuting a campaign for legislation designed to protect the people from the evils of bossism and special privilege. He was impeached by a Tammany-controlled Assembly. He was convicted by a Tammany-controlled court, three members of which had collected the evidence used against the governor and had then sat in judgment on that evidence. Another member of the court stood to gain the lieutenant governorship by Sulzer's removal. Without the votes of these four men, he could not have been convicted on the two major counts of his indictment.

No wonder Sulzer called it "Murphy's High Court of Infamy!" No wonder that when he appealed to that higher court, "the court of public opinion," and was nominated for, and elected to, the Assembly, he counted his victory a vindication! He had, moreover, the satisfaction of knowing that such a champion of social justice as Theodore Roosevelt was convinced he had been garroted by a political ring; and that, aside from independent Democrats and liberal Republicans, he had the confidence of distinguished rabbis, priests, and ministers. Except for some of the prominent New York dailies, antagonized by the full-crew bill, the liberal press, including such periodicals as the *Outlook* and the *Review of Reviews*, took up cudgels in his behalf.

Yet all this must have been cold consolation for Sulzer. Politically, he was through. Running for the Assembly was but a gesture. After the first enthusiasm of his advocates waned, he was practically forgotten. Only once more did he come prominently to public notice. In 1916 the American Party nominated him for President—an honor, if it can be called such, he declined to accept. When Tammany marks a rebel for oblivion, there is an admirable efficiency in its method of procedure. Osborne's political career, as such, ended with this dramatic incident. It had been a harsh schooling. He had learned that, however *right* a gentleman of the minority felt himself to be, *might* invariably prevailed. Yet even in his defeats, disillusioning as they often were, he saw some gain, a slow, almost imperceptible, awakening of the public conscience. He had a long-distance view that saved him from discouragement. In a new field of endeavor he was to experience the same hopes and disappointments; he was to come to grips once more with unscrupulous politicians bent on destroying him; and persecuted and finally crucified, he was to die before the full significance of his crusade was apparent.

2. THE CITIZEN

CHAPTER I

"YOUR PA"

IN 1905 Osborne had received an offer which, if accepted, might have changed the whole course of his life. Spencer Trask, at whose estate, Yaddo, he had so often enjoyed the companionship of men and women gifted in the arts, begged him to take an important position with the banking house of Spencer Trask & Company, New York. It was a flattering proposal involving transactions of an international nature that meant great responsibility, to say nothing of handsome remuneration. Though he professed ignorance of the ins and outs of high finance, he had confidence in his ability to learn quickly. It meant besides a safe, substantial life, free from the alarums which had kept him in a perpetual state of tension. There would be the thrill of power, the sense of being a highly respected citizen in one of the world's great financial centers.

For several months he pondered the matter, torn this way and that. It occurred to him that Mr. Thomas Mott Osborne of New York might not be so conspicuous as plain Tom Osborne of Auburn. He thought of his work with the George Junior Republic and wondered if after all he could not serve his fellow men better where he was. His mother was growing aged and infirm. And what about his dream of chastening the political bosses and retrieving for the people the power they had usurped?

All of these things entered into his study of the question; but it was another consideration that finally prompted his refusal of the offer. Living over again the anguish of those last days before the death of his wife, he wrote in reply:

I do not wish to seem to pose as a martyr; I have not expected
the world to put on mourning for my sorrows; I am glad for all the
brightness and joy there is about me; but life could never be the
same again. During those five months of ordeal it has seemed to
me as if all personal ambition was burned up within me; and as if
with that destruction I had acquired a clearer vision with which
to test values. For myself I should feel only too glad to lay down
my burdens and test the great truths of futurity tomorrow—but my
boys need me. . . . Our home, which is now in the house which
their mother planned and which is still filled with her dear presence,
is here and can never be anywhere else quite the same.

When Mrs. Osborne died, she left four sons, one a mere babe
of seven weeks. It was a terrifying responsibility that fell
upon the stricken husband, and he felt it more than most men
who have experienced a similar loss. Perhaps if he had been
less sensitive, it would have been better for his own peace of
mind and for that of his boys. All the affection he had felt for
his wife was now concentrated upon his children. Had he
remarried, this emotion might have been diffused; but he
could not bring himself to think of another woman in a marital
relationship. Still young, virile, wealthy, and talented, he
caught the fancy of many a lady who set her cap for him in
vain.

The story of these years is a story of abrupt transitions
from rapture to despair. However far afield his crusades took
him, he always felt the tether that held him to his home. It
was there his heart lay. Somehow he must take the place of
the mother who was gone. Remembering his own sheltered
boyhood, he allowed his boys a greater freedom than he had
enjoyed. Remembering too his opportunities and his capacity
for making the most of them, he expected of his sons an equal
eagerness for the things he had loved. It was inevitable that
often he should be disappointed, for the ideal in his mind was
his own ideal, the product of his own individuality. When one
of his boys showed tendencies at variance with his preconcep-
tions, he was plunged into the depths of despondency. When
one of them met a situation as he would have met it, a wave of
pride swept over him. So great was his sense of responsibility
that any delinquency seemed to cry at him that he had failed

as a parent; that he had been untrue to the trust his wife had confided to him.

I am often sorry that I have not talked more to you boys of your dear mother. But I have been afraid to do so. In the first place, it is very hard for me to reopen the old wounds. In the second place, the only time she ever said anything that would indicate that she realized how ill she was was when she asked me never to have you boys think of her as a stern monitor. I don't just recall the words, for I could not trust myself to answer—hardly to listen—but what she foresaw was the danger of saying, "Don't do that—your mother wouldn't have liked it," etc., until you would have thought of her as a sort of grim dragon. So I have tried never to say anything that would have that effect, and perhaps I have erred on the other side. . . . It is a cruel, cruel loss to a boy—to have no mother.

Yet there was even greater anguish than this. More than all else he wanted to make confidants of his sons. They were to take the place of the only one to whom he had ever been able to open his whole heart. He craved their companionship as he had craved nothing else in life. It became a necessity. Again it was inevitable that the very urgency of his love set up barriers. His demonstrativeness was too overwhelming to strike articulate response from boys passing through the various stages of adolescence. Often they withdrew into their own embarrassment, leaving a father distracted with frustration.

Though each boy had something of his father in him, the traits were so combined with contrasting features that it was unthinkable they could be molded in one cast. One especially seemed more like his mother than any of the others. Yet it was this boy who was most remote. Osborne felt that a curtain was falling between them. The more he pleaded for confidences, the thicker became the blanket of reserve with which the boy surrounded himself, until the father declared bitterly that he was unloved. Sometimes he was almost abject in pleading for admission into a heart that seemed forever locked.

I have looked forward to the time, as I have so often said to you, when my boys would be also my friends—when I could meet them on the same intellectual level. . . . I can do that with other boys of your age. Why should I not expect to do it with you? . . . You say that I seem to be on a "much higher altitude . . . and cannot

see your points of view or have regard for your opinions." . . . I
have the utmost sympathy and regard for your opinions—*if you will
only let me know what they are.* . . . But do, my dear son, realize
that I don't stand on a pedestal. I am battling every day with
problems that are *just like yours,* involving the same mental processes and the very same temptations and trials. I need help from
you—and I think you need help from me.

There were times when the barriers seemed to fall away and
father and sons came into close comradeship. As children the
boys had addressed their father circumspectly as Papa. When
at last they reduced it to that simple monosyllable which suggests a relationship both patriarchal and intimate, Osborne was
delighted. He encouraged them by referring to himself as
"your Pa." Even when the boys reached manhood, they clung
to this form. It seemed to connote all that was best in their
association with their father. Often, too, when speaking *of*
him in later years, they adopted a nickname that had come
into wide use among Osborne's acquaintances—T. M., the first
two initials of his name.

From the first, Osborne encouraged his boys in athletics.
Behind his house there was a large lot where scions of South
Street families mingled with neighborhood urchins in the only
true democracy—sport. Baseball was the favorite. Watching
a scrub game one afternoon, Osborne had an idea. "Get organized into an association," he told the youngsters, "practice
hard, choose a team, and I will furnish you with regular baseball uniforms." There was a whoop of joy, and out of the discussions of that day grew the O. A. C., the Osborne Athletic
Club, which flourished for many years. Even if it had accomplished nothing else, it demonstrated to Osborne the value of
the gang spirit when guided in the right direction.

Proud of its spick-and-span uniforms, the O. A. C. nine looked
about for competition. Although it played games with a number of amateur outfits, its chief opponent became the George
Junior Republic at Freeville. It was a hardy bunch that came
from the Republic to cross bats with the Osbornes, boys who
had learned how to take knocks and how to give them. Thinking to stimulate competition between these two teams, Osborne

offered a cup, which was to become the permanent possession
of the first club to win it for three seasons.

Never was Newcastle in less need of coals. When, to celebrate the initial game of the first season, he invited the two
teams to play at Willow Point, with a substantial repast as
reward for both victors and vanquished, the game ended in
such a general free-for-all that by the time the viands were
rushed on, bulging lips and sore noses made mastication difficult for many of the contestants.

"Competition?" thought Osborne. "Good God!"

It was with deep respect, however, that the boys saw their
father in perfect control of the mysteries of a box score—a
gadget here and a do-hickey there. He was the official score-
keeper, and it turned out to be no mean task. Being more or
less of the sand-lot variety, the games produced tallies with
such rapidity that it needed a public accountant to keep them
straight. Sometimes in despair, he was obliged to note the final
score as follows:

"O. A. C.'s, 44 plus; G. J. R.'s, 30 something."

Sport was not the only diversion. Osborne saw to it that his
sons had every opportunity for cultural and educational development. They were sent to the best academies—among
them the Adirondack-Florida School. There were travels in
Europe and trips round the world. All but one of the boys
had musical talent. "Learn the cello so you can play duets
with me," Osborne would say, "and you shall have five thousand dollars." Or it might be the reward was offered for pro-
ficiency in a foreign language. He made it a point also to
take his sons to every musical and dramatic entertainment that
came to Syracuse, though in those days it meant staying overnight at a hotel. That, undoubtedly, was part of the thrill for
the boys, in spite of the fact that they rebelled violently at
their father's principle of always choosing the *second* best
hostelry. "The best is never any better," he would say, "and
a lot more expensive."

At home the quartet were for some years under the supervision of William O. Dapping, an older boy in whom Osborne
had become interested. An outstanding leader in the George

Junior Republic, Dapping had accepted Osborne's invitation to live in Auburn and was completing his school and college education under the latter's guidance. During the summer there was always something forward at Willow Point. Scarcely a week-end passed without its crowd of guests, interesting people with the average quota of robust sons and, equally important, attractive daughters.

When the time came for the boys to leave home for preparatory school, their father's thoughts went with them. So did his letters of admonition. Strict in many details, especially in regard to an accurate accounting of expenses, he was fundamentally generous and infinitely forgiving. One son, who made the mistake of running up debts and borrowing money secretly, was finally compelled to confess all in a pathetic letter. The reply came promptly:

You say, "I know and realize what a fool I am."—No, my dear boy, you are not a fool by any means but you are very lazy and indifferent. . . . You do not use the brains the Lord has given you.

Then, after itemizing scrupulously the lad's sins of the past year, the letter concluded:

Send me a complete list of all your indebtedness. I will clear it all up and we will begin over again—although I think I shall expect you to pay it back little by little.

Even though the lectures were often too pointed for comfort, and though it seemed at times that gradually sons and father were drifting further apart, there was a quality in the letters that made them cling in the memory. There was a blind reaching out for intimacy along with verbal chastisement.

So often such messages go astray. One writes something which comes from the bottom of the heart; and then, just because of some unfortunate turn of a phrase . . . the message never gets to the heart of the other.

Honor and stability of character were the things he preached. Sometimes, though infrequently, a religious note crept in:

As I get older I'm getting a good deal of comfort in finding how I can let the unimportant things drop away; then the vision clears. I am getting to *understand* Lincoln and Jefferson as I never did before—yes, and Jesus too. He seems so human. It seems to me so childish to make a God of him when he is so much bigger as a *man*, with the spirit of God moving him as it moves in all of us only we are not strong enough to let it guide us.

A touch of Unitarian doctrine perhaps, yet not compelling. The boys were free to go their own way to faith. Self-searching was the important thing. When a boy complained bitterly because he had failed of election to an important office in college life, Osborne suggested that the probable reason was that he did not deserve the honor, and quoted Shakespeare's Wolsey:

Had I but served my God with half the zeal
I served my King, he would not in mine age
Have left me naked to mine enemies.

These extracts give only one side of the picture. Osborne's letters were witty and gay as well as wise. Not only was he a master of apt quotation but he had a genius for coining pungent phrases and epigrams. Even his serious thoughts often ended with a humorous quirk that saved them from mere didacticism. After three years in Harvard one young Osborne began to be bored by the solemnity with which the Boston aristocracy regarded themselves and their place in nature's scheme. Confessing to his father that there were altogether too many Lowells and Cabots and Lodges for comfort, he received the following reply:

Your real true Bostonian is a queer party, and Boston is certainly the most provincial of places—but a pretty nice place after all. There is a fine side as well as a humorous side. . . . Mr. Eliot is a product of the New England Brahmin Caste—and you see you belong to it yourself if it comes to that. Your ancestors on both sides have been New Englanders for two hundred fifty years—except the dash of Pennsylvania Quaker which comes in Grandpa Wright. Do you know the story of the man who returned from Philadelphia and taking a friend aside, said, "For heaven's sake, what is a biddle?"

As the years passed, his sense of responsibility toward his sons increased rather than lessened. Manhood brought its own problems for them, one of the first being the choice of a career. It was then Osborne was struck with the terror of loneliness. The eldest son, David, who had been christened after his grandfather, married and took up his residence in New York City. Charles, the next in line, planned to take a position with a Boston firm. Lithgow selected the diplomatic service. Robert, the youngest, entered business in New York to support his young bride. It was a great comfort, therefore, when Charles yielded to his father's wishes and returned to Auburn to carry on as publisher of the family newspaper, the *Citizen*, bringing with him as wife the daughter of Barrett Wendell, celebrated professor of English at Harvard.

With the exception of Lithgow, all the boys saw military service in the World War. The former left Harvard in his senior year to become private secretary to James W. Gerard, ambassador to Germany. This was in 1914. Attracted by the exciting drama of diplomacy that was going on behind the curtain, he decided to take up a diplomatic career in his own right and succeeded in obtaining a post as third secretary of embassy under Gerard in Berlin. After three years of thrilling intrigue in war-mad Germany and a brief interlude in Havana, Cuba, he was transferred to Copenhagen, Denmark, as secretary of legation. It was there he met Lillie Raben, daughter of Count and Countess Raben-Levetzau, whose residence was the ancient castle of Aalholm. By a curious coincidence, the Countess, an American whose maiden name was Suzanne Moulton, was second cousin to Agnes Devens Osborne, Lithgow's mother, and had been her inseparable companion in their childhood days in Cambridge.

The romance which began against this background of world upheaval ended in the marriage of the young secretary and the talented daughter of the House of Raben-Levetzau. In 1922, after assignments with the American Peace Commission in Paris and the Arms Limitation Conference in Washington, Lithgow brought his wife to live in the old home in Auburn, where he joined his brother Charles in journalism and that more precarious vocation, politics.

Perhaps nothing in Osborne's relations with his sons was so remarkable as his fairness in judging disputes between them and others. He did not allow his natural prejudices to determine his position and would even take the part of an outsider against his own flesh and blood, if in his judgment justice lay on that side. The same trait was conspicuous in his attitude toward his daughters-in-law. During the inevitable discords that belong to the period of readjustment in married life, he played the rôle of an impartial adviser. If a misunderstanding threatened serious estrangement, he intervened with such sympathetic counsel, balancing the virtues and foibles of each party so justly, that even the wife could not look upon it as an intrusion. She soon learned that in him she had an honest arbiter and, if her cause justified it, a stanch advocate.

This fine balance is the more striking because of Osborne's own tendency toward pettishness in disagreements. He would haggle over a trivial point; his vanity was easily insulted; he played the game his way or would not play at all. The result was that his participation in the lighter activities of social life frequently led to squabbles. Yet this discrepancy is not uncommon in dynamic personalities. A true nobility in affairs of moment is often compensated by a petulance in trifling matters.

In a material way also Osborne showed his devotion to his sons. Some years before his death he settled upon them a large portion of the patrimony that would be their share of his estate, intending to leave the remainder to them in his will. Yet as he saw his grandchildren growing up, he suddenly felt a responsibility to the new generation. They were the important persons now, and their future should be taken care of, whatever happened. Only a few weeks before he died he changed his will, making a trust of all the property, the income to be used for the support and education of the grandchildren.

To evaluate Osborne's influence as a father would be impossible. One can only guess at it from little words and acts that betray how vividly he lives in the memory of the second and third generations. His sayings are treasured up and often quoted; his letters are carefully preserved that his children's children may yet have his guidance in time of trouble. Not always were the sons and daughters-in-law enthusiastic about his social experiments. They were often the victims of embarrassing situations arising directly from the use of his home as a laboratory for demonstrating the innate goodness of confidence men, forgers, and murderers. It has taken time to achieve a detached point of view and to correlate the man who signed himself "Your Pa" with the crusader the world knows. Now, aside from the clannish solidarity of the Osborne family, one cannot fail to be impressed by the unifying power of one man's example.

CHAPTER II

EXCURSIONS IN LITERATURE

IF catholicity of taste in reading were to be reckoned on the variety of books in one's library, Thomas Mott Osborne would be counted a man of diverse interests. In that spacious hall which in 1913 he added to his house in South Street to accommodate his large collection, there were books on nearly every subject under the sun—thousands of them, all neatly arranged in metal stacks and classified in an arbitrary fashion not recognized by professional librarians. Here was a first edition of Samuel Johnson's Dictionary; here a bound set of *Punch*, complete. Here were the Victorian novelists he so loved and the historians of many countries and numberless works on penology. The classics and the recent moderns had their place. Books on art, travel, and natural history—not forgetting Audubon's classic paintings of birds—filled the shelves. It was a book-lover's paradise.

Although Osborne loved books and took pride in the degree of Doctor of Literature conferred on him by Hobart College, he was not a bibliophile in the usual meaning of the word. He lacked a certain quality in his acquisitiveness. First editions were not sacrosanct unless the author and content won his admiration. Then they became memorials. He had a first edition of practically every book written by Scott, Dickens, Thackeray, and Trollope; but rare volumes by lesser authors interested him no more than first imprints of the works of most modern writers. For mere *curiosa* he had no inclination; and he was only mildly concerned about incunabula. Your passionate book collector, aghast to see hundreds of precious first editions bound uniformly in calf, might have been relieved had he looked inside. The original board or paper covers had been carefully preserved in rebinding. To Osborne it seemed quite fitting that a fine piece of literature should have a worthy covering.

In literature as in other fields he had strong prejudices. It was not indecency alone that disgusted him. His standards of excellence were largely Victorian, and he had little sympathy with those writers who were trying to break ground for a truly native literature, whether in romance or in realism. "It irritates me dreadfully," he wrote in 1899, "to think that 'Richard Carvel' and 'David Harum' are selling so like fury everywhere. They will all be consigned to what Carlyle calls the 'Limbo of forgotten vanities' long before the great books have lost their flavor." "The Honorable Peter Stirling" was "an irritatingly poor, good book." He hated the gloomy Russians and could not bring himself to read Tolstoi or "that man who wrote 'The Deluge' and 'Quo Vadis.' " Yet when "Trilby" appeared, he carefully clipped the sheets from *Harper's Magazine,* sent them to Henry Sotheran & Company, London, with an order that they be bound "in crush Levant, in brown, with the edges tooled on the inside in as artistic a manner as possible." Then he wrote Du Maurier and obtained from the author an autograph inscription on the title page. *There* was a masterpiece!

For all his fondness for reading, Osborne was never a prisoner in the world of books. It was not a refuge from reality he wanted, but a better understanding of reality. Books stimulated him, keyed him up to action. In one of the less quoted passages of his famous essay, Francis Bacon says, "Studies themselves do give forth directions too much at large, except they be bounded in by experience. . . . but that is a wisdom without them, and above them, won by observation." There is the secret to much of Osborne's influence on his generation. Men of action respected him because of his great store of learning. Men of learning respected him because his life was so largely a life of action.

It is only natural that one who so relished literature should feel the urge to create it himself. As a boy in his teens he showed considerable talent in his letters. Later he dabbled in comic opera lyrics. Even before he acquired the Auburn *Citi-*

zen, he was an inveterate writer-to-the-newspapers. Experiences abroad or adventures at home were likely to be recorded in a series of letters, sometimes published at a later date in book form. Interest in politics brought a number of magazine articles from his pen. Finally, the prison crusade gave him a subject on which he could speak with authority and with passion.

Yet, in general, he was better as a speaker than as a writer. When he wrote for publication, with, say, the *Atlantic Monthly* in mind, his style tended toward the verbose, especially when dealing with abstract themes. The frequency of literary allusions and favorite quotations was sometimes distracting and gave a rather formal note to the composition. Before an audience he spoke more naturally. It is significant, I think, that his best published book, *Society and Prisons*, should be a reworking of lectures delivered at Yale.

His letters and journals, however, have a genuine charm. In them a scholarly allusiveness is pleasantly combined with an easy, often colloquial, diction. They have the intimacy and the flavor of early nineteenth-century essays—something of Lamb's sensitiveness and Thackeray's humor. Unfortunately, being privately printed, these delightful accounts had small circulation. Osborne never seemed to consider them as a natural entrée into the profession of literature; rather as by-products for the amusement of his friends. Whether thoughts of publication made him grow serious or whether serious ideas made him think of publication, I am not sure; but the light vein in which he excelled manifested itself too infrequently in his published works. As his writings on penology form a special study, they will be excluded from the present chapter.

One of the first articles he succeeded in placing was an anonymous review of two books on football published in 1893. Just why Wendell Phillips Garrison of the *Nation* selected T. M. Osborne to comment on Walter Camp's "Book of College Sports" is a little obscure until one learns that the ex-Harvard contributor and the ex-Harvard editor had both a theory and a grudge. The theory was that football was being turned into a rough, bloody game by the abolition of the rule against "off-side play." The grudge was that Yale, by systematic violation of the rule, had brought about its abolition. Between them, they made Walter Camp the evil genius of football, a czar who had altogether too much power in the realm of sport. The brutality of "the shoving wedge," the malignancy of the low tackle, and the lack of delicacy exhibited by charging "rushers" they laid at the doorstep of the unsuspecting Mr. Camp. Lest it be imagined that Osborne did not realize how much he was influenced by the ancient feud between Harvard and Yale, it may be well to note his confession to Mr. Garrison. I feel, he wrote, much like the Englishman who exclaimed: "Thank God I am not prejudiced, but I hate a Frenchman!"

Most of his political writings got no further than publication in newspapers or in pamphlets for private distribution. In 1908, however, a few months before the national conventions, he was delighted to have the *Atlantic Monthly* accept an article entitled: "Has the Democratic Party a Future?" Needless to say, the answer was an emphatic *Yes*. It was rather a scholarly effort, somehow managing to trace the development of the party of Jefferson from the dawn of history to William Jennings Bryan. Every ointment has its proverbial fly, and much of Osborne's elation evaporated when ruthless *Atlantic* editors used the shears on his "choicest bit," a vitriolic assault on Theodore Roosevelt. He never quite forgave them; but then, he never could leave that man alone.

In the summer of 1907 Osborne took five young men, including his sons David and Charles, on a motor trip through Europe. At odd moments he jotted down notes of their wanderings—scraps of history, comment on customs and monuments and mountains, anecdotes of people. These were mailed home and appeared as a series of letters in the *Citizen*. In response to numerous requests, he had them printed in book form under the title, "Adventures of a Green Dragon"—the Green Dragon being a snorting Stevens-Duryea of the Noah's Ark variety capable of carrying a whole menagerie with room to spare. People of the countryside through which they passed would rush out to gape at this juggernaut, though amazement

sometimes changed to wrath when a dog or a hen showed its
religious zeal by committing suicide beneath its wheels.

Written "in all sorts of odd places—seated by the roadside
while tires were mended, in crowded hotels, in silent places
of the mountains, in the stuffy cabin of a steamer," these
articles show Osborne at his best as a writer. Even to-day, sur-
feited as we are with travelogues, they make pleasant reading;
for Osborne's nature had so many facets that he reflected an
experience from many angles. For him Europe was filled with
voices from history. Imagined characters from his reading
made every quaint village a meeting place with old friends.
"Oh, ye poor people that haven't read or 'don't care' for
Dickens, never come to England; for you will lose half the
fun."

It is not the narrative that makes these sketches live; it is
the personality of the writer. He laments blocking up beautiful Westminster Abbey with a lot of memorials of people who
are not buried there at all. As he contemplates the surrounding
effigies, one is reminded of Washington Irving standing in that
very spot nearly a century before, musing over "these casual
relics of antiquity . . . telling no tale but that such beings
had been, and had perished; teaching no moral but the futility of that pride which hopes still to exact homage in its
ashes, and to live in an inscription." Writes Osborne:

> Here lie those—kings and nobles, who with the largest oppor-
> tunities in life made the greatest failures; and here lie those who
> with the least advantages made such success that we still thrill with
> the glory of their deeds. Here, side by side, lie the warrior, honored
> for his success in destroying his fellowmen, and the physician
> honored for his success in saving them. Here is the politician who
> played upon the weakness of human nature, rising to power only to
> corrupt and degrade,—and here is the statesman, the record of
> whose long life is one of wisdom and purity.

Turning whimsical, he anticipates the doom of the British
nation:

> If it had been suggested to me six years ago that I should live to
> see discarded the sacred fatigue cap of the British soldier—that
> little round cap perched jauntily over one ear, with a narrow black

strap under the lips, and kept in place only by some extraordinary and unique application of the law of gravitation . . . and . . . replaced by a miserable imitation of a German military hat, I would have sworn that such a change could not take place without undermining the whole British Constitution. I think the Constitution must be in peril, for the change has taken place; and only the little messenger boys are left to save the country—they still wear their caps perched sideways over their right ears, as British soldier boys should. Tommy Atkins is no longer the soldier of my heart, now that his cap has gone. I wonder how the housemaids like the change. They certainly must miss that fascinating roll of the hair which went curling up on the left side.—But there! the subject must be dropped; it won't bear thinking of.

He lectures, in imagination, a young fellow who turns up at a drug store in search of a headache remedy, following a too strenuous night of "seeing Paris." For that sort of thing Osborne has the most profound scorn. It is all fake, anyway, from the fake students of the fake Latin Quarter to the fake riots quelled by fake policemen. Besides, there is nothing that can't be found in any other tenderloin; so why not gather headaches nearer home? In this "city of the average sensual man" he discerns everywhere a false note, now loud, now soft, but always present.

It is in the faces of the people, it is in the jokes of the comic papers, the pictures in the shop windows, on the stage and in the streets; it is in their art and their literature—a taint in the blood which it will take generations to wipe out.

So much for that thing called "the Gallic spirit"!

Before guiding the Green Dragon into Switzerland, he stands before the Cathedral of Reims, gazing moodily at the mass of scaffolding which indicates the structure is being "restored"— the beautiful old sculpturing being replaced by "smug, smooth, and uninteresting modern work." Why don't they preserve the old carvings? They have suffered enough from destruction without adding restoration.

Everywhere we go the demon of restoration pursues us. We could not see the great tower of Canterbury—they were restoring it; we could not see the front of Rouen Cathedral—they were restoring it; now we can't see the special glory of Reims—they are restoring it. Thank Heaven, they can't be restoring the Alps!

The joke of it is they are. Instead of driving leisurely through the clean valleys, and then climbing on foot up and up past ribbons of waterfall that flutter on the sheer mountain side, the party is hauled aloft by dirty, puffing engines; and Osborne pauses long enough to hurl anathema against all the efficient Swiss railways that have sacrificed a paradise to save time and shoe leather. To cap it all, at Mürren, where, before, the reward of hard climbing was solitude, there are hotels and dancing and tennis courts, and you have to dress for dinner. Ah, the pleasures of such hating! What a disappointment if you could not tell your young friends how much better were the old days!

So the Green Dragon, having spouted fire all over Europe, was at last stabled docilely in the hold of an ocean liner and transported to its native shores. If its memoirs have not the notoriety of that other monster slain by St. George, at least they have delighted a small and no doubt prejudiced public. As noted by the author in the foreword, his wares are not for all markets—but "them as don't want 'em needn't have 'em."

The same was true of "The Tale of a Green Duck," a serial narrative Osborne contributed to his paper three years later. Though it was never embellished by cloth covers, this story of a canoe (christened as a marine partner of the Stevens-Duryea) surpasses its predecessor in familiarity of style if not in interest. Written at leisure in moments of recollection, it follows the agreeable tradition of Stevenson's "Inland Voyage."

Osborne detested "roughing it." A passion for sailing he considered one form of insanity. He never felt impelled to give "that hitch to his trousers, which is a trick all seamen larn." "I was perfectly satisfied to stay on land and leave my trousers alone." Fishing belonged in the same category:

Many people apologize for themselves by saying that what they really enjoy is not so much the hooking of fish as it is "the breezy tramp along the streams and over the hills . . ." Then why fish? If what you want is a tramp over the hills, why not take a good walk and leave at home all those baskets and rods and pails and fish hooks and angle worms and things?

There was in him, however, a romantic gypsy craving. For a brief period it found satisfaction in wholesome outdoor jaunts whose discomforts he accepted with a jest and a laugh. The first of these was a canoe trip on the Susquehanna River from its source in Otsego Lake to Chesapeake Bay. It was in the summer of 1909, during his residence in Albany as public service commissioner. In the heat his duties began to pall, and the restlessness of his familiar, Louis Schaedeline, became irresistible. They had played the hobo together along the railway lines; now came a longing for the smell of damp earth and pine trees, the stillness of quiet valleys, and the glint of sun on the rapids.

It was with mingled emotions, nevertheless, that Osborne found himself dressed in khaki shirt, overalls, and high moccasins, squeezed between all sorts of duffel in the bow of a canoe—that most "preposterous sailing craft"—sometimes paddling with the current, sometimes pausing to cast a lure at a supercilious bass, and occasionally bowling along with sails set and the lee rail flirting with Susquehanna undines—or mermaids to that effect. He did enjoy it, though. Even the long hard hours of paddling, the foraging for straw to make a pallet, the unending warfare with mosquitoes, and "the total depravity of inanimate things," such as rocks that crept under your straw at night to poke you in the ribs or canoes that pushed themselves into the water at no provocation and left you stranded—even these things failed to destroy the fascination of that river odyssey. And what a curiously assorted pair they were—Schaedeline the Tramp, and Osborne the Millionaire! One, a healthy animal with an inborn lust for things of earth, untroubled by dreams; the other, interpreting every experience in the light of its cultural or ethical values.

"Tramp," I remark, as I extend myself at full length for a slight siesta, "what after all is better than a quiet conscience and a nap?"
"Lots of grub and a good digestion," replies the Tramp promptly.

Sometimes Lithgow or Bob would join the party for a while; sometimes Bill Dapping. Osborne could not absent himself from Albany for long. He would pick up the expedition at various points and stay with it until the call of duty grew too imperious. Then he would rush back to the state capital by train. One day he would be sweating over portages, getting lost at night in a swamp, or taking a sudden bath in the Susquehanna after shooting a rapid; the next, he would be the well-dressed, businesslike commissioner making up reports for the governor.

It is possible that the reader who likes an author to stick to his last may quarrel with one digression in "The Tale of a Green Duck." The New York *Sun* was to blame. One installment of the story evidently came into the hands of the editor. Now the *Sun* never had liked the Public Service Commission Law and was always eager to take a pot shot at anyone connected with it, especially Thomas Mott Osborne. He seemed to be the backbone of the system. Here was a chance to spear him and rub a little salt into the wound. In an editorial lampoon, the *Sun* ridiculed the Green Duck, the narrative, and the author. Characteristically, Osborne interrupted his story to strike back at the enemy, an action which provoked another editorial, this time tainted with malevolence. After enumerating all the less reputable varieties of duck, from mock to harlequin, in a pseudo-scientific attempt to arrive at the exact nature and species of the Green Duck, the *Sun* concluded:

In the end, however, we confess that all resemblances suggested in the foregoing varieties of duck fail. We know the Green Duck is accustomed to employ many disguises, but we suspect him in none of these. There remain, however, the *Erismatura rubida* or fool duck, and *Anas obscura* or dusky duck. All we know of "The Green Duck of the Susquehanna" stands forth unmistakable when we say softly the happy words *Anas obscura*.

Apropos of digressions, nearly half the narrative has a by-the-by quality. The actual events of the journey serve chiefly as an excuse for anecdote and incidental observation. Osborne had an amazing faculty for illustration, for apparently he remembered everything he saw or read, and could somehow find a neat application for it. The Tramp, for once having succumbed to a digestive ailment, is asleep in the bow of the canoe and Osborne wields the paddle alone through a long afternoon. The hills cast premature shadows over the valley, through which the Green Duck travels with its inert Tramp, its perspiring Charon.

"And the Dead, steered by the Dumb, went upward with the flood." So I muttered to myself, and added: "Except that he isn't dead and I'm not dumb—and we are going down stream, not up—and there isn't any tide or flood—that is a singularly apt quotation." It is odd how sometimes the musical flow of a line will haunt the brain as an appropriate accompaniment of a situation even when the words are quite out of keeping.

So he runs on, amiably inconsequential (except when the *Sun* blisters him), playing the noble savage with his body, the gentleman of culture with his brain. One might follow this pair through "The Adventures of Two Dragon Fliers," an account of a motorcycle trip in Europe, with Osborne reveling in the sight of the Tramp, now appropriately rechristened Logan after the famous Cayuga Indian, bringing something aboriginal to the effete civilization of the Continent; rocketing through remote provinces where motorcycles had never even been heard of; commenting in his freest vein on the passing panorama. He will never be so unpreoccupied again. There will be no more rambles for pure joyousness. Thoughts assail him. Purposes twist the sinews of his heart. He writes with his fist, exhorting and denouncing. And when, his strength spent, he sees men tearing down what he has built, he takes his pen for the last time, dips it in gall, and writes a book justifying himself, execrating his enemies—a bitter book and, from his point of view, a just book. But you will look in it in vain for the author of "The Green Dragon" and "The Green Duck."

CHAPTER III

THE KINDLIER HAND

THIS chapter shall be largely anonymous, as Osborne would wish it to be; for it will deal with the subject of benefactions —a delicate theme for both donor and recipient, particularly in this case. Many wealthy men are content to make partial payments on their debt to society through contributions to organized welfare agencies. Though Osborne participated in more charitable enterprises than his purse warranted, the major part of his beneficence was personal. It was always the individual rather than the institution that interested him. Besides, most of the social service of the day was directed to relieving distress. He was more concerned with preventing it. Even that is too negative a statement. He was concerned with potentialities—with young men and young women who, given the training and opportunity, might find a useful place in society.

It is true that persons with artistic talent attracted him; yet he did not make his generosity contingent upon marks of genius. Individuals of average intelligence who were denied privileges of advancement through lack of funds outnumbered the prodigies. It would be idle, even if it were possible, to list those who have been educated in their respective vocations in part or in whole at Osborne's expense. In most cases the philanthropy was unobtrusive, almost surreptitious. There are doctors, lawyers, newspaper editors, business men, politicians, and others who owe their present standing to opportunities for development provided by their benefactor.

Not always, however, has gratitude been his reward. In later years he frequently found among his foes the very men to whom he had reached a helping hand. Osborne would have been the last to presume that charity obligates servility. Nevertheless, he had the right to expect a certain amount of forbearance from those whose opinions were held in respect chiefly because of his own services in their behalf. Sincere opposition did not hurt him; it was the personal rancor that sometimes embittered an otherwise impersonal dispute. Learning the truth of Emerson's surmise that "we do not quite forgive a giver," he was perhaps less inclined to consider betrayal at the hands of a convict as an exclusive sign of criminality.

He was criticized, of course—sometimes quite honestly. Once a friend overheard a man complaining that, though Osborne was undoubtedly generous, he never did much to help local people. Knowing that most of the philanthropy was secret, the friend determined to discover just how extensive it was. A check-up revealed that in Auburn alone Osborne had about $75,000 outstanding in small loans, the majority of them averaging only a few hundred dollars each. In the course of time many of these debts would be written off—unable to pay; or the canceled notes presented as graduation or wedding presents—frequently with a substantial gift thrown in.

The character of his assistance varied with the individual. One he would establish in business by advancing unsecured loans. Another he would send to school or college. Those who showed special promise were enabled to carry on their studies here or abroad. Osborne had a flair for recognizing talent. Prominent among his protégés is the American tenor, Charles Hubbard, who resides in Paris. Born in Auburn, Hubbard has become the popular choice of leading French composers for creating the first interpretation of their work. He is the first American to be appointed judge of the Paris and Lyons conservatories of music. In 1928, Sarah Bernhardt's château on Belle-Ile-en-Mer off the coast of Brittany was opened for the first time since the actress's death for a summer school under Hubbard's direction.

In spite of the extent of his charities, Osborne took good care that there was no pauperizing. He did not encourage pensioners. When he advanced a loan or gave outright, it was for an emergency. If the recipient showed no inclination to help himself, he was crossed off the list. Generally a careful record of how he spent his money and how he used his spare time was required. In judging the temperament of those he aided Osborne showed an uncanny shrewdness. To some he granted considerable latitude; others he put through a strenuous training.

One day he discovered that a young German immigrant who was working in an Auburn shoe shop could play the violin surprisingly well for one of his years. The boy's name was Peter Kurtz. Osborne took him home, played Beethoven for him, and was delighted to find an eager response. Fearing that Peter might injure his fingers in the shoe shop, he gave him a minor position in the collection department of D. M. Osborne & Co. Though he kept close track of the boy and encouraged him in practicing, he was careful not to give him much money.

"Peter," he said, "you're the sort of fellow who goes along easy, thinking you'll always find a pillow to fall on. I'm the pillow. You've got to learn to get ahead by yourself."

So Peter kept at it, lugging his violin to the office and playing during the luncheon hour—until the catastrophe. D. M. Osborne & Co. was about to institute a suit against a debtor. Young Kurtz was deputized to send all the evidence against the debtor to the defendant's attorney, and all the possible arguments in reply, to the company's lawyer. The amazing thing about farces, as Chesterton said about miracles, is that they happen. Peter mixed the envelopes and all hope for winning the suit went glimmering. So did the boy's chances for holding his job. His boss raved. Osborne called in the culprit and regarded him with a rueful smile.

"I guess," he said, "that business and fiddling don't mix after all. Well, one can't have everything."

The upshot of it was that Osborne sent Peter Kurtz to his old friend Walter Damrosch, conductor of the New York Symphony Orchestra. Peter left Auburn for New York with less than three dollars in his pocket. Osborne's share in that capital was one silver dollar; but he had arranged to have the composer, Arthur Farwell, another protégé in the shaping of whose career he had much to do, meet the boy and get him a job.

Kurtz became bell-boy and odd-job man in a wealthy private family, doing the most menial tasks all day, practicing on the violin much of the night. Besides, he had a few hours off each week for lessons under David Mannes, the Concertmeister who had recently married Damrosch's sister. In the summer, he joined the Damrosch-Mannes ménage at their summer home on Long Island, where he worked for his board and continued his violin lessons.

In a year Kurtz had made such progress that Mannes made him his assistant instructor. A few years later, shortly after he had turned twenty, he received a call from Richard Mansfield. Mansfield had invested $60,000 in what was perhaps his most ambitious enterprise, the first American production of "Peer Gynt." Looking about him for a conductor who had youth and poetry, he selected Osborne's protégé. The play opened in Chicago. When the curtain rose on the first-night performance in New York, Peter Kurtz felt his knees sag. There were all the famous conductors, critics, and music pundits of the East. And there too was Osborne. But he survived, and toured the United States with "Peer Gynt." Just before the company was to set out for London, Richard Mansfield died.

If the story is not unique, it illustrates the attention Osborne paid to individual traits of character. It was no accident that Kurtz had to fend for himself and undergo hardships from which his benefactor might easily have saved him. It was part of a training that Osborne realized this easy-going dreamer needed. But he did make sure that the boy would lack no opportunity for the best possible instruction. Not until later did Kurtz realize that his service in the Damrosch home would scarcely pay his board, to say nothing of recompensing the great Mannes.

On two things Osborne insisted: honesty and industry. A suspicion on either count, and financial aid ceased. One young man lost a college education because of evidence that he cribbed in a high-school examination. There was no appeal from Osborne's verdict, once given. When he came to deal with prison inmates, it was a different matter. *Unconvicted* culprits were rarely offered a second chance. Right and wrong were so plain to him that the slightest obliquity signified moral corruption. Whom he could not trust, he would not aid.

He drew also a sharp line between charity and commercial transactions. The two did not blend. When he contracted for the performance of a service, he expected to receive full value. He would enter into protracted correspondence over a matter of a few cents' difference in a small bill. If a purchase did not measure up to specifications, there were sharp and insistent demands for a rebate. Generous to a fault, of his own volition, he demanded an exact accounting of business affairs, great or small.

A now famous American painter, low in funds after a course of study abroad, received his first important assignment from Osborne. He came to Auburn to do the latter's portrait, glad that someone had recognized his talent. Just before the final touches were put on the painting, he ventured to ask for his pay, confident that the work already done and his own lack of funds justified the request. Instead of cash he received a solemn lecture on the ethics of delivering goods in perfect condition before accepting any payment. Chastened in soul, the artist went back to his easel and set to work. Now that he can name his own price for a picture, he is inclined to believe that this early lesson in business ethics was one of the more valuable experiences in his career.

There was a sanity in Osborne's homilies that took the sting out of reproof; yet he knew when the time for words had passed. One evening a local artist whom he had often befriended came to him with a tale of woe. It was a case of blues aggravated by artistic temperament and high-strung nerves. Life, apparently, had nothing to offer. All hope was dead. But Osborne failed to be deeply impressed.

"All right!" shouted the artist. "I'm going to kill myself!" And he started for the door.

"Well," observed his friend reflectively, "it's a great night for it."

Nevertheless he sent Louis Schaedeline to trail the man and make sure the suicide threat was not carried out. It wasn't. After a few blocks in the direction of the river, the painter's steps lagged, stopped. He turned back and got a drink. The black cloud had passed.

Injustice made the surest appeal to Osborne's sympathies. Just prior to the turn of the century there was working in one of the Auburn shoe stores a young clerk whose comic antics made him locally popular in amateur theatricals. Before many years passed the shoe clerk became America's favorite star of the musical comedy stage—Raymond Hitchcock. Osborne had watched his rise with satisfaction, and was delighted when "The Yankee Consul" took the country by storm. At the very height of his career, Hitchcock was threatened with absolute ruin. Charges were lodged against him of so vile a character that conviction meant a long prison sentence.

Osborne could not believe the charges. Neither could his friend, Frank W. Richardson. Together they employed an able and unprejudiced investigator to learn the truth. When the report came that all evidence pointed to Hitchcock's innocence, Osborne lent the actor $10,000 with which to defend the suit, and was almost as gratified as the defendant himself by the verdict of acquittal which the jury rendered. Afterward he kept in close touch with Hitchcock and was always ready with advice or funds in case of need.

The impulse to give and the impulse to instruct were closely associated in Osborne. Invariably a present was accompanied by a moral discourse, either oral or written. Those who were enjoying his generosity were supposed to write him regularly, reporting their progress and their difficulties. In return they received advice—not simply abstract principles, but suggestions as to the immediate problems confronting them.

This didactic urge found expression in still another way. For years Osborne taught a men's class in the Universalist Church. It proved so popular that over a hundred members, recruited from various denominations, attended the Sunday meetings. Caring little for doctrine or for the formalities of religion, he was still deeply religious at heart. He had no doubts on the fundamentals. There *was* a divine presence. There *was* a benevolent force in the world. Call it what one might, a Something was at work in the souls of men, urging them to better living. Conduct that was antisocial was therefore anti-God. Here was the starting point of his class lectures. He presented concrete problems, involving morals and ethics. Academic the arguments might be, but they were pertinent enough to hold the interest of a large body of men over a long period. Old members will still tell you that nothing in their religious experience made so deep an impression as these Sunday discussions under the guidance of Thomas Mott Osborne.

Time and money. Osborne spent freely of each—too freely for his own good. Other men have contributed larger totals to philanthropy, but few have given so great a share of their principal. When D. M. Osborne & Co. was sold to International Harvester, his share was over one million dollars. Added to his other reserves, it represented a good-sized fortune for those days. But there was one thing he preached that he did not practice: living within one's income. By degrees the fortune shrank until there was danger it might vanish completely. His secretaries did what they could to stop the trickle that was sometimes much more than a trickle. But what can you do with a man who one day goes out and for purely sentimental reasons buys a bank? Even if it happens to be a very old bank, one of the oldest in the state in fact; and even if there are rumors it may have to close its doors—is that any reason a man should risk his independence to preserve a landmark? In this instance, as if to put his critics out of countenance, it turned out to be not a bad investment. Reorganized, with new officers and a complete overhauling of the books, it kept its head above water and now, consolidated with another bank, is one of the outstanding institutions of its class in the region. That, however, is incidental and fortuitous. Osborne bought it because he loved Auburn.

Not many of his ventures turned out so happily. In order to provide the city with a supply of pasteurized milk, he sank over $100,000 in the Cayuga County Dairy Company. The project was too far ahead of its time. When failure loomed, Osborne began buying back from his friends and acquaintances the stock they had purchased. In the end he lost every nickel he had put into it.

Another project, though manifestly impracticable, was close to his heart. He kept recurring to the idea of making his old home into a school for boys. The fact that it would be difficult if not impossible to cut the large, high-ceilinged rooms into sufficient compartments to serve school purposes did not deter him. It was his plan to bring boys from the slums and establish them as non-paying students. The total expense would be borne by another class—paying students of wealthy families. Even if wealthy fathers and mothers could be found who desired their carefully nurtured offspring to be educated among and by urchins from the slums, the accommodations after the influx of the non-paying pupils would be so limited that cost of tuition would be well-nigh prohibitive.

Still Osborne was not deterred. He was continually inviting prospective headmasters to look over the plant, and was prevented from hiring them on the spot only by the vehement protests of his boys. Once he actually went so far as to engage one. Then his secretary took a hand. Suggesting that Mr. Osborne was suffering from a heart ailment and was likely to drop off any day, leaving chaos and financial ruin behind, he threw such a scare into the pedagogue that the latter promptly withdrew from the enterprise. Still, the subject kept coming up. Until his death the school idea fascinated Osborne.

Among other properties, he had inherited the town's chief hostelry, the Osborne House. He now had a newspaper, a bank, and a hotel. How he would have liked to touch a match to that hotel! Every day, what with repairs, and taxes, and the like, it was growing more and more to resemble the sacred beast of Siam. But he didn't burn it. Instead, he built a theater. It was a nice theater, well arranged and equipped, and dedicated to the proposition that an intelligent public will support the best in musical and dramatic entertainment. For a time it served a good purpose, but eventually it went the way of all provincial playhouses; first the silent flickers supplemented by vaudeville; then the talkies.

With all his charities and his investments, most of which were made for sentimental or philanthropic reasons, Osborne was rapidly depleting his principal. He would invest $10,000 or so in almost any business, provided it appealed to his imagination, or the entrepreneur to his sympathies. The prison crusade was to cost him several hundred thousand dollars. Fortunately, the newspaper was making money; and at his death, despite previous allotments to his sons, there was enough left to provide a number of bequests of the sort one would expect from such a man. Typical of these is the fund he established for aiding community enterprises of a cultural nature. Originally part of a sum advanced by him and his two sisters for sustaining the Woman's Educational and Industrial Union in Auburn, it was later withdrawn and set aside for its present purpose. Under the broad terms of the foundation, the income has been used in recent years to help finance community concert courses and to provide scholarships for deserving children in an experimental grade school. So, in a sense, though not exactly as he had dreamed, his desire to promote an educational project has been posthumously gratified.

Perhaps behind the largess and the preachment there was the same impetus that in his later years was to manifest itself in prison reform. If so, it was not particularly noticeable to Osborne's associates. He seemed a man acutely conscious of the obligations his wealth and culture imposed upon him, but scarcely a crusader. In 1909, at the twenty-fifth anniversary of the Harvard class of '84, his friend John Jay Chapman delivered an address of which the following stanzas were a part:

> *Osborne, of thee we had expected much;*
> *Even in thy youth, before the fates declared*
> *The meaning of a brow that wore a touch*
> *Of sadness and of talent, we had dared*
> *To prophesy some mystic gain for thee;*
> *I know not what,—some palm, some victory.*

And thou hast overrun all expectation,
Not in the brightness of a single deed,
But in the wealth and richness of donation
That has a hand for every human need;
And like a vine that hangs above the street
Blossoms in charities that make the world smell sweet.

"Not in the brightness of a single deed." No, that was still to come; but all were aware of "the larger heart, the kindlier hand" which responded to human need.

CHAPTER IV

THE GEORGE JUNIOR REPUBLIC

OSBORNE's conception of good citizenship included the responsibility of developing good citizens. The missionary spirit of the Coffins and the Motts made it impossible for him to rest content with being a passive model; he had to preach the gospel. Yet his first efforts left a feeling of disappointment.

Charity alone did not build good citizens. He found many of those whom he had helped financially coming back for more with uncomfortable regularity. One young graduate of Elmira Reformatory attracted his attention by writing a farewell editorial in the institution's paper, *The Summary*. Having undertaken to guide the boy's destiny, Osborne was at first irritated and finally discouraged by repeated demands for "loans." "After many unpleasant experiences in trying to help one and another," he confessed, "I have been driven to the belief that help in money is nine times out of ten a mistake."

Good advice, even when eliciting promises of exemplary conduct, he discovered equally ineffective. Too often disappointed by relapses, he at last took refuge in the philosophy, "Fair words butter no parsnips."

In the meantime, William R. George had arrived at the same conclusion. George had been born on a farm in West Dryden, New York, not many miles from Auburn, and at the age of fourteen removed with his family to New York City. Rebelling against the set regimen of preparatory school and college, he had turned his energies directly to things that interested him, chiefly social work among small boys in the slums. It was in August, 1890, that he began what was to develop into the most interesting social experiment of the time. With the help of the

Tribune Fresh Air Fund he took about fifty boys and girls into the country, housing them in a building which a friend had turned over to him. This was at Freeville, in the region where George had spent his boyhood.

At first there was nothing to distinguish it from other fresh-air camps, except that the children lived under one roof instead of being farmed out to neighborhood families. During the next few years the size of the settlement increased, several cottages being added to the plant. Still, George felt something was lacking. The more he did for the boys, and the greater the generosity of the people in the neighborhood in contributing clothing, pets, and playthings, the louder the urchins clamored for more. He came to the astonishing conclusion that not only was he doing them no good but he was actually doing them harm. They had come to estimate their good time by the amount of things people gave them. Something had to be done, or he would give up the experiment.

When the allotment of children arrived in 1894, they were confronted by a pile of picks and shovels. It was to be something for nothing no longer. Work or go without. How the rebellion against such an idea was finally checked, and how in the following years there developed a self-containing republic modeled, in its "restricted geography," after the large republic has been told too well in Mr. George's own book, "The Junior Republic," to be rehearsed here in detail. People who had scoffed when he first unfolded his plan became enthusiastic supporters. The fame of "Daddy" George and his Republic spread over the country and across the water.

Osborne first heard of the experiment in 1896. During a trip abroad following the death of his wife, he read an account of it in a magazine. It was something of a coincidence, therefore, when shortly after his return he was approached by his old friend, Frank W. Richardson, already a member of the governing board, with an invitation to visit the Freeville settlement. Osborne's reaction to what he found in the Republic was immediately favorable. Here was the principle toward which he himself had been groping for a number of years. Give youth responsibility, and it will rise to the emergency.

No pauperizing. No fair words and unbuttered parsnips. Instead, a system of rewards and penalties based on individual effort, the important feature being that such rewards and penalties were not the result of interference by outsiders but of the operation of economic laws and the direct decree of the citizens themselves as in the greater republic.

When Osborne accepted a post on the Board of Trustees, the Republic had been under the new policy for two years. From a place of recreation for the underprivileged it had changed to an educational *gymnasium*. Attendance of boys from good families was solicited, with the promise that the training they would receive would be unique, and that for many a college education would be made available through the generosity of philanthropic backers. Because many of the citizens were boys of high ideals, a system of self-government was in successful operation. All officers except the president were elected, and soon even the chief executive was chosen by popular vote. The Republic had its own code of laws, a police force, a judge, trial by jury, and a jail for convicted offenders. Even those citizens who had been considered difficult at home responded to the new responsibilities citizenship placed upon them.

It all began with the sense of private property. When a boy received a commodity in return for work accomplished, he looked upon it as peculiarly his own, and he was unwilling to let it out of his possession without adequate compensation. That led to the idea of laws, for as one East-sider expressed it: "It ain't right for guys what work to get things swiped by guys what don't." In reform schools, inmates are accustomed to boast of the bold, bad things they have done. A newcomer to the Junior Republic tried that only once. Instead of finding open-mouthed awe at his exploits, he discovered he was an outcast among his fellows. "Better watch that guy," the citizens would say to one another; "he's liable to steal yer coat right off yer back." They had earned those coats and weren't going to have any hard guys swiping them. By a natural progression they advanced from an attitude of doing right for policy's sake to that of doing right for right's sake.

Osborne took office in the middle of a campaign that had for him a peculiar significance. While the country at large was fighting over the free-silver issue, the Junior Republic was in the throes of what Daddy George christened "the free-tin movement." The citizens had a currency of their own which consisted at that time of tin tokens representing the various coins of the realm. As more and more of this money came into circulation in payment for work done on the premises, and as there was no outlet for it save in the Republic, inflation was inevitable. Values became meaningless, and the government in power was inclined to play free and loose with its accumulated funds. The Free Tinners favored maintaining this arrangement and found inspiration in the oratory of a young Irish lad named Jimmy Dolan. The opposition, known as the People's Party, desired to retire a large portion of the currency. Their leader was Jacob Smith, whose judicious conservatism had led to his appointment as first president of the Republic. Although the Free Tinners won the first battle in a bitterly contested election, the abuses became so apparent that eventually a majority of the sober citizens appealed to Mr. George to abolish the system. Since then "sound money" has been the Republic policy, with an aluminum currency taking the place of the old tin tokens.

It was a relief for Osborne to throw himself into the Republic work. Not only did it take his mind off his sorrow, but it provided an ideal in which he had absolute faith. In behalf of the project he lectured throughout the country, wrote articles, gave generously of his own wealth, and became the most active member of the Board of Trustees. In 1897 he was elected president of the Board, an office which he held until 1913. As head of the Executive Committee, he was largely responsible for administrative policies. Always he stood with Daddy George against any proposal that threatened to institutionalize the Republic. So far as possible there was no interference with the self-running machinery which had been set up. Even when there was danger that the citizens would act unwisely or unjustly, he would not abrogate their rights.

One of the functions of the Executive Committee was to act

as a Supreme Court. It was a privilege of the defendant to appeal from the verdict of the lower court and ask for a review of his case. In one instance the lower court had found a citizen guilty as a third offender. The case was appealed. Now the laws of the Republic are based on the New York State code, and the accused knew his rights. He brought out that a careless clerk had lost the records of his second conviction; therefore he could not be tried as a third offender. Though it was a technicality, and though everyone knew the boy was guilty of the violations charged against him, Osborne admitted the legality of the plea, and prevailed upon his associate judges to set aside the verdict. He did, however, administer a thorough tongue-lashing.

It was this spirit of absolute fairness that won the boys' hearts. Besides, he was so often among them that they accepted him with Daddy George as an intimate part of the Republic. Before his political activities put extraordinary demands on his time, it was often his custom to wheel over the miles from Auburn to Freeville on his bicycle and arrive in a whirl of dust. There would be shouts of "Here's Uncle Tom!" and in a moment he was surrounded. It made no difference how bad a boy's reputation was; he received as warm a greeting. In fact, one suspects Osborne was delighted when the Republic began to accept unmanageable sons of good families, and even more when it took youthful offenders who otherwise would have been committed to a reform school. Already badness was interesting him as a phenomenon.

"It's funny," one citizen remarked, "but if a fellow's in jail or is awful tough, he's just Uncle Tom's kind."

He did not, however, make the mistake of pampering culprits by trying to save them from the results of their wrongdoing. His attitude is best expressed in a letter to a citizen who for good reasons was sojourning in the Republic jail. "Not that you don't deserve your punishment," he wrote, "for you do; but I wish that you did not have to be punished."

Osborne was not so preoccupied with young scapegraces that he overlooked boys of more admirable character. Out of his associations with the citizens of the Republic came a lifelong friendship. Qualities of leadership always attracted him, especially when accompanied by a courage that mere numbers could not daunt—the courage of the minority. He respected Jacob Smith for his cool judgment and dependability; but his heart went out to another boy—one who could always be found leading the liberal wing.

William O. Dapping was one of the boys who at Daddy George's invitation had come to the Republic for an education in practical civics as well as in book learning. Earnest and studious, he entered eagerly into the life of the community, and before long had built up such a following that he defeated Jacob Smith in a presidential election. Dapping took his new responsibilities seriously. Through his efforts the unwieldy system of representative government was changed to that of the town meeting, a method far better adapted to the conditions of so small a republic.

Osborne's first impressions of this young man were borne out by the close associations of three decades. After Dapping had served as instructor and librarian at the Republic, with a year of study at Dryden High School, Osborne invited him to Auburn. The program of education he mapped out for his protégé was nothing if not comprehensive. Building upon the foundation established in the Republic, he sent the boy to Auburn High School, later to a military academy at Fort Plain, New York, then to the Hackley School, and finally to Harvard. During school and college vacations, the boy lived at the Osborne home tutoring his patron's sons. Immediately following his graduation from Harvard in 1905, he returned to Auburn to work on the *Citizen,* the newspaper which Osborne had just established.

Since 1915 he has been managing editor, and though he has never entered active politics, his fearless and often pugnacious editorial policies have had a great influence in the region. In the main he has fought for the principles Osborne stood for, among them nonpartisanship in municipal elections. In the field of journalism he has won distinction outside the small territory covered by the *Citizen.* It was he who first flashed to the world the news of the Auburn Prison riot of December,

1929, an account of which prefaces this book. For that reportorial feat he received signal honors from the Associated Press and was awarded the coveted Pulitzer Prize. As founder and director of a coöperative buying association of New York State dailies, he is now revolutionizing the purchasing processes of the newspaper business.

In a life which has been full of industry, Dapping has not forgotten the George Junior Republic. Fifteen years as president of the Executive Committee have discharged the debt. This was as Osborne wished; for when the latter severed his connection with the Republic, he wanted a proxy who could keep him in touch with affairs at Freeville.

Such a revolutionary experiment as the George Junior Republic was bound to bring criticism. As early as 1897 a hostile article in a newspaper brought an investigation by the State Board of Charities. The report was unfavorable. Accustomed to the disciplinary methods of the reform school, the investigators could not comprehend what was going on under the surface. They saw boy merchants retailing goods for little tin disks, boy farmers tilling the fields, boy workmen laboring in the shops, boy policemen arresting boy malefactors, boy lawyers arguing cases before boy judges, and boy guards chaperoning prison squads. That was dangerous. Where were the adult keepers? Why, there might be a general uprising! Besides, at that early date, the physical plant was not impressive. Conditions should be improved.

For a long time the Republic was the center of numerous controversies. One of the most vexing attacks, because of the position of the critic, occurred in 1903. The Rev. G. M. Newman, a former assistant of Daddy George's, lodged a charge of cruel treatment and insanitary conditions. Though the accusations, except in respect to the condition of the jail, were indignantly denied, the effect on public sentiment was unfortunate.

Of far greater notoriety, however, was the case of Alexander Stewart. Osborne was largely responsible for that. Stewart had been committed to the House of Refuge in New York City. While there he had slashed a boy's throat, and at the age of fifteen or sixteen was sentenced to serve forty years in state's prison. To George's astonishment Osborne suggested taking the youth into the Junior Republic. Fearing the effects such publicity would have, George at first demurred but finally gave his consent. The Board of Trustees were not so amenable. It seemed to them a fantastic thing to do, full of peril for the future of the Republic. Ex-citizens, many of them college men, protested. It was not the purpose of the Republic, they argued, to accept boys of violent criminal tendencies. To do so would put a black eye on both the settlement and the citizens.

Nevertheless, Osborne won his point. Obtaining from Governor Higgins a conditional pardon for Stewart, with the understanding that the Republic should take full responsibility, he brought the young murderer to Freeville. The results of attempting such a drastic experiment in reform were not too encouraging. Several times Stewart ran away, and until he was captured the neighborhood was terrified with the thought of a killer on the loose. Once or twice a knife was discovered on his person. He was found to be a dope fiend. At last it was necessary to send him to Auburn Prison. In spite of public criticism Osborne stood by the boy through thick and thin. He would never admit that Stewart was irreclaimable.

Mr. George was undeterred by the obstacles he encountered. Aside from a loyal Board of Trustees who stood by him on most matters, he had the personal encouragement of Jacob Riis and Theodore Roosevelt. Gradually, as money came in, the Republic extended its area to many acres of good farming land, built new cottages, barns, shops, and "hotels." Professors and students of the College of Agriculture at Cornell University coöperated with advice concerning farm problems. In New York City the National Association of Junior Republics, with Osborne as president, was organized with the purpose of establishing other republics in different parts of the country.

Though the extension idea was a logical development of the Junior Republic experiment, it was to widen a breach between Daddy George and Osborne that had started during a crucial period of the Republic's history. At first there had been two phases of the work: the summer camp and the permanent settlement. As time went on, it became apparent that for efficiency's sake the two projects should be separated. Dropping its "summer residents," the Republic carried on as a permanent organization. With Mr. George's marriage in 1896, girls were accepted as residents and housed in a cottage under the maternal eye of Mrs. George. Without female population and natural social contacts between the sexes, argued Mr. George, the Republic would not be a true republic at all.

At first only girls of good family and high character were admitted, but as the coeducational idea expanded, the Republic accepted a number of girls who had been ticketed as wayward. A flareback was inevitable. There were those who felt that the original intent of the Junior Republic idea was being perverted. The very thought of bringing young persons of such character into contact with adolescent boys was shocking. They suspected goings-on, and their suspicions developed into rumors. Although in the long history of the Republic but one or two cases of immorality have come to light, the situation encouraged the presumption. It ended with charges being lodged against Mr. George himself.

From the outset Osborne was convinced of his colleague's innocence. The accusation had come from a malcontent citizen. Everything in the past argued against the truth of the allegation. Still, as president of the Board he was compelled to conduct an unbiased investigation. This in itself caused a tension between the two men that was increased by interference from certain wealthy backers who disapproved of George on grounds of Republic policy.

However mistaken Osborne may have been, it was with the best of intentions that he tried to keep the probe secret among Board members and friends of the Republic. It could not be kept secret. A New York newspaper got wind of it and sent a reporter to Auburn. He arrived with a batch of data he had collected as a foundation for his story. When Osborne heard what the reporter proposed to write, he was aghast. Much of it was false; some of it so unfair to Mr. George that it was libelous. In distress he undertook to point out the manifest injustices of the account, referring to his own notes on the investigation. Relying on the integrity of the newspaper, he explained in confidence the background of the case. At least he could save his friend from malicious falsehoods.

It was a sorry effort. When the article appeared, its intimate treatment of many angles of the investigation made it look as if Osborne himself had released the whole story. Mr. George could put no other construction on it. Neither man ever recovered from the bitterness of this parting. As for the Republic, it received a setback not alone from the unfavorable publicity but from the rift between its two best friends. A controversy developed, with adherents on each side adding fuel to the flames. Even the final repudiation of the charges failed to bring about the solidarity which had previously existed.

In spite of this, Osborne continued in his position as president of the Board, working in comparative harmony with Daddy George. For many of the boys he found jobs in his own factory, D. M. Osborne & Co. In time the number of Republic graduates in Auburn grew so large, with new recruits being added yearly, that he founded the Auburn Junior Republic Club with comfortable headquarters close to the Osborne works. Though the ultimate purpose was to maintain Republic ideals, the activities of the A.J.R.C. were largely of a sociable, even picaresque, character. Osborne himself invented some satanic initiation rights, drawing freely on the Dickey Club formula, still well remembered after these many years. His own part in the ceremonials may be guessed at. He was "the unknown stranger." Again he had found an excuse for his repertory of impersonations.

Initiations, however, were too far apart to satisfy his fondness for masquerade. One day he disguised himself as an Italian organ grinder—old corduroy breeches, tattered shirt, flowing mustachios, swarthy complexion, and all. Dressed in this outfit, and carrying an old hand-organ he had managed to pick up somewhere in New York, he bought a ticket for Freeville and boarded the train at Auburn. Dapping, who alone was in the secret, caught the same train in order to keep an eye on him. Everything went along smoothly until the conductor caught sight of the itinerant Italian. Then Osborne was ordered to quit the coach and make the trip in the baggage car. He complied with a full display of Latin protestations and gesturing.

At the Freeville station Dapping lost sight of the vagabond, but as he trudged up the hill he could hear the notes of the organ grinding out its tinny tunes through the village streets. It was afternoon before Osborne arrived at the Republic, the proud possessor of some thirty cents he had collected on the way. Immediately a throng of citizens gathered about him.

"Where's a da monk?" shouted someone.

"Aw, leave him alone," another protested. "Look at the poor wop. Why, he ain't hardly got any shirt at all."

Some sympathetic soul, struck with the Italian's pitiable condition, disappeared for a moment. When he returned he carried a clean shirt that still had some good wear in it. The organ grinder accepted the donation gratefully, with tears in his eyes—though possibly they were tears of laughter.

If such eccentricities had been merely the stock in trade of a practical joker, the finales would have been different. Few could have resisted the lure of the great revelation scene. Not so Osborne. He was the artist, and would not drop out of his rôle for a cheap theatrical effect. Bidding adieu to his charmed audience, he picked up his barrel-organ and started down the hill, a wandering minstrel to the last. As they heard the music die away, not one of the citizens guessed they had befriended their own patron. Even when the identity of the organ grinder was at last revealed, they could scarcely believe it until Dapping produced some snapshots he had taken of the scene and told the whole story.

Unfortunately a new point of friction developed between Osborne and George with the expansion of the Junior Republic idea. The plan was for George to resign and devote his full time to developing similar projects in various sections of the country. A part of the Freeville grounds was set aside for experimental use by organizers of the new republics. Officers were to bring their charges to Freeville and begin their work under the eye of those trained in the system. When they had grasped the idea, they could then move to their permanent location. This probationary period was considered essential to the success of the extension idea.

As Daddy George continued to make his headquarters at Freeville, where he could keep close watch over the experimental colonies, his relations with the original unit were still intimate. In fact, so long had he been accustomed to directing the destiny of the Junior Republic that he just couldn't keep his hands off. It was habit. Besides, his chief interest was there. When he saw his successor introduce some policy which he believed unwise, he naturally stepped in and countermanded the order. Was not this his brain-child?

Osborne was exasperated by such interference. He had a definite object in wishing to make the Republic independent of George. Was the success of the experiment, he wondered, the result of sound underlying principles or of the magnetic personality of one man? It is rather curious that some years later others were to ask the same question concerning Osborne's own prison system. Was it the principle or the man that counted more?

With Daddy's influence still pervasive at the Republic, it was impossible to determine the answer to such a question. No amount of admonition or rebuke dismayed George. So apprehensive was he that the new superintendent would run the place as an institution instead of as a free republic that, however earnestly he promised to keep hands off, he could not resist the temptation to intervene.

In the increasing tension which developed, Osborne was not wholly blameless. Even those members of the Board who sided with him recognized an acerbity that bred contention. He was often high-handed, carrying out his own ideas without regard for the opinion of others. Crossed, he was apt to show an almost childish peevishness. If this streak annoyed his colleagues on the Board, at times it must also have proved a vexation to Mr. George. The time came when a new president of the Republic was to be inaugurated. Tim O'Connor was the boy's name. All was ready for the ceremony. The only hitch was that the president of the Board had not arrived. Osborne, traveling by automobile, had been delayed. For a long time the gathering waited, Tim growing more and more uneasy as the moments passed. At last, in despair of Osborne's arrival, the order was given for the ritual to proceed. In the middle of it Osborne drew up. He looked at the group as if he could scarcely believe his eyes. They had started without him! Mad as a hatter, he sought out Mr. George.

"Daddy," he cried, "this is the end!"

Even then, but for an untoward circumstance, it is probable that the rancor of the moment would have evaporated. Unluckily the Ithaca paper of that evening carried a scathing article concerning the president of the Board. This time it was Osborne who was convinced his old friend had used the press to prosecute a personal quarrel.

The combined bitterness of many misunderstandings finally brought about an absolute separation. It was a blow to both men, for at heart each respected and loved the other. For a decade the estrangement endured; then fate intervened. On the deck of a homeward-bound liner in the middle of the Atlantic Ocean they met face to face. Suddenly it all seemed a tragic mistake, this nourishing a grudge which neither relished. With a silent handclasp they agreed to let bygones be bygones. Though they could not begin where they had left off, at least they could look each other in the eye with mutual understanding.

Osborne's work with the George Junior Republic was in the nature of a prelude to his prison crusade. It demonstrated both a principle and a method. In 1913, but a few months after he severed his official connections with the Republic, he startled the nation with an experiment that was to become as conspicuous a landmark in the history of penology as the signing of the Magna Carta in the development of popular sovereignty.

3. THE PRISON REFORMER

CHAPTER I

"ROLAND TO THE DARK TOWER"

THE stranger who steps off a train at the New York Central station in Auburn is immediately confronted by the gray pile of the State Prison. It is the first thing he sees when he arrives and the last when he departs. Unless he is extraordinarily immune to sense impressions, he will feel a vague unease steal over him, as if the sorrows of the thousands who have lived beneath that dome had left their trace upon the walls. For more than a century the prison has stood there, until the very stones seem to have lost their identity in one monstrous corporation having an atmosphere of its own.

Perhaps a knowledge of its inhabitants has something to do with it—human beings pent up in dark, ill-ventilated cells, deprived of all soft things, the friendly earth, the touch of women; of all color, save that of the drab walls about them—the pigment of life withdrawn and only the tissue left. Yet it is not those most familiar with the place who feel the dark spell, but strangers and children.

For children it has always a grim fascination. They recognize a mystery. As a boy, Tom Osborne often wondered what lay beyond the massive gates and grated windows. When at length his curiosity was gratified by a trip through the prison with a party of sight-seers, he was left with a sense of terror. Night after night his dreams were haunted by the figure of an escaped convict as De Quincey was pursued by the relentless Malay.

He chased me along dark streets, where I was unable to run fast or cry aloud; he peeked through windows at me as I lay in bed, even after the shades had been pinned close to escape his evil eye; as I ascended a flight of stairs in dreamland and looked back, he would come creeping through an open door, holding a long knife in his hand, while my mother all unconscious of danger sat reading under the shaded library lamp.

It was years before he was liberated from this nightmare. The departure of the phantom was at last accomplished by intimate associations with flesh-and-blood convicts both within and without prison walls.

Although the reform spirit was bred in Osborne, its direction was unquestionably determined by his proximity to Auburn Prison. He could not forget the old bastile if he wanted to. He saw it daily. For a time he could put it out of his mind and burn his energies in other fields; but it was always in the background of his thoughts. Even his other activities seem now a preparation for his great work.

Perhaps one reason why his entrance into penology was so long delayed is that, while he recognized the evils in the existing prison system and often spoke of them privately and publicly, he did not know the remedy. He hated the stupidity of it even more than the brutality. Men "spiritually sick" could not be healed by blows and solitary confinement. Yet where did he fit into the scheme? What was his mission, if indeed he had one? He could diagnose but not prescribe.

Of one thing he was convinced. The attitude of the prisoner upon release was one of resentment. Instead of being restored to society as a useful citizen, he was let loose upon society with revenge in his heart. The inevitable result was more crime. Osborne saw clearly that the blame could not be laid wholly at the door of administrative officials, or even of legislators for all their obtuseness in framing prison laws. The trouble lay deeper than that. Public opinion, if not actually favorable to the existing system, was complaisant toward it. Until he found a workable substitute, it was useless to appeal to the public for support.

His first inkling of the solution came from his work with the George Junior Republic. As early as 1905, in a public address in Syracuse, he said:

Prisoners are treated now like wild animals and are kept in cages. Here men try to study criminals. You might just as well try to study polar bears from one bear in a zoölogical garden. It is a mistake. The system brutalizes the men and the keepers. . . . [The inmates] are forced to work, and this is not reformatory. It does not create in the criminal a desire to work and respect the law. Virtue is also forced upon him, which produces no lasting effect after he is released. . . . I would propose a system like that of the George Junior Republic. The prisoner's sentence would be indeterminate. He would work for a living or starve, and if diligent would be allowed to save up and purchase luxuries and possibly freedom. He would be self-governing and learn to respect law.

This, so far as I have been able to discover, was his first public utterance on the subject; but by September of the following year (1906) his position as an advocate of prison reform had been sufficiently recognized to bring him an invitation to speak before the Congress of the National Prison Association at Albany. At this important meeting Osborne elaborated his views and summed up by offering three basic principles for rebuilding the prison system:

First—The law must decree not punishment, but temporary exile from society until the offender has proven by his conduct that he is fit to return.

Second—Society must brand no man as a criminal; but aim solely to reform the mental conditions under which a criminal act has been committed.

Third—The prison must be an institution where every inmate must have the largest practicable amount of individual freedom, because "it is liberty alone that fits men for liberty."

Although he had formulated in the rough the underlying principles of his prison creed, still the method of approach to the problem seemed obscure. Eight years were to pass before he found the key. In the meantime he felt an increasing responsibility. His activities in connection with the Junior Republic brought him into contact with a number of reform schools, and the contrast he found between these nurseries of crime and the Freeville democracy was a prod to action. Invariably the trail of reformatory graduates led to state's prison. In 1909, in his preface to Mr. George's book, "The Junior Republic," Osborne wrote:

Mr. George opened my mind to the possibility of the same principles [self-government] being used as a basis for an intelligent and reforming Prison System—a system which should be a social sanitary drainage—not merely a moral cesspool. At first I laughed at the idea; then I saw the Truth.

The turning-point came almost through an accident; yet it is evident that if it had not been one thing it would have been another. It needed only an emotional experience to transform Osborne from a protestant into a crusader. During an illness in 1912 he read Donald Lowrie's "My Life in Prison," and his mind was made up. That book jolted him out of his irresolution. Somehow, God helping, he would change such conditions. From this moment on he was militant, preoccupied, almost embarrassingly earnest. He had found his mission.

The first concrete evidence of this new incentive was his application for the appointment of Charles F. Rattigan as warden of Auburn Prison. Here was a change in tactics. Not long before, Osborne himself had sought the post of Superintendent of Prisons, but Governor Dix had shelved him into the Forest, Fish, and Game Department. If he could get Rattigan appointed warden at Auburn, perhaps he would have a chance to put some of his ideas into operation. It might even be better to work from the outside than from within.

Knowing the pressure Tammany was putting on Governor Sulzer, Osborne was agreeably surprised when Rattigan was named. Immediately he gave his support to the proposal of Dr. George W. Kirchwey, dean of the Columbia University Law School, for the creation of a State Commission on Prison Reform. Sulzer not only complied but made Osborne chairman of the Commission. Among its ten members were Dr. Kirchwey, vice chairman; and Dr. E. Stagg Whitin of New York, secretary. At last the way was opened to constructive measures in dealing with the prison problem.

The Commission, however, had no easy task. It could conduct its investigations and make its report of the evil conditions in the prisons, but it had no aroused public opinion back of it to insure remedial steps being taken. Besides, at the very outset Osborne disregarded the wishes of several of his most intimate counselors, liberals who were heart and soul with him. He had been most vehement against the part politics played in prison affairs. Prisons, he declared, were fattening grounds for local politicians. The first step was to free the system from this sinister and grossly incompetent domination. Yet, ostensibly, his first step was an example of the very evil he had been denouncing. At least, so thought such men as Oswald Garrison Villard of the *Nation*, who wished to see Osborne get off to a good start.

For a dozen years Rattigan had been Osborne's right-hand man in political campaigns. Everywhere he was accepted as the latter's unofficial representative. Though Osborne would have decried the term, Rattigan was in effect the Democratic boss of Cayuga County, one of "the local politicians" whose selection for prison jobs had seemed so obnoxious. When Osborne prevailed upon Sulzer to appoint Rattigan warden at Auburn, he gave the politicians a weapon they were quick to make use of. Foreseeing this, Villard had tried to dissuade him from the choice—not because Rattigan was not qualified but because it was asking for trouble.

An intimate friend has said of Osborne that if you could only reach him before he had made up his mind, you could influence him; but that once he had reached a decision no amount of reasoning could move him a particle. It was so in this case. Indeed, he was so wrathful at interference that he broke relations with a man whose help in guiding public opinion was invaluable. His absolute conviction of right made it impossible for him to brook opposition even from a well-wisher, and another friendship was jeopardized.

There was some justification for the choice of Rattigan. With a startling and highly unorthodox plan forming in Osborne's mind, it was essential that the man in charge of Auburn Prison be wholly in sympathy with the program. The slightest doubt or sign of hesitancy would ruin it. He could depend on Rattigan. Of course, it *looked* like a political appointment; but realities, not appearances, were what counted. It is this point of view that distinguishes the reformer from the politician. Osborne's failure to advance further in politics may be attributed to his refusal to concede that appearances are important. It complicated but could not wreck his prison crusade.

With his usual restless energy, Osborne threw himself into the work. A contemplated trip to Europe was postponed. Busy though he was, he could not resist accepting the chairmanship of the National Committee on Prison Labor, a body interested in substituting character-forming tasks for the traditional chain-gang type of manual labor. He spent most of his time, however, in investigations for the governor's commission— visiting the state prisons, talking with officials and inmates. Naturally the Auburn institution held his chief interest, and with his friend, Warden Rattigan, he attacked the immediate problems. Franklin D. Roosevelt, hearing of his activities, wrote from Washington:

> You must be having a delightful time with the cunning little incendiaries who were transferred from Sing Sing to Auburn, and I have a feeling somewhere at the back of my head that you are really enjoying your burglarious business more than if you were taking a trip to Europe.

Undoubtedly. And yet it was difficult to see just what good was being accomplished. Something drastic was needed to give impetus to prison reform. Suddenly it came to him—an idea so fantastic, judged by conventional standards, that even he was momentarily staggered.

CHAPTER II

TOM BROWN: AMATEUR CONVICT

At ten o'clock Monday morning, September 29, 1913, Thomas Mott Osborne walked through the big gate of Auburn Prison, mounted the steps to the main building, and entered the office of the Warden. Half an hour later, booked as Thomas Brown, No. 33,333x, he was indistinguishable from nearly fourteen hundred other gray-clad inmates. He was to spend a week within those walls, a prisoner subject to the same discipline as his fellows, eating the same food, working at the same tasks, and feeling at least some of the hopelessness of being buried alive.

It was with great excitement that he had first conceived the idea. When he actually came to the point of carrying it out, he was rather appalled. He had no idea what the results might be. It was only an experiment. Though he was prepared for ridicule, he trembled to think that the prisoners themselves might not understand.

There was one significant feature in his preparations for imprisonment. Originally he intended not only to be booked under an alias but to enter in disguise! No one except the Warden was to know that Tom Brown was really T. M. Osborne. The idea fascinated him, as such masquerades always did. He thought of himself accepted by the prisoners as one of them, and the guards exercising no particular discretion in dealing with his case. A chance to learn the truth, and a new rôle for the Caliph of Bagdad! Fortunately he was dissuaded from this scheme through the combined efforts of Warden Rattigan and one of the convicts who had been taken into his confidence. They pointed out that the sharp eyes of the prison world would soon penetrate the disguise, and that when that happened the inmates would never trust him again. He would be ticketed as a spy. It would be better to lay his cards on the table at the outset. Sound advice, as Osborne later admitted, but a note of regret is distinguishable in his yielding. He did insist on using the Tom Brown alias, and he did try—futilely— to keep his experiment from the press until after it was completed.

Osborne was not unknown to the inmates of Auburn Prison. Two months earlier he had appeared before them as chairman of the State Commission on Prison Reform and asked for their coöperation in the investigations that would follow. The nature of his own personal investigation he had not then disclosed, but the day preceding his voluntary durance he explained his purpose before the convicts assembled in the chapel.

Osborne has been called a visionary, a sentimentalist, a publicity seeker. These indictments are impeached by a few paragraphs in his address to the prisoners that September Sunday. They show not only the genuine sincerity of the man but the practical nature of his proposal. With one gesture he swept aside the whole body of penological writings based largely on assumption and substituted the direct experimental method. He said to his audience:

> Most of the books that have been written about you by so-called penologists and other "experts" are written, so far as I can determine, from such an outside standpoint and with so little intelligent sympathy and vital understanding that I am inclined to the belief that very few of them are of any particular value. Indeed, many are positively harmful; for they are based upon the false and cruel assumption that the prisoner is not a human being like the rest of us, but a strange sort of animal called a "criminal"—wholly different in his instincts, feelings and actions from the rest of mankind.
>
> I am curious to find out, therefore, whether I am right; whether our Prison System is as unintelligent as I think it is; whether it flies in the face of all common sense and all human nature, as I think it does; whether, guided by sympathy and experience, we cannot find something far better to take its place, as I believe we can.
>
> So, by permission of the authorities and with your help, I am coming here to learn what I can at first hand. I have put myself on trial in the court of conscience and a verdict has been rendered of "guilty"—guilty of having lived for many years of my life indifferent to and ignorant of what was going on behind these walls.

I have sentenced myself to a short term at hard labor in Auburn Prison (with commutation, of course, for good behavior). I expect to begin serving my sentence this week. I am coming here to live your life; to be housed, clothed, fed, treated in all respects like one of you. I want to see for myself what your life is like, not as viewed from the outside looking in, but from the inside looking out.

At first his hearers did not comprehend. They cast furtive glances at one another, wondering. Was he just another crank, meddling out of morbid curiosity, or did he have some selfish reason for exploiting their misfortune? When it finally burst in upon them that this wealthy, cultured gentleman actually intended to join their gray brotherhood and exchange freedom and comfort for iron bars and drudgery, they were enthusiastic in a bewildered sort of way. Osborne, however, anticipated the doubts that were sure to arise in their minds.

Of course I am not so foolish as to think that I can see it from exactly your point of view. Manifestly a man cannot be a real prisoner when he may at any moment let down the bars and walk out; and spending a few hours or days in a cell is quite a different thing from a weary round of weeks, months, years. Nor is a prison a mere matter of clothes; they cannot make a convict any more than they can make a gentleman.

What he did maintain was that this very detachment might give him an insight denied to others. Moreover, if in spite of his knowledge that at any time he could put an end to his imprisonment he felt despair and resentment welling up within him, how much more magnified must such feelings be in those who had no hope of liberty!

The experiences of Tom Brown's week in Auburn Prison are told in Osborne's volume "Within Prison Walls," a day-by-day diary of the period with comment interpolated after the end of his term. In some respects a naïve book, "Within Prison Walls" shows the shock of a well-bred man, accustomed to all the creature comforts, when confronted by a primitive mode of living. Having no army experience, Osborne objected to sleeping in his underclothes. Why didn't the State of New York provide its lodgers with pajamas? And there was no linen on the beds! His nostrils were offended at certain prison aromas; he carefully laid aside one bone and one piece of gristle that appeared in his ration of hash; he resented carrying his slop bucket to the disposal building, though it was the thought of the sewage of 1,400 men dumped into the river and carried downstream that disturbed him most. That any man, whether prison guard or potentate, should have the right to direct his comings and goings violated his sense of human dignity. The double locks and the great iron bar that fell with a thud across a whole tier of cells produced an attack of claustrophobia. At night the bars seemed to close in upon him till they pressed upon his forehead: "It is of no use to shut your eyes for you know they are still there; you can feel the blackness of those iron bars across your closed eyelids; they seem to sear themselves into your very soul." This and the loneliness afflicted him most:

My God! How do they ever stand it? . . . I am my own master in a world of four feet by seven and a half, in which I am the only inhabitant. Other human beings are living all about—on either side, at the back, above, below; yet separated by double thick stone walls from every other living creature in this great community, I am absolutely solitary. I have never felt so curiously, desperately lonely. The loneliness in the midst of crowds is proverbial; but the loneliness in the midst of a crowd of invisible human beings—not one of whom do you even hear—that has in it an element of heavily weighted horror which is quite indescribable. It can only be felt. . . . If I were just to let myself go, I believe I should soon be beating my fists on the iron-grated door of my cage and yelling.

Possibly a few traces of sentimentality may also be observed —chiefly in his point of view. There is no blinking the fact that Osborne was unscientifically predisposed to sympathize with the prisoner. For the guards he had a chip on his shoulder. Half consciously, half instinctively, he adopted the inmate attitude toward those in authority. At this stage of the game it was probably a wise method of procedure, for in a day or two he had won the confidence of practically every convict in the institution. Any doubts that may have survived vanished when Tom Brown took his medicine in the "cooler." If he was inclined to overemphasize the good qualities which he found in his prison companions, and pass lightly over their shortcomings; if he failed to realize fully that most of the inmates were eager to put their best foot forward in the hope of personal benefit when Osborne went out a free man— at least he did not lose his perspective in important matters. In extenuation of the readiness with which he accepted the fair promises of the inmates, it should be added that the one man for whom he did offer to intercede with the governor promptly turned down the chance of a pardon.

Outside the walls there were many only too glad to cull out of Osborne's report of his experiences those features which indicated the ultrafastidious or sentimental man. They chose to ignore what anyone reading the book to-day cannot fail to appreciate: a passionate sincerity and, considering the circumstances, an extraordinary insight into the psychology of prison life. So sensitive a man as Osborne was bound to be affected by the evidences of brutality he witnessed. It was not, however, the physical suffering in itself that lay upon his conscience, but the effect of brutality on the minds and souls of the victims. The entire system, as he saw it, was stupid because it was a failure. It punished but it did not reclaim. It did not even deter.

Tom Brown took up his life in prison as any other new recruit would do. Shorn of his mustache, he was finger-printed, measured, and photographed by the Bertillon clerk. Not the slightest blemish was overlooked. Into the record went the football scar Osborne had received more than thirty years before, together with mention of six peculiar brandings on his upper left arm—marks which the puzzled clerk might better have understood had he been a Harvard graduate.

Completion of the identification check-up left Tom Brown with the fear that his chances of earning an honest living by burglary had been considerably reduced. Outfitted with prison underwear, socks, cotton shirt, heavy shoes, and a suit of rough gray cloth, he began to feel every inch a convict. Only trivial exceptions to the rules were made in his case. He was allowed to retain his wedding ring. He was permitted to have writing materials and toilet articles in his cell. And he could have his morning newspaper.

At the very start he was placed with what was reputedly "the toughest bunch of fellows" in the prison—the basket-shop gang. This was an unexpected development, for the plan had been to put him with the Idle Company. By a curious coincidence, however, he landed in the right spot. Years before, while spending the summer on the New England seacoast, he had been taught basket-making by an old Indian. For the first time in his life, the knowledge came in handy. Moreover, it was out of the associations with the members of this shop that the Mutual Welfare League idea developed.

Most of the guards coöperated by treating this prisoner with official candor. Not so the Principal Keeper. He seemed to feel the necessity of making a good impression on a man who in his eyes was little else than a spy. Pausing at the basket shop on his rounds, he was overwhelmed with a sense of solicitude by the sight of an open door.

"Don't you feel a draught?" he inquired of the workers. They were much too surprised to make any response. It was Tom Brown who finally confessed to a great fondness for fresh air.

"Well now," cautioned the worthy P.K., "I don't want you men to catch cold. I think you'd better have that door shut and perhaps the windows farther open. I'll just speak to the Captain about it."

"I'm wise," whispers Convict No. 33,333x after the P.K. has gone, and Tom Brown's stock rises to a new high among the inmates in the shop.

To this impersonation as to all others Osborne brought an eagerness that helped him live the part. On the second day of his imprisonment a party of newspaper men paid a visit to the institution hoping to catch a glimpse of Tom Brown at work. Interviews were forbidden, but the reporters were permitted to make the rounds of the prison exactly like any other group of sight-seers. The Warden himself conducted the tour. When he came to the basket shop, he volunteered the information that here they would find Tom Brown. Though they passed within a few feet of Osborne not one of the party recognized him. The curious thing is that Warden Rattigan him-

"TOM BROWN"

Portrait by Orlando Rouland

self was unable to spot the man he knew so well. The day
after that, another party came through the shop. Much to his
annoyance, Osborne saw they were all intimate friends, among
them his own nephew. Carefully they scanned the face of
each inmate, once looking directly at the man they were seeking. Still his identity was not discovered. Commenting on this
incident, Osborne wrote in his journal:

I must have the marks of "the Criminal" unusually developed,
or else criminals must look a good deal like other folks—barring
the uniform. If I had the ordinary theories about prisons and
prisoners it might seem rather mortifying that, in spite of every
effort, not one of these intimate friends can spot me among the
toughest bunch of fellows in the prison.

Tom Brown's working companion was a Jack Murphy, generally considered "a bad actor." Yet his complete naturalness
appealed to Osborne from the start. There was no servility,
no currying favor. By the time they had woven a few basket
bottoms together, sweated over a couple of coal cars that had
to be pushed upgrade, and sounded each other out with decent
caution, they became fast friends. In those moments when it
was possible to whisper over their work without fear of detection, Osborne plied Murphy with questions. From casual subjects of routine he gradually worked the subject round to
possible remedies for some of the inmate grievances.

His frequent utterances on the subject make it plain that
Osborne already had his own plan roughly developed, but he
was too shrewd to force it. He wanted the initiative to come
from the convicts. It was the long dreary stretch of confinement from the conclusion of chapel service Sunday morning
until seven o'clock Monday morning that gave him his opportunity. In Auburn Prison the day of rest was the day of
torture. As a reward for their week-day labors, the inmates
could look forward to twenty hours in their cells, without exercise, with nothing to occupy their thoughts except their own
condition. Except that the arrangement permitted the guards
a day off, it was a physical and mental strain without sense or
justification. Osborne decided to broach the subject to
Murphy.

"Well, Jack," I say, "from what I have heard Superintendent Riley say, I feel sure he would like to give the men some sort of exercise or recreation on Sunday afternoons; but how could it be managed? You can't ask the officers to give up their day off, and you don't think the men could be trusted by themselves, do you?"

"Why not?" says Jack.

I look at him inquiringly.

"Why, look here, Tom!" In his eagerness Jack comes around to my side of our working table. "I know this place through and through. I know these men; I've studied 'em for years. And I tell you that the big majority of these fellows in here will be square with you if you give 'em a chance. The trouble is, they don't treat us on the level. . . . If you trust a man, he'll try and do what's right; sure he will. . . . Of course, there are a few that won't. There are some dirty curs—degenerates—that will make trouble, but there ain't so very many of those."

Secretly Tom Brown thrilled to those words. It was the very answer he wanted, but his cue was to cast doubts, to prod his partner into serious thinking. Could the Warden trust the men to be alone in the yard Sunday afternoons? Murphy was sure of it, and Osborne suggested that on rainy afternoons he and Peter Kurtz might give a violin and piano recital in the chapel. But, he added, what about those bad actors? Wouldn't they raise a rumpus and try to escape? The reply was prompt.

"But don't you see, Tom, that they couldn't do that without putting the whole thing on the bum, and depriving the rest of us of our privileges? You needn't be afraid we couldn't handle those fellows all right. Or why not let out only those men who have a good conduct bar? That's it," he continues enthusiastically, . . . "that's it, Tom, a Good Conduct League. And give the privilege of Sunday afternoons to the members of the league."

Osborne was well content to drop the subject right there and let his friend ponder it for a time. Though they were on the right track, the plan was still visionary in some respects. On the following day the discussion was resumed as they bent over their basket-weaving. Murphy was positive the members of a Good Conduct League could take care of themselves without any trouble. The time had come for Osborne to take the lead.

"Yes, but how?" I persist. "You'd probably have an occasional fight of some sort, and you'd have to have some means of enforcing discipline. Could each company have a convict officer, a lieutenant to assist the regular captain?"

Jack looks grave. "That would be too much like Elmira," he says. "I'm afraid the fellows wouldn't fall for it. You know they just hate those Elmira officers; they're nothing but stool-pigeons."

Right here is where my Junior Republic experience comes to our aid.

"Yes," I say, "but we wouldn't have any Elmira stool-pigeons. Down there the inmate officers are appointed by the prison authorities, aren't they? Well, here we'd have the members of the League elect their own officers."

Jack stares at me a moment, and then his quick mind grasps the point. "That's it, that's it," he assents eagerly, "we've got it now. Of course, if the men elect their own officers they won't be stool-pigeons."

The basic principles of the Mutual Welfare League have been drafted—ostensibly by a convict, in reality by Osborne himself.

Tom Brown was determined to experience in one short week every phase of prison life that it was possible for him to do. He had weathered that first devastating attack of claustrophobia, and though he was occasionally tormented by a desire to shriek aloud when the great iron bar slid into its brackets at night, he was growing used to the routine. Rather it was incidents out of the ordinary run that now threatened to shatter his self-control. He saw four convicts carrying an oblong box from the hospital. A coffin. Somehow a death in prison brought home to him the forlornness of existence within prison walls—the living dead waiting for release. Again, the notes of a violin played by some invisible musician shook him with their nostalgic spell. It was Mendelssohn's "Spring Song"—an unexpected reminder of that other life of his which now seemed so remote. The player was a real artist and the voice of his instrument seemed trying to frame a message of good will to Convict 33,333x. Suddenly a bedlam of noise drowned out the violin. It was the twenty-minute evening period in which the prisoners were allowed to do what they chose—within narrow limits. A burst of discords bore witness to unpracticed hands manipulating jew's-harps, harmonicas, and other musical instruments of the garden variety. Reinforced by a wailing cornet and a New York Central engine blowing off steam outside, the impromptu concert seemed like a musician's nightmare or a performance in a madhouse.

From manhandling by officers Tom Brown was secure. No guard would lay a finger on him—even if ordered. Yet if he was not to learn violence at first hand, he was to be an earwitness to one of those incidents which were only too frequent under the old system. One night the silence of the cell block was broken by a terrific uproar—at first confused cries, then the shouting of many voices, out of which rose a few distinguishable words. "Leave him alone!" "Damn you, stop that!" Finally some dull thuds and a groan.

From his position Tom Brown could not see what was happening; but he was aware of cold shivers running down his spine. He felt the terror of the unknown, and long after the cries had died away sat brooding over the inhumanity of man. Later he learned that a thin, undersized youth, recently transferred from Sing Sing, had been sent down to the punishment cells for impertinence to an officer. Five days in the dark, with only bread and water, had weakened his frail constitution and all but undermined his reason. On his return he had suffered a severe attack of diarrhea and had been left without medical aid in spite of repeated requests for a doctor. Eventually he went "bughouse," and on the night in question created a disturbance by shouting remarks in his cell. He seemed to think his life was in danger. "If you want to kill me," he yelled, "why don't you do it at once, and not torture me to death!" The remedy for such misconduct was a blackjack. He went down with a thud. Keepers flung him from his cell, and beating and kicking him, dragged the now witless devil down to the dungeon for another taste of solitary—on the apparent assumption that the very thing which had destroyed his reason would somehow restore it. Reliable evidence is still lacking to prove that the gentleman who jumped into a bramble bush and scratched out both his eyes actually did reverse the process with any appreciable amount of success.

This incident led Osborne to a conclusion whose truth he had long suspected. He himself had been inclined to look on prison guards as a peculiarly brutal type. It seemed almost as if they were chosen for their lack of all humane qualities. Experience taught him different. There were a few who seemed to derive pleasure from inflicting injuries upon defenseless convicts. Most of them, however, were a decent sort. Then why the brutality? It was a by-product of the System. Never for a moment could an officer relax in confident security. Always he must be prepared for a knife thrust, a concerted ganging of his charges when he was off his guard. This constant nervous apprehension of danger and the necessity of being prepared to fight for his very life at any moment naturally increased his severity. It was a psychological reaction. Then and there Osborne laid down the principle that *"in prison, as elsewhere, when men are dominated by fear, brutality is the inevitable result."*

There was another result of the fracas in the cell block. Now more than ever Tom Brown was determined to test the horrors of the "jail," those punishment cells where men went in, sane, and came out, raving. It was a prospect for which he had no liking, but if he hoped to understand convict psychology, he would have to suffer as so many of them had suffered. Three hours, he thought, would give him a rough notion of what solitary was like. He ought to be able to stand it that long.

Warden Rattigan was apprehensive. Business necessitated his being out of town over the week-end, and he did not relish the idea of what might happen to Tom Brown in the "cooler." Besides, Convict Brown was ill, the prison bootleg coffee having brought on an attack of indigestion. Even Jack Murphy urged his bench-mate to think it over. "You don't know what it means," he insisted. "One hour of that misery is worse than a week of the worst kind of pain."

Such remarks, whether or not exaggerated, could not deter Osborne. He insisted on the arrangements being made. By chance, however, his opportunity came before the zero hour arrived. Reprimanded for stepping out of place by the captain in charge of the basket shop, Tom Brown went boldly on strike. The lot of rattan with which he was working was a poor one, so stiff and rotten that his fingers were badly swollen and blistered. That made a good pretext for insubordination.

The captain was taken by surprise. He had had no warning of such a development, but like a good officer stuck to the rules.

"Do I understand that you refuse to work?"

"Well, that's about the size of it."

There was a moment's pause; then, quietly:

"Go and get your coat and cap."

Tom Brown was sentenced to jail for one of the serious prison offenses—strike.

Osborne called that experience "a night in hell." It was not so bad at first. Even the dim cage into which he was thrust, with its insufficient supply of air and its crawling vermin, did not immediately break down his morale. As the outer door of the jail clanged to, he was again conscious of that hysterical urge to cry aloud, but he fought it down. Except for the occupants of the other cages, there would be none to hear him, even if he went mad. Well, it was only for three hours. If others could endure it for a dozen or even a score of days and nights, he should be able to stick it out.

His cell was bare. No chair or cot on which to recline; only the floor—and that until a few days ago had been studded with rivets! What fiendish architect could have devised a sheet-iron torture chamber in which such meticulous care was taken to prevent sleep? The sole objects in this metal cell were the inevitable bucket and a small tin can. The tin can contained exactly one gill of water, a night's ration. Three gills for twenty-four hours. Until Superintendent Riley and Warden Rattigan had come into office a few months before, the limit had been one gill for twenty-four hours! Of other than drinking water the prisoners in the jail had no need. They were not allowed to wash.

In this place of extreme punishment Tom Brown was sure he would find the most debased creatures of the world of crime —men in whom every decent instinct had long since been stamped out. The "tough gang" of the basket shop had proved a disappointment, but this would be different. From down the row came a voice.

"Number One! Hello, Number One!"

Tom Brown's cell was nearest the door; he must be Number One.

"Hello!" he called back, and in reply to another question added the information that he had come from the basket shop.

"Say! Is that guy, Tom Osborne, workin' there yet?"

It was so unexpected that Number One was taken unaware. They really were interested in him then; they had understood.

"Yes," he said at last, "he's working yet."

"Well, say! He's all right, ain't he? What's he doin' now?"

"He's talking to you."

"Gee! You don't mean to say that you're the guy?"

"Well, I'm Tom Brown; it's pretty much the same thing, you know."

With that the bars—the invisible bars—fell away. Tom Brown was one of the brotherhood at last. He had challenged the powers of evil. He had come to the Dark Tower. Probably not one of the five culprits buried in those dungeons divined his purpose; it was enough for them that he wanted to understand. Never before had an ambassador from Outside brought them a message of hope, much less plumbed the abysses of their misery.

It was four o'clock in the afternoon when Tom Brown became Number One in the jail; yet the time did not matter. Day and night were the same in that corridor to the lower world. For three hours he talked with his invisible comrades. He was learning a lot; besides it kept up his spirits. There was Number Eight, a husky chap who had dared talk back to a citizen instructor. Number Four and Number Five had been jugged for roughing it up with each other, though they were apparently on the best of terms. Number Three, suffering from a bad cold, had laid a crowbar over the head of another inmate. That was serious; yet Tom Brown, brooding there in the dark, was inclined to be lenient toward all who had to undergo the tortures of solitary. Even if the deed had been done with murderous intent, what sense was there in meting out the same type of punishment for all offenses? One convict stabbed a fellow prisoner, and he was flung into jail. Another, cracking under the high tension of prison discipline, spoke a single hasty word and was condemned to the same punishment as the would-be killer. It was ridiculous, such lack of discrimination.

Nor was solitary confinement on bread and water the only penalty. It was expensive for the offender. Each day in the jail meant a fine of fifty cents. Since convicts were paid at the rate of one and one-half cents per working day, a ten-day sentence meant that the malefactor owed the State of New York considerably more than a year's pay when he returned to his own cell. He was deprived of all marks of good behavior, and a portion, if not all, of his earned commutation time was taken away from him. Attempted murder or impertinence—it was all the same except for some variation in the length of the sentence. A spell or two in jail reduced a prisoner to such a state of hopelessness that there was no more incentive to good conduct. Financially and morally, he was in the red so far that chronic bankruptcy was easier than futile striving.

There was one more member of the condemned party. Number Two was hardly more than a boy, being only twenty-one years old. Four days ago, the prison doctor had operated on his ear, already deaf from an injury received prior to his conviction. Day before yesterday he had been discharged from the hospital, unable to work and the wound not yet healed. Yesterday, following a report that he had been a troublesome patient and had broken rules by talking to another inmate in the hospital, he had been ordered to a punishment cell. All of Tom Brown's sympathies went out to this youth. Here he lay, sick and untended, clad in filthy clothes, without nourishment except a little bread and three gills of water a day, not daring to use the precious drops to wash out his ear and not permitted even a handkerchief to sop the running wound. Already he had passed thirty-six hours in this condition, and he had at least as many more to go.

Although the time was speeding far more tolerably than

Tom Brown had ventured to hope, a horror of the place was growing upon him. There was something foul in the very atmosphere, and he longed for the sound of the key in the outer lock that would signify his punishment term was over. It seemed as if that last hour would never end. Yet when the final moment came and the door creaked open and the electric light bulb was snapped on, a perverse impulse possessed him. Had he really tasted the bitterness of solitary? He knew that he had not. Buoyed up by the novelty of the situation, the interest of his invisible companions, and the realization that in a short space he would be rescued from this dark pit, he had not actually plumbed the depth of that torment which makes strong men weak, and weak men gibbering idiots. It had been more like a play than reality. When the face of the Principal Keeper was silhouetted against the bars of his cell, Tom Brown fought down an urge to shout curses at it. He could feel the man's eyes searching for him in the dim light, and more than ever he experienced the sensation of a caged animal. A fierce anger blazed through him. Perhaps already the bacillus of revolt had eaten into his veins, for it was not wholly a scientific eagerness that suddenly determined him to remain. It was obstinacy. He would not go because that man out there, that uniformed agent of imbecile society, wanted him to. For the moment it was not Osborne who glared back at the face pressed against the iron bars—it was Convict 33,333x, pal of murderers, product of the underworld, feeling all the blind resentment with which his borrowed personality endowed him. Go with that man? He'd be damned if he would!

The Principal Keeper was aghast. This was something outside his calculations. He had always thought Osborne was half-crazy. Solitary confinement had only completed the process. Deeply agitated, he telephoned the Superintendent of Prison Industries, who came down posthaste and was visibly relieved to find in Cell Number One a reasonable creature instead of a raving maniac. Thereupon it was arranged that Tom Brown's punishment should be extended until six o'clock the next morning.

This was at seven o'clock in the evening. Eleven hours more

to go—this time with no hope of relief. Whatever terrors the night might bring, he would have to see them through.

When the Superintendent of Industries left, there was complete silence in the jail. The inmates of the punishment cell were listening.

From Number Four came an anxious voice: "Has he gone?" No answer.

Then from Number Two: "I think he went with the officers. I don't hear anything in his cell. . . . Yes, he must have gone."

But Tom Brown has not gone, though his fellow prisoners can scarcely believe their ears when they hear his voice assuring them he is still there. They are even more amazed than was the Principal Keeper. Conversation picks up for a while, then droops. Someone starts singing a ragtime ballad. Someone else strikes up the Toreador's song from "Carmen" in a clear tenor voice. Now it is Osborne, not Tom Brown, who regrets more than ever before his inability to sing. He feels out of it somehow. Perhaps he can sleep. Following the directions of his companions, he rolls up his shirt and places it on top of his shoes for a pillow. His coat serves as a coverlet; the rough pine boards are his couch. But he is not the only occupant of that cell. He feels something crawling on his neck and remembers that *his* cell has been given a special cleaning for the occasion. Exhausted but not sleepy, he sprawls on the hard floor and falls into a state of semiconsciousness.

"Tom! Tom Brown!"

He hears but cannot answer. His brain is befuddled with the fetid air and phantasies of the borderland of dream. The cry comes again, followed by a pitiful wail: "My God! I've tipped over my water!"

It is Number Two in the next cell, the boy with the wound in his ear. In turning over on the uncomfortable floor he accidentally kicked over the tin can containing his precious ration of water. Now he has nothing to quench his fever thirst. He begins to grow delirious, muttering wildly to himself. On his side of the iron cage Tom Brown wipes the perspiration from his face. His eyes are filled with tears—more of rage and futility than of anything else. He cannot even share his own meager portion, carefully saved for a time when thirst might become overpowering. He would like to batter down the iron walls with his fists. Only the strongest effort of self-control keeps him from shrieking aloud. That way, he knows, lies dementia.

It is Number Four who comes to the rescue. Talking quietly to the raving boy, he persuades him to tell his story and follows that with other tales so much more atrocious that, whether imaginary or not, they sink Number Two's sufferings into insignificance. Before long the boy is induced to sing a sentimental ballad. The treatment is effective. For the moment the crisis is forestalled.

Once more Tom Brown tried to sleep. Gradually the taut nerves relaxed and he sank at last into restless slumber. But not for long. In half an hour he was awakened by the rattling of his cell door, and a gruff voice:

"Here! Answer to your name! Brown!"

Out of a fog Osborne answered, smothering an impulse to curse the man for breaking his first rest. Instead, with all the politeness he could muster, he begged that the boy who had tipped over his can be given a little more water.

Preposterous! With a curt, " 'Fraid I can't; 'gainst the rules," the officer passed down the row to awaken the occupants of the other cells.

Osborne was raging now, and sleep was impossible. The episode had jolted him out of that half-coma in which sensations were at least deadened. His brain worked tirelessly, refusing to rest. If on this single night such a thing could occur, how many ghastly scenes had this dungeon witnessed! The thought tortured him until his nerves were at the breaking point and his head felt as if it were being slowly crushed by a steel band. He could tell that he too was growing feverish. The very location of the jail aggravated his anguish. On one side the dynamos of the prison hummed their endless song, driving one near madness with their incessant roar. On the other there was—the death chamber, with the fatal chair and its horrible accessories. "The hot seat," the underworld had nicknamed it with grim and realistic humor. Nor did it contribute to Tom Brown's peace of mind to remember—one of his jailmates had taken pains to furnish this information—that not long ago in his very cell one poor chap had cracked under the strain and committed suicide. He could well believe it!

Suddenly, in the midst of his whirling thoughts, he heard a familiar sound. Click! Click! Click! The levers in the galleries! That was queer. It couldn't be later than four-thirty at the most. And how could one catch the noises of the distant wing through yards of passages and solid masonry? But it came again. Click! Click! Click! Perhaps the kitchen force going to work.

He turned his aching body on the hard pine, and immediately another sound was plainly perceptible, the dull thud of marching feet. Tramp! Tramp! Tramp! The tread rose in crescendo, ceased, and began again in another quarter. How many companies were there? And at this hour! Tom Brown was listening intently now. Other vague noises mingled with that steady tramp, filling the cell with curious vibrations. He staggered to his feet, and a shower of sparks fled across his vision. But there was no longer any sound. Only the silence of the dungeon. It came to him in a flash. God, he was going mad! There were no clicking levers, no tramping feet. They were but the hallucinations of a disordered brain. The realization almost severed the last tie with rationality. He could feel himself slipping into a world of phantasmagoria and being engulfed in an ocean of chaotic sights and sounds.

"Joe! Are you awake?"

"Hello! What's the matter?"

"For God's sake talk to me!"

"Sure! What shall we talk about?"

"Anything. I don't care. Only something."

And so Number Four began to talk, as he had talked to the sick raving boy in Number Two. Osborne never could remember what was said. He lay tense, his hands clenched, his teeth gritted together, trying to measure the minutes that trickled so slowly, praying for delivery before he should lose all grip on himself. An hour left, maybe. Half an hour now. Or no? One must only wait—and listen.

It came at last, a sound, a real sound—the six o'clock train blowing off steam at the station. Six o'clock! Yet he found he had no capacity for rejoicing left. Something had been crushed out of him. The guard who opened the iron door of Cell Number One saw a different man from the one who fourteen hours earlier had entered it almost eagerly. He walked as in a trance, obeying automatically the officer's commands. Only when he whispered a good-by to the boys did a flicker of the old spirit revive briefly. The jail door clanged behind him, and he was in the passage, stumbling toward the prison yard. With a quick intake he drew his lungs full of the keen fresh air of the morning. Yesterday's morning seemed a thousand years ago. Sidereal time marked the interim as a single day, but experience had made it an era. Yet he felt that he had come closer to the heart of the prison problem than ever before—perhaps closer than he ever would come again. Back in his old cell—incredibly comforting after the horrors of the jail—he fell on his knees and dedicated himself to a task that he knew he could no longer evade:

May I be an instrument in Thy hands, O God, to help others see the light, as Thou hast led me to see the light. And may no impatience, prejudice, or pride of opinion on my part hinder the service Thou hast given me to do.

The rest is soon told. It was Sunday morning. Dulled by exhaustion, Tom Brown automatically answered the summons to chapel exercises. Strive as he might, he had been unable to put in writing the words which should be his farewell to the Gray Brotherhood. Even when he took his place on the benches, other thoughts kept intruding. A week ago a man calling himself Osborne had spoken from that platform while hundreds of curious eyes gazed up at him uncomprehending. Yet for the past seven days that man had ceased to exist. Another personality had entered his body. Somehow that transition had seemed easier to effect than the reversal of the process now. When the Chaplain asked Convict Number

33,333x to come to the platform, Tom Brown still had the upper hand. Only when he began to speak, touching upon the future and what it held for those within prison walls, was the spell broken. Yet even then the rows upon rows of gray-clad inmates saw the comrade of their despair rather than the crusading reformer.

Some have eulogized Osborne for conducting his Tom Brown experiment. Some have ridiculed, and some have reviled. What few seem to realize is that, regardless of results, Thomas Mott Osborne was probably the only man who could have conducted it at all. Any one else would have been met with cold rebuffs or open jeers by the prison populace. With his extraordinary capacity of exchanging his own identity for that of another, he did not *act* Tom Brown. He *was* Tom Brown. The convicts felt it and accepted him as one of themselves. Though there were many things they could not understand, and though some were undoubtedly moved to self-pity, thinking more of their immediate plight than of conditions inherent in the system, all of them knew instinctively that Tom Brown was a friend who could be trusted. When he left the prison that Sunday morning, the hopes of fourteen hundred men went with him.

CHAPTER III

THE MUTUAL WELFARE LEAGUE

"DAMN Fool! Pity you are not in for twenty years."

This unsigned note Osborne found lying on his desk the Sunday he came out of Auburn Prison. The New York City postmark was that of the substation nearest to the Fourteenth Street headquarters of Mr. Murphy's political organization. A coincidence maybe; but with vivid recollections of former passages between the Tammany chieftain and himself, Osborne felt justified in assuming a connection.

Not that it worried him. He had been pilloried too many times for that. No sooner had the news leaked out that he was voluntarily spending a week as an "amateur convict" than the press of the country jumped into action. Tom Brown was swell front-page copy, and streamer headlines told the story of his incarceration. The reporters were followed by the editorial writers, paragraphers, and cartoonists, whose comment, verbal and graphic, ranged from eulogy to denunciation. It is hardly necessary to add that the prevailing attitude was one of skepticism, if not outright ridicule.

The periodicals were the kindest. The *Outlook*, which had followed Osborne's political career with an occasional favorable notice, applauded now. So did the *Saturday Evening Post*. *Current Opinion* linked his report on prison evils with the more bitter attack of Julian Hawthorne, whose celebrated name had not saved him from a term in Atlanta Federal Prison. "The time is coming," it predicted, "when men will come out of prison sounder in body and mind than when they went in."

Osborne did not fare so well at the hands of the metropolitan newspapers. True, the New York *Tribune*, Boston *Transcript, Christian Science Monitor*, and a few others came

261

whole-heartedly to his support; yet even the New York *Evening Post,* in principle an ally, qualified its endorsement. It may be a mistake to consider that the prisoner is not a human being like the rest of us, was its dictum, but "it would be fully as grave an error to assume that he is just like the rest of us." If Osborne had acquiesced in this precise footnote, it would have been with the reservation that the prisoner *could* be like the rest of us if we gave him the chance.

Of all the New York City papers the *Sun* was the most vindictive. Perhaps it still nourished the "Green Duck" grudge. When first it heard of Osborne's intention to spend a week in Auburn Prison, it remarked that "the self-sentence is ridiculously inadequate." A little later it reported in mock sorrow that "the self-reformation of Thomas Mott Osborne, alias Tom Brown, is not proceeding as rapidly as a sympathetic public hoped." Hundreds of other newspapers followed the *Sun's* lead in declaring that no good whatever could come from Tom Brown's experiences in prison. "New York papers," observed the Bridgeport (Connecticut) *Standard,* "seem to believe it is not necessary to wallow in a mud hole to know how a pig feels." Such phrases as "playing at prisoner," "futile quixoticism," "cheap press-agenting" and "to-day's best laugh" reflected the general opinion. One cartoonist depicted a striped Osborne sitting in his cell smoking a cigarette, while a fair damsel manicured his nails, and a butler served caviar.

Sometimes an echo of Osborne's political conflicts crept into the comments. "Trying to be a regular convict," vouchsafed the Lockport *Journal,* "is about as difficult for Thomas Mott Osborne as being a regular candidate." The New York *Sun* was confident that "for a second term in his latest office the Hon. Thomas Mott Osborne can count on the enthusiastic support of a united Democratic Party."

Next to flippancy, evasiveness was the popular keynote. Carefully charting the middle path which it was to follow for twenty years, the New York *Times* captioned one of its editorials on Osborne's experiment: "Well-Intended, and Yet Ill-Advised." But smugness was the most irritating, that complacent assurance that everything is lovely just as it is. It remained for the Rochester *Herald* to interpret this point of view in a homily on the contentment of the depraved:

> It is a sad fact, but one that cannot be denied, that some people enjoy the most squalid kind of surroundings. These people would not emigrate from their hovels to a palace, if opportunity were given. . . . They even prefer food that is badly prepared to food that is well prepared, and when they drink whiskey, they prefer the very worst.

In other words, the State of New York is doing the prisoners a favor by leaving the cells foul; they like the stench. And a certain sour tang to the hash is the best of fillips to the appetite!

Far from being abashed by the attacks upon him, Osborne was inclined to relish the prominence given his exploit, for aside from his natural enjoyment of the spotlight he realized that the controversy was furnishing the first factor essential to the success of his prison program—public interest. Already we are beginning to forget the extraordinary impact his Tom Brown experience made on society. For months it was the chief topic of discussion in gatherings where conversation turned to social subjects. In the college centers especially excitement ran high.

I well recall Osborne's first visit to the small New England college which I attended. We gathered—some five or six hundred of us—in the chapel to which each morning by fiat of the authorities we were herded in various stages of dishabille to hear divine service. How long the fifteen minutes of compulsory attendance used to seem! Yet in those same straight-backed, wooden benches, where the more godless had whiled away the moments by betting on the length of morning prayers, the entire college body sat transfixed for two solid hours listening to a story of stupidity and barbarity as told by a master of pathos, a dramatist who was leading actor in his own play.

What happened at Wesleyan was duplicated wherever Osborne went. In a flash society had become prison-conscious, and he hastened to take advantage of the new spirit. Meanwhile, further discussion had been aroused by the exploit of Madeleine Z. Doty, a member of the New York State Commission for Prison Reform, and Elizabeth C. Watson, investigator for the National Child Labor Committee. A few weeks after Tom Brown's release, these women spent four days in the Women's Prison at Auburn. They had intended to stay a full week as Osborne had done but broke down under the strain before their time was up. Except for Warden Rattigan and the Head Matron, no one in the institution knew that Miss Doty and Miss Watson were other than they seemed— new recruits for the prison population. The report these women issued corroborated Osborne's account of prison evils and impressed on the public the necessity of reform.

Now was the time to act. As Osborne wished, however, the first move came from "inside." It was Jack Murphy, his bench mate, who had suggested a Good Conduct League and had been led through Osborne's adroit guidance to the idea of League officers elected by the convicts themselves. Murphy was desperately serious. When Osborne suggested that a pardon from the governor might be forthcoming, Murphy rejected the implied offer almost roughly.

"Put that right out of your mind, Tom," he said. "I am ready to stay behind these walls all my life if I can help you and the Commission bring about some of these reforms you have in mind. That's all I want."

The record of succeeding days testifies to his sincerity. At his instigation a resolution pledging loyalty to the cause was drafted and signed by the most earnest of the inmates. Interviews with Warden Rattigan and Superintendent Riley brought permission to start at Auburn Prison a Tom Brown League—though Osborne was quick to protest a name which had too much of the personal element in it. In the latter part of December, when Osborne returned from a six-week business trip to Europe, all was in readiness for launching the project.

Free balloting in the various shops had resulted in the election of forty-nine inmates to serve as a general committee. On December 28, this body met in the chapel. After the meeting was called to order by Warden Rattigan, the guards and the warden retired. For the first time in prison history a large group of convicts, many of them notorious criminals under severe sentences, met unattended by any person of authority to discuss their own problems.

Only one of their number was not a bona fide member of the prison clan, and he could not be called an outsider. That was Thomas Brown, No. 33,333x. By unanimous vote Tom Brown was elected chairman.

Aside from routine matters pertaining to the machinery of the proposed organization, this Committee of Forty-nine took one important step. Originally, both Murphy and Osborne had assumed that membership in the League would be determined on a basis of good conduct. In discussion, however, one of the convicts inquired who was to be the final judge of what constituted good conduct. Hard put to it to find an answer, Osborne was forced to admit that the prison authorities would probably set the standards. The answer was prompt: "We don't recognize those standards!"

The point could not easily be dismissed. If the League were to elect its own officers in order to prevent prison authorities from appointing "rats" and "stool-pigeons" to important posts, the right of establishing membership qualifications must also rest with the inmates; otherwise it would not be a prisoners' league but a warden's league. So vital did this principle appear to the Committee that it was unanimously voted that membership should be open to all and forfeited only through bad conduct. The League itself should determine the standards of behavior.

If the December meeting was unique, the first League assembly on Lincoln's birthday in 1914 was dramatic. In all prison records there is nothing to equal it. In the interim a Subcommittee of Twelve had drafted a code of by-laws, selected a name and a motto, and after several conferences secured the sanction of the committee of the whole. On January 11 the results were reported to the entire prison population gathered in the chapel. At this time the old system was still in operation, and the guards, stationed at their usual posts, watched curiously and perhaps apprehensively nearly 1,400 convicts planning to take from them their old authority and assume it themselves. It would be interesting to know what passed through their minds as the by-laws were adopted by unanimous acclamation.

The structure of the new organization was simple enough: a governing body of forty-nine delegates elected by League members every six months; an Executive Board of nine chosen by the delegates from among their own number; a clerk, a sergeant-at-arms, and deputies appointed by the Executive Board; and eight Grievance Committees composed of five delegates each to hear and dispose of all complaints against members of the League.

On the Sunday following the first election the new officers were sworn in by Warden Rattigan, who read to them this oath of office:

You solemnly promise that you will do all in your power to promote the true welfare of the men confined in Auburn Prison; that you will cheerfully obey and endeavor to have others obey the rules and regulations of the duly constituted prison authorities, and that you will endeavor in every way to bring about friendly feeling, good conduct and fair dealing among both officers and men to the end that each man, after serving the briefest possible term of imprisonment, may go forth with renewed strength and courage to face the world again. All this you promise faithfully to endeavor. So help you God.

It is probable that not until this moment had the forty-nine newly elected officers, the hundreds of their fellows who heard them swear to the oath, and the guards who watched the proceedings realized the full import of the step that was being taken. The solemnity of the occasion brought understanding. To some it also brought doubts—not to the guards alone, but to the inmates. The latter had been accustomed too long to the old system with its harsh, indiscriminate discipline to adopt so revolutionary a change without misgivings. They were afraid. In some of the negotiations Osborne had had to force the issue, because the prisoners hesitated to go so far as he did in reforms. Even on this day it was difficult to believe that the brief rites they had witnessed meant the end of the old order. It seemed as inexorable as ever. About them stood the guards, still watchful, still with authority to consign any one of them to "jail" for a whisper or an attempted murder—it wouldn't matter which. Yet there was an atmosphere of expectancy—of suppressed excitement—as the men filed out of the chapel and were marched back to their cells.

And then came the first official meeting of the League on February 12. Osborne himself could scarcely credit the changes he saw. He stood on the rostrum in the prison chapel, now curtained like a stage. On the curtain was painted a large shield bearing the monogram MWL, signifying the official name of the organization, Mutual Welfare League, with the motto, suggested by one of the prisoners: "Do Good. Make Good." The hall itself was gayly decorated with the colors of the League, green and white. On the back wall of the stage over the national flag hung a portrait of Lincoln, peculiarly appropriate not only to the holiday but to the new emancipation of which it was a witness.

Presently the distant tramp of marching feet was heard, and through the door came the first column of Mutual Welfare League members. They were followed by others and still others, until about 1,350 convicts had taken their seats in the chapel. All but seventeen of the prison population had voluntarily joined the order and were proudly displaying the insignia of membership—a small green and white shield worn on the coat.

Osborne gazed down on these hundreds of eager faces with a strange mixture of emotions. He thought of that Sunday when, standing in this very spot, he had first unfolded his plan of spending a week in Auburn Prison. Then he had been struck with the indescribable drabness of the scene—the surroundings, the men, the very clothes they wore. "Gray and faded and prematurely old," he had written in his journal. How could he ever have thought of this audience as gray and faded? They were so no longer. They chatted and laughed among themselves, their eyes alight, their movements natural and unrestrained. It suddenly occurred to Osborne that this scene was alive with color, and that the audience before whom he was to speak was as good-looking a body of men as one could ask to see. Not a guard or keeper was in sight, yet there was perfect order among these hundreds of criminals ranging from first offenders to notorious killers. The only sign of officialdom was the Deputy Warden, and he stood by the door merely as an invited observer.

There was little business to come before this first meeting. A program of music including selections from Bach, Beethoven, Sullivan, and Strauss (obviously the choice of Osborne) followed by a few speeches, and the lines of men began to file out. Not a whisper. Not a sign of insubordination or sullenness. Watching with amazed eyes, a prison keeper was moved to ejaculate: "Why in hell can't they do that for us?" And Osborne echoed, "Why, indeed!"

Astounding as had been this spectacle of an entire prison body meeting in perfect order under no supervision except their own, a severe test was at hand. Not long after the convicts returned to their cells, the lights began to flicker and wane. In the past that had always been a signal for vindictive shouts, bronx cheers, and general disorder. Richards, the inmate secretary of the League, had been cynical from the first. He could not believe that any large group of convicts could be trusted for long. "Now you will have the other side of it," he told Osborne.

The lights grew dimmer and dimmer, and finally went out. Listening at the window of the great iron door leading to the north wing, Osborne felt his brow damp with perspiration. He fervently wished that this unexpected test had not come so soon. For a half-minute he waited there in the darkness, fearful of the outcome. Yet not a sound disturbed the silence. Presently there was a faint glimmer from the bulbs. It wavered, went out, and then came on full.

I look at Richards. He is paler than usual, but there is a bright gleam in his eyes. "I would not have believed it possible," he says impressively; "such a thing has never happened in this prison before. The men always yell when the lights go out. In all my experience I have never known anything equal to it. I don't understand it."

To Osborne it meant one thing above all else: the confirmation of his belief that prisoners are like other men and should be treated as men. There was nothing marvelous in the change which had come over the inmates of Auburn Prison.

When a man, treated like a beast, snarls and bites, you say, "This is the conduct of an abnormal creature—a criminal." When a prisoner, treated like a man, nobly responds, you cry, "A miracle!"

What folly! Both these things are as natural as two and two making four.

The new order which came with the establishment of the Mutual Welfare League brought many revolutionary changes in prison life. Among them was the abolition of the terrible rule of silence. Condemned to perpetual muteness, prisoners had lived in a cheerless vacancy that bred more evils than it cured. In place of healthy greetings and responses there came evil communications, surreptitiously maneuvered by the "grapevine" telegraph that flourishes in all prisons. Osborne himself had witnessed the functioning of this prison wireless and during his week's term had gleefully confounded the Warden by his knowledge of what was taking place. Once, when Mr. Rattigan came to his cell with an apology for forgetting the evening newspaper—one of the exceptions allowed Tom Brown—Osborne had been able to reply, "Don't worry. It doesn't make any difference. I've read it." And to the astonishment of the Warden he produced the paper.

Such suppression was bound to cause rebellion, for men must have communication with their fellows or go mad. Even the threat of a stay in the "cooler" for a single whisper could not deter, and ten to one there would be mischief behind secret contacts. The only way to check violations was through constant supervision. The guards did their best, but it was not enough. It was folly to think that a handful of officers could keep tab on fourteen hundred men. Faced with an impossible situation, officialdom resorted to a compromise of the worst sort—the "stool-pigeon" system. Every prisoner knows the fear of the "inside" spy—the "rat" who in return for certain privileges will inform the authorities of secret infractions. As it is the nature of a "rat" to be treacherous, old grudges were frequently paid off by casting suspicion on innocent men. Lying and deceit flourished. Between the diligent alertness of the guards and the under-cover spying of the stool-pigeons, an inmate was denied all sense of security. Every moment of the day he could feel prying eyes following his every movement, waiting for some unguarded act. Innocent or guilty, he was kept in a perpetual state of nervous tension that might snap under any unexpected strain. Then hell would break loose—the flash of a knife, a groan, and another prison murder!

All this was banished under the new deal. A different atmosphere pervaded the whole prison, and the sound of laughter and talk in recreation hours must have struck many a veteran guard as incongruous in the extreme. He had known only the strained hush of enforced silence. In the past, noise had meant trouble. It might, he feared, mean trouble again. It is a tribute to the practicability of Osborne's system that the new freedom reduced violence, and that life in Auburn Prison approached closer to sane, normal living than anyone had believed possible.

Another of the ancient institutions that went into the discard was Blue Sunday. For over a century the Lord's Day had been the Devil's Day in Auburn Prison. Beginning with a divine service that seems almost blasphemous in the light of what it prefaced, Sunday became a nightmare of torture, restlessness, and that inevitable concomitant of close confinement, vice. Locked in their cells all day long, except for a few moments granted for the emptying of the buckets and a bite of breakfast, the inmates had nothing to do except think of their lot and hatch mischief. Around them the damp and corrosion of bleak walls breeding rheumatism and tuberculosis. Walls so close than an occupant dare not extend one hand swiftly for fear of hitting the opposite side of his cubicle. Walls that seemed to press down and in like the terrible torture chamber of Poe's "Pit and the Pendulum." No chance for a breath of fresh air to filter through. No hope for what exercise the shops afforded on week days. Nothing to interrupt the deadly monotony of the prison Sunday. And when a holiday and a Sunday happened to come together, the evils of inaction were doubled. Small wonder that most of the prison fights occurred Monday morning. Small wonder too that the vilest things were nurtured in the long gloomy hours of the day that is to be kept holy.

Both Osborne and Jack Murphy agreed that the Sunday confinement was one of the worst features of the prison system. As soon as the Mutual Welfare League was perfected, that was the first abuse to go. The Sunday afternoon assembly, inaugurated at that first meeting of the League, was made a regular part of the schedule. There would be a musical program or a lecture or a movie to break the long grind. The Lord's Day was no longer a horror that hung over the whole week, but a respite in a very real sense.

Most revolutionary of all reforms, however, was permission for the Mutual Welfare League to have outdoor sports in the prison yard. It began with a request for an inmate athletic program on Memorial Day. Why Warden Rattigan was not challenged by his superiors when he gave his sanction to the plan is not quite clear. Certainly within the prison all the officers and many inmates looked with misgiving approaching dread to the coming holiday. The Sunday afternoons in chapel had turned out all right—but this yard business!

Osborne himself realized the perils of the proposed field day. There were prisoners who had been waiting years for the chance of "getting" an enemy. Perhaps it was some rival gangster who had murdered a friend; or some former pal who had framed him and put him behind the bars; or a "rat" who had squealed to the Warden. The animosities of a prison are deep and enduring. What would happen when the whole prison community was let loose in the open yard for the first time in history, with old scores to be wiped out, hated "screws" to be slugged or knifed? More than one guard and inmate wondered.

Memorial Day dawned warm and sunny. In his tiny cell each man waited for the signal that would announce his temporary release from the dank air of his cage. When it came, every door was thrown open, from somewhere a band began to play, and under the command of their own delegates and sergeants-at-arms, 1,400 men marched through the corridors and out into the yard. It was typical of Osborne that he should see the beautiful side. Let him describe the picture as he saw it:

Each group stood at attention until the last man was in the yard; then at the trumpet call ranks were broken, friends rushed across the yard to greet each other, and brothers who for long years had never been able to speak, clasped hands and walked away together, their feelings too sacred for the common gaze.

In many another witness the scene aroused different emotions. One of the oldest guards, watching with unbelieving eyes, exclaimed, "Good God! Who would ever have believed this a few years ago!" One of the convicts confessed years later that he had concealed a heavy iron bolt in preparation for the general mêlée which he feared might develop. But there was no knifing, no cracking of skulls. Throughout the afternoon athletic contests, enlivened by a rivalry between the North and South wings, alternated with band music, group singing, and dancing. And at last, still under their own leaders, the men marched back to their cells in perfect order.

A single blast of the trumpet had demolished the old penology.

It was the sanity of it that was most encouraging. Like boys out of school the men had forgotten their troubles in healthy play. No longer were they sullen, cringing creatures, beaten into submission, nourishing hatred, waiting only for an opportunity to wreak vengeance on their oppressors. Life meant something still. They laughed and sang. Moreover they discovered a latent sense of humor and could joke about themselves and their plight. When a group of inmates had submitted a list of the proposed events to the Warden and had received his approval, one of them, a third-termer, drily suggested an additional feature—a wall-climbing contest! The very atmosphere of the prison and the character of the inmates had been changed—not miraculously but by the application of a little common sense.

All these changes came gradually, giving both prisoners and

officers a chance to feel their way. It was difficult for both, but every day brought new evidence of the feasibility of inmate responsibility. Even many of the guards were finally reconciled to the new régime. Some of them, at first honestly skeptical, became enthusiastic supporters of Osborne; others, admitting that the Mutual Welfare League was working for the time being, could never quite free themselves from the prejudices of the old system. Perhaps it was difficult for them to accept as bona fide converts some of the more notorious characters in "Copper John." * Perhaps Osborne's own attitude —he was often scathing in his criticisms of guards as a class— bred antagonism. Although he asked them for suggestions, it is yet to be demonstrated that, with the exception of a few tips on arranging schedules, he ever adopted their recommendations. The two systems were as far apart as the poles, and advice from a product of the old school he naturally regarded with suspicion. In fact, he implied that eventually his system would do away with guards entirely—a prospect for which the latter showed no enthusiasm whatever!

All was not easy sailing. Often there came seemingly insuperable obstacles. For one thing, as in the George Junior Republic, the inmates had to earn their privileges. Osborne would never countenance the policy of bribing prisoners to be good. The initiative had to come from the inmates. When they showed themselves capable of accepting responsibility, it would be conferred. Even the Memorial Day record did not suffice. For a time, because of a prison quarantine for scarlet fever, daily recreational hours in the yard were continued. When the quarantine was lifted, the privilege was withdrawn. That first day the prisoners were marched directly from the shops to their cells emphasized the value of yard liberty as nothing else could have done. They petitioned for a regular daily schedule of outdoor exercise and got it—though not without some grumbling from "a few of the stupider guards."

It was the same with the motion pictures. A full-length feature lasted half an hour longer than the allotted hour, and any sign of disturbance brought a prompt cancellation of the spe-

* Auburn Prison.

cial privilege. The League officers took charge of maintaining discipline. Once, at the conclusion of a showing, a brawny sergeant-at-arms warned his section: "If you don't quit chirpin' when a dame is flashed on the screen, you don't get no extra half-hour, see!" The chirpin' stopped.

But the greatest threat to the survival of the Mutual Welfare League was the problem of dealing with offenders against prison rules. It will be recalled that the by-laws provided for Grievance Committees to take charge of all complaints against League members. Originally Osborne contemplated the establishment of a prisoners' court modeled after the system in operation at the George Junior Republic. On second thought he changed his mind. The men who would appear at these trials—accused and accusers alike—had had their fill of the rigmarole of courts and judges and lawyers. So vivid a reminder of the machinery responsible for their present predicament boded ill for the dignity of a prisoners' court or the respect of the inmates.

The Grievance Committees avoided this pitfall and reduced procedure to simple terms. A League member charged with violation of prison rules was summoned before the Committee having jurisdiction over his case and examined. His accuser and other possible witnesses were also heard, and from the information thus obtained a verdict was arrived at. The first two men to be brought before a Grievance Committee followed the old tradition and lied like troopers. To their amazement, however, several of the witnesses who had caught the spirit of the system told the truth. Before the case was concluded, both culprits made a complete confession and took their punishment uncomplainingly.

This example would have proved more effective had it not been for one flaw. While the Grievance Committees were functioning, prison officials were meting out justice in the old way. The Principal Keeper still sentenced inmates to solitary on bread and water for minor offences. Afterwards the same culprit was hauled before the Grievance Committee and disciplined by the League. As a consequence inmates were getting double punishment for the same infraction. Such a situation was intolerable. It was worse than before, and being only human, offenders began to lie out of their trouble rather than pay double penalty. Witnesses refused to testify, and even members of the Grievance Committees objected to serving.

Something had to be done and done quickly. Either the whole project of prisoner responsibility in disciplinary matters had to be discarded, or independent action had to be granted the League. For Osborne there was only one possible choice. He took up the matter with Warden Rattigan, and arranged that the League should have full jurisdiction over all cases of violations except five major offences: assault on an inmate, assault on an officer, refusal to work, strike, and attempt to escape.

Here was a definite division of authority, and what is more the proposal had the approval of Superintendent of Prisons Riley. The men themselves were not so sure. They shrank from accepting a responsibility that had unknown possibilities, for it is a delicate matter for one malefactor to pass judgment on another. The convict's instinctive repugnance to being mixed up with the disciplining of his fellows had been aggravated by the "double penalty" abuse, by gossip and petty jealousies. Realizing the seriousness of the crisis, Osborne called a mass meeting to debate the question. Unattended by any guards, the inmates argued the matter pro and con for three hours. In the end, the progressives won. When a vote was taken, all but about a score of the fourteen hundred men present had been persuaded that the only hope for the League lay in trying this extraordinary experiment.

Osborne credited the success of the League in its early stages to four men. They were Jack Murphy, to whom he always referred as the founder of the League; Billy Duffy, the first sergeant-at-arms; S. L. Richards, the first secretary, better known as Dick both to his companions and to the police; and "Canada Blackie."

Every worthy cause needs a martyr. Canada Blackie, bandit and bank robber, played that rôle. He was a sample of the finished product of the old prison system. Serving a term of life *plus* ten years, he had reached such a point of hopeless-

ness that he would balk at nothing. A desperate attempt at a
break had failed. There had been rumors of a hidden store
of dynamite with which he was plotting to blow out the end
of the cell block. Steps must be taken.

When Osborne found him, he was in solitary confinement,
the most feared man in Auburn Prison. For three years he
had been held in isolation, one year and eight months of which
had been spent in the dark jail where a few hours had been
sufficient to make Osborne fear for his own sanity. During
those weary months he had clung to his reason by stripping the
buttons from his coat, throwing them at random about his
cell, and then hunting for them in the dark. It was not a game
of solitaire; it was One against the Gods—the Gods of Darkness. If all the buttons were found, victory for the One. If a
button rolled away and hid itself in a crack and you couldn't
find it, indeed suspected it had a locomotion of its own and
ran sneering from place to place as you fumbled after it, the
little evil gods chuckled maliciously in the deeper shadow
of the corners.

Yes, Canada Blackie kept his reason; but he came out of his
torture cell blind in one eye and stricken with tuberculosis.
And still, because he was feared, he was segregated under
strict surveillance. Even when the Mutual Welfare League
obtained yard privileges, he was excepted. Too dangerous,
everyone said. But one day he asked to see Osborne—in private. Osborne came to the cell, was admitted by an officer,
and heard the lock click behind him. From some secret recess
the prisoner brought forth a rude key.

"See," he said with a certain pride, "that fits the door of
my cell." Then he produced a wicked-looking knife fashioned
from a piece of steel.

"I intended to use this, too. But not now. Give them to
the Warden and tell him not to worry about me any more.
I'm going straight."

Canada Blackie kept his word. The next day, June 3, 1914,
he walked with the others into the yard. He saw the sun. He
breathed the clean air. He took in all the changes that had
taken place during his exile. It seemed too good to be true.

That evening he wrote a letter to Donald Lowrie. Reprinted many times, that letter is documentary evidence of a resurrection, physical and spiritual.

"Dear Friend Don," he began. "The above is the date of my new birthday. . . ."

For Canada Blackie there were to be no more birthdays. Pardoned too late, he was to die before another year rolled round; but the inspiration of his example was to sustain the League through many a crisis.

To an outsider the penalties which the Grievance Committees might impose will probably seem inadequate. Suspension from the League was the one punishment. Only the length of the period was discretionary. What few persons realize is the almost pitiful reverence in which the prisoners held the insignia of League membership. It was not simply that suspension meant loss of all the privileges which membership in the League conferred, though that was an important factor. It was also the disgrace connected with it. Hitherto the man who had been disciplined by prison authorities was a hero, and there was a certain glory in his martyrdom. But when his own fellows deemed him unworthy of participating in their organization, he became an outcast. He was a danger in the prison community, for he threatened the existence of the League itself. To be deprived of the right to wear the little shield on his coat was a stigma which even the most hardened convict felt.

There were occasions on which officers of the League used unorthodox methods to preserve order. Both Jack Murphy and Billy Duffy were husky individuals, packing a wallop in either hand. Moreover, they were so intensely earnest that they would go to almost any lengths to maintain League discipline. Mutual Welfare League records do not contain accounts of *all* the disciplinary measures applied. Once in a while the stubbornness of one of the less enlightened members brought prompt retribution in a form which the offender could not fail to understand. In all justice it should be added that the need for such direct methods was rare. Except in the case of a few chronic troublemakers who could not quite forgo the pleasures of insubordination, the regular system of penalties sufficed.

Although the course of inmate self-discipline had its ups and downs, depending largely upon the group in control of League affairs, the earnestness of the majority was demonstrated too many times to justify condemnation for occasional miscarriages. Several times the League was instrumental in preventing attempts at escape. Once it conducted a search of prison premises for a missing member and after twenty-four hours found the fugitive shivering and half frozen in the top of the big ice box, with some bread and a ham for provisions. What is more remarkable, it sometimes brought about the voluntary return of inmates who succeeded in "taking it on the lam."

Even in later years, when its character had been changed by administrative pressure from without and by psychological disturbances from within, the League justified its existence at critical moments. In the July, 1929, riot it was a League official who quieted the prison community during the excitement caused by blazing buildings and random shooting. Nevertheless, there was an immediate cry for suspension of the organization. People who never had believed in the League were quick to cast on it the entire blame for the insurrection. Perhaps some of the agitation would have subsided had it been known publicly that Principal Keeper Durnford himself rejected the suspension idea. He may not have approved of all the activities of the League, but when it came to a showdown he realized that in spite of its drooping morale it was better than no League at all.

In the following December a few of the most notorious convicts, none of whom was an official of the League, staged their desperate attempt at delivery. It happened that the "idle company," composed of the riffraff of the prison, were in the prison yard under the command of their sergeants-at-arms. During the tumult they maintained perfect order and, upon the signal, marched quietly to their cells. Only fifteen or sixteen prisoners took part in that bloody mutiny.

Osborne himself was the first to admit certain inherent difficulties in the functioning of such an organization as the Mutual Welfare League. He would be the last to admit that they could not be overcome. To begin with, the criminal "honor code" enjoins silence. In the ethics of the underworld the unforgivable sin is "squealing"—whether by accusation of, or bearing witness against, one of the profession. To overcome this reticence by showing the delicate distinction between blabbing and reporting offenses to an authoritative body composed of one's own peers was by no means easy. It took time and patience. Fortunately the few who immediately appreciated the difference were leaders whose influence counted for a great deal in the prison.

This hesitation to inform Grievance Committees of infractions was strengthened by another consideration. Convicts who were haled before the prisoner tribunal sometimes harbored resentment against those who imposed sentence. Who were these judges but outlaws like themselves? What right had they to assume superiority over their fellows? The hell with them! Now a prison feud is a nasty thing. It thrives on trivialities. Under the continual tension the merest accidental jostle becomes an overt act. The grudge turns into an obsession. Even when it is discovered by the authorities and for his own safety the threatened man is transferred to another prison, the vengeance of his enemy is likely to follow him. News travels quickly in the underworld, and the end of the story is often a knife in the back and a thousand prisoners who saw nothing, heard nothing. That too is part of the code. It was a lot to ask of an inmate that he should serve on a Grievance Committee. That the risk was accepted without grievous results speaks well for the new spirit which had come over the ancient prison.

Perhaps this is best illustrated by an incident that occurred during the discussion in one of the early meetings of the League. Under the new régime, argued the spokesmen, there must be no more fights or disorders in prison. Although all agreed, an undercurrent of uneasiness was plainly perceptible. It was Tony, an Italian, who renewed their confidence. Rising in his place, he said, "Let me tell you something."

"Two months ago at Sing Sing I did have a quarrel with my friend, and this is what he did to me." And the speaker pointed to a large scar which disfigured his left cheek. His "friend," when Tony was lying asleep in the hospital, had taken a razor and slit his mouth back to the cheek-bone.

A hard glint of light came into Tony's eyes as he said, "And I have been waiting for my revenge ever since. And he is here—here in this prison."

Then the light in the eyes softened and the hard look on the face relaxed as Tony added, slowly and impressively, "But now I see, Mr. Chairman, that I cannot have my revenge without doing a great wrong to fourteen hundred other men.

"So I give it up. He can go."

Wherever money or power is at stake there will be politics. The Mutual Welfare League had its share. Authority in League councils was the one prize worth striving for in prison, and the men fought, argued, bribed, and dickered for it exactly as do their brother politicians outside. It was of course unavoidable that at times a none too respectable clique should gain control. A man who has been a leader outside the walls is likely to be a leader in prison, for the qualities that made him a power in criminal circles cannot be hidden by a gray uniform. So long as Osborne was in personal touch with affairs in Auburn, he capitalized such leadership by winning it to the League. Often the very men who had been a center of trouble became under his influence the chief pillars of the prison society. Exceptions, however, were bound to occur, and occasionally the wrong type of leader rose to a commanding position in the League.

The problem of proper leadership was complicated by the fact that membership in the Mutual Welfare League had been thrown open to every inmate. Many critics, friendly as well as hostile, have picked out this indiscriminate eligibility as a flaw in Osborne's system; but none of them has yet suggested a practical way of limiting membership without changing the organization from a prisoners' League to a warden's League. The whole program was built on inmate responsibility. If the personnel of the League had been subject to the prejudices and predilections of an agent of the state, few convicts would have had confidence in the scheme. Whatever its draw-backs, the right of members to establish their own qualifications of membership was the backbone of Osborne's system.

Finally, as time passed, the first flush of enthusiasm for the new system was bound to fade. The novelty wore off. Some of the new men had a tendency to look upon the comforts and the privileges which came with the League not as something struggled for, sacrificed for, and won through a critical probation testing the capacity of prisoners to discipline themselves; but as the natural order of things, their inalienable right for which they need feel small gratitude. When the magnetism of Osborne's personality, felt spasmodically during the busy years that followed, was finally removed by death, the Mutual Welfare League lost not only a friend and adviser but a dynamic, inspirational force. It is not prejudicing the principles on which the League was founded to say that without Osborne's guidance and example it became more vulnerable to the perils just noted.

The League is still a controversial subject. For some it is synonymous with pampering and mollycoddling of prisoners. Osborne hated pampering only less than he hated brutality. To others it seems a great humanitarian project that miraculously turns murderers into saints. Osborne was often irritated by well-intentioned friends who sentimentalized his work. All he asked was that the Mutual Welfare League be judged fairly by its results as a practical system of dealing with convicts. Observed dispassionately, it was an inmate organization that for fifteen years functioned effectively if not perfectly—assisting in disciplinary problems; providing healthful exercise and recreation for its members; demonstrating its value as a preserver of order and security in times of emergency; and through substitution of self-discipline for the often stupid brutality of the old system preparing prisoners for law-abiding citizenship when their terms ended.

The most conclusive evidence of the League's value is to be found in the record of its "graduates." Some, it is true, returned to the old life; but there are hundreds now holding positions of usefulness and responsibility who look back on their experiences in the Mutual Welfare League as the turning point in their career. For Osborne, that was compensation enough. It justified his faith in "the enormous capacity of man to recover his moral balance after the commission of sin."

CHAPTER IV

WARDEN OF SING SING

OSBORNE was not content with the revolutionary changes going on inside the prison. He had other projects in mind. One of these was the establishment of a convict "honor camp" for road construction. In the summer of 1914 twenty inmates were placed in such a camp located near the little village of Meridian, about sixteen miles north of Auburn.

If the villagers and the farmers in the vicinity were terrified, who can blame them? There had been convict road camps before, but never one like this. Usually the personnel represented the pick of the prison, men considered safe and trustworthy. A corps of guards, heavily armed, was always on hand to discourage thoughts of escape. The twenty members of the Meridian outfit, on the other hand, had been elected by the Mutual Welfare League according to standards of which no warden of the past would approve. Only one was a first termer; one was doing his seventh stretch. Their unserved sentences ranged from one or two years to natural life.

Even greater cause for alarm could have been found in the nature and variety of the crimes for which these twenty men had been convicted: murder, first and second degree; manslaughter; rape; arson; sodomy; assault; robbery and grand larceny. The thought of children passing such notorious criminals on the way to and from school brought hysterical protests from parents. It might not have been so bad had a full quota of prison guards been on duty. The road work spread the convicts over an area of several miles, yet the camp was in charge of a single guard. And for an entire week even he was withdrawn, leaving discipline and administration to the prisoners. Not a bar or bolt, day or night. Not a person standing between these men and liberty. Yet not one of the group, whose sentences totaled over 221 years and averaged eleven

283

years each, took advantage of this extraordinary opportunity to escape. Loyalty to Osborne and to the League sustained their morale during the three months the road gang was in camp.

As the days wore on, the attitude of the people in the region underwent a radical change. Panic and suspicion abated. Convinced at last that they need fear no harm from this honor camp, they began to grow embarrassingly hospitable. Frequent invitations for one or more of the convicts to visit various homes presented so perplexing a problem that the men finally decided not to accept unless all the members could go in a body. The wisdom of such a course was indicated in the comment of one of the prisoners that "there are some women who will run after a uniform, even when it's a prison uniform."

On the night before the convicts were to break camp and return to Auburn Prison, they were invited to supper by the Assistant Town Superintendent in charge of road work. During the course of the meal word came that one of the members of the gang was wanted on the telephone at camp headquarters about a mile away. Although it was an unusual occurrence, the sergeant-at-arms gave the man permission to return and delegated another of the prisoners to accompany him.

Why should a convict member of a road gang be walking through the growing dusk to answer a long-distance telephone call? The mystery evaporates when it is learned that the man in gray was Tom Brown doing another bit. A repeater if there ever was one. For a week he had wielded pick and shovel on that very road he was now traveling. Dressed in the old uniform of Convict No. 33,333x, he had sweated under the sun, unrecognized by passers-by. After an interval of three weeks he had returned for another seven-day stretch, and after that for a day or two at a time. To-morrow the honor camp would disband, and the "dangerous" criminals who had proved that length of sentence or nature of crime is no true index of character would be back in their little cells in "Copper John."

Osborne had a shrewd idea of what that telephone message would be. For several weeks the question of a new warden at Sing Sing had been hanging fire. Two months earlier, Charles

S. Whitman, Republican nominee for governor, had visited Auburn Prison and expressed amazement at what he had found there. A little anxious about addressing an audience composed of hundreds whose presence was a direct result of his activities as District Attorney of New York, Whitman had been surprised by the hearty welcome he received from the inmates. Here was something outside his experience, wide as it had been. If he should win the election, he might follow Hughes' example and disregard party lines by naming Osborne to an important post.

Then had come the Sing Sing investigation by a special commissioner appointed by Governor Glynn. Certain unwholesome aromas resulting from this probe recommended a house-cleaning, and Glynn had suspended the warden. The place was now vacant. Without being an applicant for the position, Osborne could not help feeling he was the logical man to be chosen. His only doubt concerned the advisability of relinquishing his rôle as unofficial adviser of the Mutual Welfare League in Auburn for an official appointment that would have political complications.

So matters stood that evening when Tom Brown trudged along the road toward the honor camp headquarters. The chill of late October was in the air. Winter would soon be upon them. Involuntarily his thoughts turned toward those notoriously dank, dismal cells of Sing Sing. Even an indifferent public and a still more indifferent officialdom were becoming aroused over reports of evil conditions at the largest of the state prisons. Did he not have a moral obligation to accept the post? He confided his thoughts to his convict companion.

"What do you think I ought to do, Bill, in case the offer is made?"

"Take it."

"But think of the difficulties."

"Yes, but think of the good you could do."

With this cheering corroboration of his own belief, Osborne answered the telephone call. It was Dr. Whitin, secretary of the Prison Commission, who reported that Governor Glynn was expected to act favorably and soon on the wardenship. Osborne replied that he thought it would be a good move to make the appointment *before* election, now only a few days away.

That was that, but the question of accepting or refusing still bothered him. Upon his return to Auburn, he decided to ask the advice of his friends in the Mutual Welfare League. They knew the obstacles even better than he. Calling together his companions of the honor camp and five of the Executive Committee, he explained the situation. At first, opinion was about evenly divided. Some thought no good would come of it. There were too many first-termers in Sing Sing to appreciate all the League meant. Others were fearful of political treachery. "You'll be framed, sure as the world," they told Osborne. For two days they debated the matter. When it came to a vote, eighteen of the twenty-five went on record as favoring acceptance of the wardenship. For Osborne that was enough, and he decided to take the risk.

The mills of politics, however, grind slowly. Election Day came, and still there was no appointment. Whitman's victory at the polls meant that Glynn would probably consult his successor before naming a man for warden of Sing Sing. Superintendent of Prisons Riley would naturally have a part in the discussion. After several interviews with Glynn, Whitman, and Riley, Osborne suggested Everit Macy, Superintendent of Charities of Westchester County, as an alternative. Macy refused to consider. Finally, on November 19, the Governor, the Governor-elect, and the Superintendent of Prisons joined in asking Osborne to take the post; and on the same day Osborne wrote his letter of acceptance.

There could have been no misunderstanding about Osborne's purposes. He had the solemn assurance of Governor-elect Whitman that there would be no politics in the Prison Department, and that he could remain at Sing Sing unmolested as long as he chose. It was understood also that the old system at Sing Sing would be done away with and a branch of the Mutual Welfare League established there. To his surprise and chagrin, Osborne learned in confidence from Whitman that the Superintendent of Prisons was slated for removal. Judge John B. Riley had coöperated splendidly at Auburn, and Osborne hoped to have his support in this new venture. Later he was to wish that Whitman had stuck to his original intention.

Osborne took up his duties at Sing Sing on December 1. If he needed a reminder of the forebodings of the eight dissenting members of the Mutual Welfare League at Auburn, it was provided by an article in the *New York Tribune*. When the news of Osborne's appointment broke, a staff correspondent had been sent to Auburn for a special story. Although invited by Warden Rattigan to inspect the workings of the prison, the correspondent never entered the gate. Contenting himself with picking up gossip and rumor in the city, he wrote a two-column article, beginning as follows:

In Auburn bars do not a prison make. Coddled by Thomas Mott Osborne, who until he was made warden of Sing Sing, unofficially ran the institution here ostensibly directed by Charles Rattigan, the appointed warden, a majority of the 1,300 male convicts are permitted more liberties than boys in a boarding-school.

Coddling of prisoners. How that phrase was to stick! Invented by a reporter unacquainted with the actual reforms accomplished, it was to plague Osborne for the rest of his career. With this threat of misinterpretation at the very outset, Osborne wished he had given more publicity to the Mutual Welfare League development. After the spectacular Tom Brown exploit, he had worked quietly within the prison, organizing, testing, perfecting the inmate society. As a consequence, the public knew little of what was happening. There were few headlines in the newspapers. Time enough, he had thought, to publish the details when the experiment had proved itself.

There was another disconcerting result of this policy of unobtrusiveness—one that had a great deal to do with Osborne's eagerness to become warden of Sing Sing. A few months before his appointment, the press had suddenly burst into columns of print. It seemed that revolutionary reforms were taking place in the old bastile up the river. A new era was beginning. The then Warden had formed the Golden Rule Brotherhood, membership in which conferred a variety of privileges. Who said New York State was not progressive in penological matters?

Osborne was first exasperated, then furious. He realized that the Golden Rule Brotherhood aped the Mutual Welfare League in everything but the important things. It put the cart before the horse, granting privileges before they were earned. And yet people called him a sentimentalist, a coddler of prisoners! He was human enough, too, to resent the stolen publicity. Obviously based on his system, of which the general public had little accurate information, the Golden Rule Brotherhood was apparently an attempt to distract attention from what was going on at Auburn and to forestall the criticism of Sing Sing implied by the successful operation of the Mutual Welfare League.

An even more ghastly parody, to Osborne's way of thinking, was being tried out at Great Meadow Prison, situated at Comstock about seventy miles north of Albany. There Warden William J. Homer, whose years of experience as a railway ticket agent had evidently impressed the authorities with his fitness for his present assignment, was running what he called an "honor prison." Of all the prison experiments, this seemed to Osborne the grossest fraud. Honor? The system was distinguished by a lack of it. Only first-termers and men with excellent records were admitted. Men convicted of violent crimes were barred. This picked population was supposed to be on its honor, for there were no walls at Great Meadow. Except for the prison buildings, the only structure in sight was a small railroad station.

To give credit where credit is due, it should be stated that there were few attempts at escape. But there are substitutes for walls. Warden Homer dispensed special favors to those inmates who would spy on their fellows. It was his boast that nothing could happen in the prison without his being aware of it in a few minutes. The efficiency of this espionage system was rather alarmingly demonstrated to Dr. George W. Kirchwey and Miss Doty of the Prison Commission. As they were passing through the kitchen on a tour of inspection one day, Miss Doty made some casual comment not particularly favorable to the Warden. No sooner had they returned to the main office, than Mr. Homer taxed her with her very words, more in glee at his achievement than in pain at the criticism.

There were, however, more tangible evidences of the effort to instill honor into the criminal breast. Cordons of armed guards watched over the prisoners with unremitting caution while they were at work in the quarry or on the farm. If these measures failed and some desperate inmate succeeded in making a break for liberty, he rarely got far. The reason is all too clearly explained in the annual report of Great Meadow Prison, dated November 1, 1915. Only twice that year had there been attempts at escape, and both of those occurred on the same day. Of the bolters the report said:

They were captured some five hours later about four miles from the institution, where they had been trailed by the bloodhounds. These dogs have on several occasions demonstrated their worth and the wisdom of their purchase.

Admitting that there was less brutality at Great Meadow than in Clinton and Sing Sing, Osborne was nevertheless disgusted by the inherent hypocrisy of the "honor" claim. Such a system, he declared, might make good *prisoners;* it could never make good *citizens.* He took up his duties at Sing Sing with the determination to expose this false penology and demonstrate the feasibility of his own program—the treatment of convicted men as individuals capable in varying degrees of assuming responsibility for prison routine and prison discipline.

It was a delicate task that faced him. On the one hand were conditions so appalling that only radical revision of the existing system could hope to be effective in changing them. On the other was a prisoner organization, already functioning, already owning the loyalty of many inmates—especially a favored group who found the Brotherhood much to their liking. He would have to move slowly and with consummate tact if he hoped to apply his own theories without alienating the men.

Sing Sing is situated on the east bank of the Hudson River about thirty miles north of New York City. Built on a sort of promontory that overlooks the village on one side and the river on the other, it is typical of the prison construction of a century ago. The original cell block, constructed by a draft of convicts from Auburn in 1825, still stands, forbidding in spite of windows that have been cut through the solid masonry to admit light and air to the unfortunate occupants. The walls are three feet thick. The cells, twelve hundred little burrowings in this mountain of stone, are seven feet long, three feet three inches wide, and six and one-half feet high. "Twenty Thousand Years in Sing Sing" is the provocative title of Warden Lewis E. Lawes' recent book. He might have added a subtitle to the effect that the first ten thousand years were the hardest. Hardly a ray of light had filtered into those dungeons. One can imagine the jailer going his rounds, his lantern casting grotesque shadows on the wall; the prisoners, with shaven crowns and zebra clothing, disconsolately beating out the rhythms of the lock-step; and over it all the atmosphere of hopelessness, obsceneness, and cruelty.

Although some of the worst conditions had been remedied by the time Thomas Mott Osborne took charge in 1914, Sing Sing was still a byword for all that is evil. The record of its wardens during the past century told all too plainly the futility of hoping for amelioration of the prisoner's lot through wise administration. Politics had been the determining factor. Captain Elam Lynds, warden of Auburn Prison and the man in charge of the draft that had built the Sing Sing cell block, was the first to take office in the new prison. Notwithstanding the fact that in those days wardens were expected to be hard-boiled, charges of extreme cruelty were lodged against Captain Lynds. He was exonerated by a "select committee" of the State Senate. Yet he must have been a man of strong character—and that is more than can be said of the majority of his successors. In most cases brutality and incompetence seemed to go together—so much so that suspensions and removals were incredibly frequent. Excepting three men whose terms ran over five years, the average tenure of office for thirty-one Sing Sing wardens was only little over a year. The roster included a steam-fitter, a coal dealer, a horseman, a drunkard (by avocation if not by profession), and a flock of ward heelers—anybody, it seems, except a man whose qualifications might lead one to believe he could exercise an intelligent direction of the institution.

Osborne was apparently the first warden whose appointment had not been dictated by politics. The responsibility of it rather oppressed him that first night he spent in the warden's aparument in Sing Sing; nor did his surroundings contribute to a cheerful frame of mind. Looking out of his window, he could just see the roof of the death house. More than anything else connected with prison work the idea of capital punishment repelled him. Although he was convinced that society had no right to take a life for a life, his revulsion was more biological than intellectual. The thought of the electric chair sickened him. Many a time he sat up all night in the death house with a man condemned to die the next morning, but not once during his whole career would he consent to be present at an execution.

If the outlook from his room was not inspiring, the interior arrangements could scarcely be called cozy. Massive furniture, the product of prison labor, stared at him stonily. On every drawer and every cabinet he saw lock and key, reminders of a pervasive suspicion. The bureau alone, with its many compartments, resembled a locksmith's display. On the spot he decided to change all that. From now on no more locked drawers and bolted doors. He kept his promise. When he resigned two years later, he looked back with satisfaction on the results of his first reform in Sing Sing. Nothing was ever stolen. Once, though, thirty dollars disappeared. Then he remembered he had left it in the pocket of a pair of white duck trousers that had gone to the prison laundry. Before he could make inquiries, the convict in charge of the laundry brought back the money.

Osborne began his official duties the next morning. First of all, he visited the mess-hall and watched nearly fifteen hundred prisoners march in for breakfast. At the advice of Harry Bolasky, a "graduate" of the Mutual Welfare League whom recently and almost involuntarily he had added to his household, he went alone. "Show them you're the boss," Harry had advised. Walking along the aisles, he was pleased to note that the convicts seemed more interested in the new Warden than in the breakfast; but when he glanced at the food he could well understand that—hash that turned the stomach just to look at it.

After breakfast in the Warden's house, a meal prepared by a prisoner cook who had once been chef at a leading New York hotel, the day's routine began: visits of friends to congratulate him; interviews with newspaper reporters, eager to get a line on the new Warden's policies; inspection of the various departments of the prison. What struck Osborne most was the filthiness that seemed to be taken for granted. Not only the kitchen but the cook was dirty. Even the hospital, with its operating room and nurses' dormitory, seemed to be in need of a cleaning. In the school for illiterates, an atmosphere of listlessness matched the dullness of the "professor's" elucidations. A visit to the death house reminded him that the State Legislature had recently passed a law requiring all executions to take place at Sing Sing, and he shuddered to think of the impending increase among the occupants of this place of doom.

Osborne's first official act was the appointment of a "confidential clerk." That title was a substitute for Deputy Warden, for the law made no provision for an official assistant to the Warden. With his innate dislike for the details of routine, Osborne was determined to have someone in charge of the business part of the job, leaving him free to undertake the reforms he had in mind. For this assignment he chose Charles H. Johnson, superintendent of a Westchester orphan asylum and previously head of the Albany Orphan Asylum. Johnson had been the choice of the New York Prison Association for Warden of Sing Sing. Without prison experience, he had seemed to Osborne ill fitted to assume full responsibility for the state's greatest penal institution, a belief which made Osborne all the more willing to accept the appointment himself. In a spirit of fairness, however, he decided to make Johnson his deputy. He was even more generous than that, allocating to his subordinate $2,000 of his own $3,500 salary, leaving himself only $1,500 a year and bringing Johnson's pay up to $3,500. Moreover, he promised to recommend Johnson for Warden if he made good.

Osborne lost no time in putting his ideas of reform into effect. The first afternoon he called a meeting of the Board of Delegates of the Golden Rule Brotherhood. Treading cautiously, he explained that he was not so familiar with conditions at Sing Sing as they were, and that he would have to rely on them for suggestions and advice. In the evening the president of the Brotherhood and the Executive Committee met with him in the Warden's office. As Osborne scrutinized the six men before him, he wondered whether or not it would be possible from such raw material to build real leaders. Although his hopes rose a notch in the discussions that followed, he felt that the task he had undertaken was even more difficult than he had anticipated.

The results of that first day seemed far from exciting, yet in a negative way it could be counted a victory. At least some of the newspapers thought so. The *New York Times* commented the next morning:

> The first day was a success in every way. There were no incendiary fires, no riots, and no strikes—all marks of coming and going of wardens in the past.

Osborne had not thought of that!

In the days that followed he mingled freely with the prisoners, especially in the yard, chatting with them in direct defiance of the old rule that forbade a convict to approach within fifteen feet of the Warden. The guards were amazed to find that he went unarmed, even when alone, for the custom had been for the Warden to carry a loaded revolver on his rounds. Osborne scarcely thought of any risk. As Tom Brown he had lost all fear of convicts, and in turn prisoners trusted him completely. His absolute confidence was all the protection he needed.

The effects of this new attitude soon showed themselves. On the sixth day after his arrival, the Principal Keeper came to him in a state of bewilderment.

"Warden," he said, "I have to tell you a piece of most remarkable news. There isn't a single man under punishment!"

"Well, why should there be?" was the quiet response.

"Why, in all my experience at Sing Sing I have never known such a condition. I don't believe it's happened before since the prison was built, certainly not in my time."

And the Principal Keeper was just rounding out a quarter of a century of service at Sing Sing.

Osborne had asked the Executive Committee of the Golden Rule Brotherhood to draft a formal petition embodying the changes that in their judgment were advisable and practicable. As a result fifteen requests were submitted. A day or two later came the first mass meeting of the Brotherhood. It was Sunday, and for the first time Sing Sing prisoners assembled without guards. Because the chapel did not accommodate all the prison population, only half of the inmates could attend. One after another, the requests were formally presented, and all but two granted. Frank Marshall White, the only outside witness, wrote a vivid account for the *Outlook,* stressing the difference between this scene and the mutinies and fires that had been the rule only a year before.

The thirteen reforms which were authorized by Osborne at this meeting changed the entire atmosphere of Sing Sing. Prisoners were allowed to have visitors Sundays and holidays, for many relatives could not make the trip to Ossining on work days. They could purchase postage stamps and write necessary letters to persons whose names were not on the official correspondence list. Hitherto, for some unknown reason, inmates had to rely on friends from outside to furnish stamps, although they could buy groceries and other things. Lights were left on a half-hour longer at night to give opportunity for reading. The moving picture shows were transferred from Saturday afternoon to Sunday afternoon, thus providing an interlude in that most terrible of days. The recommendation of the inmates that places in the dormitory, used to house the prison overflow, be given first to cripples or those suffering from some illness indicated a concern for the general welfare that was most gratifying to Osborne. So too was the objection against "doubling up" of prisoners, and he determined to remedy that as soon as conditions permitted. The only requests that he held in abeyance concerned the removal of the screens separating prisoners and outsiders in the visiting room, and permission for inmates to receive Sunday newspapers.

There was one recommendation that had been inspired by Osborne himself. In that first meeting with the Brotherhood Board of Delegates he had declared that in his opinion the thing most needed was a tribunal of the prisoners to deal with disciplinary matters. From that suggestion came the following request:

> We ask that the system of discipline be materially altered, and that the Executive Committee of the Brotherhood, sitting as a court, shall be allowed to examine all minor cases of discipline and determine, if practicable, the nature and extent of the penalties to be inflicted for violation of the prison rules or the rules of the Brotherhood. . . .

In this recommendation one divergence from the system in operation at Auburn is to be noted. Instead of the Grievance Committees of the Mutual Welfare League there was to be an inmate court. Osborne had returned to the George Junior Republic idea. In his mind, however, it was not a backward but a forward step. He had a plan so daring that in comparison his other reforms seem mere child's play. It will be remembered that in Auburn the Mutual Welfare League had excepted from its jurisdiction five major violations: assault upon an officer, assault upon another inmate, refusal to work, strike, and attempt to escape. In Sing Sing there would be no exceptions. The Prisoners' Court should deal with *all* cases, from minor infractions to attempted murder! That meant that if an inmate wielding a huge knife attacked an officer, he would be judged by his fellows, not by the Warden.

Osborne's plan did not entail an absolute transfer of authority from the prison officials to the prison inmates. Rather it was a division of authority, a coöperative effort, with the prisoners assuming the initial responsibility. The Court consisted of the Executive Board of the Golden Rule Brotherhood acting as a Judiciary Board of five judges, and met each afternoon in the chapel. Charges could be brought against an inmate by any other inmate or by any one of the guards. The accused had the privilege of taking charge of his own case or being represented by "counsel" of his own choosing. Both sides could summon witnesses and take testimony, and the sessions were open to all prisoners who wished to attend.

The keystone of this structure was the presence in Court of a representative of the administration. Designated by the Warden, he was a spectator only, except that he had the right to appeal any case if in his judgment justice had not been done. Privilege of appeal was also open to the accused. When a case was appealed it went directly to the Warden's Court, composed of the Warden, the Principal Keeper, and the prison physician. Ultimate control, therefore, rested with the administration. Without relinquishing adequate safeguards, Osborne had abolished the secret inquisitions conducted by the guards and had established a self-governing prison community that challenged whatever remained to its members of honor, fair play, and capacity for sound judgment.

The alacrity with which the prisoners in Sing Sing adopted this suggestion was in striking contrast to the hesitation of the inmates of Auburn Prison when they were asked to assume responsibility for minor violations alone, and the first session of the Court was held exactly one week after Osborne became Warden. From that time on it functioned efficiently if not perfectly; better in fact than the administration of justice in New York City—though that can scarcely be construed as high praise. In spite of the reluctance of some of the guards to appear as witnesses before a court of their own charges, cases were heard and disposed of with surprising expedition; nor was there evidence of a tendency toward undue leniency. Of the thirty-four malefactors haled before the Prisoners' Court in that first month of December, twenty-eight were convicted and sentenced. Only three were found not guilty. The other three cases were dismissed.

There was no pretense of following the legal formula. The

judges passed their verdicts, without benefit of jury, on the merits of the cases. None of the punishments meted out by the Prisoners' Court was entered upon the prison records. On this Osborne had insisted. So far as society went, a convict upon his release would have a clean record unless the Warden's delegate in the Court appealed his case to the Warden's Court. Judge Garvin once visited Sing Sing with a party of friends and was surprised at the simplicity of the legal machinery. Congratulating the presiding judge at the conclusion of the day's session, he remarked:

"I was very much interested to notice that apparently you have no code of law and no rules of procedure."

"No, Your Honor," was the naïve reply. "You see, in this court we try to manage things by common sense."

The Court, however, should not be considered as an isolated factor. It was part and parcel of the new system as a whole. The important thing was not that the Court functioned well but that it was not called upon to function more strenuously. Compare the record of those thirty-four cases which were handled that December with the record of the preceding December. A year before, 117 men had been reported during the same period. Instead of such minor infractions as smoking, profanity, or occasional rough-housing—the grist the new court had to deal with—the roster of violations had included twenty-eight fights, ten strikes, one case of felonious assault, twelve cases of insubordination, and several of immoral conduct. Although the penalties under the new code were negligible as compared to the old schedule of fines, loss of good time, and solitary confinement—suspension from the Brotherhood for various periods being the only punishment—they were doubly effective. Violent crimes in Sing Sing were reduced to the vanishing point, and insubordination was practically nonexistent.

Osborne had objected to the "honor prison" and to the Golden Rule Brotherhood as he had first found it, because each of the two systems was an attempt to bribe prisoners to be good. Coddle them first; then maybe they will behave. It was a sort of gentlemen's agreement between the Warden and the inmates, with the implicit understanding that the parties of the second part were anything but gentlemen. Osborne's program was more like a business contract—something for something. Before giving formal sanction to the changes asked by the prisoners, he demanded a return in kind.

First of all, there should be better general discipline in the prison and better order in the cell block. He asked that the men cultivate a more alert bearing, especially in marching, and that whether in the shops or in their cells they show consideration of others by silence and good order. Coupled with this, a courteous attitude toward the prison officers was essential. Any attempt to encroach upon their lawful authority would jeopardize the success of the Brotherhood and bring a return of the old regulations.

Cleanliness was another thing the Warden insisted upon. He had been troubled not only by the appearance of the men but by the litter in the prison and in the yard. There must be an end to such conditions. Barrels would be provided for waste, and every inmate would be held personally responsible for maintaining cleanliness and orderliness.

Some have thought that Osborne was not practical; yet he succeeded, where others had failed, in increasing the industrial output of Sing Sing. He demanded not only greater efficiency but longer working hours on Saturday. That was only fair, he contended, if the moving picture entertainments were to be shifted to Sunday afternoons. "I must urge the importance of this to the men themselves," he told them. "The worst thing a man can learn in prison is to do inefficient work."

That the justice of these demands was immediately recognized indicates how firmly Osborne had planted his feet on solid ground. It was the realist in him shrewdly coöperating with the idealist.

His common sense was shown in other ways. For nearly three months he made no attempt to change the structure or name of the inmate society. Using the Golden Rule Brotherhood as an instrument, he effected reforms without giving the prisoners cause to feel that he was upsetting an established organization for the sake of his own pet ideas. Yet all the time he was building up a personal following who could be counted on to support him. Nearly every day brought new evidences of progress.

Christmas, like all holidays, had meant a stretch of loathsome confinement. The one relaxation open to the men was that of hearing the chaplain preach on "peace on earth, good will toward men," while they wondered "What peace?" and "Toward what men?" No doubt the critics who were watching for traces of sentimentality in the new Warden's policies sneered at the innovations Osborne introduced. For every inmate there was a gift, made possible by generous friends in New York, intrinsically of little value yet significant enough to make Christmas spirit seem less like a bedtime story than ever before in that Big House. In the afternoon, through the courtesy of William A. Brady, Owen Davis's new play, "Sinners," was performed in the chapel with Alice Brady making her début as a star. Special scenery had been brought from New York. In spite of the accidentally pertinent title, the prisoners were delighted. There was also keen competition among the inmates for the prize of $100 which Mr. Brady had offered for the best written account of the performance, and it is worth recording that the winner promptly turned the money into the treasury of the Golden Rule Brotherhood. Some idea of the relative magnitude of the gift may be gained from the reflection that at inmate wages it would take the donor twenty-two years to earn that amount in the prison shops.

It was typical of Osborne that in trying out his theories of greater liberty for prisoners he should choose the toughest gang in the institution for his experiment. Even in Auburn he had been warned against the "Knit Shop." It was there, Mutual Welfare League friends had told him, he would have the greatest difficulty. The men in the Knit Shop hated the work, and many a bloody assault had been recorded against them. Yet there was good psychology in tackling the hardest problem first. The so-called hard-boiled convicts were often easiest to approach; and once they were won over, the rest was easy.

Osborne put it up to them. On their marches to and from the shop and the mess-hall the guards would be withdrawn.

Their delegates on the Board of the Brotherhood would act as marshals.

The arrangement worked perfectly, and the men strode along with a new lift to their shoulders. Next day Osborne told them how proud he was of them. "I have heard," he said frankly, "that your company is the worst behaved in Sing Sing; but there has been no trouble yet, and I don't expect any. But as I wish to make certain there will not be any, I am going to take all your guards out of the shop; for, of course, if there is no one to make trouble for, there won't be any trouble."

For a moment there was absolute silence; then a gasp followed by a roar of laughter; and finally a cheer—a progression of emotional reactions that was particularly pleasing to the Warden. He was genuinely surprised, however, when a delegate of the Knit Shop called on him next morning with a request from the company that one of the guards be retained as assistant foreman. The men liked him, and he would be a good influence in maintaining discipline and increasing production. Although this proposal represented a departure from his original plan, Osborne accepted the judgment of the prisoners and gave his approval, with the result that only once thereafter was there the slightest trouble. Months later there was a threat of a strike in the Knit Shop, but the difficulty was ironed out by the men themselves before the Warden could intervene. And this was the company with the bloody record!

Osborne spent New Year's Day with his family in Auburn. When he returned on the morning of January 4, he felt a curious tension in the air—not of alarm but of secrecy. It was explained that noon when in response to a summons he went into the yard. The noon whistle blew, and the prisoners came marching out of the shops in double column. Osborne's first thought was that he had never seen them march so well before; then suddenly he realized there was not a guard in sight! All the companies were in charge of their own delegates. It was the same in the mess-hall. In place of the usual corps of thirty-five or forty guards lined up against the wall and carrying heavily loaded canes, there was only the inmate sergeant-at-arms and his deputies. Yet the discipline was flawless.

"What did you think of that surprise, Warden?" asked a convict later that day. "Wasn't that a swell New Year's present?"

Osborne admitted it was the best he ever had, for the suggestion had originated with the men themselves and had been sanctioned by Mr. Johnson.

Before many days had passed all the shops were operating without guards. In some cases, however, the guard was retained as foreman to help with production problems; but usually he discarded his uniform and wore civilian clothes. It is significant that the officers as well as the inmates realized the benefits of the new system. At a special mass meeting the keepers and guards drafted a communication to the Warden expressing their appreciation of his efforts to change the revolting conditions in Sing Sing. They characterized his plans as "practical" and pledged him their loyalty. This was more than Osborne had dared hope. What could he not accomplish with both guards and inmates coöperating with him?

Toward the end of February he decided the time had come to effect the complete transformation of the Golden Rule Brotherhood into the Mutual Welfare League. Really the process had been begun months before. When the Brotherhood adopted the Prisoners' Court, it had automatically discarded one of the cardinal features of the old organization. According to the system established by Osborne's predecessor, inmates were to report all violations of rules—to the guards! Osborne knew the folly of that. On the one hand, spying and grudge-paying; on the other, silence in accordance with the criminal code. The one was vicious; the other, impenetrable. He remembered the words of the dying lad who stubbornly refused to reveal the identity of his assailants: "If I live, I'll get 'em, and if I die, I'll forgive 'em." Those words epitomized the unwritten law of the underworld.

Built on such foundations, the Brotherhood was doomed to failure from the outset. There was little real prisoner responsibility; and what trust there was, the men abused. Some of the worst evils even increased. More drugs and liquor were smuggled in than ever before. When Osborne took the helm, he attacked this problem with uncanny subtlety. He knew that many prisoners were getting their "snow" regularly. He knew also that some of the guards were purveyors of the dope. Yet he made no dismissals on that score, and refused to listen when a guard or inmate wanted to name names. "I don't care what has happened in the past," he said. "That is over and done with. It is the future that counts. All I ask is that from this moment there be no more peddling of drugs and liquor."

The immediate results of this announcement were a bit staggering. Osborne received a visit from the sergeant-at-arms, a mere youth whose innocent face had induced the Warden to intrust to him an extraordinary amount of responsibility. He brought with him three other convicts, all of them looking very sober indeed. There was an embarrassing silence for a moment; then the sergeant-at-arms struck in desperately:

"Warden, we thought we ought to come and tell you that you are trusting us too much."

Taken by surprise, Osborne asked what he meant.

"Well, it is only right that you should know what we are. I have been one of the chief dope peddlers here, and this fellow" —pointing to another of the quartet—"has been the worst of the lot. We don't think you ought to go any further without knowing who you are dealing with."

It was a delicate situation, but Osborne met it promptly.

"That," he said, "was before I became Warden, I suppose. I am not interested in that. The question is, what are you doing now?"

"We're on the level," was the solemn response.

Evidently they were, for a few days later a group of convicts held up one of the "crooked screws" known to be peddling liquor and dope, searched him, found a bottle of whisky, smashed it, warned the guard, and let him go. Osborne never asked the names of the inmates or of the guard involved in this fracas.

Some weeks later the sergeant-at-arms reported to the Warden that except for small amounts that new men might sneak in, there was no more dope traffic in Sing Sing. Osborne refused to be convinced, knowing only too well what the situation had been. He was astounded as well as pleased, therefore, when a prisoner who had been a drug addict testified voluntarily that he couldn't get the stuff, and that if he couldn't, nobody could. The stream of drugs which had been smuggled in, in a thousand crafty ways, had been checked at last.

With such revisions of the old system already a fact, all that remained was the formal change of the Brotherhood to the Mutual Welfare League. The inmates were loyal, and showed it by living up to the bargain Osborne had made with them at first. With greater liberty had come increased industrial production. Some of the men, after working a whole day for one and one-half cents, sacrificed their evening leisure to knit garments for the Polish war sufferers. The guards, too, had their faith in the Warden confirmed in a very practical way. Because the Brotherhood had taken over so large a part of the responsibility for discipline, Osborne was able to change the two-shift system of ten to fourteen hours for guard duty to three shifts of eight hours each, without hiring a single extra man.

One day in the mess-hall, Osborne found a favorable opportunity to state his case. It was undesirable that the new system now in operation at Auburn and Sing Sing should become confused in the public mind by two separate organizations with different names. As the original unit, the Mutual Welfare League should give its name to the Sing Sing branch. With the change of name would also come a change of structure, the office of president being abolished, the Executive Committee increased from five to nine, and voting suffrage extended to include all inmates in good standing. Would they like that? He would abide by their decision.

Until the overwhelming vote in favor of the change showed how strong was his support among the prisoners, Osborne was anxious. He looked upon this move not as a technicality but as an essential step, for there were certain abuses he could not reach through the Brotherhood. With the abolition of the presidential office, his way was cleared. Yet he knew there was trouble ahead. Already there had been menacing signs of a conspiracy against him. Soon, he was sure, his enemies would come into the open.

CHAPTER V

THE TRAP IS SET

AT six-thirty o'clock on the morning of July 30, 1915, the Warden of Sing Sing threw himself on his bed in a state of utter exhaustion. For twenty-four hours he had had no rest. With the possible exception of the night spent in the Auburn Prison jail, no experience in his prison career had been so grueling; and now, sick at heart, he sought oblivion in sleep.

Charles Becker, twice convicted of the murder of the gambler Herman Rosenthal, had just gone to his death in the electric chair.

When Becker first came to the death house in Sing Sing, Osborne had not liked him. In spite of the handsome face and splendid physique—he stood six feet four—there was a hardness about the eyes and mouth that spoke of unscrupulousness, even cruelty. Such a man, thought Osborne, would commit murder if driven to it.

Gradually, however, he changed his mind about Becker. The doomed man would sit for hours at the door of his cell reading aloud to his fellow prisoners, whiling away the dreadful monotony of that period between sentence and death. There was, too, something manly in his attitude. He liked to talk with Osborne about his own case, yet never tried to appeal for sympathy by hypocritical avowals of repentance. He admitted certain crimes—chiefly concerned with graft—but not the murder of Rosenthal. The more Osborne saw of him, the more clearly he realized that certain features of that crime were not 'n keeping with Becker's character. If such a man had set his mind on murder, he would have made a better job of it. Certainly he would never have put himself at the mercy of several accomplices. Against his own inclination, Osborne came to

304

believe that the gangsters who had turned state's evidence were sacrificing Becker to save their own skins.

Corroboration of this theory came unexpectedly. A prisoner named Murphy asked for an interview with the Warden and told this story. Nearly three years before, while in the Tombs Prison awaiting trial, he had heard the men who later testified against Becker planning the testimony they should give. "That won't do; we want Becker!" was one of the remarks. Murphy was sure it was all a frame-up and did not want the blood of an innocent man on his conscience.

Still Osborne was not deeply impressed. Why had not Murphy come forward with this story long before? The answer to that seemed reasonable: Murphy had been afraid he might "get the chair" himself, and he did not dare antagonize District Attorney Whitman. Besides, he shared the opinion of most people that Becker could not be convicted.

Although last-minute testimony from a convict is usually looked on with suspicion, Osborne felt the matter important enough to obtain Governor Whitman's consent to hear Murphy. Leaving his assistant, Mr. Johnson, to conduct the prisoner to Albany, he caught the train for Auburn to spend the week-end. The next day came a telephone call from Albany. It was the Governor in a boiling rage. He demanded to know why prisoners at Sing Sing were allowed to go into the death house and talk with the men awaiting execution. When Osborne denied such a practice, Whitman said Murphy was there in his office and had confessed he had made contact with Becker.

Osborne was both amazed and alarmed. He had never extended the inmate privileges to include men in the death house and he knew violation of the rule of isolation was a serious offense. A telegram from Superintendent Riley, ordering him to report at Albany immediately, arrived that very afternoon. The mystery was finally explained. According to a custom which had existed long before Osborne took charge, the condemned men were permitted to hear concerts on Sunday evenings, sometimes a chorus of inmate voices. About a month before these events, Murphy had confided his secret to another prisoner, who, instead of advising him to go to the Warden or communicate with Bourke Cockran, Becker's attorney, suggested that he try to get into the death house and see Becker himself. Murphy accomplished this by arranging to change places with one of the Sunday evening singers. Somehow or other, he managed to pass the Principal Keeper, find a place near Becker's cell, and during the singing explain his errand. Becker, however, was wise enough to tell Murphy to get in touch with Cockran if he knew anything about the case.

All this came out at the interview between the Governor and Murphy. Whitman was so angry that he would scarcely listen to the new evidence, and the convict was glad to escape to the greater security of Sing Sing. For once, however, Osborne was lucky. The records showed that on the day Murphy made his way into the death house, the Warden was in Auburn. Some one else had signed the order and approved the list of singers. Responsibility for permitting another inmate to double for a singer rested squarely on the Principal Keeper. Still, it was a close call; for had Osborne been present, an adequate excuse for dismissing him would have been provided. Already Osborne knew that plans were afoot to get rid of him.

On the day before the execution, Sing Sing was in a hubbub. The Warden had canceled all passes, but there were crowds of reporters hanging about the prison entrance, men coming and going on errands, and a general air of excitement. By coincidence, there was also an election of the new Board of Delegates of the League, and a postponed visit of Samuel Gompers and a party of friends. In the midst of this confusion Murphy appeared again, sobbing hysterically, with a written plea for intervention in Becker's behalf:

> Won't you make a final plea to the Governor in Chas. Becker's behalf? I know positively, absolutely, that he is an innocent man. . . . I overheard the plot of the real murderers . . . who are now sacrificing Becker to save their own worthless lives. . . . If he goes to the chair I can never forgive myself for concealing what I knew for three years, but I could not believe he could be doomed.

It was too late now to hope for clemency. Governor Whitman had already shown extreme annoyance at Osborne's repeated attacks on capital punishment, and in Becker's case he was obdurate. The wife of the doomed man arrived at Sing Sing late in the evening after failing to reach the Governor in Albany. He was away—no one, apparently, knew where. With the minutes slipping by, the woman made frantic efforts to reach Whitman by telephone and finally discovered him at a hotel in Poughkeepsie. The answer to her plea was *no,* and it was final.

For all Osborne's disbelief in capital punishment, he realized how difficult it is for a governor to decide an issue of life and death when death has been decreed by the state; but in this instance he felt injustice had been done. In the first place, he was now fully convinced of Becker's innocence of the murder. Secondly, it seemed hardly fitting that the man who as District Attorney had convicted Becker, not only once but again after the first verdict had been reversed by the Court of Appeals, should have the right to pass judgment as Governor on the merits of the case. However honest and discerning Whitman might be, he could scarcely help being biased. To pardon Becker or commute the sentence would have meant a reflection on his own conduct of the trial as District Attorney.

After Becker had bidden his wife a last farewell, the Warden entered the death house. White shades were drawn before all the cells except that of Becker, and it seemed to Osborne that he was walking down some ghastly gallery that led into the Realm of Death. It was not mere fantasy. That little green door at the end of the corridor was the entrance to the execution chamber. In an hour or two a man—an innocent man, he sincerely believed—would walk that way and never return.

Osborne entered the one lighted cell and heard the lock click behind him. He sat down beside Becker on the cot, and the big man grasped his hand, as one instinctively reaches out for warm human contact when facing the unknown. For a long time they talked—of many things, but mostly of this experience and its significance. Becker, firm in his declaration of innocence till the last, wanted Osborne's belief, too; and he wondered if perhaps his sacrifice might not hasten the end of capital punishment.

It was nearly dawn. Father Curry, who was to give what

consolation the Church could offer, waited behind the curtains until Warden and prisoner had said good-by. In those last minutes of solemn confessional, Becker swore under the sacred vows of the Church that he was not guilty by deed or by conspiracy or in any other way of the death of Herman Rosenthal.

The troubled sleep into which Osborne fell after that nerve-racking night was interrupted less than two hours later by a knocking at the door. It was Timmie O'Connor—the same who had been president of the George Junior Republic. This young man, later to fall in action in an assault on the Hindenburg line, was studying at the Albany Law School. Every vacation he spent with his old friend in Sing Sing—sometimes, as on this occasion, accompanied by his brother Joe.

Timmie announced that a Mr. MacDonald insisted on seeing the Warden, and before Osborne could learn why he had been disturbed at such an hour the voice of MacDonald was heard from the hall. Why couldn't he get into the prison? What was the idea of keeping out an agent of the superintendent's office, pass or no pass? Wearily Osborne scribbled a pass and lay down again to sleep. Yet no sooner had his head touched the pillow than he was wide awake. What was that man doing in the prison at such an hour? Previous passages with MacDonald had not inspired him with any confidence in Riley's confidential agent. It was barely possible that this particular morning had been chosen for the visit on the assumption that the Warden would be away, for his abhorrence of executions was well known.

Dressing hastily, Osborne went down for a bite of breakfast. Before he had finished, an inmate appeared with a letter from Superintendent Riley. It directed the Warden to hand over to Mr. MacDonald all the written orders concerning assignments of prisoners on file in the Warden's office.

"Where did this come from?" he asked.

"Mr. MacDonald just gave it to me as he was leaving."

Osborne rushed down to the P.K.'s office. For a moment he could scarcely believe his eyes. Every drawer in the filing cabinet had been swept clean; not a single paper of any kind remained. MacDonald not only had delayed delivering his letter until he could make his get-away, but had decamped with the whole batch of records without asking the Warden's permission. Osborne was furious. Calling the two O'Connors he dashed for the station in his car.

Too late! The train had pulled out. As they were about to depart, Timmie sang out: "There he is!" Sure enough, seated on the farthest bench of the upper platform was Mac-Donald, a handbag between his feet, his head hidden behind a newspaper that was shaking like a leaf. He had missed the train.

Things began to happen—melodramatic things. Osborne demanded the papers. MacDonald refused. He had a right to take them. It was the Superintendent's order.

"I don't care if you had an order from the President of the United States. No one takes any papers out of Sing Sing while I am its warden, without my knowing what they are. I shall obey the Superintendent's order, but not before I know just what it is he wants. Give me those papers!"

"You shan't have them!"

"We'll see about that!"

Osborne snatched the handbag and started for the stairs with MacDonald in pursuit. It was then the two O'Connors put their football training to practical use. Forming perfect interference, they gave Osborne time to open the bag and take out the package of papers. MacDonald, a short, puffy man, nearly exploded with wrath. He ran after Osborne, grabbed his throat, shook him futilely by the necktie, and succeeded in tearing a few buttons off his shirt. Although the little man could not possibly have inflicted any serious injury upon the Warden, reinforced as he was by the O'Connors, this personal attack so enraged Osborne that he drove directly to the police station and swore out a warrant for MacDonald's arrest on a charge of assault.

When he had time to inspect the recovered papers, he found there were six hundred seventy-six separate items—all kinds of orders and memoranda pertaining to prison administration.

Dick Richards was set at the job of making individual copies which Osborne sent to Riley with the ironic comment that if the superintendent needed the originals, they were always at his disposal. Riley never took advantage of the offer.

There was one paper missing from the files. Osborne felt it was no coincidence that it should be the order of June 20 admitting the singers to the death cells—the occasion on which Murphy had managed to sneak past the P.K. in place of one of the entertainers. He was inclined to believe that when MacDonald found it did not bear the Warden's signature, he had destroyed it, his purpose being to make Riley think that Osborne himself had guiltily done away with it. Else why all this mysterious conspiring—the early morning call on the day of the execution, the postponed delivery of the letter, the absconding with *all* the records, not merely the papers called for in the superintendent's order?

Only one answer seemed reasonable. His enemies had come into the open at last. He was well aware of their presence, but hitherto they had been working in subterraneous ways, plotting to discredit his administration, especially the League; and inventing the vilest slurs upon his character.

Osborne had been at Sing Sing only a few days when he realized that hostile forces were at work against him. It was difficult to locate the focus of the trouble, for most of the officials in charge of departments were political appointees who counted prison jobs as part of the spoils system. Unless there was conclusive evidence of negligence or incompetence, he had retained these men as a matter of fairness: but he did not know how far he could trust them. Instead, he had to rely on the small group he had assembled in the Warden's house as private assistants.

First of all, there was Mr. Johnson, for whom he had created the post of Deputy Warden. Upon urgent invitation, Donald Lowrie, whose book, "My Life in Prison," had made such an impression on Osborne, had come in the capacity of secretary and stenographer. As a general man of all work, from valet to courier, there was Harry Bolasky, who after release from Auburn had attached himself to his benefactor. The chauffeur, Jack, had been an employee of D. M. Osborne & Co. The enthusiasm of Dick Richards, secretary of the Mutual Welfare League in Auburn, had resulted in his being added to the Warden's ménage to assist in the development of the League in Sing Sing. Another old friend was also on hand—Billy Duffy, the first sergeant-at-arms in Auburn, and now transferred to Sing Sing to nurse Canada Blackie, dying of tuberculosis in a little room on the third story.

It was upon this group that Osborne pinned his faith. Not until too late did he find out that there was one among them on whom he could not depend.

Trouble had first arisen when Osborne began to shake down the favorites of the old system—prisoners who because of their position outside or because of certain services to the Warden had been allowed to live almost sumptuously at Sing Sing. Ringleaders of these privileged few were William J. Cummins and William Willett. Cummins was a banker whose operations in New York City and elsewhere had resulted in conviction and sentence. Willett was an ex-Congressman convicted of bribery to secure a judgeship. "Silk-stockings," they were rated by the prison population. Their own opinion was that they should never have been in "stir" at all.

It was the banker who exercised the greater influence. When Osborne arrived he found this man sitting comfortably at a desk in a special room *outside the bars*. This was known as "Mr. Cummins' office," and here he transacted his own private business without let or hindrance. His business agent had access to him without bothering about visitors' rules. Although the preceding Warden had assigned him the official title of record clerk, the work of this position was taken care of by an assistant, leaving Cummins free to carry on his financial operations. From the very beginning things had been made easy for the banker. While at the Tombs he roomed in the Warden's apartment: at Sing Sing he was assigned to a bed in the nurses' dormitory. To him a cell was something he had heard about. He had never occupied one. His prison clothes were custom-made, and he wore white shirts and neckties that were denied to the "common trash."

Although such favoritism was anathema to Osborne, he did not at once cancel all of Cummins' privileges. In fact, at first he had a real sympathy for the man and for the devoted wife and daughters who visited Sing Sing regularly. He did, however, move forward the screen partition so that "Mr. Cummins' office" was actually behind the bars, and the business agent had to apply for the usual visitor's permit. Even that apparently did not destroy his agreeable relations with the banker, who in florid eulogies professed tremendous admiration for the new Warden and his policies. The first real break came when Osborne refused to appeal to Governor Glynn for executive clemency. Cummins produced letters from some of the most distinguished men in the country petitioning that he be pardoned. On the list were the names of senators, governors, and judges representing thirteen states. Knowing nothing of the case, Osborne fell back on the rule forbidding wardens to make such appeals; and from that moment the banker became a vindictive enemy.

Before long the Warden realized that the banker was in reality the dictator of Sing Sing. One of the chief promoters of the Golden Rule Brotherhood, he had used that organization to extend his power. In drafting the constitution of the Brotherhood he had disfranchised nearly half the prison population by incorporating an article restricting the Board of Delegates to those who could "speak, read, and write the English language." By shrewd political bargaining he had been able to dictate the election of presidents and appointments to the Executive Committee—a control that permitted him to hand out special favors to members of his own clique. Usually content to keep in the background and pull the strings, he came into the open a few months after Osborne's arrival and maneuvered his election as president of the Brotherhood by promising to hire no one except "cons" at his works and to give them all jobs when they got out.

This development helps one to understand why Osborne hastened to replace the one-man rule of the Brotherhood with the greater democracy of the Mutual Welfare League's elective Board of Delegates; but if he thought he had put an end to the banker's régime he was soon disillusioned. By accident he discovered that Cummins' office was the center of a secret propaganda. Unauthorized letters, circulars, and telegrams were being sent in the name of the League to members of the Legislature and other influential persons, with pleas for the passage of certain laws favorable to prisoners. It was an offense of the most serious nature, for surreptitious contacts between inmates and outsiders might lead to fearful consequences. For the first time, Cummins found himself confined in a prison cell with charges preferred against him. To Osborne's dismay, however, the League Court, still controlled by the banker's intimates, refused to convict. It was a serious blow to the new system and to the authority of the Warden, for the accused had been caught red-handed.

It is strange how little things play such an important part in a man's life. Instead of having the case appealed to the Warden's Court, where conviction and sentence would have been certain, Osborne had the banker and several of his cronies transferred to Great Meadow Prison. Perhaps he was reluctant at that stage to supersede the action of the inmates' own court; but too late he realized he had made a serious mistake. Rumors soon came from Warden Homer's "honor prison" that Cummins was carrying on a campaign of slander against the Warden of Sing Sing. From certain prisoners embittered by their transfer to Great Meadow he had obtained statements reflecting upon Osborne's character. Dick Richards, who went down to investigate, brought back a report so disquieting that Osborne sent a private detective—the same he had once employed in Auburn—to discover what was actually going on. Introducing himself to the Warden as a writer anxious to learn conditions at first hand, the detective was referred to the inmate banker himself—the very man he wanted to see.

Mr. Cummins proved not only exceedingly voluble but extraordinarily familiar with what was happening at Sing Sing. Apparently he was on intimate terms with Warden Homer and with Mr. MacDonald, confidential agent of the Superintendent's office. In the Warden's presence he launched into an attack on Osborne and his Sing Sing administration, charging favoritism, double-crossing, dealing with "rats." "Osborne is a visionary," he said, "and he lets his rats get the best of him. He wanted me to be his rat, but I wouldn't, so he shipped me up here."

A curious assortment of charges from the man who had had his special privileges curtailed, who had been disciplined for double-crossing, and finally who, in a last plea to be allowed to remain in Sing Sing, had offered to serve as Osborne's spy! But this was the least unpleasant part of his confidences. "Sing Sing is a hotbed of sodomy," he told the visitor he thought was a writer. "Osborne himself is a pervert and spends much of his time with the younger boys. Some of the boys claim Osborne is 'there' himself."

The nature of the attack was now disclosed. It was to be a campaign of deliberate calumny with a few disgruntled prisoners—men who had refused to accept in good faith the new reform—making accusations of homosexuality. The filthiness of the charges sickened Osborne. During his political career he had been undaunted by defamation, open or whispered; but this was different. The alignment against him was the vicious part. Of the prisoners alone he had little fear. Their unsupported charges were harmless except as they might poison the minds of persons eager to believe the worst. But now he was convinced of what he had long suspected—a conspiracy that reached to the office of the Superintendent of Prisons and perhaps even to the gubernatorial chamber itself.

Trouble between the Warden and Judge Riley had started almost immediately after Osborne took charge at Sing Sing. The man who had coöperated with such apparent willingness in the reforms at Auburn Prison suddenly turned about-face. By continual criticisms, countermands of the Warden's orders, and secret dealings with subordinate officers and prisoners he succeeded in making Osborne's administration one long series of controversies that were promptly reflected in the press. If Superintendent Riley actually had been acquainted with what was being done at Sing Sing, there would have been less ground for complaint; but after four casual visits during the first few months he never appeared again. Even at the wardens' meetings in Albany he rarely spoke to Osborne or showed the slightest interest in the progress that was being made. Could it be that his only reason for approving Osborne's appointment was the removal of a possible candidate for his own job? He could not know, of course, that Governor Whitman had already offered the superintendent's post to Osborne, or that Osborne had refused it because he would not displace the man to whom he owed, nominally at least, his appointment as warden.

In the rehearsal of the events that followed one thing is to be borne in mind. At any time Superintendent Riley or Governor Whitman could summarily have removed the Warden of Sing Sing. They did not do it. Instead, he was subjected to the most cruel persecution that could be devised. Osborne was not one to resign under fire. For one thing, he knew that his record at Sing Sing would vindicate him. He did not have to rely on the general improved tone of the institution, though that was apparent to all who took the trouble to investigate. There were figures that could not be disputed. The increased output of the industries, for instance. Even Judge Riley, amazed at the improvement of the shop work, unbent so far as to write a note of congratulation, observing that "the industries now being carried on at Sing Sing are making a better showing than at any time during recent years." Just six weeks later, when the attack on Osborne was gaining momentum, he contradicted himself with the following: "I am satisfied for the past year or more the inmates of Sing Sing have not rendered efficient service in any of the departments."

Yet these inconsistencies were minor irritations compared with the attacks upon the League itself. The Superintendent, having no personal knowledge of what was taking place at Sing Sing, took his cue from articles in hostile newspapers and from the gleanings of his confidential agents. As the latter's source of information was Banker Cummins and his gang, Riley became the willing victim of gross misrepresentation. A fracas between two prisoners that ended harmlessly became a "deadly riot." A story in the New York *Sun* to the effect that "Battling Nelson" was scheduled to put on a bout with a Sing Sing "White Hope"—absolutely without foundation because the League itself had turned down Nelson's offer—was picked up as gospel by Judge Riley and used as a sermon against the Warden. The curious thing about this episode is that until Osborne took charge boxing bouts had been allowed. Judge Riley knew this, because he had once written his regrets that he could not attend a performance.

Hardly a day passed without a letter from Superintendent Riley complaining about conditions in Sing Sing. He seemed to think life in that institution was a continuous round of felonious assaults and disorders. If he had wished, he might easily have learned the truth, for there is one infallible yardstick of prison discipline—the hospital record of emergency cases. From the number of treatments for bruises and wounds resulting from accidents and assaults it is easy to deduce the extent of disorders. In 1914, with a prison population of 1,466, 372 emergency cases were treated at the hospital, or more than 25 per cent of the total population. In 1915, when the number of convicts had increased to 1,618, only 86 emergency cases were treated, or about 5 per cent. The figures speak for themselves. In spite of, perhaps in compensation for, the efforts of Cummins and his confederates to cause trouble, the great majority of the inmates rallied to Osborne and his program. Their loyalty changed Sing Sing from a prison notorious for its bloody affrays to a self-governing institution in which violence was the exception. It was one of the exceptions, however, that gave Superintendent Riley the chance he had been looking for.

One inmate had assaulted another. The case was handled by the Mutual Welfare League in the usual way, with the suspension of League privileges for one culprit and transfer to another prison for the other. More than eight months after this occurrence the Superintendent demanded to know why no reports of assault had been made by the Warden. Osborne replied that the records of the League Court proceedings were held inviolate, and that all such cases had been satisfactorily taken care of. For Judge Riley's own information, however, he enclosed the Court abstract. To his chagrin, the Superintendent immediately sent the confidential records to the district attorney with orders to prosecute. Not only was this a violation of the understanding Osborne had with the Superintendent about disciplinary cases and a direct blow at the heart of the League, but it was a departure from the practice in other prisons.

This extraordinary act was followed by a surprise "frisking" of the Sing Sing cells. Two of Cummins' old gang had written a secret warning to the Governor that he had better visit Sing Sing at once. When Whitman's delegate arrived, they charged that they had seen six revolvers and three boxes of cartridges in a certain cell. To Osborne's relief the hunt for weapons disclosed nothing of importance. Some time before this he had appealed to the inmates for the sake of the League to give up any concealed weapons they might have in their possession. The result was a voluntary contribution of about 150 knives of various sorts and sizes, which the sergeants-at-arms consigned to the river. It was something to know that since that time the men had kept faith, but he could not help wondering whether one of the disaffected group had planned to "plant" a few revolvers for the special benefit of the Governor.

Against such attacks Osborne's administration was practically invulnerable, but there was a more insidious campaign under way. One of the constant causes of friction between the Warden and the Superintendent of Prisons was the transfer of convicts from Sing Sing to other institutions. Crime was on the increase, and all the state prisons except Great Meadow were overcrowded. Osborne did his best to keep down the Sing Sing population by recommending increasingly large transfers, although it meant aggravating the overcrowding in other prisons. Still Judge Riley complained that Osborne was not complying with his orders and made repeated demands for bigger drafts. Eventually he sent two agents to Sing Sing to take the transfers out of the Warden's hands entirely.

At this insult Osborne lost his temper. To him the problem was simple enough. At Great Meadow there were enough empty cells to absorb most of the overflow at Sing Sing. Superintendent Riley, however, would not consent to use the

space at Great Meadow. That was the "honor prison," and he
would take no chance on a large and heterogeneous population.
The bloodhounds might not be able to stand the strain. Finding no hope for relief in that quarter, Osborne renovated a
space over one of the shops and fitted up a dormitory that
would accommodate all the overflow and do away with the
abominable practice of "doubling up." As the new room was
clean and sanitary, and the League could be counted on to
maintain discipline, he was nonplused when Superintendent
Riley forbade its use. Why, in Auburn and Clinton inmates
were sleeping in the corridors!

The Warden's temper was by no means improved by a series
of letters from the Superintendent denouncing him for the
"outrageous practice" of doubling up prisoners. It culminated
in a visit by Governor Whitman, who had been primed by
Judge Riley concerning the dreadful conditions in Sing Sing.
When the Governor was shown the orders for large transfers
and the neat dormitory with its 200 empty beds, it was his turn
to be surprised. Growing confidential, he admitted that he was
having a great deal of trouble with Riley and wished to remove
him as quickly as possible. Did Osborne have any suggestion
for a substitute?

This was the opportunity Osborne had been hoping for, and
he immediately suggested Dean Kirchwey.

"If he will accept it," said Governor Whitman, "I will appoint him."

From that moment Osborne lived in the hope that his worst
troubles would soon be over.

In the meantime, he had other worries. The ultimate authority for designations of transfer rested with the Superintendent. Although the changes which Riley often made in the
recommended list irritated the Warden, he could not justly
complain. That was the Superintendent's prerogative. It soon
became evident, however, that an effort was being made to crip-
ple the Sing Sing industries. Osborne was at first curious and
then angry to find that the names of his best workmen were
being regularly added to the transfer list. A suspicion that all
was not as it should be became a certainty when on a visit to

Auburn Prison he was approached by a group of inmates who recently had been transferred from Sing Sing. Why, they wanted to know, had they been shifted to Auburn? They were acknowledged to be among the best workmen in their respective shops, and it seemed unjust to punish them without cause. A great many things suddenly became clear. Osborne had received written applications for transfer from these men. Although he had been loath to let them go, he had acceded to their requests. Now, upon investigation, it developed that the applications were forgeries. It explained in part the steady drain upon his most dependable workers. It revealed, too, that there was a traitor in his own circle. There was no doubt about that; but who was it?

In the midst of this turmoil a prisoner escaped, and a few weeks later another one. A more inopportune moment for such occurrences could scarcely be imagined. The story, seized upon avidly by the press, made plausible some of the editorial attacks upon Osborne and his system. Not long before, for example, the Brooklyn *Times* had descanted on "Mr. Osborne's Show Shop." "It is gratifying to learn," it observed, "that Governor Whitman intends to investigate the noisome scandal at Sing Sing Prison, which is being openly paraded under the guise of humanitarian and criminologist reform." Declaring that crooks no longer dreaded sentences if they could spend their term in Sing Sing, the *Times* called for the summary ousting of the Warden.

What such critics did not realize, or else purposely ignored, was the decrease in attempts at escape which had come with the new régime. Unorthodox though Osborne's methods seemed to those trained in the old school, they had proved their practicability. Once Osborne gave permission to nearly sixty of the delegates, who had been busy until midnight counting ballots in a League election, to have a little tea in the Warden's kitchen before retiring. He himself hardly realized the risk at first. These "dangerous criminals" would be outside the cell block, and there would be no guards on the wall. Escape would be as simple as the opening of a door. Standing in the inner room, Osborne felt an impulse to run outside and keep watch; instead he determined to try the issue. An hour later every man marched back to his cell. Henry, the butler, told the Warden next morning what had occurred. Occasionally several of the prisoners would wander over to the door and look thoughtfully into the darkness. "Gee!" said one. "It's a fine night."

Again, an inmate had come to the Warden's office with the news that four desperate criminals were planning a break that evening. Osborne did not ask their names; not simply because he himself did not approve of spy methods but because he would not put a prisoner in the position of being a squealer. When the men had finished dinner, he appeared in the mess-hall and told what he had heard. "It may lead to my dismissal as Warden," he said, "but I can go home. . . . there are other ways in which I can make myself useful and contented. But what of you? You are the ones who will suffer, and all because four men are willing to imperil the interests of the other sixteen hundred."

Osborne took no extra precautions that night. Everything was the same as usual. And nothing happened. Some months later a young prisoner mentioned this incident to the Warden. "I happen to know something about it," he confessed, "because I was one of the four who was going."

"Why didn't you go?"

"Well, in the first place we didn't know how much you knew about it. And besides, we couldn't have made a get-away anyhow. Every damned fellow was on the watch!"

In spite of such examples of disciplinary control, the League was still on trial so far as the public and prison officialdom were concerned. Two escapes in quick succession indicated trouble somewhere. Osborne blamed the Principal Keeper and his own assistant, Mr. Johnson. The Principal Keeper, who had already been warned that his authority over the men was not all it should be, was dismissed in the face of strenuous objections from Superintendent Riley. Johnson, with an offer to become head of the Cheshire Reformatory, resigned in favor of Elihu Church, and Osborne was not sorry to see him go. When the private detective sent to investigate affairs at Great

Meadow had quoted Cummins as saying that Johnson was only pretending to believe in the Sing Sing reforms, Osborne had discounted the statement because of its source. Even when his friends warned him not to trust his assistant because the latter was forever trying to get his job, he was only mildly disturbed. But things were happening that were difficult to explain. Somewhere there was disloyalty in his own ranks. To cap everything, Johnson was held personally responsible for one of the escapes. Warned that a certain inmate could not be trusted, Osborne ordered his subordinate to hold him in the cell block. Upon his return from an interview with the Governor, he discovered Johnson had disobeyed instructions and put the suspect to work on the tennis court. The man had vanished. It would have been disheartening at any time, but at such a crucial moment it was a staggering blow.

Among the official family at Sing Sing was Luther C. White, Superintendent of Industries. White was Osborne's second choice, Riley having refused to approve the first man selected. He had rather bookish leanings, combining a love for poetry with more practical talents, and had not unexpected revelations disturbed their relationship, Osborne would have found the man much to his liking.

The Warden was trying out another George Junior Republic idea at Sing Sing. In addition to the one and one-half cents a day the state was accustomed to paying for prison labor, he instituted a wage of nine dollars a week in token money. Out of this income an inmate was required to pay for everything he received—board and room. Breakfast and supper cost fifteen cents; dinner, twenty-five cents. Room rent was based on location. Pending the organization of a prison bank, the aluminum currency was kept in Superintendent White's home in Tarrytown. As the sum grew in size, Osborne decided to have the money transferred to his own quarters for safekeeping and sent Harry Bolasky and Jack, the chauffeur, to obtain it. Now Harry was going straight, but when he discovered letters signed by Willett, Johnson, and others lying on White's desk within easy reach, his loyalty overcame his scruples. Detailing Jack to engage the maid in conversation, he collected the correspondence and made off with it.

Never before had Osborne been so tempted. Perhaps his whole career rested on what those letters contained; but when Harry Bolasky presented the loot, he fought down an impulse to take advantage of the opportunity, and ordered his valet to return the batch immediately. "Gee, boss!" said Harry. "You don't know what you're turnin' down."

He didn't then. But later, years afterward, those same letters reappeared. Dick Richards, whose ideas of rectitude did not always square with the copy-books, had intercepted Harry, confiscated the correspondence, and made copies. Having gone thus far, he decided he might as well keep the originals too. When eventually they came into his hands, Osborne found White had been going over his head to Superintendent Riley with reports on the Warden's activities. There were also letters to an ex-convict revealing that the admiration White professed for Osborne's reforms was pure hypocrisy.

For the moment [one letter read], I seem to be in the good graces of T. M., and he is to dine here with my family and some other guests next Sunday night. I hope to Gawd I shan't put his nose out of joint somehow between now and then.

A letter from Willett offered to provide White with witnesses and testimony against Osborne in the impending clash. Still another letter from White to his ex-convict friend, dated Thanksgiving Day, 1915, ended with this holiday thought:

I fail to see what can save him [Osborne] now. It seems to me it is up to his friends now to get him away. But, Hell, let him stay and take his medicine, he has got it coming to him.

How out of sympathy White really was with the new spirit in Sing Sing is indicated in the following excerpt from a note to the same correspondent:

Things are going so dam badly that I reckon they've reached close to the bottom limit. But you just ought to see the banners and flags and things that are to be raised to welcome back Tom Brown to his own. They've got the average campaign banner nailed to the cross and pleading for mercy. The sign of the sacred League appears upside down and Hindside to and every other way on 'em all, and now I've just had to give the band the Lawd knows how many yards of white cloth for sashes to be worn on the memorable occasion.

Although at the time Osborne was ignorant of these passages, he learned enough from Harry to convince him that White was a stool-pigeon for Riley. Whether his suspicions were right or wrong, it was obvious the Superintendent of Industries did not approve of the system at Sing Sing. Again the Warden thought of those mysterious forged transfers and to be on the safe side, he dismissed White and brought down upon his head the maledictions of Riley. But he had expected that.

White's reply to the dismissal order was characteristic:

"Banished from Rome? Banished? My Lords, I thank you for't. What's banished but set free from daily contact with the things I loathe? . . . And now my sword's my own."

It always seemed appropriate to Osborne that of all the noble Romans whose words White might have quoted he had selected the words of Catiline!

Everything seemed conspiring to bring the Sing Sing administration into discredit. Everything and everybody. More and more Osborne became convinced that he was ringed in by a gang of conspirators. He became distrait, suspicious. Evil lurked in the shadows. Sometimes he caught glimpses. . . .

Philip Braun ran a saloon in Ossining, just outside the precincts of the prison. "Come In, You're Out" was the invitation displayed, and many took him at his word—incoming convicts, eager to solace themselves with one last drink before being thrust into a dark cell; outgoing prisoners who had served their terms and wanted to celebrate; visitors trying to shake off the incubus of dejection caused by a brief sojourn within those walls; and, not infrequently, prison officers on their way home. In fact, it was a thriving business conducted with more than customary decency.

One day a visitor appeared at this establishment and asked for the proprietor. He presented a card bearing the name of a man connected with the office of the Superintendent, and Braun immediately recognized him as a previous employee of Sing Sing. The visitor went directly to the point. "I am very close to the Governor," he said, according to a statement Braun later swore to, "and he wants to get something on Mr. Osborne. If we can smuggle a couple of girls into your back room and lure some of the convicts working on the road to come at them, we could have an agent from the Superintendent of Prisons' office spy on them." Braun refused to enter into any such arrangement and communicated with Osborne.

Less than a fortnight later the same agent of the Superintendent appeared again. This time he brought a camera and urged Braun to assist in getting pictures of prisoners and prostitutes together. When Braun persisted in his refusal, the agent went to the telephone and called up someone at the prison. The proprietor heard him tell the person at the other end of the line that it was all off. Braun would not consent.

Philip Braun was just a saloonkeeper, but he had a code of honor that did not include frame-ups. The nauseous character of this particular plot so disgusted him that to protect Osborne he immediately made written statements vouching for the truth of the above incidents. Subsequent events, however, were not calculated to convince his neighbors behind the walls that honesty is the best policy. A brewing company held a second mortgage on the Braun property. Because of certain services the saloonkeeper was rendering, the company had orally agreed not to claim the mortgage. For nine years it had run without a question; but immediately after Braun had sworn out his statements regarding the attempted frame-up, the brewers started foreclosure proceedings, dispossessed Braun, and ruined him.

Cause and effect? What else could Osborne think? . . .

William Trefry, the inmate telephone operator in the front office, reported to Osborne that an agent connected with the Superintendent's office had offered him ten dollars to steal the Warden's private diary. Instead of refusing, he had been shrewd enough to say he would consider the matter. Now what should he do?

"Go through with it," was Osborne's advice. "Get your money, and take the book. It will be ready for you any time you want it."

Purchasing a duplicate of his diary, Osborne made a number of entries—some of them correct, some of them false—and substituted it for the original. Thereafter he kept two diaries —one for the inquisitive agent, and the other for himself. . . .

Harry Bolasky, Osborne's valet, was on the train bound for New York. Suddenly from the seat ahead he heard a familiar voice. It was the same man in conversation with a Sing Sing official. "We must try to get four cons to play tennis," Harry heard the agent say, "and then have someone take a picture."

A day or two later a young prisoner, Paul Vogel by name, appeared in the Warden's office with the request that he and a few other inmates be allowed to play tennis on the Warden's court. It was an extraordinary thing to ask, for League privileges did not extend to the use of the tennis court. Osborne refused as a matter of course, and smiled. But the smile was grim. . . .

Fat Alger, who had been a member of the Board of Delegates, was transferred from Sing Sing to Great Meadow. In twelve days he was back again on a transfer order. He wore an inscrutable smile and refused to say why he had been returned. That evening Joe Rotolo, inmate record clerk, burst into the Warden's office, trembling with anger.

"What do you think that —— Fat Alger has come here for! He wants me to give him the names and addresses of the wives of some of the prisoners. Then someone is going to try to get these women to swear that when they have come up here to visit their husbands you have let them in the Warden's house. And Alger says some of them can be got to charge you with making improper advances to them. I may be a thief, but I don't know what I have done to make anyone think I would do such dirty work!"

After thinking it over a moment, Osborne decided to let Rotolo give the names and await developments. He then took into his confidence the husband of one of the women, Minnie Gross. This inmate wrote his wife what to expect and told her to let him know if anything happened. Something did happen. A few weeks later Minnie Gross visited Sing Sing and reported that a man who gave his name as John Hogan had called on her and represented himself as an agent of the Prison Department at Albany. First he had asked if Harry Bolasky (Osborne's valet) had ever come to her house and insulted her. When she answered in the negative, he had sought to play on her resentment by declaring that Harry was an ex-convict, and that he and the Warden would have transferred her husband to Clinton, only the Prison Department wouldn't stand for it. (It was not for nothing that Clinton was known as the "Siberia of America.") Hogan also tried to induce Minnie to say that she knew something about Warden Osborne; but when she insisted she would be glad to give him information if she had any, he gave it up as a bad job and departed, leaving an address at which she could reach him if she changed her mind.

And so it went day after day—attack and repulse, attack and repulse. Osborne wondered how long he could keep it up. No prison was perfect, and no warden could make it so. Thus far his alertness, combined with good luck, had been sufficient to forestall the machinations of his enemies, but sooner or later, by the law of averages, they would catch him unaware. He himself might have taken the offensive and gone directly to the Governor with a demand for a show-down; but all this time he was hourly expecting the dismissal of Riley and the appointment of Kirchwey. Relying on Whitman's repeated assurances that this substitution would be made soon, he preferred holding the fort until a change in supervision should put a stop to the intrigues. As the weeks and months dragged by without action, the tension became almost intolerable. He could never tell from one day to the next what villainy was being hatched.

Then, unexpectedly, the blow struck.

A prison is an institution in which are segregated certain members of society who have disobeyed man's laws; but if that were the whole story decent, law-abiding citizens could rest more peacefully. It is ridiculous to be deceived into think-

From "Puck," 1914, 1915. Now the "Comic Weekly Puck."

THE CHALLENGE

ing that men are in prison because they have committed crimes; they are there because they have been caught in commission of crime. If one subscribes to the truism that there are more criminals outside prison walls than inside, one must also concede the corollary that the group segregated from society is not so different from society itself as most people like to believe. In spite of the restrictions and the "limited geography," there is the same play of human emotions inside as outside: ambition, jealousy, hate, love—in fact, all the individual and collective impulses common to man.

Of all these various factors the one most difficult to control is the sex impulse. Isolated from normal contacts with the opposite sex, the prisoner fills his long hours of confinement with brooding, and it is inevitable that at times his pent-up passions should induce voluptuous reveries which in turn demand gratification. The result is sodomy. No prison is free from it. It is the curse of the institutional system. With the overcrowding to which all our prisons have been subjected in recent years, perversion alone would be difficult to combat; but the problem is complicated by the presence of inverts. The invert in prison becomes a focus of vice, for to him sodomy is not an unnatural act. Science belatedly recognized this difference, but in 1915 the topic was taboo in polite conversation. Wardens, fully aware of conditions which made their prisons breeding grounds of immorality, did their best to check the evil and kept silent.

Osborne approached the problem from two angles. To begin with, he tried to reduce opportunity by abolishing the doubling-up of prisoners in the same cell. In that effort he was defeated by the refusal of the Superintendent to make use of available space in Great Meadow or to approve the new dormitory at Sing Sing. From the first, however, he had realized that no warden could cope with sodomy simply by proctor methods. The confidence and coöperation of the majority of the decent inmates were essential. To that end he worked through the Mutual Welfare League and was rewarded with the definite knowledge that vice at Sing Sing was under better control than in any other of the state penal institutions. Yet he was never blind to the fact that it persisted in spite of all he could do. It will persist as long as there are prisons.

Nevertheless, it was with a sinking heart that he received intelligence from one of the Executive Committee of the League that a young prisoner who had been brought before the Court on suspicion of immorality had confessed to conduct so flagrant that League officers thought the Warden himself should deal with the case. Even then Osborne was unprepared for the enormity of the offense. In a private interview the culprit, James Harvey, admitted with perfect composure that in the three months he had been at Sing Sing he had sold himself to twenty-one inmates. The complacency with which he enumerated his unnatural acts was revolting. Here, surely, was a man who should never be in prison at all—a degenerate who was a menace wherever he went. Only a hospital for the insane could cope with such a case.

Osborne was aghast, but there was one consolation. The League, not he, had uncovered this corruption and brought the offender to book. He was proud of that. It justified his faith. And with his talent for getting into trouble he proceeded to do the most indiscreet thing he could have thought of. At the meeting of the Parole Board next day he confided the news to one of the members. In his position, any other man would have played safe; yet Osborne never thought of his trust being betrayed. The information went directly to the Superintendent's office where an entirely different construction was put on the matter.

In the meantime, the men whom Harvey accused denied the charges flatly both to Osborne and to the five judges of the League. Even when confronted by their accuser with details of time and place, they swore to their innocence. Osborne was in a dilemma. He hated to force conviction solely on the evidence of a degenerate, and yet he could not ignore the possibilities. The impasse was suddenly terminated by the confidential admission of guilt by Jack the Dropper. All but three of the others followed suit, giving their admissions to the Warden upon pledge of secrecy.

Now, however, the predicament was even worse. As he

would not violate the pledge of confidence he had given, the case could not be handled in the usual way by the League; and yet he was determined the malefactors should be punished. In the end, he took matters into his own hands, reported to the Judiciary Board that for the good of the League all the accused men should be deprived of their privileges, and placed under special surveillance. In addition, he assigned them, not without a grim thought as to its peculiar appropriateness, to the hardest and most disagreeable labor—digging a sewer. That, he thought, settled the matter.

Early in October, upon motion of Dr. Rudolph F. Diedling, the State Commission of Prisons decided upon an investigation of Sing Sing.

A few days later Dr. Diedling appeared at Sing Sing with a stenographer, questioned a few men, subjected the Warden to a catechism regarding alleged improper conduct in administration, with special reference to the Harvey sodomy case, and reported to the Commission with two recommendations:

First, that the proper steps be promptly taken to remove Thomas Mott Osborne from the position of Agent and Warden of Sing Sing Prison.

Second, that this Commission lay this report before the District Attorney of Westchester County and seek the indictment of Thomas Mott Osborne on the evidence contained therein.

On December 28, the Grand Jury of Westchester County brought two indictments against Osborne—one for perjury, and one for neglect of duty. Of the six counts contained in the latter indictment, the first five charged willful and unlawful violation of prison rules, together with a general breakdown of discipline and morale. The sixth and last count alleged that Warden Osborne "did commit various unlawful and unnatural acts with inmates of Sing Sing Prison, over whom he had supervision and control." The grand offensive had begun.

CHAPTER VI

THE TRAP IS SPRUNG

IF they were not a matter of record and had not been preceded by a series of equally fantastic episodes, the events leading to Osborne's indictment would be incredible. Although it was not generally understood at the time, the private "investigation" undertaken by Dr. Diedling was wholly unauthorized, the Prison Commission having refused to give its sanction. As a member of that body, he had the right to inspect the prison, but it was not within his jurisdiction to take testimony on oath. The men he interviewed were with few exceptions discharged or disaffected officers, prisoners bearing a grudge, and mental defectives, some of whom were degenerates.

Aside from this, Dr. Diedling was the last man in the world fitted to conduct an unbiased investigation. He had no sympathy whatsoever with the new system and subscribed to the doctrine that the only way to reform a prisoner is "to hit him on the nut with an ax." Because immediately after graduation from medical college he had spent two years at Elmira State Reformatory, he considered himself as something of an expert on penology. In his opinion, Osborne's methods were sheer lunacy, and he agreed with Judge Riley that the sooner this "reign of Bedlam" at Sing Sing ended, the better. It is not to be wondered at that a man with such views should accept as gospel some of the stories told him. How was he to know that the yarn about a gang of prisoners carousing and drinking punch with the Warden until the small hours of the morning had grown out of that incident of the League election: Board members counting ballots all evening and allowed a cup of tea; Osborne wondering about the temptation of easy escape; inmates looking into the encompassing dark and thinking what a fine night it was!

330

Upon his first arrival at Sing Sing Prison Dr. Diedling had ordered the Warden from the room during the conduct of the inquiry. Osborne refused to budge. As head of the institution he had the right and the duty to be present. This not only offended the good doctor's dignity; it circumscribed his activities. His choice of witnesses indicated that he intended to get what he came for: a blasting report of conditions that would justify putting the case into the hands of the District Attorney. Yet when he came to the questioning, his witnesses showed reluctance to depart very far from the truth. Dr. Farr, the prison physician, ventured an understatement in regard to the progress made. Asked to give his opinion about the number and severity of the assault cases, he replied that he did not think there were more than in previous years or that they were more severe. Had he forgotten that, according to his own records incorporated in the annual report for the Superintendent, assault cases for the year had decreased from twenty-five per cent of the population to only five per cent?

Ostensibly gathering data concerning management of the industries, discipline, efficiency of staff, and suspicions of immorality, Dr. Diedling practically ignored all but the last item. Obviously he was going to make the Harvey sodomy case, so luckily discovered through Osborne's own indiscretion, a *cause célèbre*. If he failed to elicit testimony to his liking from the doctor and the nine inmates he questioned from the community of 1,618, it was not for lack of trying. Curiously, it was the Warden himself who provided the opening needed; and even that hinged on a mechanical mistake. When the records of the examination were perused later, it was found that the stenographer had made so many errors it was difficult to discover the exact meaning of many of the passages. The omission of a single word led to Osborne's indictment on a charge of perjury. According to Dr. Diedling's report, the following dialogue took place with the Warden:

Q. Have you a record of sodomy cases?
A. It has never been before the court.
Q. Why?
A. There are no sodomy cases as far as the prison is concerned.

Even in this form, the meaning of the last statement is clear to anyone who knows how the perversion cases were handled. In a moment of exultation at his success in punishing the offenders without destroying the inmates' confidence in their own disciplinary body, Osborne had related the incident to a member of the Parole Board. The Superintendent of Prisons knew about it; and so, assuredly, did Dr. Diedling. To base a charge of perjury on a question of fact known and understood by all parties was in itself a prostitution of justice; but Osborne was misquoted. "There are no sodomy cases as far as the *prisoners' court* is concerned," the Warden had replied—a statement impossible of misinterpretation. Dr. Diedling chose to construe it as a flat denial that any cases of vice had come to light! If at this time he had any pangs of conscience at the course he was taking, they evaporated upon his next visit to Sing Sing. Osborne defied his authority by flatly refusing to surrender the records of the Mutual Welfare League Court.

At Great Meadow Prison, Dr. Diedling had better luck. There he found Fat Alger, who testified that he had free access to the death house both by day and by night and had been there about fifty times; that he knew of fifty or more sodomy cases that had been hushed up (fifty seemed to be his favorite round number); that he had been on the Warden's porch until two in the morning drinking wine and claret, and had enjoyed Osborne's hospitality in the Warden's room until three A.M.

This from the man whom Osborne had never been able to trust, who had been disciplined, who had been ringleader in the plot to suborn women to confess immorality with the Warden, and who of all inmates in Sing Sing would have been the last to see the inside of the Warden's quarters on any excuse!

There too was the ex-congressman, Mr. Willett. What was he doing at Great Meadow? Only a few days before, he had been at Sing Sing. Summoned by Dr. Diedling, he had refused to testify, and Dr. Diedling had not insisted. The next day, for reasons Osborne could not fathom, orders had come from the Superintendent's office that he be transferred. Now he was prepared to expatiate at length on his grievances. He was followed by another man who had not forgiven the Warden for curtailing his privileges—Mr. Cummins, the banker. It is curious how these two names keep creeping into the record. Cummins' chief contribution to the testimony was his complaint that Osborne had taken control from the "silk-stockings" and placed it in the hands of the "rough-necks." That left the banker in a humiliating situation. Why, he was no better than a common jailbird! In addition, he volunteered the information that sodomy was rampant, and that at night the cell doors were often left unlocked so that the inmates could get together at will.

The very extravagance of the charges, to say nothing of the impossibility of their truth without the connivance of every official and guard on the Sing Sing roster, should have damned them utterly; yet they were incorporated in the Diedling report as the sworn statements of trustworthy witnesses. Other charges were added, dealing chiefly with Osborne's alleged failure to report to the proper authorities (for example, the District Attorney) felonies and misdemeanors committed in the prison; his refusal to answer certain questions and to surrender the records demanded of him; his general conduct of the prison, on the ground that it permitted disorder and immorality, facilitated escapes, and transferred authority from civilian keepers and the better element of the prisoners to vicious and degenerate inmates; and finally the accusation that he had illegally permitted inmates to visit condemned men in the death house and even to leave the bounds of the prison without proper guard. Upon this mixture of falsehood and of truth falsely presented, District Attorney Frederick E. Weeks of Westchester County was asked to undertake a Grand Jury investigation. In the meantime, three of the seven members of the Prison Commission issued public statements endorsing in the most emphatic terms Osborne's administration of Sing Sing.

Connected with the District Attorney's office in the capacity of assistant was a tall, red-headed young man, not yet turned thirty, with a tremendous yen to get on. William Joseph Fallon had already made a name for himself as a trial lawyer, and in his two years under Weeks had chalked up a nice list of convictions. Before long he was to be known as the Great Mouthpiece of the underworld, defender of crooks and Big Shots, a brilliant strategist, a ruthless enemy, and a convivial friend.

District Attorney Weeks put most of the burden of the Osborne case on the shoulders of his young assistant. And willing shoulders they were. It was the red-headed young man's first big case, and he was determined to show the boys. When William J. Fallon decided to go places, he usually went; and he didn't always care how he got there.

For his defense Osborne had obtained the services of some of the most distinguished lawyers of the day, among them Huntington Merchant and George Gordon Battle, the latter acting for the National Prison Reform Association. Besides, he could count on his friend, Professor George W. Kirchwey, recently resigned as dean of the Columbia Law School, for advice. George W. Wickersham also coöperated with defense counsel.

Osborne was cut to the quick by the charges against him—in fact, was closer to panic than he had ever been before. Any doubts as to what was in store for him soon vanished. On November 3, while taking a much needed rest at his home in Auburn, he received an S.O.S. call from Dr. Kirchwey, unofficially in charge during the Warden's absence. Hastening back to Sing Sing, he found waiting for him an order to produce at White Plains five prisoners, among them Harvey, the cause of all the trouble, and Kaplan, or Jack the Dropper—the man who had first confessed to the immorality charges. To the Warden's dismay, he discovered upon motoring to White Plains with the prisoners that the District Attorney had no intention of having these witnesses examined before the October Grand Jury, then in session. Furthermore, the convicts were to be lodged in White Plains jail under the eye of District Attorney Weeks. In spite of strenuous protests, Justice Morschauser upheld the state's right to detain the men.

To Osborne this seemed a gross encroachment upon his rights. He was still Warden even if he was under fire, and proved it a few weeks later. Weeks, emboldened by his first success, had a warrant of criminal contempt sworn against a Sing Sing inmate who refused to testify against Osborne before the Grand Jury, and dispatched a sheriff to bring the man to White Plains. Osborne charged kidnaping, obtained a writ for the custody of the prisoner, and was upheld.

It was on November 9 that the November Grand Jury got down to business. If the members had conducted an investigation, Osborne would have welcomed it. He had no fears about the outcome. But though he pleaded with them to make a personal visit to Sing Sing, inspect everything, question anyone, and learn conditions for themselves, not one of that body, so far as Osborne could discover, went near the institution. They preferred to judge the conduct of the prison, the charges of neglect of duty and immoral conditions, on the testimony of certain convicts who, defense counsel believed, had been handpicked by the District Attorney because of known grudges against the Warden.

A commentary on this plan of procedure was offered by the voluntary action of the Kings County Grand Jury. In December the members visited Sing Sing in a body, inspected every section and department, talked with guards, shop foremen, and inmates. They were so impressed that they drafted a set of resolutions endorsing whole-heartedly the reforms which had been introduced, with specific reference to the Mutual Welfare League and the improved morale of the men. The publication of this document came as a complete surprise to the harassed Warden and reinforced his determination to fight this thing to the bitter end.

Osborne had good cause to be anxious. Evidences of a conspiracy came pouring in. Affidavits of convicts privy to the scheme left no doubt in the minds of Osborne's counsel that the whole thing had been engineered.

A man named Brooks had been transferred by Osborne to Clinton for writing crooked letters to his wife in the Women's Prison at Auburn. Suddenly he appeared at Great Meadow, where he was given the cream of the jobs in that institution. Why this promotion instead of the punishment Osborne directed? Brooks' sworn statement explains:

Cummins had Riley bring me down from Clinton Prison . . .
ostensibly to get the basis for a frame-up for Mr. Osborne. . . . At
this time my mind was very much inflamed against Mr. Osborne.

In spite of his grievance at being transferred to Clinton, Brooks
rebelled when he learned the details of the plot.

Another prisoner testified that Cummins had predicted Osborne's political ruin before the 1st of January; and still another quoted him, the banker, as saying that "in case they
could not get Osborne on any misdemeanor charge, they were
going to get him on some other charge."

If the conspiracy had been confined to the prison group
alone, it would have been easier to fight; but unsuspected
ramifications were developing, linking, in Osborne's mind at
least, the District Attorney's office with his enemies. It appeared that undue pressure was being put on prisoners to make
them "come across" with incriminating testimony. Mr. Merchant produced evidence to show that inmate witnesses were
being promised speedy parole if they would testify against
Osborne, and severe additional sentences if they refused. The
special victims of these coercive measures were the twenty
inmates Harvey had implicated in the sodomy scandal. Threatened and manhandled, they resolutely refused to speak the
single line of perjury that would have saved their own skins
and ruined Osborne.

Weeks and Fallon could scarcely believe it. Such loyalty
from criminals was outside their experience. It was obvious
now that before Osborne was put on the rack, these men must
be indicted. After a few sessions, the Grand Jury accommodated. It indicted twenty-one inmates of Sing Sing without
asking for a single word of testimony from the Warden!

Not until close to the end of the Grand Jury proceedings was
Osborne allowed to testify. In the meantime he was kept in
ignorance of the testimony to which the jurors had listened.

He did not know that ex-Congressman Willett had told how
shocked he was that the Warden should try to "hush up" the
Harvey case. There was no one there to point out that it was
Osborne himself who had first told the facts to a member of the
Parole Board.

He did not know that Convict James Connolly, removed as house orderly for disobedience, had sworn the Warden had the words *Tom Brown* tattooed on his body—with the implication that inmates had been permitted to prick them there. In 1908, while engaging in those investigations for the Public Service Commission, Osborne had felt the need of some mark of identification in case of accident and had had "T. M. O., Auburn, N. Y." tattooed on his left side.

He did not know that Charles H. Johnson, his former assistant whom he had appointed out of a spirit of fair play and to whom he had assigned the major share of his own salary, had shown his gratitude by giving testimony open to foul interpretation; or that Dr. Farr, Fat Alger, Luther C. White, and the rest—all of them nursing their own personal grudges—had elaborated the vicious legend to a point that should have made even Osborne's most bitter enemies incredulous.

Yet if he was unaware of how deeply the sewer was being dredged, he guessed much. The very names of the witnesses were significant of the type of inquiry that was being conducted. What he did not know then he learned later when, after a long legal battle, he obtained possession of the Grand Jury minutes. Although it is impracticable to follow all the strands to their conclusion, several deserve special mention. Among them is the case of Joe Rotolo, record clerk.

Joe had been loyal to his warden; but when it came to meeting a real crisis, he couldn't face the music. In a few weeks he was due for parole. He must get out! What would happen if he refused to testify as desired was all too clear. When brought to the stand, he swore on oath that Osborne had had "one of the boys" transferred from Auburn Prison to Sing Sing, and quartered in his private residence. The Warden's excuse, he testified, was that the man was suffering from t. b.

Possibly nothing in all the falsehood and filth that was dragged before the Grand Jury cut Osborne so deeply as this. For Rotolo had perjured himself to win his freedom. The story he told was the story of Canada Blackie dying of tuberculosis on the third floor of the Warden's house; but the name he used was that of an inmate nurse whom Osborne had assigned to take care of the sick man. Rotolo knew the truth. So did every prisoner at Sing Sing.

Does any doubt of a conspiracy still linger?

In the Westchester County Jail waiting for trial was lodged a man charged with the revolting crime of assaulting a child crippled with infantile paralysis. In his attempt at rape, he had torn off the straps and supports of his victim. Once before he had been convicted of a similar crime; now he was summoned before the Grand Jury that he might swear to having witnessed improper relations between Osborne and Jack the Dropper. He did his dirty work, and when brought to trial for his own outrage was let off with sixty days in jail, as if he were a common drunk!

Paul Vogel was the youth who had asked for permission to play tennis on the Warden's court—just after Harry Bolasky discovered the plot to take pictures of Osborne hobnobbing with convicts in a tennis game. As he was one of the more prepossessing boys in Sing Sing, the Grand Jurors, their minds already filled with obscenities, were unquestionably influenced by his preposterous story. Vogel testified that on a certain night he was awakened by a special officer and conducted to the Warden's bedroom, where improper advances were made to him.

Any prison official could have exposed the absurdity of this story. In the first place, such conduct would have meant flaunting immorality before the eyes of all the officers and inmates in Sing Sing. No man in his right senses, however depraved, would have been so indiscreet as to make accomplices of the entire prison population. Even assuming the Warden's insanity, there was one bit of evidence that would have riddled Vogel's story completely. The prison records showed that on the very night named as the date of the assignation, Osborne was keeping a speaking engagement in Germantown, Pennsylvania!

After MacDonald's attempt to steal these records, Osborne, it will be remembered, had had copies made and sent to Riley. They would have cleared up many mysteries and refuted much false testimony. Why did the District Attorney fail to produce them? Why did he not let the Grand Jury know what he and

Riley already knew? Osborne's guess is as good as any. As the Warden still had the originals, it would have been difficult to falsify the copies. But suppose MacDonald had been successful in securing the originals and that among the papers there miraculously appeared a note from Vogel bearing a hastily scribbled "O. K., T. M. O." in what looked like Osborne's handwriting! By this time, Osborne did not put forgery beyond his enemies.

Although he did not realize it, retribution was waiting for one of the principal witnesses. In his effort to denounce Sing Sing as a place of unspeakable conditions, Judge Riley had gone in so deep that he himself was caught in the mire. Why, suddenly asked a juror, if you knew of these conditions and disapproved of Osborne's work, did you not remove the Warden?

There is no question that Riley was taken unaware. He had never guessed that after he had been used he would be destroyed. Before his ordeal was over, he was a broken man. With but a short time to live, he saw his reputation shattered at a single stroke, his work discredited, and his last days embittered by disgrace and suffering.

From some of his own witnesses, whose names he had given the District Attorney, Osborne learned a little more of the way things were going. The District Attorney and his assistant took good care that these witnesses should not offer evidence that might raise doubts in the minds of the jurymen. When one of them attempted to contrast conditions at Sing Sing with those in other prisons, he was promptly told his testimony was irrelevant. Miss Doty, whose intimate knowledge of affairs both at Auburn and at Sing Sing qualified her to speak with authority, was side-tracked for ten minutes by innocuous questions and then dismissed before she could give any of her data.

Of all outsiders, Dr. Kirchwey was probably most familiar with the Sing Sing administration. He had often taken unofficial charge at the institution when Osborne was absent and knew the problem from the Warden's angle. When he was called to the stand, he did his best to justify Osborne as a man

and as a warden. Dr. Kirchwey might have succeeded in coun-
teracting the prejudicial testimony of previous witnesses, had
not the District Attorney modified the effect of his evidence by
a clever trick. Mr. Weeks began his questioning as follows:

Did [Mr. Osborne] tell you that eighteen of these twenty-one
men who were indicted in the sodomy cases were either executive-
committeemen, sergeants-at-arms, assistant sergeants-at-arms, delegates, or gallery men?

Dr. Kirchwey did not know this and had never been told
this for the simple reason that it was not true; but his surprised "No," left standing without comment by the District
Attorney, gave the impression that this witness was not in close
touch with Sing Sing affairs after all. The same question, in a
slightly altered form, also staggered Richard M. Hurd of the
State Commission on Prisons when he entered the witness box,
and the jurymen were allowed to believe the implication was
based on fact. In their eyes the Mutual Welfare League was
forever discredited.

As most of the witnesses Osborne had named were not examined until toward the end of the inquiry, the Grand Jurors
would have had to be more than human to keep their judgments unbiased. The resourceful Fallon had regaled them with
every sort of calumny and innuendo before allowing his case to
be jeopardized by friendly testimony. By the time the accused
took the stand, they were ready to immolate the fiend that had
been conjured up.

Osborne's demands to appear in his own behalf were evaded
as long as possible. Finally he was informed that he would be
heard if he would sign the usual waiver of immunity. The
document District Attorney Weeks prepared, however, was
far from "usual"; it was in fact a tacit confession of guilt that
Osborne was asked to sign. He refused, and Justice Morschauser himself stepped in and compelled Weeks to make the
proper changes.

At the twenty-first session, only a few days before the indictments against him were brought in, Osborne was called as a
witness and sworn in.

With what emotions he took the stand may be well imagined. Here was a man whose education from childhood to maturity had been drawn from those things we hold the finest in our culture; whose tastes had ever been fastidious, tending toward the finical; whose public service had been marked with unselfishness almost to the point of folly, so great had been the inroads upon his private fortune; and whose devotion to Purity was almost fanatical. Scores were eager to testify to his blameless life—men of unimpeachable character who had played football with him, roomed with him, traveled with him, seen him under all sorts of conditions and in innumerable situations with never a hint of a dark thought or an ignoble deed. Yet here he sat, surrounded by suspicion and malevolence, accused of selling a calf for fourteen dollars and appropriating the money, of luring women into his quarters and insulting them, of carousing with convicts and committing unmentionable iniquities with men of foul lives and diseased bodies!

But the trumpet and the thunder were not silenced. In the third degree to which he was subjected, he was still the intrepid champion. He gave blow for blow, and defied them to indict him. Of the Harvey case he refused to speak. He had given his word to hold the confessions confidential. Because the men were convicts, could he break faith? For the moment Weeks was baffled; but there were other ways. He recalled that about three months before, Osborne visited him, hoping to convert the District Attorney to his way of thinking in regard to the assault cases.

WEEKS: The thing that brought you to see me was to get me to condone these sodomies.
OSBORNE: That is a lie. . . .
WEEKS: You came to me and tried to feel me out and see what you could do with me toward letting those sodomists go?
OSBORNE: You are a damned liar!

There are limits to human endurance. No man can keep his temper forever—under such provocation. Once again Osborne was to lose command of himself. Fallon, failing to shake the Warden's resolution in regard to the confessions, resorted to abuse. He charged the witness openly with immoral relations with two convicts, one of whom Osborne had never even heard of.

"We have numberless affidavits," continued Fallon relentlessly, "testimony that we have not introduced, that shows this man to be the worst kind of a degenerate."

This was too much for Justice Morschauser, and Fallon was rebuked for injecting improper material into the discussion. The harm, however, had already been done. It was too late now to win over the jury. Not Osborne's spirited defense; or the telling statements of Principal Keeper Dorner of Sing Sing and Warden Rattigan of Auburn; or the honesty of Mrs. Minnie Gross, who still refused to be intimidated by the ring that was trying to force her testimony, could be of any avail. Not even the exhaustive brief filed by Mr. Merchant and Mr. Battle accusing the District Attorney's office of coercion and prejudice in the conduct of the inquiry. Three days after Christmas the Grand Jury brought in the two indictments, perjury and neglect of duty. And Osborne found himself classed as the vilest criminal enjoying personal liberty only by virtue of $2,000 bail.

CHAPTER VII

OUT OF THE CLOUD

In Albany there was undisguised satisfaction. As soon as he heard of the indictment, Superintendent Riley announced his intention of removing Osborne immediately. If he expected this would bring an offer of resignation from the Warden, he was disappointed. Osborne curtly refused to resign. "Let them kick me out if they want to," he said. There was one rational solution to the problem—leave of absence. That was honorable and practicable for a man in his position; but some imp of perverseness prevented him from applying, even when Dean Kirchwey obtained the Governor's assurance that the request would be granted. He hated to put himself in the position of asking a favor, however reasonable, and delayed so long that Whitman became exasperated. If he doesn't have his application for leave in by nine P.M. on December 31, the Governor told Kirchwey, I'll have to order his removal.

The evening of the 31st came, and still no word from Osborne. Outside the executive mansion a group of reporters waited for the decision. Inside, the Governor fumed while a state dinner waited. At nine o'clock Mr. Battle telephoned that his client would not agree to the terms. At eleven there was a conference. Some time after midnight, just as the Governor was on the point of informing the press that the Warden of Sing Sing had been removed by official edict, Osborne capitulated on the understanding that Dean Kirchwey would act as Warden during his leave of absence.

The compromise had been agreed to, but from the legal point of view the situation was confused. Osborne said he was still warden. Whitman wasn't sure. Riley asserted he was out for good and issued an order prohibiting him from setting foot

343

within prison bounds. Although the order was never enforced it had one unexpected result.

News that the Warden was never again to be permitted to visit the prison came by the grapevine route to Tony Marino, Sing Sing inmate—Tough Tony, the Italian who in those first days of organizing the Mutual Welfare League in Auburn had given up his revenge that there might be an end to prison feuds. "He can go," he had said of the fellow convict who had slashed his face from mouth to ear. Tony's face was still disfigured. No surgery could remove that telltale gash, though his one-time enemy had offered to pay the best doctors to attempt an operation.

Recent events had shaken Tony's faith—not in Osborne, "the Big Boss" whom he looked upon almost as a god, but in society. Society, it seemed, had no use for either Tony or Osborne. If it treated its great men as shabbily as it treated its criminals, what was the use of going straight? Being no philosopher, Tony could find only one answer to that problem. The hell with it! They got you either way, straight or crooked. And the straighter you were, the dirtier the double-cross. So on New Year's Day, Tony disappeared.

· For Warden Kirchwey, who had been appointed just twenty-four hours before, it was a severe blow. With a show of confidence, however, he told the reporters that Tony had not actually escaped. It was just a psychological case. Tony had wandered away, but would return—voluntarily. This bit of idealizing sent the newspaper scribes into spasms of mirth. Tony would return, would he? Yes, indeedy! He and the lost Charley Ross! And they proceeded to write derisive columns about the unmasking of Osborne's system of mollycoddling prisoners. Yet scarcely had the ink on the newsprint dried when they were collared by frantic editors; for, wonder of wonders, Tony had returned—and voluntarily! They had to eat their words, and eat them quickly. To do the reporters justice, they did it willingly, for the incident sobered them as it sobered many another thoughtless critic.

But what would they not have given for the news behind the news! They may have guessed that Osborne, learning of the escape while spending the holiday at Auburn, had been nearly distracted. It was the best possible break for his enemies. But they did not know that Harry Bolasky had begged and received permission to hunt for the fugitive; or that he had shoveled his way through snowdrifts that blocked the road between Auburn and Syracuse, had swung aboard the last train for New York just as it pulled out of the station, and had run Tony to earth in an underworld dive. A different set of headlines would have topped their stories if they could have seen the big touring car in which Tony and his pals, packing guns equipped with Maxim silencers, were just starting for Cheshire, Connecticut, to wipe out the man whom Tony, in his blind anger, considered responsible for all of Osborne's troubles— Charles H. Johnson! There was murder afoot that night, and all that saved Johnson, blissfully unaware of impending danger, was the intervention of ex-members of the League he had sought to discredit. For five hours they pleaded with Tony; and it was no small favor they asked. He still had two years of an eleven-year minimum sentence to serve. To go back now would certainly mean an additional sentence. And then there was that Cheshire job.

It was Harry Bolasky who broke Tony's defense: "The Boss said that the District Attorney in White Plains could not have harmed him more than you have."

Tony, with money in his pocket and friends to protect him, gave up his only chance of liberty.

"It means about four years more for me," he said with tears in his eyes, "but if I have to do every day in solitary for it, I won't throw down the Boss. I see where I have made a big mistake. I am going back, and I'm going alone."

There was consternation in Albany when Tony returned. Riley apparently took it as a personal affront, for he immediately demanded additional sentence. Governor Whitman had other ideas. Ten weeks later Tony, stricken with tuberculosis, was given his freedom, and Osborne at his own expense sent the lad to Saranac.

Osborne was fortunate in his choice of a successor. With the aid of Spencer Miller, a young Amherst graduate who had succeeded Church as assistant warden, Dr. Kirchwey continued Osborne's policies, and introduced ideas of his own. The honor camp system was extended with gratifying results. The Sing Sing Institute, an educational organization with inmate directors, was developed to include classes in literature and art as well as in vocational training such as engineering, mechanical and architectural drawing. Several "graduates" of the telegraphy class went directly from Sing Sing to Western Union.

Dean Kirchwey had been in Sing Sing scarcely a week when he ran foul of Riley. The Superintendent ordered him to reinstate the prison officials Osborne had dismissed. Kirchwey said he would resign first. Moreover, he flatly refused to obey Riley's order to keep Osborne out of Sing Sing. Then one day Warden Kirchwey received from the Superintendent an order for the transfer of sixty-six men from Sing Sing to Clinton. That list included a number of delegates and committeemen of the Mutual Welfare League, the leader of the prison band Osborne had organized, the head of the Educational Committee, and nearly every inmate who had held a responsible position under Osborne.

It meant that the League was being wiped out; that the Superintendent was using the same tactics against Kirchwey as he had used against his predecessor. But at last he had overstepped the bounds. The new Warden went directly to the Governor and showed the order. As a result Riley was put on the mat. His excuse that the transfer was advisable because of congestion was riddled when Whitman produced a subsequent order from the Superintendent transferring a score of Clinton inmates back to Sing Sing.

"And wasn't it strange," the Governor added, "that of the fourteen witnesses who were to be called by Warden Osborne in his defense, eight of their names appear on this transfer list?"

It was more than strange; it was diabolical. A few days later Riley was removed, a sinister yet pathetic figure, maintaining his sincerity to the last. Within the year he was dead. Osborne's own sentiments concerning the long postponed ouster were echoed by an editorial in the New York *Call:*

Whitman isn't a great Governor, not even a fairly decent Governor—he's just a temporizing, fence-fixing little politician—but even he may be thanked for kicking Riley out.

The repercussions which followed the indictment of Osborne were a surprise even to the instigators. Defenders arose on all sides to champion the man who had brought to prison reform not simply new methods but a new spirit of understanding and sympathy. The public was by no means ignorant of what had been going on at Sing Sing. Osborne and the press had seen to that. During the years 1915 and 1916 more was written in the newspapers about prisons and prison reform than in any other similar period in the history of penology. Never one to hide his light under a bushel, especially when inspired by a great cause, Osborne had preached his gospel from the housetops. When he spoke, crowds flocked to hear him; and often the S.R.O. sign was hung out a quarter of an hour before he was scheduled to appear.

In Osborne's indictment there was a double jeopardy: the attack against prison reform, and the still more bitter, more ruthless attack against the man who had dared to throw out the old abuses. Assurances of faith began to pour in—from schoolmates of the old Adams Academy days, from Harvard classmates, from associates in business and politics. Resolutions upholding the Sing Sing administration were adopted by the Grand Jury Association of New York. From Auburn came a testimonial signed by one hundred leading citizens, many of whom at one time or another had been active political adversaries.

The greatest demonstration of all was a mass meeting held at Carnegie Hall on January 16. Thirty-five hundred people answered the call of a Citizens Committee composed of two hundred sixty men holding distinguished positions in the varied life of the metropolis. In the audience creatures of the underworld rubbed elbows with ladies and gentlemen of the upper social stratum. Isaac N. Seligman presided in the absence of the Hon. Joseph H. Choate, who had suddenly been taken ill; and the speakers included such men as Charles W. Eliot, president of Harvard, Dr. Charles H. Parkhurst, Felix Adler, and

Judge William H. Wadhams, who had sentenced many a convicted felon to Sing Sing and knew whereof he spoke. Although a feeling of delicacy prevented Osborne from attending, he must have harked back in memory to that meeting in Cooper Union a few years before when he had stood on the platform to champion another victim of conspiracy—Governor Sulzer.

Of even more dramatic interest was the meeting held a month later in the same hall. Ex-convicts engineered the whole thing, with Dick Richards presiding, and half a dozen graduates of penal institutions telling their story of crime, conviction, and regeneration in simple, straightforward terms. "The last time I spoke in public," confessed one embarrassed orator, "was to the judge who sent me up." Only two men on the program had no criminal records, and one of these was in immediate jeopardy of state prison—Osborne and Principal Keeper Dorner. Through all the turmoil and intrigue of the preceding months Dorner had stood courageously by his chief. Neither threats nor bribes had moved him a particle, and it was he who sounded the keynote this evening. Glancing about him at his fellow speakers—possibly the strangest assemblage that ever appeared on a public rostrum—he said with a smile:

"Under the old system I wouldn't have dared to come to New York—the ex-cons might have got me. Now look at 'em!"

Heartening as these evidences of confidence were, Osborne found his greatest encouragement in the attitude of the men within the walls of Sing Sing. When he first reported his indictment to the inmates, they had received the news in stunned silence. Familiar as they were with the methods of crooked politicians, they had never really believed the gang would "get" him. But when he told them he was still warden, that he was going to fight this thing to the bitter end and that they must help by giving the new warden the best coöperation, they lifted a cheer that shook the mess-hall to its foundations. Except for the clique that was party to the conspiracy, and one or two who succumbed to the coercive methods of the District Attorney, they were loyal to a man.

Previous mention has been made of the captious attitude Osborne had occasionally taken toward prison guards. All the more significant, therefore, is the following letter to Governor Whitman signed by eleven men on the office staff, the Superintendent of Industries, eight foremen, the Principal Keeper, and ninety-nine keepers and guards:

Hon. Charles S. Whitman,
Governor of the State of New York.
Your Excellency:
Owing to the fact that the impression has gone abroad that the guards and other employes of this institution are unfavorably disposed to the new order of things installed here by our Warden, Hon. Thomas Mott Osborne, and further, that we are resentful toward him and deplore the lack of discipline now alleged to obtain because of his placing the same, as is slanderously said, in the hands of vicious inmates, we feel it our duty to protest these statements, to repudiate them indignantly and to state most emphatically that never in the history of this prison have such cordial and kindly relations been established and maintained between the Warden, the inmates and ourselves.

Very respectfully yours,

This letter alone should have been sufficient to spike the false propaganda that had been spread. It was not; and Osborne, always loath to leave others to fight his battles, entered the arena himself. At colleges, in churches, on the platforms of public forums he pleaded his case. The chief issues involved are summed up in a statement he made at the time of his indictment. Characterizing the work of the Grand Jury as a conspiracy, not an investigation, he declared:

Because I have run Sing Sing with business honesty and efficiency I have made myself hated by the corrupt political element that have long utilized the prison for their own foul purpose.

Because I have reduced vice and disorder to a minimum within the prison, I have incurred the hatred of the few prisoners who had long enjoyed special privileges at the expense of their fellows.

Because I have served the state to the best of my ability, the very machinery of law intended for the protection of society has been prostituted from its high purpose to serve the vilest end by means equally vile.

This is not my personal fight. It belongs to every citizen in the State of New York. It is not one innocent man alone that has been indicted. The attack is directed against every honest office holder in the state, every other believer in decency in private life, every other believer in fair dealing between man and man, every other man who has endeavored to make his faith in God a living principle of action.

I have no fear of the result. No jury will be blind enough, no court unfair enough, to carry this conspiracy to ultimate success. The real question is: What do the people of New York State propose to do about it?

Of the twenty-one inmates who had been convicted of assault, only one was arraigned—Kaplan, or Jack the Dropper. He was to be tried first as a test case, the outcome of which would have also a distinct bearing on the Osborne trial. There was little to admire about the Dropper. A husky, thick-headed gangster, he was quite capable of committing all the crimes attributed to him—and more besides. But he had guts. When the third degree failed to break him, he was shipped to Clinton, the punishment prison. A writ of *habeas corpus* brought him back to White Plains. Once more he was shipped to Clinton, and once more his lawyer secured his return. Fat Alger was doubled up with him in the cell jail. The Dropper reported to defense counsel that Alger urged him to testify against Osborne on the promise that "the District Attorney will take care of you." He was starved—even the Sheriff admitted on the witness stand that he had not treated the Dropper as gently as the others—until his belly ached for food, and then on the promise of a chicken sandwich brought to the District Attorney's office.

"We have got you for two assaults," Kaplan later quoted a member of the District Attorney's staff as saying, "and we have you indicted for attempt at sodomy; maybe now you will turn around and not be a fool and come and make a statement that the Warden had immoral relations with you."

Kaplan went back to his cell—hungry.

When the defense sprang a surprise and called the accused to the stand to testify in his own behalf, Fallon jumped at the chance to trip the witness; but in the cross examination the Dropper stood his ground, became in fact the accuser. Once he rounded out a reply with the charge: "Then you turned around and told me, 'If you make a statement against the Warden we won't indict you.'" Again, when asked if he recalled a certain conversation, he retorted: "Yes, that was the time when I told you that before we got through with the thing, we'd have you down at Sing Sing carrying your bucket yourself."

It was of course a shot in the dark, but in 1923 the Great Mouthpiece just missed joining the bucket brigade. Indicted for conspiracy to obstruct the administration of justice—to wit, bribing a juror—he learned what it meant to be a fugitive from the law, to be double-crossed and captured, to see the walls come crashing down upon him, demolishing fortune, security, and professional reputation. There is irony in the fact that in his extremity, possibly through some faint tingling of the memory, he should have protested bitterly: "This is not prosecution. It is persecution!"

That it was persecution in the case of Jack the Dropper, the jury was soon convinced. The Sheriff confessed under pressure that while Jack and his counsel were conferring he had sneaked into an adjoining room to listen to the conversation. Harvey, the pervert responsible for the revolting mess, was caught in a deliberate lie. He swore he could identify "Yusky Nigger," an inmate whom he had implicated with the Dropper, because he had recently seen him again in Comstock. "Yusky Nigger" had been in Sing Sing all the time, as the Principal Keeper's records showed. With the chief witness discredited; with the methods employed to force Jack the Dropper to testify against Osborne brought to light; with the testimony on which Fallon asked conviction a stench in their nostrils— what could the jury do but bring in a verdict of "Not Guilty"? It was really Osborne's victory, for the conduct of the trial left no doubt that Fallon had attempted to stage this drama as a curtain-raiser for the big show. To the Assistant District Attorney the outcome was unforeseen. He had expected the twelve actors in the jury box to speak the lines that he pronounced to them, and they had gone back on him. Fallon was not used to that.

Osborne's trial was scheduled to come before the Court immediately. Instead of asking for a change of venue, the defense decided to fight it out at White Plains, where the charges had first been made; a bold stroke, for evidences of bias and hostility were all too plain. Acquittal, however, was not the only objective. Osborne wanted complete vindication, and the only place to make sure of that was right in the enemy's own territory.

The first step taken by the defense was to offer the usual motion to set aside the two indictments. Although the motion was denied, Justice Morschauser did strike out two of the six counts in the indictment for neglect of duty: one charging that Osborne had absented himself from prison, on the average, three days a week; and another alleging his failure to report violation of prison rules to Superintendent Riley.

Shortly before the trial began, a bizarre interlude threatened to blow the lid off a number of political pots and kettles. Osborne and melodrama were never very far apart, but in this instance he put the hack mystery and detective writers to shame. It came about as a result of increasing evidence of the stratagems adopted by his opponents. Thus far he had merely attempted to defend himself against the onslaughts; now the time had come to strike back, to fight fire with fire.

Into the case came one of those fictional characters you read about but can't quite believe in—a descendant of Sherlock Holmes. Val O'Farrell, former lieutenant of detectives in the New York Police Department, is a confidential investigator whose exploits have already passed into legend. O'Farrell engaged quarters under the name of Colonel Trout in the building where the District Attorney had his offices. One bitter February night one of his operatives sneaked up a scaling ladder to the roof and succeeded in stringing wires from a dictograph installed in Mr. Weeks's office to a detectaphone four floors below. For several days agents of "Colonel Trout" took stenographic records of all conversations between the District Attorney and his visitors—among whom were witnesses, assistants, and politicians.

An ordinary sleuth would have been quite content with his work, but Val O'Farrell is not ordinary. He likes to be more than one step ahead of his opponents. Perhaps, too, he has the makings of a dramatist in him. At any rate, after the authentic records were removed to safety, he sat down and composed a fake set of the most extraordinary character. There being nothing to hinder his play of imagination, he brought in the names of men prominent in public life, not forgetting the Governor himself. It was a masterpiece. He then secreted the fake records in various places about his "office," substituted for nis own staff a group of innocent employees who had not the slightest idea of what it was all about, and had an intermediary tip off Weeks and Fallon that someone was tapping their conversations by detectaphone. Val didn't have to wait long. Weeks flew into a passion and ordered an immediate raid on the Trout establishment. Sure enough, there were the records and a group of completely mystified employees.

When the records were perused, Fallon nearly broke a blood vessel. Here were the most preposterous accounts mixed with plausible-sounding conversations. For the life of him, he couldn't tell what was true and what was false. In righteous indignation that anyone should beat him at his own game, he threatened to prosecute O'Farrell.

"Go ahead," said the detective. "Why not? Of course, there's no law against using a dictagraph. And by the way, why don't you publish the detectaphone records? Or are you afraid to let the public know what goes on in your office?"

It was a complete checkmate, for the District Attorney could only guess how much the Osborne forces knew. Not daring to reveal the details of O'Farrell's fantastic imaginings, he was left in the position of appearing to conceal incriminating evidence.

O'Farrell, however, had more than one string to his bow. Not until Dr. Rudolph Diedling took the stand did the District Attorney realize the resourceful Val had been paying attention to his chief witness. While the detectaphone staff was busy taking down records of conversations in the District Attorney's office, another operative was on his way to visit the prison commissioner whose report had led to Grand Jury action. With him—of all things!—he carried a dozen violet ray lamps. Representing himself as a salesman, the detective soon disposed of several machines in the neighborhood—at less than cost price. Then he tackled Dr. Diedling. Both the lamp and the price appealed to the physician.

"Doctor," said the pseudo-salesman after reciting a panegyric on the qualities of his commodity, "if you'll come in with me, we can make a lot of jack. With your name it ought to be easy to sell a flock of lamps. Now, to begin with, if you'll write me a nice testimonial, I'll give you one free. What say?"

Dr. Diedling vouchsafed that he would be tickled to death, and accommodated with a signed statement that he had been using the lamp with gratifying success "for several years."

O'Farrell's operative neglected to tell Dr. Diedling that the machine had been on the market *only a few months!*

Such was the situation when the trial on the perjury indictment began on March 13 before Justice Arthur S. Tompkins of the Supreme Court. Although the testimony was largely a repetition of that taken before the Grand Jury and in the Kaplan trial, Mr. Fallon discovered his job was getting harder every minute. Under cross examination, his witnesses broke down badly:

Harvey admitted that he had been coached for his testimony by ex-Congressman Willett. . . . Willett was forced to confess he had been living like a king at the White Plains jail, sleeping and sometimes dining in the comfortable quarters of the hospital while Jack the Dropper was being browbeaten and half starved. . . . Dr. Diedling collapsed on the stand when confronted with his testimonial for the violet ray lamp and several other incidents of alleged unethical conduct in the practice of his profession. . . . Thompson, the Mutual Welfare League stenographer, tried to make the Court believe he had not sworn under oath at the Kaplan trial that Willett might have said, "Now let us see how we are going to fix it to convict this fellow"—insisting that the court record was wrong, and that he had actually said, "Now, let us see how we are going to *fit* it to *connect* this fellow.". . . Clifford Young, Dr. Diedling's stenographer, was shown up as egregiously inefficient, unable to remember accurately any of the answers Osborne had given to Dr. Diedling except—so he swore—the alleged statement, "There is no sodomy case as far as the prison is concerned."

As the whole case hinged on Osborne's contention he had said "prisoners' court," not simply "prison," the discovery that no one could tell the difference between Young's stenographic symbols for "prison" and "prisoners" made a deep impression on the jury.

As it turned out, most of this evidence was superfluous. In the first place, Dr. Diedling had never been authorized to take testimony on oath. Therefore there could be no perjury. Yet even if the Doctor had had full authority, the element of willful deception was lacking. Diedling's testimony showed that he had heard about the sodomy cases and had questioned witnesses about them in Osborne's presence. Since both Diedling and Osborne shared this knowledge in common, any attempt to give false witness was absolutely impossible, whether or not the stenographer had made an error. The defendant's refusal to answer certain questions was for the purpose of keeping his promise to the men that he would go to jail before betraying their confidences. That was Justice Tompkins' ruling as he threw the case out of court. Osborne had won another round, and his acquittal was hailed with rejoicing from one end of the country to the other.

There remained the indictment for neglect of duty, including the immorality charge. Impatient to try the issue, Osborne clamored for an immediate trial. District Attorney Weeks demurred. The state was not ready. For two months legal technicalities blocked action, while Mr. Battle and Mr. Merchant chafed at the delay. At every point they were checkmated. The District Attorney's office refused to produce the minutes of the grand jury proceedings. Even when ordered by the judge to give the defense a copy of the records, Fallon found the most exasperating excuses: His typist was sick—he had a luncheon engagement—the judge's order must be verified. He waited so long before complying that there was talk of contempt proceedings. When that matter was cleared up, other delays were maneuvered. The truth is, Fallon was in a funk. He saw the case slipping through his fingers and wanted to postpone the trial until he could buck up his demoralized witnesses.

Still another rebuff was in store for the Great Mouthpiece.

According to the law, if Osborne were found guilty of any one of the remaining four charges, he would be convicted. As that would leave the general impression that he was guilty on all counts, his lawyers sought to have the immorality charge divorced from the others and tried under a separate indictment. Thwarted in this by the desperate opposition of Weeks and Fallon, Mr. Battle finally moved that the count be stricken out altogether. Again the legal machinery began its slow pace, with Fallon protesting every inch of the way, until at last the motion reached the Appellate Division of the Supreme Court. By unanimous decision of the five judges the count was ruled out. But, more important, Weeks and Fallon received one of the severest rebukes ever administered to public prosecutors; the summation read in part:

The sixth count contains no statement of acts constituting a crime. It contains characterizations that are legally meaningless . . . but oppressively injurious by suggestion. . . . The Legislature having failed to prescribe the method of expunging from an indictment containing a good count, irrelevant, scandalous and prejudicial matter stated in a separate count professing to charge, but not charging a crime, we are unwilling to concede that the court in which the indictment is tried is powerless to protect the defendant from so gross an injustice.

Now that the indictment was stripped down to three counts dealing with the general management of the prison, the District Attorney and his ambitious assistant were only too anxious to drop the case. They were well aware that public sentiment was swinging toward Osborne. Their conduct of the investigation and trial had been conspicuous only in its flouting of decency, and at the last had brought a scathing rebuke from the appellate bench. Some newspapers were calling for an investigation of the District Attorney with a view to his removal from office. Still Weeks could not well back down. He had to save his face. Through further delays he managed to postpone action until his successor took office. Then the case was withdrawn in short order, as were also the charges against the twenty prisoners indicted with Jack the Dropper.

Osborne hardly knew whether to be glad or sorry. He had

spent $75,000 in the effort to clear his name, and though legally he was vindicated, he wondered whether a trial and acquittal would not have been more impressive. Dean Kirchwey was more practical.

"You know," he said, "you are guilty of one crime charged against you."

Osborne bridled at that. It was like a stab in the back to have his friend, the man who had carried on so ably in Sing Sing, believe a single one of the fabrications.

"And what crime is that?" he asked.

"Insubordination," replied Kirchwey cheerfully.

Osborne's features relaxed, and his mouth twisted into a rueful grin. "I guess you're right," he admitted. He never had liked the details of the administration end, and Riley's flood of picayune memoranda, orders, and what not was a perpetual irritation. Sometimes he would not bother to open letters from the Superintendent's office. They were too insulting, he said. By the time a subordinate got round to perusing them, Riley was raging. But even granted that superiors always found Osborne hard to deal with, why should there have been such a concerted effort to destroy him? It had not been simply an agitation for his removal from Sing Sing, but a plot to shatter his reputation so that he could never again aspire to public office.

Only a genius could have marshaled against himself so many powerful forces. Not one, but many, factions were eager to get rid of him for good. There were the prison favorites, the men of influence who had been permitted to live almost in luxury. When Osborne canceled their special privileges, the squawk they lifted rallied allies from the outside who tried to square things with the Warden. Their surprise at finding the Warden could not be reached through the usual channels—crossing the palm with silver or threatening personal discomforts—soon changed to vindictiveness. No less eager to see the last of Osborne was a group of crooked contractors and purveyors whose fat slices of graft from prison jobs ended when he took charge of Sing Sing. As the sum of money involved was by no means small, almost any means would justify their ends.

Ostensibly the political phase was mere jealousy. In the publicity which centered about the Warden of Sing Sing one may find a partial explanation for the pertinacious hostility of Superintendent Riley. He rarely missed an opportunity to proclaim that *he* was responsible for all the innovations. One of his numerous statements to the press was headlined in the New York *Sun* as follows: "Osborne Lied, Says Riley; Prison Reforms Are Mine." Queer, that he should have found no inconsistency in damning before the Grand Jury the very reforms for which he was so anxious to have the credit! Occasionally, too, Governor Whitman seemed to resent the attention given to Sing Sing; yet neither Riley nor Whitman dared demand Osborne's resignation. They were afraid to "make a martyr of him."

At the root of the situation, however, was the fact that Osborne was a political threat. He was a far greater power now than when boomed for governor in 1910, and both parties watched his rise with deep concern. Tammany had not changed its mind. This was the old Osborne, again a Democratic officeholder under a Republican administration, and the last man it wanted to see as a candidate. On their side, the Republicans feared him as a possible opponent. Whitman was known to cherish Presidential ambitions. If he walked out on them, it would be difficult to find a man to beat Osborne. But there was one way to prevent such a catastrophe—political assassination.

To imply that the respectable element of either party lent themselves to so vile a scheme would be unjust. There were enough of the other kind to engineer it. If any blame attaches to the leaders, it is that they failed to break up the conspiracy when it first got under way. Is it any wonder that Osborne, badgered by spies, false friends, and faithless assistants, should see a traitor in every temporizing official? The *New York Times* called it "delusions of persecution"; but he knew better. It was only in the ramifications of the plot that he was deceived.

Gradually his suspicions centered on one man as the arch villain. Till the day of his death he was convinced that Whitman was mainly responsible for all his troubles. Had the Governor dismissed Riley when the nature of the attack became apparent, and had he appointed a commission to investigate Sing Sing as he had promised, the horrible scandal would have been averted. On October 25, 1916, Osborne published an open letter to Whitman in which he said:

Thanks to you, sir, the name I inherited from my honored father, and from my mother, who was your mother's friend, has been linked in people's thoughts with the vilest of crimes: I have had to fight for what is worth far more than life itself against a powerful and remorseless political organization; I have been indicted and placed on trial with the shadow of state prison sentence falling upon the court room. Yet for all this and more I not only bear you no resentment—I am deeply grateful.

You have been the means of bringing to me some of the most wonderful experiences the world can give; renewal of old friendships, and troops of new friends; appreciation of my work far beyond its deserts; increased opportunity and power to be of service to my fellowmen. I would not alter the past two years, if it were possible to do so.

But I do desire to influence the future, so far as I may, to the end that no man so weak as yourself—so shifty, so selfish, so false, so cruel, may be trusted with further power. The next public servant who stands in your way may not be so fortunate as I have been.

Osborne, so conscious of his own uprightness, was never able to conceive of genuine doubts in others. He failed, for instance, to appreciate Whitman's difficulties. The Governor was hedged in by a ring of underlings whose conflicting reports on the Sing Sing situation were so baffling that he did not know what to believe. The Brooklyn Sunday School teacher whose exceptional talent for securing convictions as District Attorney had won him the governorship may have been weak, was assuredly dilatory; but the evidence is against his active participation in the conspiracy. Both Dean Kirchwey and Leigh Bonsal, two of the Warden's closest confidants in this hectic period, absolutely absolve Whitman of intentional wrongdoing; but they were never able to convince Osborne.

There are a number of things that explain but do not wholly excuse the credence placed in some quarters upon the charges against Osborne. Most important was his utter disregard for appearances. That gave his enemies a peg on which to hang their slanders. Osborne was demonstrative. He would often fling his arms about a man's shoulders—much as I have seen a fatherly college president embrace students. In both cases the feeling was sincere, and in both cases there was some embarrassment on the part of the embraced. But to a man like Charles H. Johnson, whose emotions were rigidly inhibited, Osborne's camaraderie with convicted felons was offensive. Because he could not understand, he placed the worst construction on the most innocent scenes. He failed to perceive that their very openness should have disarmed suspicion.

Osborne was an athlete and had an athlete's unconcern about the human body. He had trained with football squads and had dressed with his fellow players in the locker room. Yet when a prison official saw him cross the hall in dressing-gown and slippers, it seemed a violation of the proprieties! This, remember, was nearly twenty years ago. The same people who raised an eyebrow at customs that would seem rather conservative to-day were shocked at Osborne's frankness in discussing the greatest of prison evils—sex perversion. Until he dared bring the subject into the open, vice had been clothed in secrecy—and had flourished because of it. Squeamishness was responsible for lack of proper preventive measures. When Osborne attacked the problem, demanding segregation and calling upon the inmates to coöperate in stamping it out, he committed the sin of mentioning the unmentionable. The fact that he came close to ridding Sing Sing of the evil and might have been even more successful had not the state sentenced a degenerate to prison instead of to an insane asylum, seemed to count little. In the first decade and a half of the new century society interpreted literally the hear-see-speak-no-evil text.

To the best of his ability Osborne strove to give a fair deal to every inmate. Yet his sympathies went out instinctively to the outcasts who had never had a chance. He believed he could trust them in the long run better than the silk-stockings, men with brains enough to know right from wrong and ability enough to earn an honest living. Possibly this leaning was felt in a rather hazy way, for the élite—the safe-crackers, embezzlers, and high-powered confidence men—were inclined to shy off Osborne, while the poor purse-snatchers and stick-up men gave him a loyalty they had hardly dreamed themselves capable of. The natural result was that the Warden's entourage was recruited largely from the lower circles of the underworld —bums and gangsters who for the first time had found an incentive to become decent citizens. Unfortunately, society was more impressed by what these men had been than by what they had become, and Osborne was condemned, as others had been before him, for associating with publicans and sinners.

Then, if ever, he learned the price one pays for venturing from beaten paths. Agents, sent to Auburn to rake up the old stories about adventures in disguise, returned with accounts so distorted that a specious credibility was put on the Sing Sing accusations. Even old friends, unaware of his Harun-al-Rashid proclivities, were momentarily put out of countenance by these embroidered tales. Yet how could he make people understand that impulse to wrench himself free from his own personality and create other selves with other lives and other horizons? He could imagine the embarrassed silence that would greet such an explanation. Helpless, he saw the lies grow, unite with other lies, and propagate a monstrous Thing that people pointed at and called by his name. The immortality of a lie is terrifying. It may be dormant for years and then spring up with renewed vitality. Osborne found that out. Even death has not freed him from its curse.

It is fitting that Fallon, the relentless prosecutor, should have the last word. Not that any pangs of remorse seared the soul of the Great Mouthpiece; he was too self-centered for that. But he realized he had overstepped the bounds and defeated his own ends. Gene Fowler, his biographer, quotes him as saying of the Osborne case: "I turned a prosecution into a persecution. And that is always bad."

How bad, Fallon was not the sort to appreciate.

The usual throng of commuters were hustling through the vault of Grand Central Station in New York on that bright morning of July 16, 1916. Intent on their own affairs, few noticed the excited group gathered about one of the train gates. Even if their attention had been attracted, they would never have guessed that the party was made up of ex-convicts or that, contrary to all experience, they were eagerly waiting for the departure of the train that was to carry them up the river to Sing Sing. For most of the group the trip was no new experience—but there was one great difference. Each had paid his own fare and had carefully tucked away in his pocket a return ticket!

This was the day when Thomas Mott Osborne was to come back to Sing Sing, and forty-one members of the outside branch of the Mutual Welfare League in New York City and the surrounding region had determined to participate in the celebration. Of that number, twenty-one were workers in the Ford assembly plant. Henry Ford may have been short on history, but he knew workmen. After witnessing the miracle Osborne had performed in "turning a scrap heap into a repair shop," he had promised to employ every able graduate of the Mutual Welfare League. And he had kept his word. There was one there that morning of whom he had said, "He's the best man we have."

When the train was called, there was a rush for places, but good care was taken not to harm the big floral horseshoe that was to be their tribute to Tom Brown. With a lurch the train started. The voices of women mingled with the talk of men, for wives, sweethearts, and sisters had come along, too. It was a lark and a triumph in one.

Sing Sing. Old friends to greet. Inmates you had known when the Hudson River at your feet seemed so far away, so unattainable. Yes, and guards, too. He was always a square guy, wasn't he! Hello, Sam. Hello, Bill.

Baseball teams are warming up on the prison diamond. The parade is about to form, with Tom Brown's Aurora Band practicing a few last bars. Banners and flags are fluttering in the breeze. There are prisoners everywhere, it seems—all over the place, even perched on roofs and hanging out of windows. You

TRIUMPHANT RETURN TO SING SING
Osborne and His Loyal Ally, Principal Keeper Dorner

have to look sharp to find a guard. Only a few of them in all that throng. Yet no trouble. Only a great gladness.

And now the reception committee starts for the station— over two hundred of them, including the Executive Board of the League, the inmate faculty of the Institute, looking very dignified in their academic gowns, and the band, all spick and span and tootling a stirring march. Out through the last gate, across the last boundary, bodies erect, heads up—a group of convicts under no officers except their own, parading through the town to welcome home a warden!

The events of that day made history. No returning college president ever received a warmer welcome from his undergraduates. There were speeches, athletic contests, instrumental numbers by the band. Listening to the cheers and songs of the inmates, Tom Brown felt that here at last was real vindication.

Osborne was not the only one to be honored. Dean Kirchwey came in for his share of the glory. During his six months of administration, conditions at Sing Sing had continued to improve. He had won the loyalty of the inmates, and the Mutual Welfare League was functioning as well as ever. More than any other man he was instrumental in answering the moderate critics who, while granting the benefits that had come under Osborne, insisted that the man, not the system, was responsible. On the afternoon preceding Osborne's return, Dean Kirchwey had been tendered a silver loving cup by the National Committee on Prisons. To-day the "faculty" of the Institute conferred on both Wardens with all due solemnity the degree of Doctor of Humanity. Although no one knew exactly what a Doctor of Humanity was, the degree was prized by the recipients as highly as more orthodox honors.

Throughout the festivities Osborne was jubilant. His face shone, and his voice trembled with emotion. Had he not come back to his own, freed from the dark cloud that had hung over him for many months? And now he had new ideas he wanted to try out. One of these he revealed to the corps of reporters who followed him about—a psychopathic clinic, the first of its kind in the country. The mentally deficient prisoners would be segregated for special observation and treatment by a corps of trained psychiatrists. Already he had engaged Dr. Bernard Glueck, of the Government Hospital for the Insane at Washington, to take charge of the clinic. And there would be other innovations. Oh, there was so much to be done!

Exactly three months later to a day, Osborne resigned as Warden of Sing Sing.

CHAPTER VIII

TOM BROWN IN THE NAVY

Osborne's resignation was like a bombshell to both friends and foes. They could not understand it, and it may be a little difficult to understand now. A hard-earned victory had been won. Not only the man but the system had been vindicated. With hopes for progressive prison reform brighter than ever before, why had the leader suddenly deserted the cause? Many of the journals that had never liked Osborne became righteously indignant and lamented loudly that he should give such a poor example to his charges by surrendering in the face of obstacles. Others gloated openly that "sanity" would now return to Sing Sing. Even the friendly press was apologetic.

Osborne had his reasons. In his letter of resignation to the new Superintendent of Prisons, James S. Carter, he bitterly assailed Whitman, charging that the Governor had broken every promise made to him. He intimated, too, that the Superintendent was in league with his foes in trying to discredit his reforms. A series of official orders had demanded a cessation of publicity in regard to Sing Sing, attributed escapes either to lax methods or to impracticability of the new system, and finally stipulated that no long-term convict should be allowed outside prison walls. This last was the straw that broke the camel's back. Experience had led Osborne to believe that neither nature of crime nor length of sentence was a true index of character; that "the enormous capacity of man to recover his moral balance after the commission of sin" is often greatest in those derelicts whom society has given up as incorrigible. To differentiate between prisoners on the basis of sentence would emasculate his program. It would mean that every trusty in the administration offices, which at Sing Sing are outside the prison walls proper, would have to be dismissed, no matter how commendable his record there had been, and sent back to his dungeon.

Osborne needed no more proof than this of the persistence of the conspiracy against him. Because he felt that much of the hostility was directed at him personally, he came to the conclusion that his usefulness as Warden of Sing Sing had ended. Now that he had established his system on a sound basis, it was possible that another would receive better coöperation from prison authorities than had ever been accorded him. And had not Dr. Kirchwey proved that any man of experience and fine perception could carry on the work?

Unfortunately Osborne was not content with resignation. Wrongs real and imagined bit like acid into his soul, and he took the stump against Whitman in the gubernatorial campaign. If only he had let others fight the political battle! Did he not see that his act would be construed as a nullification of his own plea to keep prisons out of politics? Again, at a critical point in his career, his headlong impulsiveness alienated those most anxious to serve him—men like Richard M. Hurd, who had appeared at White Plains as an Osborne witness, and George W. Wickersham. Although the New York *World* continued to defend him, it was no longer proof against the charge of partisanship. The campaign had started, and its aversion to Whitman was no secret. To the Governor's camp rallied a number of influential men who were unwilling to follow Osborne's lead now that he had entered the political arena. Osborne's defense was that the Governor had beaten him to the tape in dragging prisons into politics—a truth that did not fully absolve him of his own participation. It was, besides, a futile gesture; for Whitman was reëlected with a staggering plurality.

Government interference was probably not the only reason that induced Osborne to resign. The lure of new adventure was calling his restless spirit. He could never accommodate himself to the rut of ordinary pursuits, and even the extraordinary eventually grew tame. The world was so full of crossroads and each new turning revealed such entrancing vistas that he rarely kept to the same path for long. Yet whichever way he turned, his feet bore him unerringly toward the same goal. In January, 1917, Tom Brown was again in "uniform"—this time serving a term in the naval prison at Portsmouth, New Hampshire.

Authority for the new venture had come directly from Secretary of the Navy Josephus Daniels, who as early as the preceding autumn had asked Osborne to make a study of conditions in naval prisons. With Harry Bolasky and Austin H. MacCormick, an instructor at Bowdoin College, Osborne had enlisted in the navy and become a deserter. For this crime, of which sixty-five per cent of the inmates at Portsmouth were guilty, the trio suffered imprisonment on board the old ship *Southery*, lying at the pier. Dressed in regulation prison gray, with their hair clipped close to their heads, they were set to work with their fellow prisoners washing greasy dishes and cutting ice—the temperature hovering around zero at the time. After a few days they were transferred to the main prison ashore.

During this week's imprisonment and on subsequent visits, Osborne learned enough to convince him that Uncle Sam was making a bad investment. In comparison with other prisons, there was less actual brutality, yet here were hundreds of young men, convicted of all sorts of offenses—most of them minor—lodged and fed at the expense of the government only to be turned loose with a dishonorable discharge at the expiration of their terms. If Portsmouth Prison were to be good for anything, it should be returning able-bodied seamen to the navy.

When Osborne submitted his report, Secretary Daniels indicated complete approval by asking him to take charge at Portsmouth. The offer was a surprise to everybody, Osborne included. Never before had a civilian been placed in command of a naval prison, and many a navy officer grumbled when a mere landlubber was jumped over old service men to the rank of lieutenant commander.

It was the first day of August when Osborne took command at Portsmouth. Standing in the reception room of his new quarters, he was a striking figure in his immaculate white uniform, worn with just a touch of romantic swagger. Interviewers, anticipating a civilian type, were rather awed to find an officer who looked and acted every inch an admiral. They were impressed, too, by the program which he mapped out for them. This was not the radicalism they had been led to expect. It was common sense that many boys who had rebelled against strict navy discipline, or who had got into trouble on a spree to forget trouble, were not really bad. They simply had not adjusted themselves to the military routine. Lost man-power was the result.

Of course, lost man-power was not Osborne's chief concern; it was lost manhood. But he was practical enough to realize that many who either did not understand or did not sympathize with his ideal of regeneration would find a patriotic appeal in a project that would save sailors for Uncle Sam. Now that the United States had entered the World War, counting masculine noses was a serious business. Of Osborne's own patriotism there could be no question, for his whole family—he and four sons—were in service.

Although essentially the same as in Auburn and Sing Sing, the prison problem at Portsmouth had certain distinguishing characteristics. All the inmates were products of a single system. For that system Osborne had an undisguised loathing. Blind obedience, he believed, was useless obedience. Besides, the severity of the penalty meted out to a boy who had overstayed his leave a few hours and was rated a deserter seemed to him wholly disproportionate to the offense. Our military laws had been inherited from England in the 1770's, and England herself had long since abandoned them for a more intelligent code. Among the greatest of injustices was the lack of uniformity in imposing sentences. The court-martial system was responsible for that. Under one officer a slight disobedience would be judged mutiny and the offender would receive twenty-five years in a federal penitentiary. In a different outfit the same offense might bring only six months' confinement in barracks. The whim or the prejudice of an individual was supreme, and there was no appeal to civil justice.

It did not take long for the men at Portsmouth to discover that they had a friend in court—if they met him halfway. Osborne told them that he was going to feel his way slowly; but when he began by removing from the buildings the entire detachment of marines who had served as guards and establishing inmate control in a prison that had no walls, they wondered what would have happened had he started with a rush. As Osborne well knew, however, the very suddenness of these dramatic gestures was in part responsible for their effectiveness.

At Portsmouth much the same reforms were put into force as in Auburn and Sing Sing. For the first time prisoners were permitted outdoor recreation, with baseball and other sports in the open field outside the turreted structure of concrete and steel which is the prison proper. At one period over 2,500 men were in detention, most of whom were eligible for this out-of-bounds privilege; yet, though not even a fence barred their way to freedom, loyalty to something—a principle or a man—restrained them from taking advantage of the situation. For the two and a half years Osborne was at Portsmouth only eight men escaped. During that time sixty-six hundred jackies passed through the prison—and four thousand went back into the navy.

Such revolutionary changes were accomplished not without difficulty. Navy men were scandalized, and most of the officers assigned to assist Osborne looked with disfavor upon the liberties permitted to prisoners. Nevertheless, they found it difficult to explain away some rather extraordinary occurrences.

One of the innovations was an inmate dramatic club, which gave performances in the prison and in the city of Portsmouth. Once it went farther afield. By permission of Secretary Daniels, Osborne took about one hundred of his charges for a one-night stand at Manchester, more than forty miles distant. In the cavalcade of thirteen automobiles which transported the party there was not a single guard. On the return journey Osborne's car led the way. When at last the weary Thespians stumbled out at Portsmouth about one in the morning, the last car failed to check in. All through the night Osborne waited, hoping. Was thirteen to be his unlucky number? Dawn came, and still no word. Finally about nine o'clock there was a message. The missing men were safe. In the falling snow and darkness they had lost the road and tried vainly to find their way back to prison.

In that car there were six or seven convicts—one a lifer, another serving a twenty-five-year stretch. To escape they had only to clout the civilian driver on the head and step on the gas for somewhere. Yet every last man of them came back.

Why?

Undoubtedly the personality of the commanding officer counted a great deal. Osborne was close to every man, knew each by name until the increasing and shifting population made this impossible. He coached the dramatic club, helped supervise the educational and recreational programs, and listened sympathetically to any man who had what he considered a real grievance.

Back of the man, however, there was a principle to which the majority gave unwavering devotion. As at Auburn and Sing Sing it found expression in an inmate organization with a Prisoners' Court that handled matters of discipline. The commanding officer merely imposed sentence, according to navy law, after the court handed down its decision. At first the men had wanted to call their association the Naval Welfare League, but when Secretary Daniels objected that the title implied the whole service rather than simply the prison at Portsmouth, they agreed that the Mutual Welfare League was the logical name.

There is a temptation to picture the Mutual Welfare League at Portsmouth as one hundred per cent efficient, meeting every crisis with wisdom and unanimity. In spite of a true sense of loyalty, the members fell far short of the ideal. For instance, a few ambitious inmates succeeded for a time in counterfeiting honorable discharge papers in the prison print shop. Until discovered and brought to book, they made a handsome profit selling these forged documents to men dismissed with dishonorable discharges.

Once, in particular, the League fell upon evil days. A certain clique, by practices not unknown to politics, gained control of the court and used their authority to shield malefactors from the consequences of their wrongdoing. Now this judicial procedure was the most vulnerable point in the entire scheme, and Osborne acted quickly. Assembling all the inmates in the mess-hall, he explained the situation in terse language and summarily suspended the League. With that he left; but before his audience could recover its breath, he staged a dramatic reëntrance.

"And don't think," he thundered, shaking a finger at the amazed convicts, "that I don't realize you fellows have me at a disadvantage. Until I can get some marines here, I shall have to count on the decent element to protect me. Barney Higgins, get some deputies and maintain order!"

Order was maintained, but the League stayed suspended until the inmates themselves, with Barney Higgins at their head, petitioned humbly for its reinstatement.

In "T. M.," as Osborne was now widely called, the old sea dogs of the regular navy found they had caught a tartar. He cut navy red tape as deftly as a hot knife cuts ice cream. For the old fetishes of the service, the rules of etiquette and the sanctity of rank, he cared not a whit. They were useless, ridiculous, humiliating.

With such utter disregard for navy tradition on the part of their chief, the associate staff at Portsmouth suffered a chronic headache trying to keep Osborne out of hot water. There was Captain Hill, who as official navy adviser felt his responsibility keenly and prayed each night that the C. O. would do nothing next day to bring down the heavens; Austin MacCormick, executive officer next in command to Osborne; and Harold E. Donnell, later to become Superintendent of Prisons in Maryland. Perhaps the most useful in the group was William B. Cox, chief yeoman and captain's writer, whose special assignment was to keep T. M. from violating navy rules. More often, however, it was his talent to find a way out of trouble—thirteen years of experience having taught him most of the loopholes in navy regulations—that was in demand. There, too, was husky Billy Duffy, free once more and serving as yeoman under his benefactor.

Although the combined efforts of these advisers did not always suffice to ward off embarrassing situations, there was fortunately a *deus ex machina* to step in and cut Gordian knots.

That was Secretary Daniels; or, more frequently, his youthful assistant secretary, Franklin D. Roosevelt. Both men were stanch supporters of Osborne and could be counted on to protect and uphold. In time of trouble a letter to "Dear Frank" worked miracles, and disgruntled navy officers discovered it was dangerous to bedevil the commanding officer at Portsmouth too much.

All official communications from the prison went through Osborne's immediate superior, the admiral in command of Portsmouth Navy Yard. With embarrassing frequency, however, Osborne found it convenient to appeal by personal letter directly to his friends in the Department at Washington. If this was irritating, the open flouting of authority was much worse. One day the Commandant summoned his subordinate to appear before him at the Yard. Osborne sent word:

"I'm too busy. Come over and see me."

Discipline? Rank? Etiquette? Osborne had so little respect for any of them that it is a wonder he did not get himself court-martialed.

It was inevitable that old-time navy men should have a chip on their shoulder. Not only were they aggrieved that a civilian had been placed in command of Portsmouth Prison, but they viewed with general alarm what they considered an attack upon their cherished traditions of discipline. Sometimes they went out of their way to snub the interloper.

As director of athletics, Osborne had Louis B. McCagg, Jr., son of his old college chum. This young man had grown up with a tremendous admiration for the charming gentleman whose frequent visits to the McCagg home had always meant music and laughter. Attracted by the prospect of working under Osborne, he had obtained his transfer from the coast guard to Portsmouth.

On waking one morning, the inmates saw a battleship lying in the harbor. Immediately Osborne conceived the idea of a baseball game between the Portsmouth Prison team and a nine recruited from the battleship crew, and McCagg was sent aboard to make the arrangements.

When the Captain heard the proposition, the accumulated

dignity inherited from seagoing forbears from John Paul Jones down was cut to the quick. What, his good boys play with that bunch of jailbirds? Not while he trod the bridge on this ship! Osborne was so infuriated at such supersensitiveness that he berated the Captain, his superior officer, like a cabin boy, and not until both Daniels and Roosevelt were called in was peace restored.

Hardly a day passed without its controversy. One project brought a howl not only from the navy press agents but from the whole army staff as well. "Is the ex-convict morally unfit to fight the savage Hun?" asked Osborne. He asked it so persistently that both services began to grow uneasy. This was far more serious than a baseball game. It was an effort to smash the regulation against the enlistment of men who had prison records. Worse than that, the ultimate goal was clearly the drafting of men *now in prison* to fight for the Stars and Stripes! Against such a vulgarization of the military the *Army and Navy Register* sounded a call to arms, waxing extremely wroth that the service should be considered "a refuge for criminals." Quite suddenly hard-boiled generals and admirals became very solicitous of "the integrity of the fighting personnel."

Traditions aside, there was some reason in many of Osborne's arguments. In the first place, in a national crisis that demanded every available man it was no time to be fastidious. The country was faced with cold solid facts—a German army well equipped and well manned. Only another army likewise well equipped and well manned could hope to come away victorious. Besides, who could say that a burglar was less capable of patriotism than a plumber or a banker? For that matter, there were already thousands of ex-convicts in the army—men who had enlisted under aliases to escape detection. As crooks often made the best kind of soldiers, why not give them a chance to serve their country without resorting to deception and at the same time to rehabilitate themselves?

Even before he took charge at Portsmouth, Osborne had approached Newton D. Baker, Secretary of War, with the suggestion that an army contingent be recruited from ex-convicts.

Perhaps a recruiting officer without a bona fide criminal record would be advisable. In that case Thomas Mott Osborne would be glad to offer his services.

If Secretary Baker had any temptation to adopt this proposal, he changed his mind after a talk with General Scott. To a case-hardened military man it seemed worse than madness, and Teddy Roosevelt's idea of raising a regiment of Rough Riders mild in comparison. In a letter meant to be tactful, the Secretary assured Osborne of his own personal sympathy with the scheme but regretted that military opinion would not permit a trial. Osborne wrote in return:

> . . . The vitally serious thing that one finds between the lines of your letter is the thing which is likely to make our army a laughing stock of the nations, if it ever goes into action under men who live in such a fools' paradise as that indicated by General Scott. That thing is the inability to face facts. . . .
>
> In regard to your suggestion that it might be possible to form such a contingent later when "it would be lost among the great multitude"—that, my dear sir, would be something so far from what I suggest that under no circumstances could I recommend or have anything, personally, to do with it. An ex-convict regiment formed in such a way that every one was ashamed of it, so that the fact of its existence must if possible be hidden, would indeed be a shameful thing. . . . The only way such a plan could be carried to success would be to do it quite in the open.

Just what would have happened, had this fiery letter been delivered to the Secretary of War, will never be known. Osborne intrusted it to his son Charles, then waiting in Washington for his commission, with instructions to send it through Franklin D. Roosevelt to Newton Baker. Once he had read the contents, however, Charles took matters into his own hands and calmly pocketed the communication—a mutinous act that brought down on his head a storm of paternal wrath.

Although Osborne continued to press his plan publicly and privately, army and navy authorities succeeded in frustrating him at every point, with the result that of all classes criminals alone have been unable to boast they won the War.

And yet such things were tempests in a teapot compared to the uproar aroused by another project upon which the stormy petrel of the navy embarked—embarked figuratively and literally. On the evening of June 29, 1919, Acting Commanding Officer Austin MacCormick stood in the mess-hall at Portsmouth giving last words of advice to a quartet of inmates about to depart for service on the battleship *North Dakota*. The cheers of the men rang out with unusual fervor, for the "salvaged" group of seagoing gobs was composed of Luke Cote, Joe McShea, Billy Duffy—and Tom Brown! In the face of frantic opposition from high navy officials, Osborne had obtained the consent of Secretary Daniels to spend a month as a common bluejacket. Although it was actually his vacation, he felt that a period of active service with enlisted men on a great battleship was essential to his understanding of the naval prison problem. So the Lieutenant Commander doffed the white uniform of which he was so proud and donned the regimentals of a gob.

What the old-line admirals thought of such capers is easy to imagine. More than one would have been glad to see Tom Brown strung up to a yardarm. Here was a lieutenant commander eating and slaving with deck-hands. Why, the distinctions of rank were going plumb to hell!

As a matter of fact, the worst fears never materialized. Tom Brown took to gobhood as a duck takes to water. He stood watch, scrubbed decks, and in the stifling heat of the glory-hole stoked the huge furnaces until the sweat poured in rivulets down his back. He made a lark of the most menial tasks and fired his companions with new zeal. There were, to be sure, several trivial regulations which he regarded with skepticism. Why should there have to be exactly thirteen buttons on his pants? Why should he be called from his hammock at 5:30 A.M. when breakfast wasn't served until seven? Getting up early, he confessed, was not one of his vices, and he agreed with Huxley that early risers are "conceited all the forenoon and stupid all the afternoon."

In spite of his distaste for certain phases of discipline which he considered petty, Osborne was surprised to find how easily he accommodated himself to the routine. And he was enjoying himself to the top of his bent. As one of the crew of the *North*

Dakota he had a humble part in the great naval reception accorded the *George Washington,* bearing President Wilson home from the Treaty of Peace. He played the piano for the enlisted men's ball, and discovered that jazz and ragtime have an invigorating quality he had never suspected. He learned some of the sailors' argot and began smoking cigarettes—a habit which he had hitherto despised.

For this new impersonation there came at last the perfect tribute. Billy Duffy, following a few paces behind his comrade, heard two sailors in conversation.

"You know," said one, pointing at Osborne, "that guy's an officer—a two-and-a-half striper."

"You're a goddam liar," contradicted the other. "He's nothing but a big, greasy gob!"

Few guessed that Tom Brown, able seaman, whose industry above and below decks was a byword, was several times a grandfather and that before the following month ran out he would celebrate his sixtieth birthday.

Even in Portsmouth the "brothers" of Tom Brown occasionally put in an appearance.

It was the annual ball of the Emerson B. Hovey Post of the Veterans of Foreign Wars. As the special feature of the occasion, Lieutenant Commander Osborne was to present the Post with the colors, the gift of the Hovey family in memory of their son killed oversea. The closer the hands of the clock drew to nine, the more uneasy grew Chief Yeoman William B. Cox. It was high time the C. O. showed up. Then, as the hour struck, his attention was attracted by a commotion at the entrance of the hall. Huh! Just a bum trying to crash the gate—a terrible-looking creature who was making strenuous objection to being thrown downstairs by the police reinforced by embattled veterans.

The Chief Yeoman felt a chill of apprehension run up his spine. Surely, there was something familiar in that robust figure, those incredibly distorted features. It was—it was the C. O. himself!

Now, Cox's job was to keep his superior out of trouble, and he met the emergency by rescuing the intruder from the police.

"For God's sake," he exclaimed after corralling Osborne in a corner, "don't you know you can be court-martialed for this? You're supposed to be in uniform, and here you are in this outlandish costume. What's the big idea?"

The big idea turned out to be that handing over the colors in the rôle of a bedraggled tramp would be perfect. Cox pleaded and argued, but Osborne was determined to go through with it. Eventually, though, he gave in, and disappeared down the street still acting his part.

In the meantime the audience was waiting restlessly for the presentation. There was only one thing to do, and with his knees knocking together Chief Yeoman Cox made his first public speech.

Sometimes there was a purely picaresque touch to these masquerades. One noon the kitchen detail was busy paring potatoes for dinner. Osborne appeared for a moment, spoke a few cheerful words, and proceeded upstairs to his quarters. Several minutes later the outside door banged open and the inmate cooks beheld a marvelous apparition. It was a swarthy Greek in full costume, his eyes blazing, his right hand brandishing a huge knife.

"Where's Os-sborne?" he hissed. "I keel him"—and he darted for the stairs.

Immediately the pack was on him—whacking, thumping, kicking. Then and there the poor Greek would have suffered a sudden death had not Billy Duffy, who had a knack of being present at crucial moments, suddenly shouted, "Hey, lay off! It's the C.O.!"

Sure enough, out of the mangled disguise appeared the features of the Lieutenant Commander. After his brief salutation, he had hurried up the back stairs, donned the disguise, sneaked down the front way, and staging a theatric reëntrance, again started upstairs—to kill himself. It was a comedy that might have had a tragic ending.

Wherever Osborne went, his familiar, Trouble, followed after. It dogged him to Portsmouth. No great amount of penetration was needed to discover that the Commanding Officer was being made the object of special attention by the Bureau of

Naval Intelligence. Old-line navy men were not going to submit to the revolution at Portsmouth without a struggle. Among the incidents that occurred, however, it is impossible to cull out those that were directly inspired by the Bureau.

Through the assistance of Cox, one of the assigned officers was discovered to be engaging in espionage activities. His cheerful reports to his chief ran along this line—"Insubordination runs riot." In writing to Roosevelt of the incident, Osborne added ruefully:

The man has ability and one of the sore spots here to me will always be the fact that he made some excellent suggestions, which we are now engaged in carrying out. I hate to admit that the snake has been useful.

Criticisms leveled against the radical changes at Portsmouth came to a head in charges that the naval prison was being made a paradise for criminals instead of a place of punishment. So persistent were the authors, that in the summer of 1918 Rear Admiral Spencer S. Wood, Commandant of the First Naval District, was ordered to make an investigation.

By chance Admiral Wood popped into Portsmouth unannounced just as Osborne had finished playing the fire hose on an especially refractory offender—a form of punishment which the victim considered so unpleasant that he immediately appealed to Osborne's superior. Whatever Wood's prejudices may have been, they evaporated at this example of ready justice. It might be unorthodox but it was sound. After thorough examination of the prison and its administration he wrote a report endorsing the practicability of the reforms and commending the work of the commanding officer. From that day on he was a stanch ally against such bitter critics as Admiral Sims and Rear Admiral Thomas Washington.

Osborne had need of every ally he could muster. For the rest of his tenure he was subjected to espionage and attack at every step, and agents of the Naval Intelligence Bureau kept up a continual barrage. Rumors were spread of fraud in the commissary department. Three mysterious strangers tried to buy blankets from government stocks, with the obvious intent of

LIEUTENANT COMMANDER OSBORNE AND HIS
GRANDSON, RICHARD

catching the commanding officer in petty graft. Discharged prisoners made statements to government operatives concerning lax discipline and favoritism. Yet there was nothing Osborne could actually put his finger on. As at Sing Sing his enemies were working in the dark.

Although he could laugh at most of the inept attempts to discredit him, his heart sank when he discovered that the old Sing Sing tales were being revived. In spite of the fact that the Chaplain reported conditions had never been so wholesome since he had been connected with the institution, there was the whisper of open immorality at Portsmouth. Worse than that, slanders on his personal character were carried to such a degree of vileness that Osborne threatened the *Army and Navy Register* with a libel suit.

Ghosts! For the first time he realized he would never be free of them, that they would continue to haunt him until he was laid in his grave.

To make matters worse, Billy Duffy succeeded in getting himself into a serious scrape, and Osborne, oblivious of consequences, jumped headlong after. To the old guard in the navy, Duffy had long been a thorn in the flesh, for Osborne had succeeded in getting him a chief yeoman's rating. What was the navy coming to, anyway, with a lieutenant commander surrounding himself with ex-convicts!

For one thing, Billy took too readily to the tradition that a sailor with only one sweetheart is no true sailor at all. There were two fair lassies who wanted to play mate to his skipper, or maybe vice versa. At any rate, each thought she was the apple of Yeoman Duffy's eye, and he saw no reason for disillusioning either. He did, however, secretly engage himself to one charmer and then, inadvertently, married the other. Even before the threat of a breach-of-promise suit could splash over the bows of the honeymoon ship, Romeo realized he had mixed his Juliets. So did Osborne. Suspecting all was not as it should be, he followed in the wake of his yeoman, found him before the marriage had been consummated, and marched him straight back to Portsmouth.

Duffy came willingly enough, asserting he had been tricked

into the ceremony by the young lady and a couple of friends who had plied him with grape and alcohol. By the time he had succeeded in picking the vine leaves from his hair, he discovered that the license he had obtained for Sweetheart No. 1 was magically inscribed with the name of Sweetheart No. 2 and that according to a Justice of the Peace he had taken the latter for better or worse. With the assurance of a priest that the marriage was fraudulent, Duffy went through another ceremony—this time with the right girl—and might have lived happily ever after had not a judge unexpectedly pronounced the first ceremony legal. That made him guilty of adultery, charges for which were presently preferred.

As Osborne was fully convinced Duffy had been tricked, no amount of warning could keep him from mixing in the imbroglio. Indeed, if his guardian angel Cox had not outmaneuvered him, he would have appeared as a witness at the second marriage. Using his authority as commanding officer he held Duffy within bounds at the prison and sought legal advice. The sequel—there was always a sequel when he fought others' battles—was a $25,000 suit for "alienation of affections" brought by the first Mrs. Duffy. Again Fate seemed conspiring against Osborne, for the legal phrasing of the charge was subject to misinterpretation. Before he was acquitted of persuading a husband to leave a wife, he had spent thousands of dollars and suffered humiliating insults in a litigation that had no other basis than his desire to see justice done.

While agents of the Department of Justice were gleefully picking up the strands of Duffy's matrimonial adventures, another chief yeoman absconded with what was reported to be about $9,000 in cash and jewelry, and a lieutenant made off with some Liberty bonds. Both the money and the bonds were the property of Portsmouth prisoners. Once more the crescendo which marks each of Osborne's crusades was gaining volume, and another climax was impending. Early in 1920 a demand for a new probe resulted in the appointment of a special board, consisting of Assistant Secretary Roosevelt and Rear Admirals A. S. Halstead and H. O. Dunn, to investigate alleged "shocking conditions" at Portsmouth. It is possible that Roosevelt was biased. He was "investigating" his friend and was already a believer in the system under fire. Nothing like that can be said of the other two members, representatives of a navy officialdom that had looked on Osborne as a corrupter of discipline. Yet after an exhaustive study, which revealed how government agents had distorted the facts, they unanimously exonerated the commanding officer of all charges and sanctioned with real enthusiasm the administration of Portsmouth. Osborne, suggested one writer, should be investigated more often—*in order to learn how a prison should be run!*

For a second time admirals had put an official O.K. on Osborne—a victory not lightly to be brushed aside. Although there were still many of the old school who could not mention his name without an oath, a new tolerance was perceptible in the attitude of some officers in the navy. No one could deny that the restoration of four thousand able-bodied men to the service was something to think about, particularly as the great majority of them made good. Not that they became Galahads by any means. Roughnecks they remained, many of them, and good fighting men to boot. "Well, Mr. Osborne," wrote one lad who had gone back to his ship instead of home to his mother with a dishonorable discharge, "I was only drunk one day on my first furlough—pretty good considering the way I used to make furloughs." No heroics about that. Just a simple statement of fact. But there is a story between the lines, not the least part being that his commanding officer considered him eligible for furlough at all.

Possibly, too, Osborne's contention that a crook was capable of feeling true patriotism gained some converts. In the autumn of 1918, the prisoners at Portsmouth, led by Inmate William McColgan, had voluntarily contributed nearly $75,000 spot cash for the purchase of Fourth Liberty Bonds, and followed with an advertising campaign to spur on their more fortunate— and more prosperous—brothers outside. When it came to dying, on the field of battle or in the hold of a stricken ship, an ex-convict's blood ran as red as any man's. Thousands of letters, written from all parts of the world, during the war years and after, bear witness to the strengthening of moral fiber which association with Osborne had brought.

The war was over, the majority of service men had been mustered out, and the time had come for Osborne to take leave of Portsmouth. Secretary Daniels had refused to accept his first tender of resignation, and against his better judgment the commanding officer had consented to remain another six months. Now there was no further profit in holding a post which continued to be a center of controversy and attack. If a regular navy man, sympathetic with the reforms, could be found as a successor, progress might be accelerated. Fortunately, Commodore A. E. Wadhams, U.S.N. retired, was willing to be drafted, and on March 17, 1920, Osborne bade farewell to his boys. The sadness of his departure was tempered by a cheering note from Secretary Daniels:

The policy of helpfulness and hope will be continued, for you have taught the navy and the country that prisons are to mend the prisoners and not to break them. It must be a source of gratification to you that so many young men, who had violated navy regulations or been convicted of wrongdoing, have found themselves through your friendship and leadership, and all over the country in every walk of life are making good.

This ended Osborne's prison work in an official capacity. It was, too, the end of an epoch. During the next decade extremes of reaction and extravagance were to plunge America into a vortex of dizzy discrepancies—a mad hiatus between sanity and sanity. With a submergence of the sense of proportion, values tangible and intangible were all but lost, and prison reform suffered a temporary eclipse.

BOOK III

SPLENDID DEFEAT

Defeat, my Defeat, my deathless courage,
You and I shall laugh together with the storm,
And together we shall dig graves for all that die in us,
And we shall stand in the sun with a will,
And we shall be dangerous.
                                        —KAHLIL GIBRAN.

CHAPTER I

THE DARK YEARS

It was the night before Christmas Eve. In the big house at 99 South Street the chandeliers were ablaze, and a smell of spruce hung in the air. Occasionally the front door was opened, admitting a blast of frosty wind and people in twos and threes who bowed ceremoniously and, having disposed of their wraps, passed on to the spacious library. In spite of the affability of the host and a general festive spirit, a degree of formality marked the deportment of the guests. For this was in the way of being a solemn occasion. To-morrow the rooms would ring with the laughter of children as Punch and Judy took up their raucous feud, but this evening was given over to a gathering that had become a Yuletide rite.

Standing on the white bear rug in front of the fireplace in the library, his back to the logs that crackled and sent showers of sparks up the chimney, Thomas Mott Osborne began his annual reading of Dickens' "Christmas Carol." It was his favorite, and he read it with a feeling that left his hearers inarticulate. As they listened to the story of *Scrooge* and the Ghosts, they were aware of a certain constricting of the throat, yet would not for the world have confessed it. In common embarrassment and common emotion they sat transfixed, waiting half fearfully for the moment they knew would come, when the reader's own feelings would choke his voice and hold him silent till he could command himself again and read doggedly on. There would be several such pauses, painful but strangely gripping. And at last, when *Scrooge* went to dinner with his nephew and raised *Bob Cratchit's* salary and *Tiny Tim* did not die, they breathed a sigh of mingled relief and exaltation. Something a little too deep to be wholly pleasing was stirred by those last words, uttered in a husky whisper: "God bless us, every one."

Osborne believed that everyone should read "A Christmas Carol" at least once a year. He did his part, and at these functions, neighborly rather than social, friends felt they had recovered the Tom Osborne of the early days. Again he was the charming host, with a wealth of anecdote and a joy in the human relationships of his own circle. Living with his son Lithgow's family, he picked up the strands of his life that he had dropped a decade before. There were evenings around the piano in the music room, and friends who dropped in heard once more the titillating strains of Gilbert and Sullivan's operas.

Almost as if there had been no hiatus, his fellow townsmen reclaimed him. With Peter Kurtz he played duets at recitals. He gave lectures on music and the arts, and sometimes accepted invitations to conduct a symphony orchestra or an operetta at Syracuse. On these latter occasions he was resplendent in his naval dress uniform with its military cape. As might be expected, Osborne's interest in the Auburn Amateur Dramatic Club revived, and as its president he exercised a paternal autocracy over its activities. Of a more strenuous nature was his association with the Mynderse Rice Post of the American Legion. He adopted the local veterans, became commander of the Post, and gave freely of his time and funds. When money was needed, he would stage a benefit show, training the actors, arranging the music, and even devising the dance routines for the chorus.

Such display of vigor at his age brought warnings that he must spare himself, but he brushed them aside. Years before, the doctors had told him to slow down—heart or something. Instead, he had plunged into the most hectic decade of his career with never a thought of his health. And apparently he had thrived under the regimen—or rather the lack of one. Though the hair on his temples was graying, his figure was still erect, and his face had a youthfulness about it that not even lines drawn by anxiety could disguise. Seeing him in a moment of vivacity, the center of interest in any group as he had always been, no one could possibly think of him as approaching seventy. Strange, how kind Fate is to those who defy her most.

To the majority of the men and women who saw him almost daily, he seemed the Osborne they had known of old. He had the same inexhaustible energy, the same personal charm—and, inevitably, the same susceptibility to flattery and intolerance of disagreement. He still moved in that curious atmosphere of his own which attracted yet forbade intimacy. Perhaps this is the reason why so few perceived that it was a different man who had come back to them. Before, his participation in social and civic affairs had been spontaneous. Now there was something forced in it. It was an escape. He sought a refuge from memories of the past and a momentary release from the disheartening realities of the present.

To be defeated is one thing; to see all the things for which one has fought crushed or discredited is quite another. Partly because he had led the attack on so many fronts, Osborne tasted more bitter defeats than any other man of his time. Hardly anything was saved from the wreck.

There were his political aspirations, founded on the belief that citizens want decency in government. Tammany still exercised complete domination in New York City and had made inroads upstate. Down in Washington a series of scandals of gigantic proportions had left people breathless and apparently indifferent. Harding, affable, easy-going, not too fastidious, betrayed by those he trusted most—the Teapot Dome affair, spreading its tentacles into the cabinet. And people took it lying down!

Osborne had never made money in public service. Usually he left an office poorer in purse than he entered it. To see evidences of greed in both parties, with men of high repute brazenly engaging in raids on the public treasury, cut him to the quick. Yet he was never asked to take a position of prominence. Wilson, for whom he had labored so faithfully, passed him by in the diplomatic assignments; and the Republicans of the Harding era had no use for one of his type. In place of knee breeches in the Court of St. James's there was left for him the livery of a political underling—state committeeman, a post that brought him, however, into the counsels of Al Smith, Senator Wagner, and other Democratic leaders of New York. A taste of campaigning he did get—notably in 1923 when he took the stump in behalf of Lithgow, who tried unsuccessfully to break the uninterrupted succession of Republican assemblymen from Cayuga County.

There was some consolation in the thought that he had been in part responsible for Smith's rise. It was Rattigan, his political lieutenant, who had organized the opposition against Murphy's hand-picked candidate for governor and had accomplished the nomination of the young man from the East Side. Smith was a Tammany man, to be sure; but he was no pawn. And he was honest. For Osborne that was enough.

It was a topsy-turvy world to which Osborne returned. Engrossed in his conflicts, he had not been fully aware of the social changes which were taking place. As he saw the delirium and incoherence about him, he felt like a stranger in a world he no longer understood—*"Ich verstehe die Welt nicht mehr!"* Everywhere standards seemed to have been demolished and nothing offered in their place. It was not the disappearance of the old taboos which concerned him; that was part of his own doctrine of personal liberty. But he could find little evidence of a compensating moral growth. Little men doing little things in a big way. Women under the impression that abbreviated fashions in hair and skirts constituted a valid emancipation. Youngsters emerging from adolescence into a forced, tropical maturity.

Osborne's own intemperateness had direction and did not extend to the gestures of the new freedom. They puzzled him. I saw him once as host at a party in his home gazing with disapproval and mild astonishment at a cocktail glass in his hand. Then, as his glance traveled round the room taking in knots of people clutching the same symbol of personal liberty, he shook his head sadly. "Prohibition," he murmured, more to himself than to any one else, "is making criminals of us all." I wondered then what pictures were in his mind, what faces stared at him from the dusk of subterranean cells, and whether or not the pallid features metamorphosed ironically into the countenances of his friends. I rather think he saw himself at that moment not in the rôle of Tom Brown, but as a bona fide convict—in fact, all of us wearing the gray uniform and looking indistinguishable from a thousand other comrades in duress.

When he thought of the reaction which had set in against prison reform, Osborne was tortured by a feeling of impotence. He had done all he could, had had victory almost within his grasp, only to see enthusiasm die or turn to other things in this mad decade. Over the whole nation the doctrine of force again dictated prison policies, while on the legal side the Baumes laws and their counterparts in other states showed the trend of popular thinking.

Osborne had been succeeded as Warden of Sing Sing by a school teacher, who after two months gave way to William H. Moyer. Moyer had previously been head of the federal penitentiary at Atlanta, but had resigned following charges of extreme severity. This was the man Governor Whitman chose to carry on Osborne's work. Soon after Moyer took office, many League privileges were withdrawn, and a number of prominent League members were transferred to Auburn and Comstock. Prison reformers saw in these measures and in renewed charges of favoritism and political intrigue a definite reversion to the old system.

In Portsmouth things were little better. Commodore Wadhams' régime, based on the Osborne system, came to an abrupt end with that officer's removal following Harding's election; and the navy went back to its traditional prison system. There was another flare-back in connection with Osborne's Portsmouth period. Franklin D. Roosevelt, running for vice president on the ticket with Cox, was made the victim of severe attack during the campaign on the ground that he had jobbed the investigation of the naval prison. In an open letter to Roosevelt the Providence *Journal* accused him of having "whitewashed" Osborne, made willful misstatements, and covered up all manner of iniquity permitted to flourish by the commanding officer. There they were again—the old infamous stories—and broadcast over the nation.

Osborne needed no one to tell him how well the conspirators

of Sing Sing had done their work. The ultimate victory had been theirs, for the suspicions engendered by the trial had cut popular support from under him. He was left with a pitifully small band of earnest students of penology and a much larger group of emotional sympathizers. The latter became more and more a bane to him, for they were in large part responsible for his being catalogued as a sentimentalist. Nothing he could do or say stopped their activities. In the middle of the celebration of his return to Sing Sing he had paused in his address to say sternly: "I, for one, do not want to hear any mush about 'the dear prisoners.' I want prisoners only to get a square deal and be treated as men." Even then he feared that misguided friends would use that extraordinary spectacle as copy for lachrymose lectures, poems, and newspaper contributions.

Sometimes he wrote letters to these people, begging them not to jeopardize the cause of reform by connecting it with the gush school. But it was of little avail. Even the dean of American poetry added his bit to the sentimental literature. During his Junior Republic days Osborne had asked Edwin Markham to write a poem on the Freeville citizens, something in the manner of "The Man with the Hoe." Although I have found no record of the fulfillment of this request, Mr. Markham later came forward with some verses on Thomas Mott Osborne's prison reform work—verses, shall we say, somewhat inferior to "The Man with the Hoe" and damned by the trick title, "Our Believing Thomas."

At the other end of the scale were those who retailed with gusto the failures of convict protégés. In Auburn, as might be expected, it was generally believed Osborne was an easy mark for ex-cons. His home became a refuge for released prisoners. Some stayed a night or two before taking wing; others remained as more or less permanent fixtures. Sometimes those who left suddenly carried with them souvenirs of their visit. Those who stayed were supposed to perform certain duties, never very arduous. One helper, instructed by the mistress to take care of the shoe-shining, was wont to wander aimlessly about the house carrying a shoe with him as a sign he was on the job. At the head of this curious ménage was Mrs. Lithgow

Osborne, who found herself transplanted from her father's Danish castle, where she had acted as hostess to Edward of England and other reigning princes, to the job of hostess to mysterious figures of the American underworld. Victor Nelson, whose love for writing recently found satisfaction in an autobiographical book, appeared now and again, played the piano, and vanished. Dick Richards, first secretary of the Mutual Welfare League, still retained a position of confidence in the family—at least with Osborne senior. Yet of all those who shared in the bounty of his benefactor, he perhaps deserved least; for Dick Richards, an alias for Cornelius J. Donovan, did more to bring the League into discredit than any one else.

Leigh Bonsal, Osborne's college roommate, had come up from Baltimore to attend the vindication meeting held at Carnegie Hall following Osborne's acquittal of the Sing Sing charges. He and John Jay Chapman sat together in a box. The next day Bonsal had luncheon with Osborne at the Belmont Hotel and unwittingly came under the keen eyes of Dick Richards, hovering in the background. It was not many days later that a telegram came to Bonsal at his office in Baltimore. It was from Springfield, Massachusetts, and set forth that the undersigned, Thomas Mott Osborne, would appreciate any help given to his private secretary who was in Washington on business. After a decent interval a courteous, well-dressed man of obvious intelligence called and inquired about the wire from Osborne. There was some patent business pending, and spot cash was needed to close the transaction. Whereupon he produced a check for $2,000 bearing Osborne's signature. Knowing nothing about his visitor's prison background, Bonsal accepted the man in good faith, took him to the National Bank of Baltimore and endorsed the check. The bank officials cashed it without batting an eyelash; but Dick Richards, with twenty hundred-dollar bills in his pocket, took the Blue Bus to Washington and vanished.

When the ruse was discovered, a group of ex-members of the Mutual Welfare League, knowing Richards' weakness for the ponies, started on his trail and caught up with him at a racetrack near New York. The curious part of the tale is that in his pocket were found $1,700 in cash and $300 worth of receipted M.W.L. bills. Although Richards had spent the money given him to pay those bills, a sense of honor, not quite defunct however perverted, had prompted him to cheat Osborne's best friend that he might make payment in the name of the League. Just how he fitted the $1,700 balance into this ethical program is not clear.

Down in Baltimore Bonsal had a telephone message from Osborne that Richards was coming back to surrender himself voluntarily and would arrive at four-thirty. Skeptical about such matters, the Baltimore police arranged a little reception party at the station and prepared to pounce on the prodigal. But when the four-thirty pulled in, there was no Richards.

Bonsal had not enjoyed the notoriety the case had brought him. Now it was worse. Sitting in his office with the first editions of the evening papers, he saw screaming headlines, "Bonsal Again Duped." Suddenly the door opened and in walked Dick Richards, debonair as ever. He had jumped the train at the outskirts and outwitted the coppers he rightly suspected would be waiting for him. With his customary loyalty, Osborne induced the judge to parole the culprit in his care; but Richards could not keep out of trouble. A short time later he was serving a two-year stretch for stealing, and this time Osborne left him to his fate—that is, until the expiration of his sentence. Need it be recorded that when Richards came out, he was presented with a new suit of clothes and given a new start? Or that when tuberculosis set in, he was sent at another's expense to take the cure in Arizona?

Richards was too clever for his own good. In 1929 he turned in the neatest confidence trick of the year by filching a valuable ring from under the very noses of the staff of Governor Roosevelt's New York City home. Run to earth, he went to Sing Sing to wait for his last release. The white plague had him in its grip.

In the meantime a new type of operator had emerged. Borrowing the organization methods of big business, the racketeer grew rich by furnishing danger and protection in one package —the ultimate in compression and efficiency. It was not always easy to determine where legitimate operations left off and the illegitimate began; but there were those who said that Billy Duffy was a smart actor. Maybe it was only envy, for Duffy was distinctly in the money. At his Silver Slipper night club lovely coryphées of Broadway gave the eye a treat; at Duffy's Tavern robust servitors ministered to the needs of the palate, particularly a dry palate. If you dropped into this latter establishment and had staying qualities, you might, some time during the evening, catch a glimpse of another of the proprietor's acquisitions—a great, good-natured mountain of flesh and bone, Primo Carnera, the Italian Alp. Primo was not then heavyweight champion—indeed was considered only a creature of the ballyhoo artists—but he was already a gold mine for Mr. Duffy.

New York is a cynical, not a suspicious town. Whether or not Billy Duffy's activities extended beyond furnishing various forms of entertainment to a generation that not only asked for it but was willing to pay for it, and pay well, may be dismissed with a wave of the hand, as most Gothamites dismissed it. All except one group of civic-minded gentlemen. They proceeded to nominate Mr. Duffy as a Public Enemy, and in that rôle his picture appeared in the public prints. People began to talk. Billy Duffy, the first sergeant-at-arms of the Mutual Welfare League. Billy Duffy, Osborne's familiar at Sing Sing and Portsmouth, and fellow gob on the U. S. S. *North Dakota*. Billy Duffy, Public Enemy!

But there were a lot of things that the wiseacres didn't know. From whom did a released convict, facing a world that wanted none of him, seek help? Who gave him his first few meals and a flop, remembering the time when he too was trying to get a grip on himself and might have failed but for one man's encouragement? Here was one of Billy Duffy's activities that never got into the newspapers. Maybe it was just as well; people would have misunderstood. Some of the men who were tided over those first unsettled days after release went looking for jobs with renewed hope. Others drifted—God knows where. Nevertheless, the word was passed along: "If you need a hitch up, see Billy Duffy and his West-side mob."

Then there was Owney Madden, another racketeer enjoying the spotlight of notoriety. Owney, a graduate of Hell's Kitchen, was resting at Sing Sing when Osborne met him. Twelve good men and true had decided he knew too much about the sudden passing of Little Patsy Doyle, a professional rival, and had him sent up the river. Mr. Madden would say "railroaded," for he avers that of the many charges brought against him during his spectacular career, he knows less about this—indeed, practically nothing—than any of the others. When Owney emerged from the portals of Sing Sing, he found to his surprise that the millennium had arrived—prohibition. Prohibition made him rich, brought him a penthouse, lifted him to the aristocracy of racketeerdom where he need fear only a small group of accountants checking up on income taxes for Uncle Sam. And the tongues continued to wag. Owney Madden, another protégé of Osborne's. Owney Madden, beer baron, night-club operator, fight promoter—and what else?

Osborne knew what people were saying. Some were reviling him as a dilettante whose theories about prison reform were breeding more crime. Others were lampooning him as a fairy godmother to roughnecks who played him for a sucker and then stabbed him in the back. He could not stop the tongues. He could not explain that failures were bound to be remembered and successes forgotten. He thought of those early days in Auburn Prison—of Canada Blackie, dead now; of Jack Murphy, holding a position of trust in a great bank; of young men in the navy and older men, ranging from taxi drivers to business executives, who owed their rise to the Mutual Welfare League. If only some of his thoughtless critics could have been present on the evening of October 5, 1915, in the Park Avenue Hotel, New York! Then he had been guest of honor at a dinner tendered him by twenty-five ex-convicts, men who had wiped out the past and had rehabilitated themselves as orderly, useful citizens. Yet these were but a few among many hundreds.

Sometimes witness of his impress on the underworld came in curious ways. An Auburn merchant, unpacking a shipment of clothing from a Chicago factory, saw a piece of paper sticking out of the pocket of a vest. Upon investigation, he discovered a note bearing a message in rude scrawl:

FINDER

Regards to Tom Mott Osborne

P. S. The only white man God put into this world.

Charles Osborne, invited one evening to a neighbor's house, left his new car parked at the curb. When he came out, it had vanished into thin air. Automobile thieves. News of the theft came to an ex-convict who had set up in business in Auburn. Then he too disappeared. Next morning he was back again. "It'll be all right," was his laconic report. "Gosh, *they* didn't know it belonged to T. M.'s son!" A little later Charles received a telephone call from the Syracuse police chief. "Found your car," came the word. "Somebody parked it in front of Officer ———'s house while he was eating lunch."

Osborne did not have to rely solely upon his own observations or upon advocates who might be accused of bias in judging his work. Prisoners sometimes wrote glowing letters that strained the truth for the sake of a good story. Preachers and professional reformers were apt to be preoccupied with the purely humanitarian side. But there were others who were qualified to speak impartially of the system of self-government in prisons—the judges. They were the ones who heard the cases, sentenced the offenders, and only too often had to repeat the process not once or twice but many times with the same prisoner in the dock.

The judges, in the main, were with Osborne—though his recommendation that before taking office every judge should spend one month in prison, every district attorney six months, must have been faintly alarming. They believed in his work for practical reasons. When Osborne was indicted in Westchester following the Sing Sing investigation, Judge William H. Wadhams of the Court of General Sessions came to his defense with testimony that should have had a place in the grand jury minutes. In a public address Judge Wadhams said: "The

proof of the pudding is in the eating. Since Mr. Osborne undertook his noble work I have not had one man released from his
supervision brought into my court." An entire year without a
repeater, and in a court through which passed the majority of
felons bound for Sing Sing!

The memory of these things was both bitter and sweet;
bitter, because the public already was beginning to forget. A
rankling sense of injustice drove Osborne to attempt a vindication not merely of himself but of his program. Day after day
he worked upon a monumental volume that he hoped would
substantiate his principles. He wrote with asperity, damning
his enemies as enemies of the truth, laying about him with the
ruthlessness of a man who sees defeat staring him in the face
yet will not ask quarter.

It was not as a substitute for action, however, that he poured
out his disappointment in a book, or sought temporary escape
in social and civic diversions. Osborne never gave up the real
struggle, the fight against graft and special favor and vicious
cabals. Sometimes he scored a triumph.

Through his influence Charles F. Rattigan had been appointed Superintendent of Prisons, and for a time it looked as
if in New York State at least the Osborne principles would
prevail. Just before Moyer had resigned as warden at Sing
Sing it was discovered that crooks had filched over $8,000 in
checks for prison coal bills, and Judge Edward V. Brophy, who
succeeded Moyer, admitted after eight months that the job was
too much for him. At this point Superintendent Rattigan appointed to the Sing Sing wardenship a young man named
Lewis E. Lawes. Thirty-seven years old, Lawes was the youngest of all the thirty-nine wardens who had held the position
during the century of Sing Sing's existence; and he has out-
lasted them all. On taking office he announced that he would
continue the Mutual Welfare League established by Osborne,
giving it as much responsibility as in his judgment it deserved.
Disciplinary work, however, would be conducted solely by the
administration.

Perhaps Osborne was learning to accept half a loaf as better
than no loaf at all. Not that he was content with what was

happening at Sing Sing and Auburn. The suppression of the prisoners' court meant a radical change in his system. Sometimes, overcome with chagrin, he would say he would rather see no League at all than such a flimsy imitation. Indeed, he anticipated the terrible riots that were to break out in 1929. In a scathing letter to Warden Jennings of Auburn he predicted that continuation of an administrative policy which was a compromise between warden authority and inmate responsibility would lead to serious trouble. It did, and, as he feared, the Mutual Welfare League was held responsible.

He himself, even during the darkest years, never relaxed his efforts. Upon leaving Portsmouth he had postponed his return home in order to make a tour of inspection of the penal institutions of the country. Within a few months his story of prison life, written while at Portsmouth, was offered to the public as a motion picture by Edward A. McManus, producer of "The Lost Battalion"; and Osborne, accompanied by several ex-convicts, went from city to city to lecture at showings. At one time he had planned to write a novel based on his favorite theme, but had given up the project in favor of the screen. While at Sing Sing he had produced, for publicity purposes, a few sequences presenting the Tom Brown story. The new picture, however, was a more ambitious effort. Entitled "The Right Way" and presenting a cast of more than a thousand, it had a run that, as might be expected, netted its sponsor thousands of dollars' loss! What propaganda there was in "The Right Way" was aimed at arousing public indignation at prevailing prison methods, but it had one unanticipated result.

The picture was showing at Cincinnati. At the conclusion of Osborne's lecture a young man asked for an interview with the speaker. Immediately Osborne recognized him as Victor Nelson, a former inmate of Portsmouth whose tendency to be absent without leave had brought him two terms in the naval prison. A subsequent offense after the war landed him in Charlestown State Prison, Massachusetts, and the youth was well started on a life of crime. What made his appearance at the theater in Cincinnati so startling was the fact that three months before, he had staged a dramatic escape from Charlestown Prison. In broad daylight and in a shower of bullets from the guards he had broken ranks, leaped over a high grating, jumped from a roof to the ground twenty feet below, and disappeared. The police drag-net failed to pick him up, and his whereabouts was unknown.

If Osborne felt embarrassed by the situation, he was soon relieved. Nelson had come for advice. Perhaps he suspected the police were closing in on him. Or maybe it had suddenly occurred to him that his escape meant disgrace for the League. At any rate he wanted to do something about it. What should it be?

"Give yourself up," said Osborne.

The boy swallowed hard. "I'm on," he said. Osborne took him to Auburn by train, drove him by automobile to Boston, and saw him safely lodged in prison once more.

Between 1920 and 1924, the scope of Osborne's work steadily increased. He was in demand as a special investigator from Maine to California. Everywhere he went he stirred up a hornets' nest, for his recommendations were invariably opposed to the sentiments prevailing in the communities where the prisons were located. In a moment of enthusiasm the Prison Commission of Maine offered him the wardenship of the State Prison. No sooner had he publicly accepted than the worthy body repented its action, appointed another man without warning, and left Osborne fuming in helpless wrath and humiliation. When Governor Pinchot authorized him to investigate the prisons of Pennsylvania, Osborne ran foul of Warden Robert J. McKenty of Eastern Penitentiary, Philadelphia. Charged with doling out fat jobs to members of his own family and relatives by blood and marriage, McKenty was finally ousted, and Osborne received assurance that he would be appointed to fill the vacancy. Instead, he was shoved aside at the last moment, and the new appointee found means to keep Governor Pinchot's investigator out of Eastern Penitentiary. Discovery that someone was trying secretly to rake up the old Sing Sing and Portsmouth scandals, and lack of support from the Governor, finally led Osborne to an open break with Pinchot. He withdrew from the investigation, hurt and disheartened.

During these trying times he had found encouragement in the support of Mrs. Harrison S. Morris, Quaker leader of prison reform in Pennsylvania. Always a welcome guest at the Morris home in Old York Road, North Philadelphia, he was accustomed to dropping in unexpectedly and enjoying a few hours of music and laughter with the young people who flocked about the talented daughter, Catharine. These visits cheered and refreshed him. When all his efforts seemed come to naught, it was to Mrs. Morris that he confessed his utter discouragement. In June of 1923 he wrote her:

I don't know how much longer I can keep this thing up. I really feel that it is all such a waste of time, and that we had better shut up shop, and each of us go about his business. What is the use? We can't break into a prison anywhere. All the good work we have started has been either killed or crippled.

Yet this was but a passing mood. In spite of opposition, he was responsible for exposing and remedying conditions in some of the largest prisons in the country. Governor Ritchie authorized him to conduct a survey in Maryland. Missouri employed him. At the personal request of Governor Sweet of Colorado he investigated the state prison at Canon City and turned in a report that charged Warden Tynan with brutal floggings of prisoners and other cruelties. Although Tynan succeeded in surviving the attack, he was later removed on similar charges.

By now Osborne's reputation had become international. German penologists were writing interpretations of his principles. A lecture trip through England aroused the supposedly phlegmatic British to such a pitch of enthusiasm that for weeks the press followed his tour with laudatory articles and editorials. In her first public interview after the restoration of the royal family in Greece, Queen Sophie expressed her wish that Thomas Mott Osborne could be persuaded to visit her country and superintend the revision of the penal system. This was followed by a personal invitation which Osborne accepted.

Triumphs? Yes, he had many; but he could see that in the main they were personal triumphs. And he had a premonition that as the months and years passed they would become more and more infrequent. Once he had been able to disturb public inertia and set the wheels of civilization revolving slowly along the road of reform. Then they had stopped; now they were turning in the opposite direction. Undeniably. The truth flashed at him from every newspaper, every magazine. Sometimes the utter falsity of the assumptions lashed him into a fury.

"An End to the Crime Waves!" shouted one streamer. "Courts, Legislatures, and Prison Officials Aroused to Stop the Coddling of Convicts and to Put Back into the Criminal Laws the Penalties the Reformers Have Softened." The article began:

One-thousand-dollar cash reward for every policeman who shoots a bandit.

The old-fashioned whipping post to be reëstablished for offenders.

Prisoners to be put back again into the old striped uniforms, which meant disgrace and humiliation.

A real day's work, at hard labor, in the prisons. . . .

To put an end to the parole boards and to limit the pardoning power of the governors of the states.

To put back "the teeth" into the criminal laws, which are, for the most part, now in the interest of criminals instead of the public.

These are some of the proposals of the police and judges of the criminal courts to stop the coddling and petting of professional criminals. . . . For more than ten years the prison reformers, crime sentimentalists, and friends of professional criminals have been busy interfering with prison discipline, and have succeeded in having a series of laws passed which have very largely removed the fear of punishment from evil-doers. . . . But at last the pendulum has begun to swing back. . . .

So plausible. And yet so unsound. It was Osborne who had given warning of a crime wave, even before the armies of the world had been mustered out. It was Osborne who had urged more efficient police methods, with rapidity and certainty of apprehension as deterrents, instead of the nature of the penalty or brutal treatment in prison. Though he could make no one believe it, he had campaigned privately and publicly against the sentimentalism that was undermining his own work. Yet every article was aimed at him as the most conspicuous of the prison reformers. And what had he done? Propounded the thesis that there is no such thing as a "criminal type." Argued that, since most prisoners are to return to society, the chief objective of prisons should be to prepare them for that return. Reiterated that only by treating convicts as men instead of as beasts can an attitude of coöperation on the part of the prisoners be cultivated. Demonstrated in actual practice that granting inmates responsibility after they have shown their capacity to appreciate it is the best insurance for maintaining a sense of responsibility after their release. And summed it all up in the general principle: No man can reform another man; what we can do is give him a chance to reform himself.

The public had lost sight of these fundamentals. Everything was confused, and no distinction was made between rational treatment of prisoners and coddling. That word again! He wished it had never been invented. Anything that did not jibe with prevailing notions about whipping posts, zebra clothing, hard labor, rotten food was called coddling. It was almost more than he could stand. He was tired. Never before had he been so tired. Sometimes he felt an unfamiliar weakness creeping through his limbs. But he could not stop now. He was like a clock that had been wound up and had to wait until the mainspring hung loose and pithless in its case. So with his old-time petulance he flung off the momentary weakness and joined battle for what he now feared was a lost cause.

CHAPTER II

EXIT HARUN-AL-RASHID

IT WAS early evening, and the October dusk made black squares of the window panes. Fully dressed, Osborne reclined on his bed in the downstairs bedroom, keenly aware of the silence which ruled over the house. Except for the servants, busy with their own affairs in remote parts of the building, and the grandchildren already asleep, he was the sole occupant. Only a dim light burned in the hall, but in his room the chandelier shed a steady radiance, lighting up the great bed and the heavy furniture and the family pictures on the walls. Familiar objects. Familiar room. This house was the one link that bound together his two lives.

Memories of his boyhood and young manhood thronged in upon him—of his father and mother, and of the bride he had brought home just thirty years before. Here he had first learned what contentment means. Here three of his four sons had been born. It was more than a house; it was a sanctuary filled with ikons he once had worshiped—still worshiped, only he had lost them for a while. Now he had them again. This evening, just after supper, he had played the old scores of Gilbert and Sullivan to his two young grandsons, whose mother was now deathly ill in the hospital with a son two days old; so ill that even he had not been allowed to see her. Perhaps to-morrow. But it worried him. It revived his own hurt. If *she* had lived, what would his life have been? At least not all this tumult, this ceaseless, scatheful bludgeoning! There would have been gracious moments of peace, a chance to catch one's breath before returning to the fight.

Perhaps he had been at fault a little. Perhaps he should have held fast to the strands of that old life. It was easy to say, but he knew it had to be one thing or the other. Indeed, he had tried for a time to cling to two worlds. When affairs took him to Boston, he used to stop at the Tavern Club. The atmosphere appealed to him, and he met old friends, Barrett Wendell, Arlo Bates, Charles Hopkinson; writers, artists, musicians—inhabitants of that brilliant world in which he, once, had been so at home.

There in the quaint old building in Boylston Place, whose Gothic spirit had survived the process of remodeling, he had sought to recapture the leisurely tempo of the old days. It had been a pitiful effort. His failure was written in the faces of his friends. Partly they were sorry for him. Partly they were embarrassed at witnessing an absorption in which they could not share. It was Osborne; and it was not Osborne. There was a spell on him, and he could not enter their charmed circle. After a number of visits he left off going there altogether.

No, it had been impossible. There was no golden mean for him. He had to stick to one path, and the effort had taken its toll. This faintness that was upon him: it was foolish, it was exasperating. Yesterday he had gone to Syracuse for a conference with Al Smith and Senator Wagner about the coming campaign. Before it was finished he was as weak as a kitten and had to hasten back to Auburn. He knew what that meant—had known for a long time but would admit it to no one, rarely even to himself. Why, in most ways he was still hale and hearty—stronger by far than most men of his age. And there was work to be done, lots of it! Smith would win again with the right management. And now Osborne had his boys to help him. Both Charles and Lithgow were active in Democratic politics. Some day they would carry on.

Lithgow was like his father in more ways than one. He too had the dramatic instinct and loved amateur theatricals. Was he not playing the lead to-night in the Kiwanis show? Secretly Osborne wanted to see the performance, but had refused to say definitely whether or not he would attend. In the back of his mind a scheme was forming, and the thought of it made him smile. Why not? It was not too late, and he was feeling stronger every minute. Yes, Harun-al-Rashid would come to life again and go to the play. There would be two Osbornes playing a rôle to-night; one on the stage, the other in the audience. Only the one in the audience would go unrecognized. That too had its points. As the Unknown Spectator he might hear what people really thought of that other one up there behind the footlights. Here was a droll adventure!

Osborne rose, went to the door, and listened. Not a sound. He turned back and entered the little room off the bedroom where hung his disguises. More than once recently he had visited this place. It was the rabbit's hole that led to Wonderland. Here, indeed, was his true escape. One went in with a burden of cares and issued buoyantly into a world that seemed fresh and new and full of romance. But nobody understood— the few that knew about it at all. To his family it seemed a graceless sort of diversion, even dangerous. He chuckled as he thought of what an outspoken lady, privy to the secret, had said to him a week or so ago: "Tom, you ought to stop this running around in disguises. You can't tell, you might die in one of the damn things!"

Looking over the grotesque wardrobe, Osborne made a careful selection. He took down a suit several sizes too large for him. Donning it, he stuffed it out with strips of padding. Then he began on the make-up. False whiskers. An extra set of teeth. Little spirals of wire that spread each nostril. A delicate film of some transparent substance that fitted over one eyeball, giving it a glassy look.

He was done now. He glanced into the mirror and murmured approval. Nobody could possibly recognize him; not even Lithgow. And the part he played was not mentioned in any program. Picking out a hat, he slipped quietly out of the little door giving to the side lawn, stepped noiselessly over the turf to the street, and set out jauntily in the direction of the theater. . . .

Some reporters never seem to sleep. Even when the day's work is over, they can't keep away from the scene of their labors. Something may crop up, they tell themselves; but really it is more than that. The editorial room becomes a habit. It is home and club in one.

The veteran reporter of the Auburn *Citizen* sat before his typewriter knocking off driblets of news items for the Syracuse morning papers. Nothing much to-night. Just the same old stories about meetings of fraternal orders and somebody's golden wedding anniversary. Not even any political dope worth more than a stick. Oh, well, might as well hang around a little longer anyhow. There was that Kiwanis shindig. It ought to be over by now.

The telephone bell jangled unexpectedly at his elbow. "Hello! What? On William Street? Thanks."

He shuffled into his coat and lounged down the stairs. It might make a story. Only there was nothing new about a man's dropping dead on the street. It happened nearly every day.

He had only a few blocks to go. As he turned the corner on William Street, he saw a small knot of people, among them a policeman, standing about a prostrate form.

"Know him?" asked the officer as the reporter came up. The latter looked at the inert body, noting the strange features, the curious dress; then he shook his head.

"Better take a look at his wallet," said the officer. "Maybe it'll have his name in it."

But the reporter was staring at the face of the dead man. Some elusive memory was stirring. He knelt down close, peering at the rigid features. Suddenly he rose.

"Why don't you take him across the street to the undertaker's?" he suggested hurriedly. And at a nod of acquiescence he helped the policeman carry the heavy burden up the steps and into the building. Outside, the group of curious spectators dispersed, only faintly disturbed by the phenomenon of sudden death. . . .

In the editorial room, the reporter sat once more in front of his typewriter, staring at the blank sheet of paper before him. A story? Here was one. All he needed to do was send a flash to New York and the order would come for—how many words? A thousand? Two thousand? And they would pay anything to get it. Phrases were running through his mind, little phrases that would be picked out by the copy reader and spread in a streamer across the front page. Phrases that next morning would be read by millions smacking their lips over another novel sensation.

The typewriter began to click, but it clicked out a different story altogether.

A gay party was in progress at the Osborne Hotel. Lithgow Osborne was host to the large cast of the Kiwanis show, and there was music and laughter and dancing. The play had been a great success; it deserved a celebration. Suddenly there came a word that suspended the activity with the abruptness of a broken motion-picture film. It passed from mouth to mouth. The dancers stopped. The music ceased. A quiet fell on the room, save for the repetition of the whispered words:

"Thomas Mott Osborne is dead! Thomas Mott Osborne is dead!"

PROLOGUE

PROLOGUE

I

ONE of the most difficult things in the world is to tell the difference between a beginning and an end. There is little in our experience to inform us whether defeat is the end of one chapter or the beginning of another; and even less in our perspective to indicate whether death opens or shuts a door.

Contemporaries of Osborne saw a finality in the collapse of his crusades; his death put the seal upon it. The work of half a lifetime seemed nullified, and the departure of the one man whose defiance of evil and scorn of danger had caught up thousands in the whirlwind of his enthusiasm left a void and a silence that presaged the end of hope. The trouble was that we lacked faith in the incredible; in the persistence of unseen forces after the original impetus has been removed.

Even before death put a period to Osborne's striving, there were evidences that these forces were alive and at work. From the battle over the succession of Chauncey Depew's seat in the Senate had come popular election of United States Senators. Civil Service, the direct primary, woman's suffrage—these once controversial matters had long since become part of our national life, accepted as orthodox and conservative. Orthodoxy, however, never caught up with Osborne's heresy—not during his lifetime. Yet had he lived a few years longer he might have seen more convincing proof that his defeats were but the beginning of victories.

The first cause which had really stirred him profoundly was that of Philippine independence. He had battled the imperialism whose philosophy of benevolent paternalism had to be justified by bayonet and gun. He had denounced the torturing of Filipino prisoners and the treachery by which Aguinaldo was captured, and he had heard himself denounced as one who stabbed our own soldiers in the back. Although he realized that after conquest had been effected American administration of the Islands was bringing to the inhabitants educational and sanitary betterment, the call of liberty was too strong in him to accept without protest a limitless supervision. He died without knowing that in a little over six years the Philippines would be voted independence.

Nor was it granted him to know that a legislative experiment, noble in intent but disastrous in its effects on national character, would be wiped out by a plebiscite of the people. Or that Tammany, overconfident in the long-suffering tolerance of its millions of victims, would be engulfed in a maelstrom so whelming that it would end the public career of a popular idol and establish a Fusion candidate in control of New York City.

Foreknowledge of these events would have brightened his last years; it would not, however, have compensated for the decline and the apparent suppression of that which was closest to his heart—prison reform. One more flash of clairvoyance would have been necessary for that, and an understanding that progress thrives on the defeats of its champions and is greedy of sacrifice. To-day, though it is a time when despair breeds violence and crime, the fundamental principles of Osborne's doctrines are more widely accepted than when he was alive and struggling to justify them. The supreme tribute, paradoxically, is that few realize the source of the power which wrought the changes; for the infiltration of truth is slow and often imperceptible.

Lewis E. Lawes writes a book and people say: "Now that's sound sense. The man knows what he's talking about." Without Osborne there could have been no Lawes. Without the cultivation of men's minds to receive the ideas of reform, and the incessant repetition of those ideas until people grew weary of it yet were subconsciously influenced, Lawes would have been cast out as an iconoclast, a dreamer, a danger to society. However much he has revised Osborne's program, rejecting here, adding there, translating it into practical form to meet the conditions as he sees them, Lawes is building on Osborne. Practically every warden and penologist in the country is building on Osborne. The bases of modern penology are of Osborne and by Osborne.

Even the much-disputed theory of self-government for prisoners is winning back lost ground. At the 1933 American Prison Congress, Warden F. G. Zerbst of Leavenworth rose to make a fervent plea for the participation of inmates in the conduct of prisons. Coming from one of the younger men, this utterance might not have been so significant; but Mr. Zerbst is the oldest warden in service and is head of a prison which houses criminals of all types. From such a source one might expect extreme conservatism. If the experience of many years has led him to an endorsement of what most persons consider Osborne's most radical principle, who can say that self-government, including even prisoners' courts, is a dead issue? Perhaps Thorsten Sellin has the answer. In the *Journal of Criminal Law and Criminology* for May-June, 1933, Mr. Sellin writes of self-government:

Tried with varying success in a few institutions a decade and a half ago, it is now confined in a modified and frequently emasculated form to a few institutions. That it will be more widely used in our penal institutions as a means of resocialization, there is not the slightest doubt, but since it is an eminently delicate training instrument, which requires for its successful employment fine psychological insight and broad pedagogical understanding on the part of institutional executives and their staffs, the greatly increased use of self-government programs will have to wait until the level of administrative work has been generally raised.

There was a time when the American Prison Association looked askance at Osborne. When, in 1916 and 1922 respectively, the Welfare League Association and the National Society of Penal Information were formed to promote Osborne's work, there were occasional frictions with the American Prison Association. Gradually the differences have been adjusted; and the Osborne Association, a union of the Welfare League Association and the National Society of Penal Information, now receives whole-hearted coöperation from the national body. Headquarters of the Osborne Association are the Tom Brown House, located at 114 East Thirtieth Street, New York City.

A tablet set in the wall informs the visitor that this house is dedicated to the memory of Thomas Mott Osborne, "Prophet and Pioneer of Prison Reform, Brave, Just, and Compassionate"; and bears the legend, quoted from Osborne: "We Will Turn This Prison from a Scrap Heap into a Repair Shop."

II

And so his work continues. Men who were associated with him never seem to have lost that spark which he kindled. There is William B. Cox, the chief yeoman whose watchful eye kept his commanding officer out of much trouble at Portsmouth. He is now executive secretary of the Osborne Association. There is Austin MacCormick, another assistant of Portsmouth days, whose recent investigation of conditions at Welfare Island reawakened interest in penal reform. Harold E. Donnell, Paul W. Garrett, and many others, either actively engaged in prison work or lending their influence to some phase of social betterment, are a living proof that sacrifice is not in vain.

Ever since those eventful Sing Sing days, Dr. Kirchwey has devoted his life to prison reform and crime prevention. He is now, and has been for many years, head of the Department of Criminology at The New York School of Social Work. Among the younger writers on social subjects, Dr. Harry Elmer Barnes has championed Osborne's basic principles in books, lectures, and newspaper columns.

But there are still others even more vitally concerned, though they may not know it, in the preservation of Osborne's ideals— the convicts; yes, even the criminals not yet apprehended. One could wish that all of them might have witnessed a scene in Auburn Prison, Saturday, October 23, 1926.

On the evening of the 20th a grotesque figure had crumpled suddenly to the ground. To those who knew the surrounding circumstances it seemed a ghastly way to die. Osborne himself might have chosen a different exit had the privilege been granted him; but I imagine he would have appreciated the note of fulfillment which the manner of his death provided. It integrated his life as nothing else could do. It is a clue, gratuitously offered, to the meaning of that struggle in which he was unceasingly engaged. The boy with his toy theater and puppets; the young man and his love for impersonation; the crusading mayor and the public service commissioner seeking entrance into inaccessible regions of personality; and Tom Brown, who has as independent an existence as he who created him—all are embodied in this man lying voiceless on the grass in the chill of an autumn evening. Even the picturesque adventurer is here, too—he who disguised the strength of that inner urge in sportive, often ludicrous, masquerades. It is a completion such as life, which deals out fragments, rarely permits to be revealed.

The men in gray who filed past the casket placed near the entrance to the prison chapel were not thinking of such things that Saturday afternoon. They were thinking that their best friend—some said their only friend—had been taken away from them. They came in two files, one on each side of the casket, and as they passed they took a last look at the smiling, peaceful face within.

It was a different scene from that an hour or two earlier in the First Universalist Church. There many of the nation's great had gathered to pay tribute to the man they knew as Thomas Mott Osborne. Here forgotten men came to say farewell to Tom Brown, their friend and protector. There in restrained grief men and women of the world had heard Dr. Samuel A. Eliot eulogize the dead, and had heard Peter Kurtz play the solemn music by which custom decrees that we shall usher the departed spirit into the unknown. Here robbers and forgers and killers, whose code forbade the weaker manifestations of grief, were unashamed of the tears that rolled unheeded down their cheeks.

It may be that in the days which followed many forgot the desire for better living which this moment inspired; but for the time being the emotions they experienced were sincere. They knew, none better, how unlikely it was that another would make the sacrifices which Tom Brown had made for them; and they knew how great those sacrifices had been. What they failed to realize, in common with many others, was the inevitability of permanence for the underlying principles which Osborne had enunciated. The pendulum swings to and fro, but each stroke toward reform reaches further than the last. From time to time we need a prophet, like the Syrian mystic, to tell us that by crucifying those whom the world calls madmen humanity climbs upward:

I was dumb—and I asked wounds of you for mouths. I was imprisoned in your days and nights—and I sought a door into larger days and nights. And now I go—as others already crucified have gone. And think not we are weary of crucifixion. For we must be crucified by larger and yet larger men, between greater earths and greater heavens.

It was to build a more spacious world with wider horizons and stronger men and women that Thomas Mott Osborne fought and died and made defeat a victory.

INDEX